THE GRACE OF OUR
SOVEREIGN GOD

JOHN G. REISINGER

Books by

John G. Reisinger

Abraham's Four Seeds

The Believer's Sabbath

But I Say Unto You

Chosen in Eternity

Christ, Lord and Lawgiver Over the Church

Continuity and Discontinuity

Grace

In Defense of Jesus, the New Lawgiver

John Bunyan on the Sabbath

Limited Atonement

The New Birth

Our Sovereign God

Perseverance of the Saints

Studies in Galatians

Studies in Ecclesiastes

Tablets of Stone

The Sovereignty of God and Prayer

The Sovereignty of God in Providence

Total Depravity

What is the Christian Faith?

When Should a Christian Leave a Church?

THE GRACE OF OUR SOVEREIGN GOD

JOHN G. REISINGER

5317 Wye Creek Dr, Frederick, MD 21703-6938
Website: newcovenantmedia.com
Email: info@newcovenantmedia.com
Phone: 301-473-8781 or 800-376-4146
Fax: 240-206-0373

The Grace of Our Sovereign God

Published by:

New Covenant Media
5317 Wye Creek Drive
Frederick, Maryland 21703-6938

Orders: www.newcovenantmedia.com

Printed in the United States of America

ISBN 13: 978-1-928965-39-8

DEDICATION

To the saints of God who meet as the Reformed Baptist
Church in Lewisburg, PA.
They called me as pastor fifty-eight years ago and have
continued to love and support me and my family ever
since.

TABLE OF CONTENTS

DEDICATION VII

TABLE OF CONTENTS IX

CHAPTER ONE
THE SOVEREIGNTY OF GOD IN PROVIDENCE 1

CHAPTER TWO
THE SOVEREIGNTY OF GOD IN DECREES 49

CHAPTER THREE
THE SOVEREIGNTY OF GOD AND PRAYER..........................99

CHAPTER FOUR
TOTAL DEPRAVITY 165

CHAPTER FIVE
UNCONDITIONAL ELECTION 207

CHAPTER SIX
LIMITED ATONEMENT 269

CHAPTER SEVEN
IRRESISTIBLE GRACE.. 327

CHAPTER EIGHT
THE PERSEVERANCE OF THE SAINTS 363

CHAPTER NINE
THE SOVEREIGNTY OF GOD IN PERSONAL LIFE 393

CHAPTER TEN
OUR SOVEREIGN GOD 419

APPENDIX ONE
TWO VIEWS OF THE ATONEMENT 445

APPENDIX TWO
ALL *EQUALS* MANY *BUT* MANY *DOES NOT EQUAL* ALL ... 449

APPENDIX THREE
PERSEVERANCE AND OUR BAPTIST FOREFATHERS 469

APPENDIX FOUR
THE CARNAL CHRISTIAN DOCTRINE................................ 475

CHAPTER ONE
THE SOVEREIGNTY OF GOD IN PROVIDENCE

For of him, and through him, and to him, are all things: to whom be glory forever. Amen. Romans 11:36

There are six principles that are basic to the concept of the sovereignty of God in providence that run all the way through the Word of God and undergird its message of salvation. It is essential to understand and believe these six principles in order to have a biblical understanding of either God himself or the theology of his sovereign grace. Grasping and applying these truths to your everyday life is the foundation of biblical hope that leads to true joy in the Lord. It is difficult to have a reasonable, hopeful sense of security and a heartfelt assurance while living in our present-day, crazy world without a knowledge and appreciation of the sovereignty of God in providence embodied in these six biblical truths.

Do you understand the message of hope and grace that is set forth in the Word of God, or do you have trouble putting it all together into one coherent system? Can you relate the truths of the Bible to your everyday life, or do the doctrines of Scripture seem unrelated to the real life situations of your personal world today? This chapter is written for the express purpose of giving you clear and specific help in these two areas. It is designed to help you understand what the Bible really says and means, and to apply that message to the real life situations you must face in your personal world.

Listed below are the six fundamental principles of the doctrine of God's sovereignty in providence:

I. *God has a definite plan and purpose for the world.* (Job 23:13; Eph. 1:8-12)

II. *God is always in control of all things and is constantly at work in accomplishing his plan.* (Hab. 1:1-11; Isa. 10:5, 6)

III. *God controls and uses everyone, even the Devil, in working out his plan.* (Isa. 10:7-11; Ps. 76:10)

IV. *God punishes the people that he uses to accomplish his purposes when they act out of wrong motives.* (Isa. 10:12-16; Acts 2:23, 24; cf. Matt. 27:15-26)

V. *All things are from God, but the Devil is the agent of all evil.* (II Sam. 24:1; I Chron. 21:1)

VI. *Although all sickness and affliction are part of God's purpose and under his sovereign control, it does not follow that all sickness and affliction are necessarily chastisement for sin.* (Job 1:1, 6-2:10; 13:15)

Before we look closely at these six principles, let me kick the needle of your mind so that you are mentally in gear. This will test both your basic knowledge of Scripture as well as your ability to apply it to real life situations. We are all naturally averse to hard thinking, especially about anything new. Like the needle in the hi-fi, we go round and round in the same groove. I want to be sure your mind is engaged and that you are really thinking.

Just suppose next Lord's Day morning you are shaving and listening to the radio. The newscaster announces that the night before at exactly midnight every house of prostitution, every pornographic shop, every gambling casino, and every house of any kind of sin very mysteriously collapsed and was totally destroyed. Your reaction would probably be, *Praise the Lord.* When you go to Sunday School somebody asks you, "How do you account for that? What do you think happened?" I am sure you would reply, "It was the hand of God. God was surely in that." Your explanation would be correct. Unbelievers might not accept your explanation, and the newspapers and TV newscasters might invent all kinds of theories, but you would attribute the whole thing to God and rejoice in his sovereign work.

Now just suppose the following Sunday morning you are again shaving and the same newscaster reports, "At exactly midnight last night every single Bible-believing church in the country very mysteriously collapsed and was totally destroyed." I wonder what you would say then. Would most Christians say, "Bless the Lord," or would they say, "It was the Devil"?

Why would anyone blame—or rather, credit—God for the first situation (the destroying of the bad places) and then credit the Devil with the destruction of the churches? If we understood the Scriptures clearly, especially texts like Rom. 11:36 and Rom. 8:28, we would have to acknowledge the hand of God both times. The whole burden of this chapter is to teach us that *God sovereignly controls every single thing that happens, whether it is good or bad.* God is involved, in one way or another, in every event and each minute detail of that event. If this is not true, then we really have no sure hope for our lives in this confused generation.

Dualism is Heresy

When people assign all the good to God and all the bad to the Devil, they are guilty of an ancient heresy called *dualism*. Dualism basically posits God and the Devil (good and bad) as two independent and sovereign powers struggling for ultimate control of this world. We earnestly hope our side wins, but at times, it does not look very promising. Sadly, many Christians today are guilty of believing that very heresy. This is the error of any group who emphasizes health and wealth as the birthright of every Christian and blames the Devil for everything that hinders their personal happiness. This is the heresy of dualism at its worst.

Why do sincere Christians do this? Why do they give credit for the good to God and blame the bad on the Devil, unconsciously denying the sovereignty of God? It is probably because they are trying to protect God. They are trying to make it easier to believe and love him by exempting him from anything that appears to be bad and crediting him with everything that appears to be good. A young nurse who worked in the emergency ward of a hospital told me that when anyone from a particular church in that town had an accident, the pastor would rush down to the hospital. His first words to the victim and family were, "Remember, God had nothing to do with this." I suppose the poor man was afraid the people might desert the faith. If you will just think through that preacher's statement for a moment, you can see the error in it. The man may have been trying to protect God, but in reality, he was laying the groundwork for despair and unbelief. He was leaving the injured person totally in the hands of either Satan or blind, cruel fate. He was unconsciously moving God right out of the picture when the afflicted person needed the assurance of God's sovereign control the most.

The other evening, a man gave his testimony and told of a friend that had died in a tragic Army plane crash. The officer in charge of the situation was seeking to comfort the mother and said the following:

> It is impossible for this to ever be repeated. It was a freak accident that could never occur again. No one could have predicted or controlled the events. There simply is no explanation.

The mother was a Christian who understood the truths we are presenting, and she replied:

> Sir, you may not believe that God was in that plane with my son, but I do. I have no idea why God chose to allow this to happen, but I know that this was part of his sovereign purpose, and his hand was in total control of the plane, the weather, and my son's life.

How different is that mother's theology and hope from that of the preacher in the emergency room!

How Powerful is God?

Suppose you were the victim of the accident, and you were lying there in pain. Would that preacher's theology and words of comfort help you? How would you feel if someone told you that God had nothing to do with what happened? How long would it take you to start forming some very serious and logical questions like, "Where was God when this happened? Could he have prevented it? Why didn't he prevent it? Was the Devil stronger than God in this situation? Did the Devil really cause this accident, even though God was desperately trying to keep it from happening to me?" You would soon begin to wonder whether you were on the wrong side. You might think, and correctly so, that if the preacher was right, then maybe God is not nearly as powerful as you thought he was.

I am sure you can see that if God is not big enough to control the bad things as well as the good things, we are in deep trouble. When the bad things are more numerous than the good things (in times like today), it looks as if we are losing the war. It looks like our side is the weak side. Whether you realize it or not, this is exactly what has happened in the hearts of many present-day Christians. This generation has forgotten the sovereignty of God and exalted the sovereignty of man's free will. We have forgotten the holiness of God and exalted man's personal happiness to be the chief goal and obligation of the gospel. We are so occupied with ourselves and our own pleasure that we believe that God exists for the sole purpose of making us happy by giving us whatever our sinful and selfish hearts desire. He is viewed as a heavenly bellhop who is ready to carry our suitcase of self-ambition anywhere we instruct him—we call it "praying in faith." When we do not get what we want, we either condemn ourselves for lack of faith or lose confidence in God's promises (what we *falsely believed* were his promises).

The more that sin and self appear to triumph, the more it looks like God is losing the war because he is weak and helpless. The despair, frustration, and depression of this present existential generation are in direct proportion to their misunderstanding of the sovereign control of God over all things, and perhaps the worst is yet to come. The "God wants you rich and healthy" gospel may prove to be the primary cause of the forsaking of the faith in this generation. A loving God who is supposed to give you anything your heart desires will be despised and ridiculed when he does not deliver the goodies.

If a Christian living in today's wicked times really understands the Scripture, he is like the little boy who was playing baseball. A man came along and asked, "What's the score?" and the boy replied, "Forty to nothing." The man asked, "Who's winning?" The boy answered, "The other team." The man wanted to be sympathetic and said, "You must be very discouraged." The little boy's face lit up, and he said, "Oh, no, we're not discouraged. **We haven't come up to bat yet!**"

The Christian doesn't look at the newspaper headlines, he doesn't look at the odds or the experts, he is not impressed with either the doomsayer or the false prophet;

the child of God with a clear understanding of the Scripture looks to the **Sovereign God clearly revealed in that Scripture.** A knowledgeable believer knows that **he is on the winning team** regardless of what the world's scoreboard says. He knows that Jesus Christ is Lord regardless of what is taking place either in the world or in his personal life; he is confident that everything will, in the end, be for his own good as well as for the glory of God.

Calvary was a Day of Victory

Jesus Christ was still our Lord and his Father was completely in control of all things on the day that sinners *"with wicked hands"* unknowingly fulfilled the decrees of God and nailed our Savior to the cross. Our blessed Lord was never more in control, never more sovereign and powerful, than he was the moment men cried out in derision, "Where now is your God?" and challenged him to prove he was the Son of God by coming down from the cross. If you and I had been standing under the cross on that day, we probably would have wondered whether God really was the Father of our Lord Jesus. If he was, why didn't he come and help? Why did the Father allow all of these things to happen to his dear Son? We would never have understood, apart from revelation, that this hour of this day was the specific point in time toward which God had been moving ever since the day that Adam sinned.

There has never been a day when God was more triumphant in his power, love, and holiness than he was that day at Calvary's cross. Jesus Christ was not a martyr; God's Son was not a victim. That day at Golgotha was the day of God's victory, not a day of defeat. God was the supreme commander who controlled every single detail of that event. The world and the Devil may have thought that God's plan and purpose had been thwarted, but they were wrong. Calvary was a day of glorious victory for sovereign grace. Sinners gloated and mocked without being aware that their very thoughts and actions were fulfilling God's ordained purposes.

Let us now examine the six principles of the Word of God upon which these glorious truths are built.

First Principle: God has a Plan

The first principle starts with God and his purposes. *God has a definite plan and purpose for the world* (Job 23:13; Eph. 1:8-12).

We do not want to spend too much time on this first point since chapter two is devoted to this subject. Let me just outline this truth with several verses of Scripture.

> *He is in one mind, and who can turn him? And what his soul desireth, even that he doeth.* (Job 23:13 KJV)

I. God has a plan. "He is of one mind....what his soul desireth..."

II. God's plan is unchangeable. "...who can turn him?"

III. God's plan must and will succeed. "...even that (which he desires or plans), he doeth."

IV. God's plan includes all things that come to pass.

...being predestinated according to the purpose [or plan] *of him who worketh ALL THINGS after the counsel of his own will.* (Eph. 1:11 KJV, emphasis added)

*And we know that **all things** work together for good to them that love God, to them who are called **according to his purpose*** [or plan]. (Rom. 8:28 KJV, emphasis added)

The Pelagian denies that God has a plan. The Arminian denies that the plan is specific and inclusive of all things. The Confessions of Faith state, "God from all eternity did, by the most wise and holy counsel of his own free will, freely and unchangeably ordain whatsoever comes to pass." Here are a few other texts on the same subject:

- God does everything DELIBERATELY – Ps. 115:3

- God does as HE PLEASES – Ps. 135:6

- God does all things according to his own eternal knowledge, power, and desire – Isa. 46:10 and Acts 15:18

If you feel inclined to reject what is being said, I suggest you look up some "tough" verses (Deut. 2:30; I Sam. 16:14, and Rom. 9) and try to fit them into your system of theology. A classic illustration of the sovereignty of God in accomplishing his purposes is found in II Sam. 17:1-14:

vv. 1-3	Good counsel is given.
v. 4	Absalom is ready to act.
vv. 5-13	Bad counsel is given deliberately.
v. 14	God purposed Absalom to believe a lie.

As I mentioned earlier, the above is deliberately brief and will be covered more fully in chapter two, "The Sovereignty of God in Decrees."

Second Principle: God is Always in Control

The second principle grows out of and naturally follows the first principle. God not only has a plan, but he also carries out that plan. The second principle is that *God is always in total control of all things and is constantly at work in accomplishing his plan* (Hab. 1:1-11; Isa. 10:5, 6).

Sometimes God's plan calls for revival, and as a result, there was a day of Pentecost when thousands of souls were swept into the kingdom of God. His plan calls for judgment other times. Isaiah calls God's judgment his "strange work," but it is nonetheless God's work. Just as there was a day of Pentecost when thousands were saved, so there was a day of judgment when a universal flood swept nearly the whole human race into everlasting damnation. We must see that God is just as much the author of one as he is the other. Whether it is Pentecost or the flood, whether there are the events of Acts 2 or of Genesis 6, God is in total control and is working out his plan. The rain and full harvest as well as the draught and empty barns are from the hand of the same Sovereign God. We must learn to praise him under *both* circumstances (Hab. 3:17-19).

Silence of God

The first text of Scripture we want to look at to demonstrate this truth is in the book of Habakkuk. The book of Habakkuk was written primarily to give us the biblical perspective of history. The prophet deals with a problem very much in evidence today. He tackles the question, "How can a holy God allow wicked men to triumph over the righteous?" Wicked men do triumph, and it is usually at the expense of the righteous. We could put the question another way, "Why does God sometimes appear to be deaf to the prayers of his people when they cry to him in time of trouble and confusion?" Let us look at the text for our answers:

> *The burden which Habakkuk the prophet did see. O LORD, how long shall I cry, and thou wilt not hear! even cry out unto thee of violence, and thou wilt not save! Why dost thou shew me iniquity, and cause me to behold grievance? for spoiling and violence are before me: and there are those that raise up strife and contention. Therefore the law is slacked, and judgment doth never go forth: for the wicked doth compass about the righteous; therefore wrong judgment proceedeth. Behold ye among the heathen, and regard, and wonder marvelously: for **I will work a work** in your days, which ye will not believe, though it be told you. For, lo, **I raise up the Chaldeans,** that bitter and hasty nation, which shall march through the breadth of the land, to possess the dwelling places that are not theirs.* (Hab. 1:1-6 KJV, emphasis added)

As you read this, notice in verse 2 that Habakkuk is praying to God and accusing him of either not hearing or not answering his cries. Habakkuk is pleading for God to send revival, but instead of revival, it appears that God does nothing and even allows things to get worse. Habakkuk looks around and sees violence, corruption, and injustice on every hand, and God doesn't seem to be doing anything about it. Habakkuk wants revival to come, but all he sees is increasing lawlessness.

Verse 3 states that God forces Habakkuk to look at the awful situation. It is as if God insists that he see and acknowledge the violence on every hand. "I see injustice; I see wickedness in all areas of society; I hear men blaspheming God; and worst of all, it appears that God is doing nothing." In verse 4 Habakkuk concludes, "Therefore the law is slack." He describes the society as one controlled by lawlessness, where the wicked man, if he has enough money, can get away with anything. Habakkuk is describing a situation very similar to the society of today. In the first four verses you see his accusation against God, and "accusation" is the correct word to use. Habakkuk is accusing God of either being deaf or else not powerful enough to hear and answer his prayers. God appears to be either unable or unwilling to do anything about the awful situation in society, and Habakkuk seems to be wasting his time praying.

In verse 5, God answers Habakkuk, and his answer is harder to understand than his silence. Now remember, Habakkuk is praying about God's own covenant people. He is talking about the nation of Israel. I want you to particularly notice in verse 5 where God says, **"I will work a work in your days."** Then, in verse 6, God says, **"Lo, I raise up** the Chaldeans." God responds to Habakkuk and, in effect, says, "I am very much at work, and I am not deaf, blind, or helpless." Verse 5 is very amusing: God says, "When I tell you what the work is that I am doing, you will not believe me," and sure enough, when God tells Habakkuk what he is about to do, poor Habakkuk is more upset than he was before. He was first perplexed by God's apparent *inactivity*, but now his major problem is with God's announced *activity*. God's purposes seem worse than his silence. Exactly what was God about to do? At that very moment, God was strengthening the Chaldean nation and moving them to invade the nation of Israel. It is clear from the text that the Chaldeans would be God's instrument of chastisement upon Israel. The Chaldeans are coming, and God himself is responsible for sending them.

"The Devil Did It!"

Some contemporary televangelists might have responded, "That is a lie because God is a good God, and something good is going to happen to you today!" It was true that the invasion by the Chaldeans was going to be used by God for **good purposes;** in fact, the terrible times would be the means of bringing repentance, and thus, the answer to Habakkuk's prayers for revival. Such a God, with such methods, would never fit into today's popular concept of God and his sovereignty. We simply must get into our minds that when the Chaldeans come, it is not "the Devil who is sending them" to mess up our party; it is God himself who is sending them. It doesn't matter what the thing is that perplexes us today; if it happens, then God's hand is in it and over it, or it would not have happened. God sent it to accomplish something. We must seek his face and ask him for grace to learn whatever lesson he is seeking to teach us through this particular trial, instead of blaming it on the Devil.

Blaming all of our difficulties on the Devil is a backhanded way of strengthening our own self-righteous conceit: "We really must be super-spiritual Christians to be attacked so strongly by the Devil." Until you see the hand of God in all things, you will fight both God and the very purpose for which he sends the problem. There is nothing as tragic as listening to a sincere, but misguided, believer blame the Devil for the fruits of his own stupidity, especially as he then may think the Devil did it just because he was so spiritual! It never occurs to him that perhaps he believed and expected something that God never promised, and at the same time he does not understand that God is the one who has sent his circumstances. The problem is twofold: his bad theology keeps him from hearing God speak to him in his trials; and worse yet, it hardens him in his false spirituality.

Do you see what the text is teaching? "**I** (not the Devil) **will work** a work," and this work is going to be a work of **judgment.** Notice again the emphasis in verse 6, "**I** (not the Devil) **raise up** the Chaldeans." God is the one sending that awful nation against his chosen people. Later on in the chapter, God shows that he is also going to judge the Chaldeans for what they did, but that will be dealt with just a bit later under another principle.

Because this second principle—*God is always in control*—is so important, and since it is the foundation of everything that follows, let me give you another passage that teaches the same truth. The tenth chapter of Isaiah contains at least three of the principles we want to examine. The second, which we are considering, is found in verses 5 and 6:

> *O Assyrian, the rod of mine anger, and the staff in their hand is mine indignation. **I will send him** against an hypocritical nation, and against the people of my wrath will **I give him a charge,** to take the spoil, and to take the prey, and to tread them down like the mire of the streets.* (Isa. 10:5, 6 KJV, emphasis added)

Instead of using the Chaldean, God is now using the Assyrian. In verse 5, God declares that the rod in the hand of the Assyrian is really his rod. The Assyrian may be the one who is doing the clubbing (verse 15), but behind the Assyrian is the hand and purpose of God. In verse 6 God says, "**I will send him** (that is, the Assyrian) against a hypocritical nation, against the people of my wrath, **I give him a charge.**" God, not the Devil, is sending the Assyrian against Israel. God says, "I am giving this charge to the Assyrian." This passage clearly teaches the principle that God is always in control. No matter what is going on or who is doing the acting, God is always sovereignly at work. He is in total control, and he is working out his own ordained purposes. In times of trial or trouble, it is dangerous to listen to a well-intentioned, but misguided soul who says, "My God is too loving and kind to do anything like that." Ironically, such a person is probably right. "His God" would not act like that simply because "his God" grew out of his own emotional imagination instead of the words of Scripture.

Third Principle: Everybody Works for God

Here is the third principle. *In working out his own plans, God uses everybody, even the Devil.* At first that shocks some people: "What! God uses the Devil?" That is exactly right. Everybody, even the Devil, serves God's purposes. Now a servant may serve through gritted teeth, and he may hate his servitude; but he is, nonetheless, a servant. So it is with the Devil. He has never done one thing out of love or obedience to God. He has never done one thing in order to knowingly bring glory to God. Everything the Devil does, he does because he hates God and is trying to frustrate the purposes of God. However, in the end, everything the Devil does will surely further the purposes of God. If ever there was a born loser, it is the Devil himself. In the final day, it will be shown that the Devil never won a single time. And that includes the garden of Eden!

Let us see this truth set forth in Isaiah chapter ten:

> "But this is not what he [the Assyrian] intends, this is not what he has in mind; his purpose is to destroy, to put an end to many nations. Are not my commanders all kings? he says....As my hand seized the kingdoms of the idols, kingdoms whose images excelled those of Jerusalem and Samaria—shall I not deal with Jerusalem and her images as I dealt with Samaria and her idols?" (Isa. 10:7-11 NIV)

The text is very clear; the Assyrian does not have the same thing in mind that God has in mind. In fact, it is perfectly obvious that the Assyrian is not thinking at all about God. All that the arrogant Assyrian is thinking about is destroying another nation and robbing it of its riches. However, totally unbeknown to the Assyrian, God is directing the whole situation. God is moving the Assyrian's mind and emotions. The sovereign Lord is directing the Assyrian's every action in order to accomplish his own purpose of judgment upon Israel.

Man's Wrath Glorifies God

Psalm 76, verse 10 is a very interesting verse and illustrates this same principle. The verse reads, "Surely the wrath of man shall praise thee...." and then goes on to say, "and thou restraineth the residue thereof." In other words, man is filled with wrath against God and his authority. God did not put the wrath in man, nor is God responsible for either the wrath or the actions of man that express that wrath. Man's so-called "free will" is totally controlled by his rebellious nature and is one-hundred-percent responsible for both every ounce of wrath and sin in man's heart and for every act produced by that wrath and sin. Nevertheless, God totally controls and directs man's heart. All of man's wrath that *will further God's purpose* is allowed to surface and is used and controlled by God for his own ends. However, there is a lot of wrath in man that does not fit into God's purposes, so he puts a cork on "the residue thereof" and does not allow that to be expressed. God controls man's wrath both ways. God decides when and how much of man's wrath will be expressed, and he also uses each expression of that wrath to accomplish some specific part of his ordained plan.

"The Devil is the hardest working servant that God has!" I remember how astonished I was when I first heard that statement. However, the moment God showed me the truth of his absolute sovereignty, I immediately saw how true the statement was. Granted, the Devil does every single thing that he does out of pure hatred; nonetheless, God controls and uses it all to accomplish his own foreordained plan. Perhaps an illustration will help us to see this point.

An Illustration of Sovereignty

A very wealthy man we will call Mr. Rich had a beautiful estate covered with every kind of tree. Mr. Rich did not like women, so he was a bachelor; he could not stand animals, so he had no pets. He treated his trees the way some people treat their pets. He even gave each tree a name. Mr. Rich had one particular tree that was his favorite. Unhappily, he also had an enemy (we will call him Mr. Evil) that hated him and desired to hurt him; however, the enemy could not find a way to carry out his evil desires. One night Mr. Evil thought up a way to deeply hurt and wound Mr. Rich. Mr. Evil climbed over the fence into the orchard and proceeded to chop down Mr. Rich's favorite tree. The very thought of how hurt Mr. Rich would be when he saw his favorite tree destroyed made Mr. Evil work all the harder. Finally the tree began to fall. Mr. Evil was so excited that he ran the wrong way. The tree fell on him and pinned him to the ground.

Shortly after daybreak, Mr. Evil saw two men walking toward him and the fallen tree. "I know I am caught, and I know I will be punished, *but I do not care. I ruined your favorite tree!*" The poor man was so filled with pathological hatred that he kept saying, "I ruined your tree! I ruined your tree!" Mr. Rich looked at him and said, "The man with me is a building contractor. I must cut down one of my trees to build a summerhouse for my parents, and I had chosen this spot right here. I brought this gentleman out to show him which tree we would have to cut down, but I see that you have saved me that trouble. Thank you!"

I am sure that you see the point. Everything the Devil does will always, in some way, further God's purposes. We need to remember that God accomplishes his purposes in a world of sin; because of that fact, there is a lot of dirty work that has to be done. God will never soil his hands, because the Devil will (unknowingly) take care of all the dirty work. Joseph's brothers may have done what they did out of hatred, but "God meant it for good to bring to pass…" what he had ordained (Gen. 50:15). The Assyrian and the Chaldean may have been motivated entirely by lust for power and booty, but God was in charge of their every expedition.

Fourth Principle: God Punishes the Very People He Uses!

This fourth principle is perhaps one of the most difficult to reconcile with our sense of fairness and justice. God actually punishes the very people that he uses to accomplish his plan when those people act out of a wrong motive and with no thought of God.

Look again at Isaiah 10:

*When the Lord has finished all **his work** against Mount Zion and Jerusalem, he will say, "I will punish the King of Assyria for the willful pride of his heart and the haughty look in his eye. For he says, 'By the strength of **my hand** I have done this, and by **my*** *wisdom, because I have understanding. I removed the boundaries of the nations, I plundered their treasures; like a mighty one I subdued their kings.'"* (Isa. 10:12, 13 NIV, emphasis added)

You can feel the arrogant unbelief and self-sufficiency of the Assyrian. He really believes that he has accomplished everything by his own wisdom and strength. He has no thought of God nor does he acknowledge God in any way. If we were to tell him the truth of what was actually happening, he would probably burst out laughing and then kill us for daring to imply that there was a person stronger than he. The next verse really shows his conceit:

"As one reaches into a nest, so my hands reached for the wealth of the nations; as men gathered abandoned eggs, so I gathered all the countries; not one flapped a wing or opened its mouth to chirp." (Isa. 10:14 NIV)

Here the pompous king compares himself to a man robbing the nests of helpless birds. He can laugh at the armies and navies of all nations because of his superior strength. Everyone is too afraid to even open his mouth and protest, let alone actually try to stop him. Ah, wait a moment and listen to someone else speaking. Listen to God tell why the invasion of Israel took place and what is now going to happen to the Assyrian. In verses 5 and 6, God said he would use the Assyrian to punish Israel. In verse 12, God repeats that he had indeed used the Assyrian, but then adds, "I will punish the King of Assyria for the willful pride of his heart...." God will now deal with the Assyrian for what he did! Verse 15 tells us why God is angry with the Assyrian, even though the Assyrian has just (unknowingly) completed a job that has been assigned by

God. Let these words sink into your mind and heart, and build your theology on God's revelation:

> *Does the ax raise itself above him who swings it* [Who is the ax, and who is swinging the ax in these verses?], *or the saw boast against him that uses it* [Who is the saw and who is doing the sawing]*? As if a rod* [the Assyrian] *were to wield him who lifts it up* [Can the Assyrian control God or alter his purposes?], *or a club brandish him who is not wood!* [Does a man use, control, or in any way thwart God's actions or purposes?] (Isa. 10:15 NIV)

Cut that verse any way you want, and it always comes out the same way. God moved and used the Assyrian to accomplish his plans of judgment, and then he punished the Assyrian for what he did simply because he acted out of the wrong motive and with no thought of God at all. Does it sound unfair for God to use people and then punish them for what they do? The failure to see this truth is one of the primary reasons that untaught Christians have such difficulty in believing the absolute sovereignty of God. They confuse the "free will" of man with the biblical doctrine of the "free *agency*" of man. Because they have not grasped this distinction, they think there are only two choices: (1) either man is totally free [even God's power is limited by man's sovereign will], or else (2) man is a robot [God's sovereignty somehow (?) eliminates man's need to make right choices] and therefore cannot be held responsible for his actions.

God is Sovereign — Man is Responsible

These passages of Scripture that we are examining show that both of the above options are false. The Word of God, from beginning to end, teaches that God is absolutely sovereign and controls everybody and everything as he works out his own foreordained purpose and plan. The Bible also teaches that every human being is completely responsible for every one of his actions. Our finite, limited brains may balk at that and regard it as a contradiction, but the Scripture declares both of these things to be true. The validity of these two concepts is not contingent upon whether I understand either, both, or neither of these biblical facts; they are *both true simply because God revealed them **both** in his Word*. God is absolutely sovereign and will accomplish every part of his ordained plan, and man is totally responsible for every one of his own thoughts, words, and deeds.

Does Isaiah 10:5, 6, 12 explicitly say that God controlled and sent the Assyrian to invade and punish Israel? Do verses 7-11, 15 declare that the Assyrian did what he did out of his own wicked heart and arrogant pride? Do verses 12 and 15 emphatically teach that God is going to deliberately punish the Assyrian for what he did *in spite of the fact that what the Assyrian did was ordained and brought to pass by God's power and control?*

Let us look at some other texts that teach this same truth. Acts 2:23 is a classic verse that brings together the decrees of a sovereign God and the free acts of responsible creatures. In verse 22, Peter reminds the Jews that Christ had all of the credentials to prove that he was indeed the promised Messiah. Then we read these words:

> _Him, being delivered by the determinate counsel and foreknowledge of God..._ (Acts 2:23a KJV)

The NIV puts it like this:

> _This man was handed over to you by God's set purpose and foreknowledge...._

Can you imagine some of the very Jews that several weeks before had cried out, "Crucify Him, crucify Him!" hearing Peter attribute the whole event of Calvary to God's absolute sovereign purposes? Those men would have been ready to heave a sigh of relief and say, "We thought that we were guilty and responsible for the death of Jesus, but now we realize that we are not. It was God and not we." They would have loved to get the monkey of responsibility for that awful event off their backs. Sadly, that is exactly what incorrect theology would allow them to do. Notice, however, the rest of the verse:

> _...ye have taken, and by wicked hands have crucified and slain [him]:_ (Acts 2:23b KJV)

Peter says, "True, it was God's sovereign purpose to have Christ crucified, but that in no way excuses you! You acted out of the hatred of your hearts and **his blood is on your heads!**" My dear reader, words cannot be clearer. The verse shows that God used wicked men to accomplish his sovereign decrees, and then held those very men responsible for their wicked deeds. We may not understand how these two things can both be true, but we cannot deny that the Word of God declares them **both to**

be true. Hyper-Calvinism may deny the one and Arminianism may deny the other, but we will believe and preach them **both.**

God's Decrees and Man's "Free Will"

Let me give you this truth in a classic statement from one of the Puritans. "What God sovereignly *decrees in eternity,* man will always *demand in time."* Man's "free will" will always freely choose the very thing that God has sovereignly ordained, and God's purpose will be fulfilled; just as surely, man will be responsible for his every act of sin. I know of no passage that sets forth this truth as clearly as Matthew 27. The entire chapter recounts the vain attempts by men to deny personal responsibility. First, Judas tried to deny his responsibility for the death of Christ by pleading Christ's innocence and giving the thirty pieces of silver back to the chief priests and elders. They, in turn, replied, "What is that to us? That was your responsibility." Was it not their duty to be certain that Christ was, indeed, guilty and worthy of death? Certainly it was!

The account of Jesus before Pilate contains a portrayal of a blatant attempt to sidestep accountability. Pilate knew beyond question that Jesus was innocent, and yet he deliberately distorted and destroyed law and justice in punishing him. He then tried to absolve himself from responsibility. However, Matthew makes it clear that this whole event took place because Pilate went along with the "free will" choice of the crowd. Remember, they had the power and authority to choose **anybody that they wanted**

to choose to be released. It was entirely up to them.
Notice carefully the words of the text:

> Now at that feast the governor was wont to release unto the
> people a prisoner, **whom they would.** (Matt. 27:15 [The NIV has
> "...a prisoner **chosen by the crowd,"** emphasis added])

The choice was left entirely up to the "free will" of the
crowd, and the crowd knowingly and deliberately chose a
guilty, notorious criminal named Barabbas. Over the
protests of his wife, his conscience, and both Roman and
Hebrew law, Pilate refused to stop the injustice. He caved
in to the cry of the mob. When asked what they wanted
done with "Jesus who is called Christ," the crowd
screamed in unison, "Crucify Him!" Pilate tried every trick
in the book to get the crowd to change its mind, but he only
managed to make them shout louder, "Crucify him!"

Guilty Because Totally "Free"

Pilate tried finally to deny his personal responsibility by
washing his hands in front of the crowd. He said, "I am
innocent of this man's blood. It is your **responsibility.**" The
people responded without hesitation and gladly took
responsibility for the whole thing. They answered in
defiance, "Let his blood be on us and on our children!"
Could any group be guiltier and more responsible for their
acts, than that crowd was? Did anyone ever fulfill in more
detail (although totally unknowingly) the secret purposes
of God better than Pilate and that mob did?

Carefully consider two simple questions and their clear
answers from the verses in Matthew 27.

(1) Exactly what did God Almighty eternally decree would happen to his Son? **That he would be crucified!** Exactly what did that mad crowd vehemently demand to take place? **The crucifixion of Christ!**

What God sovereignly decrees in eternity, man will freely choose in time.

(2) What is the only thing (with regard to payment for sin) that will satisfy the character of a holy God? **The shed blood of Jesus Christ!** What is the only thing that would satisfy the hate and passion of that crowd? **The shed blood of Jesus Christ!**

What God sovereignly ordains in eternity, man will choose by his own free will in time.

Perhaps an illustration will help us to understand this point. A switchman for the railroad is responsible for throwing a switch that changes the tracks upon which two trains are running. Suppose he got drunk, went to sleep, and did not throw the switch when he was supposed to; the two trains collided, and over one hundred people were killed. Could the man justly be accused of murder? I think we would all agree. Suppose, however, unbeknown to the drunken man, a flash flood had washed out a bridge. Now, because the man was drunk and did not throw the switch, but also because the bridge was washed out, a terrible train crash was *avoided*. Would it now be just to reward the man for being drunk and not throwing the switch since his behavior averted an accident?

Now think clearly. Which time was the switchman guiltier? Was it when his sinful action *caused* a wreck or when the same action *averted* a wreck? The answer is simple. If you judge the man solely on the ground of his *duty*, or responsibility, then he was just as guilty both times. God may use the worst of sins to accomplish great good, but he still holds the individual responsible for the sin. The Chaldeans, the Assyrians, and the rebels who crucified Christ are proof of this fact. We are not responsible for the *results* of what God does with our acts, but we are totally responsible for the acts themselves. That, and that alone, will be the basis upon which God will deal with us.

Before going on to the next principle, let me emphasize the practical effect that the point under discussion should have in our personal life. We must never feel that we are pawns or victims of the ungodly. We should always see the hand of our heavenly Father controlling all things. If the wicked prevail, it is only because God has purposed to use it for his own glory and for our good.

In the fifty years that I have been in the ministry, I have nearly always been able to get along with the leaders with whom I have worked. Until recently, there was only one exception to that. I worked with one particular deacon that seemed to hate me; I think he would have harmed me if he could have gotten away with it. I used to call him "Shimei" (but only when my wife and I were talking). I am sure you remember Shimei. As David was fleeing for his life after Absalom had taken over the kingdom, Shimei cursed

David and said, "You bloody man, you are getting what you deserve." One of David's men wanted to "silence Shimei's tongue forever," but David said, "If God wants me to be cursed, so be it." David recognized the hand of God.

This deacon was like Shimei. When he was on the board of deacons, he would magnify every single bad thing I did and overlook every good thing. He hounded me to death. The strange part is that he did more to help me be a better pastor than any other deacon with whom I ever served. You see, when he was on the board, I always made sure that I did everything (down to the smallest detail) that I was supposed to do. I have a tendency to leave things until the last minute, and then I miss some small details. I didn't miss anything when "Shimei" was on the board. I came to the place that I could honestly thank God for that man. I believe God knew that I needed some help, and he sent Shimei along to "help" me be a better pastor. I also knew that God was going to punish that man for all the "help" that he gave me!

Punished for "Helping God"

Do you see the point? All that the man did, he did out of hatred for me. He was not motivated by love to God or true concern for the church. He was after me! However, God used him to help me, by the very fact that he forced me to take care of details. As believers, we can be sure that everyone is under God's control. When we pray for him to teach us something, he often answers by sending the people into our lives that can accomplish that task. If we rebel against his "teachers," then we are really rebelling against God. Far too often, we would like to pick both the teacher and the study course, but when we do, we never learn the necessary lessons. God sends the people that do the job.

Fifth Principle: The Devil is the Agent of All Evil

The fifth principle is essential to help us see two things at the same time. There is a real Devil, and he is extremely busy. We have seen that God controls all things and uses everybody to work out his ordained purposes. However, even though *all sickness and affliction come from the hand of God, it is the Devil that is the agent of the evil.* In other words, we must see both the hand of the Devil and the hand of God at the same time. I have a book entitled *Sixty-five Mistakes in the Bible,* written by a liberal preacher. Here is one of the "mistakes" he found in the Bible:

> *And the anger of the LORD was kindled against Israel, and he moved David against them to say, Go, number Israel and Judah.* (II Sam. 24:1 KJV)

> *And Satan stood up against Israel, and provoked David to number Israel.* (I Chron. 21:1 KJV)

It is clear that both verses are referring to the same event (when Israel and David were punished for numbering the people). It is just as clear that one passage says God moved David and the other passage says that Satan moved David. Which is correct? If we understand the principle that I am setting forth, then it is clear that both God and Satan were involved. It was God's purpose (unknown to Satan) and Satan's hatred (which God used) that accomplished the work. God used both David's pride and Satan's hatred to accomplish his own purposes. We must see Satan's hand as the **agent who brings the evil,** but we must also see God's hand as the **sovereign mover and controller.** Let me illustrate this principle with a story.

God "Sends" All Things!

An elderly lady was praying aloud in front of an open window. She had neither food nor money, and she was pleading with God to supply her with something to eat. Two boys heard her and decided to mock her faith. They went down to the store and bought a loaf of bread and a quart of milk. Then they stealthily put the milk and bread through the window. When the lady opened her eyes and saw the food, she praised God for hearing and answering her prayers. The boys stuck their heads up above the windowsill and said, "Woman, you are stupid. God did not send those things. We put them there, and we did it just to prove to you how dumb you are. God did not bring that milk and bread; we brought them."

What would you say in a case like that? The lady smiled, thanked the boys for the food, and then said, "Maybe the Devil **brought** these things, but God **sent** them." I am sure you see the difference. When the mailman brings an electric bill for two hundred dollars, you do not get upset with him. He did not **send it;** all he did was **deliver it.** This is the principle that we must see in all of the difficult things that happen. Thomas Watson was a Puritan with the ability to put great truth into short, concise statements. If you understand the following quote, you have the whole message:

> God always has a hand in the *action* where the sin is, but He never has a hand in the *sin* of the action.

It does not matter what happened, where it happened, when it happened, or to whom it happened. If it *happened*, then God had a hand in it; he controlled it. However, God is not guilty of the sin or hatred in the hearts of men that caused the sin in the situation.

It is vital to realize how important this particular principle is in our Christian life. We are told in Scripture to "humble ourselves under the mighty hand of God" and to *submit to him.* However, we are also told to *"resist the Devil"* and never to yield to his wiles and temptations. The problem lies in knowing and recognizing the difference between these two things. Many Christians, under the guise of "resisting the Devil," are actually fighting the sovereign providence of God. Other believers, under the guise of piously "turning it all over to God," are deliberately ignoring their personal responsibility to obey principles and fight temptation. Until we learn to see both the hand of Satan and the hand of God, we may be fighting God when we think we're resisting Satan, and vice versa.

Sixth Principle: Not All Affliction is Chastisement

Our last principle strikes at the very heart of the twentieth century misconception of the gospel and its sure promises. Even though *all sickness and affliction are under God's control and are part of his purposes, it is NOT true that they are all chastisement for sin.* **Some** affliction is definitely chastisement for sin and is sent to bring us to repentance and effect specific change in us; however, that is not true all of the time. **Sometimes** God allows his people to suffer just to demonstrate the power of his grace. It is wrong for a Christian to ever feel that God is "getting even" and punishing him when affliction comes. God only punishes sin in one of two places: he either punished it in Christ and the penal debt is totally paid, or else he punishes it in the sinner in hell. Even when affliction comes into our life as chastisement, it is never penal [that is, from God as judge], but the chastisement is always remedial [that is, from a loving heavenly Father]. Our Father *teaches* us through affliction, but he never *punishes* us.

The Case of Job

In the book of Habakkuk and in Isaiah, we saw God using affliction to bring repentance for sin in order that he might send revival. The book of Job also talks about affliction, but in a totally different sense. Let us look at Job's suffering and learn this sixth principle. First of all, we must be sure we understand how to approach the book of Job. It is easy to just assume that Job was "self-righteous" and God sent the afflictions to humble him. Job's "friends" assumed this, and kept insisting it was so, though both Job and God denied that such was the case. There is no question that Job made some very foolish statements; likewise, we know that in the end he knew God in a greater way than he ever did before. These things do not change the central truth of the book. Notice what God himself says about Job:

> *In the land of Uz there lived a man whose name was Job. This man was blameless and upright; he feared God and shunned evil.* (Job 1:1 NIV)

I find it hard to believe that anyone can read those words and then proceed to disparage Job by claiming he was self-righteous. If we accept that idea, we make it impossible to understand the meaning of the book and the purpose of Job's afflictions. Lest we think verse one is not actually God's personal evaluation of Job, then read God's very own words in Job 1:8 and the added words in Job 2:3. The primary precept to follow is this: the afflictions sent to Job had *nothing at all to do with chastisement for sin.* We can go further and say that one major temptation that Job faced, and overcame, was to believe and acknowledge that the afflictions were sent because of sin. That is the heart of the book. The objective of the dialogue between Satan and God is to settle this very question. Will Job continue to admit that everything that happens to him comes from the hand of God, and at the same time still trust and worship God? The answer is clear. Job lost every single thing that he had, but he did not desert his God, even when there were no answers or explanations for what was happening to him.

Challenge and Counter Challenge

The book of Job opens with a dialogue between Satan and God involving a challenge by God and a counter challenge by Satan. Notice this in the following verses:

Now there was a day when the sons of God came to present themselves before the LORD, and Satan came also among them. And the LORD said unto Satan, Whence comest thou? Then Satan answered the LORD, and said, From going to and fro in the earth, and from walking up and down in it. And the LORD said unto Satan, Hast thou considered my servant Job, that there is none like him in the earth, a perfect and an upright man, one that feareth God, and escheweth evil? Then Satan answered the LORD, and said, Doth Job fear God for nought? Hast not thou made an hedge about him, and about his house, and about all that he hath on every side? Thou hast blessed the work of his hands, and his substance is increased in the land. But put forth thine hand now, and touch all that he hath, and he will curse thee to thy face. And the LORD said unto Satan, Behold, all that he hath is in thy power; only upon himself put not forth thine hand. So Satan went forth from the presence of the LORD. (Job 1:6-12 KJV)

In verse 10 it is obvious that Job is securely in God's hands. In fact, Satan's accusation is that the hedge God has put around Job makes it impossible to get at him. In verse 11, Satan challenges God to "...put forth your [God's] hand, and touch all that he has..." God responds by saying, "...all that he has is in your [Satan's] power; only upon himself put not forth your hand." It now appears that Job is in Satan's hand. Is Job in God's hand, or is he in Satan's hand? If you have understood these verses, you see that Job is in *both* the hand of God and the hand of Satan. However, you have also seen that the hand of God is over Satan's hand, and Satan can only do what God allows to be done. In reality, Job is just as much in the hand of God when Satan is testing him as he was before. The only difference is the degree to which God has chosen to let down the hedge he had placed around Job.

And It Was All from God!

We all know the next part of the story. A servant informs Job that the Sabeans had stolen all of his oxen and donkeys and then killed all of the servants tending them. While that servant was speaking, another one arrives and announces that fire from heaven had killed all of the sheep and the servants taking care of them. A third servant immediately appears and reports that the Chaldeans had stolen all of the camels and killed those servants. In less than sixty seconds, Job learns that he is bankrupt of all his possessions. Before the third man has finished speaking, a fourth servant runs up with the news that all of Job's children died when a great wind destroyed the house in which they were feasting. The next few verses give us Job's response to these awful events:

> Then Job arose, and rent his mantle, and shaved his head, and fell down upon the ground, and worshipped, And said, Naked came I out of my mother's womb, and naked shall I return thither: the LORD gave, and the LORD hath taken away; blessed be the name of the LORD. In all this Job sinned not, nor charged God foolishly. (Job 1:20-22 KJV)

Notice that Job never mentions Satan. Job attributes it all to the hand of God. God had given all of the sheep, oxen, camels, and donkeys to Job, and Job said, "The same God has chosen to take them all away." But what does he say about his children? Job states that their births and their deaths were from the hand of God. Job maintains his confidence in God's sovereign control and his covenant promise, even when his personal world is destroyed.

We must grasp what is occurring in Job's life. Scripture makes it clear to us that Satan and God are engaged in conversation, which results in action in Job's life. However, we must constantly remember that Job himself had no way of knowing that fact. The only way we know is because the Bible takes us behind the scenes. We see and hear both the challenge and the counterchallenge. Job neither saw nor heard either. We understand that Job's heart and life was the stage on which the drama was enacted. Will the grace of God triumph in Job's heart regardless of the tests and trials? We read the story and know what is happening, but Job knew none of this. Job had no way of knowing that his heart was being used as an arena to display the results of the conversation between Satan and God. Job did not—and could not—have any logical, rational, or even theological explanation for what was happening to him. All he had was confidence in a sovereign, holy God.

"Scene One" [chapter one] in the spectacle displays the power of the grace of God. Job maintained his faith and his integrity. "Scene Two" begins with the same dialogue between Satan and God. However, when God challenges Satan the second time, he exults over Satan in the fact that Job remained true and faithful despite terrible afflictions. The third verse of chapter two furnishes us with the key to the whole book of Job:

> *And the LORD said unto Satan, Hast thou considered my servant Job, that there is none like him in the earth, a perfect and an upright*

man, one that feareth God, and escheweth evil? and still he holdeth
fast his integrity, although thou **movedst me against him,** to
destroy him **without cause.** (Job 2:3 KJV, emphasis added)

Notice carefully what the verse says. First of all, it is God
himself who is "against Job" in sending these afflictions. It
is true that Satan has *brought the afflictions,* but God is the
one that *sent them.* It is vital that we also see the second
truth in the text. God moved against Job, *without any reason
in Job.* The afflictions were in no way connected with any
sin in Job. Job was being used as a "test model" without
any knowledge of what was happening. He was
demonstrating and proving the sufficiency of God's grace
under unexplained afflictions.

In addition to his other losses, Job also lost his theology.
Job's friends reminded him that he had believed and
taught that God blesses the "good" and judges the "bad";
since that was true, how could Job explain his present
situation? Of course, Job could not explain what was
happening or reconcile it with his own theology. Someone
has said, "The book of Job records the first time that
orthodox theology was confronted with a situation that
was too big for it to handle." The hymn writer clearly
understood that fact when he wrote:

> When all around, my soul gives way,
> He then is all my hope and stay,
> His oath, His covenant, His blood,
> Support me in the whelming flood.

There are times when everything collapses, and we have
nothing left to hang on to but God himself. We cling to the

knowledge of his character and his covenant. All of our theology and all of our experience are not sufficient to understand and explain the ways of God. However, even when we cannot understand, we can trust that God will be holy, righteous, and faithful in all of his dealings with us. It is to this place that Job came. Through the awful events, Job's faith was proved genuine, and God was proved more than worthy of his faith and hope.

Satan now responds to God's glorying over him in his failure to get Job to renounce his confidence in God's grace. Let us look at the verses that contain this second dialogue:

> And Satan answered the LORD, and said, Skin for skin, yea, all that a man hath will he give for his life. But put forth thine hand now, and touch his bone and his flesh, and he will curse thee to thy face. And the LORD said unto Satan, Behold, he is in thine hand; but save his life. So went Satan forth from the presence of the LORD, and smote Job with sore boils from the sole of his foot unto his crown. And he took him a potsherd to scrape himself withal; and he sat down among the ashes. (Job 2:4-8 KJV)

Satan is still convinced that Job is a hypocrite. He blames God for being unfair in the contest and protecting Job from personal pain. It is one thing to lose "things" and see other people suffer, but it is quite another to experience unrelenting pain day and night. Again, we must note in verse 5 that Satan, speaking to God, says, "...stretch out **your hand** and strike his flesh and bones," and in verse 6 God responds and says to Satan, "Very well, then, he [Job] is in **your hands,** but you must spare his life." God lowers the hedge a little more but clearly sets the limits. It is still God's hand that is in control, despite the fact that the hand of Satan is the agent of the affliction. Job never doubts that everything has come from the hand of God.

Verse 7 shows Job taking a piece of broken pottery and scraping off the secretion from the boils that covered him from head to foot. Boils are extremely painful things. Job could not sit, stand, or lie without pain since his whole body was covered with boils. He sat "among the ashes" because they were the softest things he could find.

"Curse God and Die!"

Verses 9 and 10 are very instructive. They give us a picture of the contrast between the crippling weakness of a faith that goes by sight and the amazing strength of a faith that sees the sovereign hand of God in all things. How would you feel and respond if this had been said to you?

> _Then said his wife unto him, Dost thou still retain thine integrity? curse God, and die. But he said unto her, Thou speakest as one of the foolish women speaketh. What? shall we receive good at the hand of God, and shall we not receive evil? In all this did not Job sin with his lips._ (Job 2:9, 10 KJV)

The remarks of Job's wife are typical of both the unbeliever and the untaught, sentimental Christian who thinks of God's dealings with men in terms of a mawkish love, and reject reality. The moment we echo Job's words and declare the principles that we have been explaining, and in which Job hoped, we hear an angry response that sounds something like this in today's language: "Are you telling me that you honestly believe that God is in any way connected with these afflictions? I would not love and serve a God like that!" Few people would have the courage to verbalize that they felt the way Job's wife did, but they are in basic agreement. "I will trust and love God as long as he gives me the goodies [that I need to be happy], but if he throws in that kind of suffering, then I am not about to trust him!" How often the Devil has whispered into the ear of a tried and tested saint this same blasphemy (to curse God and end it all)! What makes this even more painful for Job is the fact that it comes from his own wife.

Now before you judge her too harshly, remember that she had to take care of Job and listen to his complaining. That would be quite a chore! All of those children that died were also **her** flesh and blood, and all that lost wealth was equally hers.

The Essence of Faith

Job's response is classic. "Shall we accept good from God, and not trouble?" Job has no use for the heresy of dualism. God is the author of **all things** whether they are good or bad. Job would have made a very poor "prosperity" adherent with his view of sickness and trouble. I doubt that he would have supported any of the "health and wealth" preachers that dominate the TV screen on Sundays.

Now remember, Job still does not understand or have any explanation for the things that are happening to him. All he knows is that (1) God has sent every one of the afflictions, and (2) God must have had a good reason for doing so even if Job could not fathom that reason. That, my friend, is the essence of biblical faith in a sovereign and gracious God. The highest point of Job's faith is found in that great declaration in Job 13:15. Notice the whole context:

> *Keep silent and let me speak; then let come to me what may. Why do I put myself in jeopardy and take my life in my hands?* **Though he slay me, yet will I hope in him;** *I will surely defend my ways to his face...I know I will be vindicated.* (Job 13:13-18 NIV, emphasis added)

Job is absolutely certain that he will be vindicated and it will be shown that God was not judging him for sin. In the meantime, Job is prepared to trust God regardless of what may come. When he said, "Though he slay me, still will I trust him," Job is saying, "Though he who took the sheep, donkeys, camels, all my children, and my health should take the last step and kill me (which he has a right to do whenever he chooses), still I trust him and believe he has a just reason. I will not believe he is cursing me in these afflictions nor will I give up believing that I shall someday be totally satisfied and vindicated."

Let me digress for a moment and examine an easily missed angle of Job's temptation. The main purpose of Satan's attack is to prove one single point. Satan is claiming that *there is no such thing as a "genuine believer" that truly loves God for his own sake.* Men only worship God because it is to their own benefit. Without the "look what I get out of it" motive, men will renounce God and curse him to his face. That part of the temptation is easy to see; however, there is an even greater snare for Job. He believes that God is the sovereign ruler of the world. Job believes that he has faithfully served God and that he is basically an upright man. In no sense is Job claiming to be without sin or guilt, but he is claiming that he has loved and followed God with an upright heart. If this is true, then how can Job explain all of these afflictions? Obviously, he cannot even begin to explain why these things are happening.

Trying to Protect God

Job's biggest temptation is to *admit to sin of which he is not guilty as a means of getting God off the hook for sending these troubles.* God's character as a fair and honest God who rewards good people and curses bad people would then be protected. Job would have a theological explanation for why God had sent these troubles (they would now be judgments or chastisement), and his friends could then sincerely encourage him to expect forgiveness and restoration since he had come clean and confessed his secret sin. The problem with this is that Job would be lying; worse yet, the Devil would win by proving that Job was a liar and a hypocrite interested only in getting the "goody basket" to start replacing the "affliction barrel." It would have been a thousand times easier to yield to the *appearance* instead of hanging on to *reality.* It would have been much easier for Job to protect God with a few pious platitudes than it was to honestly face the unexplained facts with an undaunted faith in God himself and his sovereign, holy character.

Isn't this the great stumbling block of the cross? How can God's dearly beloved Son suffer such agony without his Father so much as lifting a hand to help? No, we did not state the case correctly! How could a holy, righteous, and loving heavenly Father actually inflict the wounds with **his own hands?** The inability of the Jews to understand this fact is what made Christ's claims appear to be monstrous blasphemies. Surely, Jesus of Nazareth must be guilty to suffer so; God does not punish the innocent.

Suppose you had been there the day those wicked and ruthless men stoned Stephen to death. What would you have said if someone whispered in your ear, "God Almighty is in charge of this charade and is using these despicable men to accomplish his secret purposes"? Stephen believed that and expressed hope and assurance even while he was being unjustly stoned to death.

God's Providence a Mystery

I have no explanation as to why God allows some of his saints to endure persecution and affliction. However, it is both a biblical and historical fact that such is the case. Job, David, Joseph, and Stephen are clear examples from God's Word; Fanny Crosby, Joni Erickson, and many brothers and sisters in our circle of acquaintances testify to the same truth. It is not ours to question God and ask "Why?" nor is it ours to deny the texts of Scripture that teach a truth we do not like. It is ours to prove God's grace and power by trusting him even when we cannot understand.

There used to be a rather silly TV commercial about a grocer named Mr. Whipple who scolded ladies for squeezing toilet paper to test how soft it was. I never once saw ladies do that in a grocery store, but I did see them squeezing lemons and oranges to see if they were soft and rotten. I believe that is what happens to God's people. He allows the world to squeeze us to see what we are made of. When God opens your heart to his amazing grace, you will open your mouth and begin to testify. You will brag about having found bread that really satisfies your hungry soul and brings real joy into your life. However, sometimes people are skeptical, and they deliberately test you to see how "satisfied" you really are!

When God is doubly gracious and teaches us the truth about his sovereignty, we often open our mouths to brag about a God that controls everybody and every event. We may even ridicule the weak God of the poor Arminian. "Our God is not dependent on man or man's will. Our Sovereign God controls every event that comes into our lives!" Now the world really becomes skeptical, and they say, "I wonder if they really believe and trust God's sovereignty. Let's cross their wills and not give them their own way; we'll see how they respond." How do you react when some mean, obnoxious individual deliberately keeps you from something that you want *and may deserve*?

If I were a skilled enough artist, I could paint the outside of a water glass to look like it was filled with lemonade. However, if I upset the glass, then whatever was in the glass would come pouring out. I could have milk in the glass, even though it looked like it was filled with lemonade. The process of upsetting would bring out the milk.

You and I may ridicule Arminians and paint ourselves with all kinds of Calvinistic labels, but the real test of our faith in a sovereign God is how we act when we are upset and do not get our own way. When that happens to you, does sovereign *grace* or sovereign *flesh* come pouring out of you? A correct theology is not enough. Job actually lost his theology. In fact, his friends beat him over the head with his theology. "Job, you have taught us that God hears and answers the prayer of a righteous man but refuses to hear the prayer of a sinner, and now when God is silent toward you and all these afflictions have come, you want to maintain that you are righteous! You are a sinful hypocrite that will not own up to his sin, and you blaspheme God with your protesting. How do you reconcile what is happening to you according to your own theology?" How could Job answer such taunts? He could not deny that he had believed and taught exactly what they said, nor could he confess sin of which he did not believe he was guilty. Job could only reply, "I cannot." The only thing left for him to do was shut up and wait on God. Job could have written the hymn we just quoted.

"It Isn't Fair!"

I am often called to counsel people who have been badly misused. In tears, they say, "But pastor, it was so unfair." I can feel for them. I just recently went through a situation where Christians that I loved and trusted deliberately deceived and lied in order to maintain positions of authority. Their behavior was worse than a secular political campaign. It was one of the most difficult experiences of my Christian life. My own heart wanted to cry out, "But Lord, they *know* that they are lying. It is so cruel and unfair."

What is the only comfort we can take when it isn't fair? First of all, we can remind ourselves that *God has never indicated that it would be fair!* In fact, if we have even a little understanding of the Word of God and take its message seriously, we realize that we should not expect the ungodly to be fair.

It was not fair that Jeremiah was put into a pit. It was not fair that Joseph's brothers sold him into slavery. It was not fair that Stephen was stoned, or that Nero fed thousands of Christians to the lions. Many of the things that have happened to godly Christians have been horribly cruel and unfair (see Hebrews 11). However, where did we even get the idea that *we should expect it to be fair?* This world is no friend to the grace of God in any sense. Read Matthew 10:16-42, and then dare to ask why it is not fair.

Yes, we will be squeezed, but we will never be "tested above that we are able." If God chooses to allow us to be put into the furnaces, let us endure as good soldiers and exhibit the power of his grace. Let us pray for that grace to believe and say, "Shall we receive good at the hands of God and not bad?" Understanding and applying these six principles of the Word of God will greatly help us to do that very thing.

One of my favorite hymns has caught the truth of what I am trying to say. It is entitled "Whate'er My God Ordains

Is Right." If we could get this truth written on our hearts in such a way that we would always be able to feel its power, we would be "more than conquers in Christ" in every situation. We would see God's hand in all things and know that his sovereign grace and love controls all things. The six basic principles we have covered would be like a Rock of Gibraltar beneath our feet. We would sing with great joy, "Whatever my lot, Thou hast taught me say, 'It is well my soul.'"

Christian, this sovereign and loving one is your God. Take courage and have hope. You are absolutely secure in the shadow of his wings. Your Lord has already gained the full victory—**and so shall you!**

If you are not a Christian, then remember, this is the God against whom you rebel. You have consciously chosen to hate his authority and despise his grace. If you have never bowed your heart and will in true repentance and faith to this great God, then of all people, you are the most miserable and the most foolish. How can you even think that you can fight against such a God and ever prevail? Turn to him in faith and discover that he is just as merciful as he is sovereign.

CHAPTER TWO
THE SOVEREIGNTY OF GOD IN DECREES

Introduction

Every historical age is labeled in retrospect with a predominant feature that is characteristic of that era. We are familiar with the labels "stone age," the "dark age," the "ice age," the "machine age," etc. I wonder what history will see as the predominant feature of our generation. I am sure it will have something to do with despair and hopelessness. The philosophy of twentieth-century atheistic existentialism, characterized by no hope, surely controls every aspect of our present society. Ann Landers was amazed that most parents say that they would not have their children if they had it to do over again. Nobody feels fulfilled today. Both men and women walk away from any and all responsibilities in order to "find themselves." Nothing shocks anyone anymore, regardless of how bizarre it is. However, neither does anything inspire. Society is jaded in both directions. Someone has said, "Girls used to blush when they were ashamed, but now they are ashamed when they blush."

The ability to understand reality and build a meaningful life is like erecting a building. When constructing a physical building, you first need a good set of plans. You then begin to build by digging down in the earth and preparing a solid foundation. Next, you choose the right materials that will stand the stress of wear and weather, and then proceed to put up your building. The successful outcome of the entire project depends on the trustworthiness of the foundation. In order to build a meaningful and God-honoring life, one must follow the same procedure. The blueprint is the Word of God, the foundation is the theology presented in the Scriptures, and the materials are biblical faith and obedience.

This is what our Lord was teaching in Matthew 7:21-29:

> *Not everyone who says to me, 'Lord, Lord,' will enter the kingdom of heaven, but only he who does the will of my Father who is in heaven. Many will say to me on that day, 'Lord, Lord, did we not prophesy in your name, and in your name drive out demons and perform many miracles?' Then I will tell them plainly, 'I never knew you. Away from me, you evildoers!'*

> *Therefore everyone who hears these words of mine and puts them into practice is like a wise man who built his house on the rock. The rain came down, the streams rose, and the winds blew and beat against that house; yet it did not fall, because it had its foundation on the rock. But everyone who hears these words of mine and does not put them into practice is like a foolish man who built his house on sand. The rain came down, the streams rose, and the winds blew and beat against that house, and it fell with a great crash."*

> *When Jesus had finished saying these things, the crowds were amazed at his teaching, because he taught as one who had authority, and not as their teachers of the law.* (NIV)

All are building a house, or a life, in which they must finally spend eternity. Some people build their lives on the sand of the lies of men, and others build on the rock of truth, the Bible. We call the foundations of life presuppositions. Everyone has basic presuppositions. They accept some things without question and proceed to base their lives on those "facts." When a person says, "Well, this is what I believe," he is giving you one or more of the presuppositions upon which he bases his life. If his life is based on anything other than a knowledge of, and commitment to, Jesus Christ as Lord and Savior, then that person is building on sand. When such a person is confronted with the storms and difficulties of existence, his life often falls apart. When he faces God in the final day, everything, his whole life, will be washed away in judgment. Likewise, the man who builds on the rock is the person who builds on the truth of Scripture. The same storms of life beat upon him, but sovereign grace keeps him believing in the truth, and his house will stand for time and eternity.

Our lives operate on the same principles as a physical building; if the foundations or presuppositions upon which our lives are built are wrong, then everything built on those faulty presuppositions is also wrong. If we follow lies, no matter how sincere we may be, our house of sand will collapse when tested by God.

This principle can be illustrated by the following incident: my wife used to have a housecoat that had twenty-one buttons. One morning, before she had her coffee, she put the number-two button into the number-one hole. Scoundrel that I am, I watched her button the entire garment, knowing full well the ultimate outcome. When she was finished, she had a button left over and no hole in which to put it. The important question for our discussion is this: how many mistakes did my wife make in buttoning her housecoat? Most people would say, "She made one mistake at the very beginning." Actually, she made twenty-one mistakes. Every button without exception was in the wrong hole and had to be undone and fastened over again. In other words, because she started wrong, everything that followed was wrong.

The same thing is true of life. My wife sailed along with twenty buttons without a single problem; so, too, we may go through life thinking all is well because we have not encountered any major problems. However, if we started on the wrong foundation, when we come to the end and face God, we will discover that everything has been wrong. I remind you that this is exactly what Jesus was teaching in Matthew 7:24-28. We either build our lives on the rock of God's unchanging truth, or we build on the sand of man's changing folly. The storms of life and the final deluge of death will reveal the truth about our lives and their ultimate end. Unlike a simple clothing mistake, we do not get a second chance to undo and redo the buttons. We only get one opportunity to build one house in which to live eternally.

It is vital that we realize that all men, without exception, base their lives on certain notions they assume to be true. As I mentioned, we call those notions presuppositions. It means that the individual "pre-supposes" some things as true and lives his life by faith in those presuppositions. For instance, the Christian believes, as a fact beyond doubt, that the Bible is the Word of God and is to be obeyed without question simply because it is God's Word. He performs certain actions and refrains from certain others, just because "the Bible says so." He literally bets both his life on earth as well as the eternal life to come on Jesus Christ the Lord. The non-Christian does not believe the Bible, nor does he really care what it commands. He may look to science, education, art, philosophy, even religion, but in the end, he himself is the final authority for all his beliefs and actions. He accepts as a fact the idea that he has a right to do whatever he wants, whenever and however he pleases. Both the Christian and non-Christian live by faith in their presuppositions; however, those presuppositions are exactly opposite of each other

Most people do not realize that all men without exception are deeply committed believers, and all men live their lives by an absolute faith in their beliefs. Every person in your hometown is a "believer" and lives "by faith" in his beliefs or presuppositions. Unhappily, most people believe lies and live their entire lives in rebellion against the revealed truth of God. Man's problem is not a lack of faith. He has plenty of faith, but it is misplaced; his faith is in himself instead of in God and his Word.

Examples of this awful fact are evident on every hand. The socialist programs of the Johnson administration that were to knit the classes together in a Great Society have not succeeded in bridging the gap between rich and poor, between privilege and privation. In 1965, eighty-nine measures which Lyndon Johnson's administration backed were passed. Among these were: Medicare; Aid to Education; creation of the Department of Housing and Urban Development; Regional Development, and a host of others. One economic consequence of this overexpanding welfarism was that by the mid-seventies, devaluation of the dollar and inflation had caused an unnamed but very real depression that lasted for almost a decade. The American people had been promised that government programs would prevent any more prolonged depressions after the great one that began in 1929. "The government programs and manipulation of the money supply did alter the character of the depression, but they did not prevent one from occurring." (Clarence B. Carson, The Welfare State 1929-1985, vol.5 of *A Basic History of the United States* [Wadley, Alabama: American Textbook Committee, 1986], p. 211). Dr. Spock and his "baby bible" were supposed to produce a generation of well-adjusted children bubbling over with "self-esteem." I may not be very good at analyzing and comparing things, but to me there does not seem to be much similarity between what Dr. Spock promised and the MTV crowd that his "bible" produced. One of Dr. Spock's adamant rules was "no spanking," but twenty-five years later, with a generation of young people in open rebellion, Dr. Spock says, "Maybe they do need a few spankings."

This principle that shaky foundations produce faulty buildings can be seen in the results of fluctuating theories that rotate in our educational system. I have two nephews who were in school when the "new math" and "new approach to English" took over. Today my nephews can neither do math nor speak correct English. The open-classroom structure of the early seventies was designed to create an atmosphere where learning was comfortable and natural. Instead, it produced students who did not practice even such basic concepts as taking turns, asking permission, and not interrupting. After enough evidence of these kinds of failures was produced, schools said, "We made a mistake" and went back to the old methods, but that hardly helps my nephews and countless others whose education was built on erroneous premises.

Let me repeat, we simply must see that all men live by presuppositions. All men are committed believers, but some men believe lies! Man's problem is not a lack of faith, but rather that he has too much faith! His problem is that his faith is in the wrong person and the wrong presuppositions. He builds on the sand of lies. We must begin with God and not with man. Our basic starting point must be a sovereign and wise Creator, not man's autonomy and ability to know what is best.

The Importance of Studying the Decrees of God

I hope no one gets frightened when I use the word *decrees*. We are not talking about abstract philosophy, nor are we arguing about fine points in theology. We are talking about real, everyday life. We are talking about personal tragedies and human destiny. Our subject affects the lives of truck drivers, housewives, store clerks, sales persons, etc. The decrees of God concern your personal life.

We are raising questions that every person has thought about at one time or another. How would you explain the many terrible tragedies that Rose Kennedy suffered in her lifetime? Where was God when six-million Jews were killed and a maniac ravaged and raped a whole continent? Did God know that the terrorists were going to fly two planes into the twin towers of the Trade Center on September 11? If so, why did he not stop them?

Years ago, I taught a Bible class, and God, in his providence, converted a woman in her early forties who attended. She grew in grace and witnessed of her faith in Christ. Within one year after being converted, she died of cancer. After the funeral, her mother asked me, with tears in her eyes, "Mr. Reisinger, why did my daughter have to die? She was a wonderful mother and wife. Her husband and children needed her so badly." She was asking the proverbial $64,000 question. It is the question that every philosopher has asked since the dawn of time—"Is there rhyme and reason to the world and the events of life, or is it all a cruel joke? Is there purpose to life, or is it all without real meaning?" Is God in control, or are we ultimately the victims of chance, chaos and confusion? If God is in total control of all things, did he not surely make a mistake this time? If God ordained this awful event, how can I ever love and trust him again?

We are not talking about abstractions or fantasies. We are talking about the realities and tragedies that make up the real world. What does a pastor say when a tearful saint asks, "Why did God take my child"? How do we respond when the doctor says it is cancer and it is inoperable? Or when the company I have worked for thirty-five years goes bankrupt and I lose every penny of my pension? We could go on and on with examples in our own lives and the lives of godly Christians close to us. I repeat, when we discuss the decrees of God, we are not talking about philosophy; nor are we talking about something that is make-believe. We are talking about reality and human destiny.

The primary purpose of this book is not to promote a particular view of theology. It, of course, does that in the same sense that every religious book that was ever written lays out a theological belief. Primarily, though, we are seeking to understand the "why" of real-life situations. Many of us are aware of the personal tragedies that Rose Kennedy suffered. She had a daughter killed in a plane crash and a grandson killed in another plane crash, a son murdered while he was president of our country, another son murdered while seeking to be president, a son involved in a girl's death at Chappaquiddick, a grandson who lost his leg to cancer, another grandson convicted of murder, and the list goes on and on. Compare that to a woman who has seven children, twenty-three grandchildren, all of them healthy and all coming home for Thanksgiving Day dinner. How do you explain the difference?

We should add that the closer one gets to reality, the more tragic and ugly life becomes. That fact is true because all of life is upside down as a result of sin. Neither life nor man himself today is even close to what they were when

God originally created them. Sin has distorted everything. Man is never more in the presence of reality than when he stands by the casket of a dead loved one. Man does all he can to not think about death, but it is the one inevitable reality that all men must face. Death is an appointment decreed by God that no man will ever avoid and for which he will not be even one second late. I do not the like the fact that life is tragic, but because of man's sin such is the reality.

The Basic Choices and Responses to Reality

One response to this unpalatable fact is to not think about anything ugly like death. You maintain a "positive attitude" and simply refuse to face reality. You put on a pair of rose-colored glasses that enables you to see only what you want to see. You turn real life into a world of make-believe that you yourself create. This method cannot possibly succeed in the long run, but still many people continue to try it. When anyone runs from reality, they need some diversion; booze, dope, unbridled sex, constant work, parties, or something else just to keep from jumping off the bridge. They might even adopt the "I love me and I feel good about myself" philosophy that is being peddled even by evangelical (?) religious hucksters. Call it what you want to, but the result is the same as sticking your head in the sand.

Another response to the ugliness of reality is to believe the world is controlled by blind fate. Life really has no rational explanation. "That's the way the cookie crumbles" is the response to "bad luck." You simply grin and bear it and hope, with no real basis, that things will get better. This is a hard stone to chew if it is your biopsy report that shows inoperable cancer.

A common response by many evangelical Christians is to blame all the bad things on the Devil. We call this the Flip Wilson response, "The Devil made me do it." As we shall see in a moment, crediting God with all of the good things and blaming the Devil for all the bad things is a heresy known as dualism.

Still other people believe that those people who suffer badly are all wicked sinners and God is punishing them for their sin. Scripture clearly contradicts this view and forbids us to think like that. Our Lord addressed this very attitude in Luke 13:4-5.

> *Or those eighteen who died when the tower in Siloam fell on them—do you think they were more guilty than all the others living in Jerusalem? I tell you, no! But unless you repent, you too will all perish.* (NIV)

The only viable answer left in the attempt to explain real life, including its tragedies, is to acknowledge God and his sovereign decrees.

The Bible Teaches that God Ordains All Things that Come to Pass

That statement may disconcert you, but it is true. The major confessions of faith all agree with it:

1. God hath (Isa. 46:10; Eph. 1:11; Heb. 6:17; Rom. 9:15, 18) decreed in himself, from all eternity, by the most wise and holy counsel of his own will, freely and unchangeably,

all things whatsoever come to pass; yet so as thereby is God neither the author of sin (James 1:13; 1 John 1:5) nor hath fellowship with any therein; nor is violence offered to the will of the creature, nor yet is the liberty or contingency of second causes taken away, but rather (Acts 4:27, 28; John 19:11) established; in which appears his wisdom in disposing all things, and power and faithfulness (Num. 23:19; Eph. 1:3-5) in accomplishing his decree. (Philadelphia Confession of Faith, Chapter 3, Section 1)

The wording is almost identical in The Westminster Confession of Faith, chapter 3, section 1, and in The Baptist Confession of Faith of 1689, chapter 3, section 1.

I admit that this view creates problems, but so does every other view. Often times we are confronted with a situation that has more than one option, none of which are satisfactory in our minds. As I mentioned earlier, I do not like the fact that I cannot paint life like a bowl of cherries, but reality demands that we face the hard facts, regardless of how much we may dislike them. Trying to understand and explain the ugliness of reality and reconcile it to our view of the love and grace of God poses difficulties for which we do not have complete and satisfactory answers.

Lastly, I often hear people say, when confronted with the sovereignty of God, "That is not my idea of God at all." Sadly, that statement is only too true of that person. It means that his ideas about God are just that: they are his ideas. This person did not get his ideas out of the Bible, but out of his own imagination and emotions.

After all the smoke clears, I think it is better to accept the statement of the Confession as that which accurately represents the teaching of Scripture on this subject, rather than to chase alternative theories. Even with all its difficulties, it is reasonable to throw yourself right into the teeth of God's absolute sovereignty and rest in confidence in his holiness and sovereignty, even when you cannot understand. The "holy, holy, holy, sovereign Lord" is our heavenly Father.

Henry Ironside was a great preacher among the Plymouth Brethren. He was known for his ability to illustrate biblical truth. One of his favorite stories concerned a rug made out of a bearskin that included the bear's head and teeth. Dr. Ironside would cover himself in the bear rug, look out through the teeth, and chase his grandson saying, "I'm a big bad bear, and I'm going to eat you." The child would run and scream. On one occasion, Dr. Ironside chased the boy into the corner of the bedroom where the boy had no way of escape. Ironside said, "Now I've got you. I am a big bad bear, and I am going to eat you." The boy was screaming as loud as he could as his grandpa got closer and closer. At the last moment, the boy threw his arms around the bear's head and said, "You are not a big bad bear; you are my grandpa, and you are not going to hurt me." That's the way to meet the subject of God's sovereign decrees in the time of tragedy. When the Devil taunts you by questioning God's wisdom and love, throw yourself right into the teeth of God's absolute sovereignty and say, "This sovereign God is also my heavenly Father, and he has committed himself to bring good out of this awful situation." That is the safest and only biblical answer.

The Place to Start

One of the first verses I memorized after becoming a Christian was Deuteronomy 29:29. I have reminded myself of its truth many times.

> *The secret things belong unto the LORD our God: but those things which are revealed belong unto us and to our children forever, that we may do all the words of this law.* (KJV)

The decrees of God are the "secret things," and they belong to God. The decrees of God, as the Confession states, include all things that will ever happen. There is no way that we can know what God has decreed unless he chooses to reveal it to us. God does not consult us about what he can or will decree to do or not to do. The decrees do indeed "belong to God" and are therefore none of my business. It gives me great comfort to know that God has decreed all things. It is reassuring to know that not one single thing happens by chance or luck. However, those secret things are locked up in the secret counsel of God.

The "revealed things" to which the text refers are God's Word, the Bible. The revealed things include the law and the gospel. The text says they are given to us and to our children so that we might know and do God's will. The decrees of God do not spell out our duty as children of God. The revealed will of God in Scripture does that. We are not responsible in any way to figure out the secret decrees of God. They are not given to us to rule our lives.

We are responsible to understand and obey all that he has revealed in his Word, but not what he has secretly decreed. Arminians have a tendency to be unwilling to go as far as Scripture does on some subjects, and Calvinists have a tendency to refuse to stop where God has stopped. The latter group tries to use human logic to unlock things that God has been pleased to simply not reveal.

The following charts give a few of the basic philosophic approaches to understanding reality. Christians should be aware of how these and other philosophies impact the society in which we live.

Basic Approaches

Chart 1

THEISM	ATHEISM
A belief in a god (monotheism) or gods (polytheism)—A religious system with belief that there is "outside" control.	No God, no "supernatural"—A "natural" explanation; science, evolution, humanism, fate (luck) or man, etc.

Chart 2

Deism	Pantheism	Dualism	Biblical Theism
God is impersonal—he is not active in human affairs—the "big clock" idea.	God IS creation—he is part of everything and everything is part of him.	Two "eternal" sovereign forces—good and evil, God and the Devil in a cosmic war.	God of the Bible! Genesis 1:1 Romans 11:36 Creator, Sustainer—history is HIS-story.
Thomas Jefferson	Environ mentalist	Charismatic	Reformed Theology

I am aware that the chart above is a gross over-simplification. A philosophy major will be tempted to quit reading at this point. My defense is that I am not writing a book on philosophy. I am merely showing a few modern examples of how various philosophies impact our life and society. Deism, pantheism, and dualism are certainly three of the major philosophies that have shaped, and continue to shape, our culture.

Deism, which began to be expressed among a small group of English writers in the first half of the seventeenth century, purports to believe in God, but not the God who has revealed himself in the Bible. In general, deism refers to the concept that knowledge of God can be acquired solely through the use of reason, and denies the divine authority of the Bible. Its adherents use what Francis Schaefer calls "God words." The purpose in using a word like "God" is not to convey a concrete piece of descriptive information but to evoke a "religious" feeling. The God of deism is an impersonal God. True, he created the world, but then he turned it over to natural law. The universe is like a big clock. God created it, wound it up, subjected it to natural laws, and then he went fishing. The universe is a "closed system," and life is controlled by man's free will. Moral principles do not originate in revelation but are inherent in the very structure of man's reason. Deism denies that there are real answers to specific prayers, the concept of the new birth, the idea that God could become flesh, etc. American deists include Thomas Jefferson, Benjamin Franklin, and William Penn.

Pantheism was coined as a term in the early eighteenth century. It refers to philosophical systems that tend to identify God with the world. Pantheistic thought deifies nature so that nature becomes God. It identifies God with his creation in such a way that everything without exception is part of God. God is not in any way separate from his creation. He is not a personal, unique, individual being who is the sovereign Creator. He is nature, and nature is God. The deer and the tree, as well as you and I, are a part of God. If you shoot a deer, then you have destroyed part of God. The extreme environmentalists of our generation are rabid pantheists. When they speak of "saving God's creation," they do not refer to the God of the Bible. He is not the God and father of our Lord Jesus Christ. These people and their cohorts write songs about nature being "My Fair Sister." Nature is neither my sister nor my mother, and time is not my father. Speaking about Mother Nature and Father Time conveys very bad theology. We gladly admit that everything in nature was created by God and created for his glory. We also acknowledge that God is active in his creation today. However, we insist that God is distinct from and over and beyond his creation. God and his creation are not the same. In no sense whatever is creation necessary to God. It adds nothing at all to him as the all-sufficient God.

Dualism, as I mentioned earlier, explains given situations in terms of two opposing factors or principles. Ethical or ethico-religious dualism has its most clear-cut expression in the ancient Iranian religion of Zoroaster, but found a supporter in the third century in Mani, who fused

Persian, Christian, and Buddhist elements into a major new faith. It is dualism as presented in the form of Mani's views that was fought vigorously by both the Roman emperors and by the Christian church, most notably by Augustine, who himself had at one time been a lower-class member of the Manichaean community. The current evangelical form of dualism views the world as being in a cosmic battle between good and evil, black and white, God and Devil. The Devil has stolen God's creation and Jesus, with the help of Christians, is trying to get it back. We are not sure who is going to win the war, but we hope it is our side. We must give God all the help that we possibly can. In this system of thought, God is credited with all the good things that happen, and the Devil is responsible for all the bad things. As we pointed out in chapter one, "The Sovereignty of God in Providence," when the bad things become more numerous than the good things, we are tempted to wonder if we are fighting on the wrong side. The movie *Star Wars* depicted the philosophies of dualism, pantheism, and deism in the concept of a universal but impersonal "Force," with its light side and dark side, each available and equally powerful to any who are gifted to use it.

The moment we acknowledge any form of theism (a belief in God or gods) and reject atheism (no god), then we must answer the next logical question. If there is "government" or "control" and not just luck or chance, where and what is the source of that outside control? There are only three basic answers if we think in the "ultimate sense."

1. Man himself: Man is the "master of his fate." His free will controls not only his own personal destiny but also future itself.

2. The Devil: He has stolen God's creation (including man), and God is earnestly seeking to get it back.

3. God Almighty: He is in total control and is working out his own decrees in his own time (cf. Romans 11:36).

As biblical theists, we can safely choose the third answer and say, "What God sovereignly decrees in eternity, man will always, in time, freely choose with his own free will" (Matt. 27:15-26, cf. Acts 2:23). We have worked out the implications of this biblical principle in chapter one, "The Sovereignty of God in Providence."

When biblical theism refers to God, it means the "God of the Bible." This God has revealed himself through special revelation and can only be known personally through that revelation. The biblical revelation of God's character does not begin with John 3:16 but with the entire being of the God of John 3:16. That verse can only benefit you spiritually to the degree that you understand who this God is, what he is promising, and whether he is able to do what he promised. The God of the Bible is personal; he is Creator, Lawgiver, and Judge. Above all, he is the God and Father of our Lord Jesus Christ. God's perspective on history is presented in Romans 11:36:

For from him and through him and to him are all things. To him be the glory forever! Amen. (NIV)

The first sentence of this verse uses three different prepositions. The purpose of a preposition is to express the relationship or function between two different things that occur in a sentence. The prepositions in Romans 11:36 instruct us of the relationship between everything that happens and God's sovereign purposes. The word *from* is the English translation of the Greek word *ek*. It is the word *exit* and means "out of." The book of Exodus uses this word in the account of Israel "coming out of" Egypt. Paul is saying that all things, without exception, grow "out of" the decrees of God. The second preposition is the Greek word *dia* and means "by means of," or "through." Paul intends for us to know that just as all things have their source in God, so all things are brought to pass through, or by means of, God's sovereign providence. The third preposition is the Greek word *eis* and means "into." Paul uses these words to communicate the truth that all things are planned by God, brought about in time by God, and ultimately bring God honor and glory. All things grow out of God's purpose, they all are brought to pass by his power, and they all move into God.

A person could believe that all of the above is true and hate the fact he cannot do anything to change it. He may admit, through gritted teeth, that God is truly sovereign and does whatever he pleases. That is not the response produced in the apostle as he considers this truth. For Paul, these facts are the cause of worship. When he says, "To him be glory forever," Paul is lost in wonder and praise to the God who has revealed himself in the Bible.

God's Relationship to His Creation — Transcendence and Immanence

We must understand and hold tightly to both of these truths. To believe either one of these truths without also believing the other one is to wander into heresy and ultimately deny the God of the Bible. Let's define these great words:

"*Transcend*: to rise above or beyond the limits or power of; to overpass; exceed.... Theological: of God, being prior to and exalted above the universe, and having being apart from it" (Webster's dictionary).

"*Immanent*: remaining or operating within the subject considered; indwelling; inherent; as, the belief that God is imminent in nature...." (Webster).

When we speak of the transcendence of God, we mean that he is "over, above, and beyond" everyone and everything. The universe is not at all essential to God's being. If God had never created the world, he would still have been just as much God as he is now. Creation is not essential to God, but God is essential for creation. The main point of this idea is to insist that God is totally distinct from his creation. He is over and beyond everything he ever created or will create. As Webster correctly says, "God has being apart from the universe he created."

When we speak of God being immanent, we mean that God has chosen to come into his creation. It is true that God is "immanent in nature," but the vital immanence of which the Scripture speaks is his choice to become man and partake of the very nature of his creation. God actually became a real, living part of the world that he created.

The Three Great "Omni's"

Theologians use three words to describe God's active day-to-day relationship to his universe. You and I as individuals are included in "his universe." The three words are *omnipresent, omnipotent,* and *omniscient.* They mean God is "everywhere present, all powerful, and all knowing."

Part of the glory of the gospel is the truth that the transcendent God of creation has become personally immanent in the incarnation of Jesus Christ, God's Son and our Lord. Two key New Testament texts set forth this amazing truth:

> *"The virgin will be with child and will give birth to a son, and they will call him Immanuel"—which means, "God with us."* (Matt. 1:23 NIV)

> *The Word became flesh and made his dwelling among us. We have seen his glory, the glory of the One and Only, who came from the Father, full of grace and truth.* (John 1:14 NIV)

The incarnation fulfills the hope of the Old Testament believer. They understood both concepts of God's relationship to his creation, but never in the personal way that we do as we grasp the gospel and are indwelt by the Holy Spirit. The New Testament Scriptures reveal the relationship of the "indwelling" of God by his Holy Spirit that certainly transcends anything experienced under the Old Covenant. This was made possible by the ascension of

Christ to the throne of David, when he then sent the Holy Spirit as his vicar on the day of Pentecost.

Christ is the "head of the church," and as such, is over and beyond us (Col. 1:18). However, he is also "one with us" as our "older brother" (Heb. 4:14-16), even though he is king of kings. We are "in him" (2 Cor. 12:2), and he is "in us" (Col. 2:9, 10; and Rev. 1:10-20).

Definition of Decrees

The Confessions define decrees this way: "God from all eternity did, by His most wise and holy counsel of His own will, freely and unchangeably ordain whatsoever comes to pass...." (Westminster & Philadelphia Confessions, Chapter 3, Section 1). I'm sure I don't need to remind you that creeds and confessions are not inspired. Granted they are often treated that way, but that is a misuse of creeds. A creed does not prove a doctrine is true; it merely means that a certain group is accepting certain tenets as true. A "confessional church" may use their creed with equal authority to Scripture, and in a confessional church you must believe what the creed states. A non-confessional church may have a creed or confession, but they do not bind your conscience to the confession in the same that a confessional church does. In such a church (non-confessional), the confession proves what the church has believed and confessed down through history.

A.H. Strong, a Baptist theologian, said, "By *Decrees of God*, we mean:

- that eternal plan

- by which God has rendered certain

- all events of the universe,

- past, present, and future.

I personally give these home-made definitions:

- DECREES: The plans or purposes of God; those things that God had decided to do, allow to happen, accomplish. Some examples are: creation, Adam's fall, redemption by blood, the flood, the cross, etc. Decrees include everything that actually happens or comes to pass.

- SOVEREIGNTY: This includes both God's right and also his almighty power to bring to pass everything that he has decreed. God can, and will, accomplish everything he purposes.

- PROVIDENCE: This is God actually bringing to pass (in time) (history), by his sovereign power, all that he has decreed.

The Extent of God's Decrees

"...He is in one mind, and who can turn him? and what his soul desireth, even that he doeth" (Job 23:13 KJV).

This text states that:

1.   God has a plan—He is in one mind.

2.   He fully intends to carry out his plan—"...what his soul desireth...he doeth."

3.   His plan is unchangeable—"Who can turn him?"

4. Nobody and nothing can stop him—"...even that (what he plans) he doeth."

It is obvious that God's plan is universal and includes all things without exception. This fact is a great comfort to a child of God, especially in times of trial. Spurgeon has pointed this out.

It is, when properly understood, a matter of unspeakable consolation that God has a plan; for who could honor a God who had no plan, but who did everything by haphazard? It is a matter of rejoicing that he has one great purpose that extends through all ages and embraces all things; for then everything falls into its proper place and has its appropriate bearing on other events. It is a matter of rejoicing that God does execute all his purposes; for as they are all good and wise, is it not desirable that they should be executed? It would be a calamity if a good plan were not executed. Why, then, should men murmur at the purposes or decrees of God? (From a sermon on Job 23:13 by C.H. Spurgeon)

One of my favorite hymns sets forth this glorious truth better than I ever could.

Whate'er my God ordains is right:
Holy his will abideth;
I will be still whate'er he doth,
And follow where he guideth:
He is my God; Though dark my road,
He holds me that I shall not fall:
Wherefore to him I leave it all.

Whate'er my God ordains is right:
He never will deceive me;
He leads me by the proper path;
I know he will not leave me:
I take, content, what he hath sent;
His hand can turn my griefs away,
And patiently I wait his day.

Whate'er my God ordains is right:
Though now this cup in drinking,
May bitter seem to my faint heart,
I take it, all unshrinking:
My God is true; Each morn anew
Sweet comfort yet shall fill my heart,
And pain and sorrow shall depart.

Whate'er my God ordains is right:
Here shall my stand be taken;
Though sorrow, need, or death be mine,
Yet am I not forsaken;
My Father's care is round me there;
He holds me that I shall not fall:
And so to him I leave it all.

(Samuel Rodigast [1675],
translated by Catherine Winkworth [1829-1878])

This hymn is describing the God of the Bible. Dear child of God, the God who is so described is your heavenly Father. Dear non-Christian friend, the same God is the Judge you must face and to whom you must give an account of your rebellion. Isn't it amazing that the very truth that brings comfort and hope to a believer is the same thing that brings terror and fear to a lost man? The truth we are discussing is what makes texts like Romans 8:28 and Habakkuk 2:20 to be more than platitudes. The absoluteness and unchangeableness of God's decrees make everything fit together. When tragedy strikes and the Devil paints the worst possible scenario, the child of God can say, "Wait a minute, you are forgetting that God is in control. He brought this to pass, and he will use it for my good and his own glory."

This is exactly what our Lord experienced as he hung on the cross. The crowd taunted him, saying, "Where now is your God?" And exactly where was God that awful Friday afternoon? He was "in his holy temple" (Habakkuk 2:20) working out his sovereign purposes. It was the Father who put Christ on the cross. Calvary was not a failure, but the greatest victory the world ever saw. It may have looked like God's plans and purposes had gone astray, but every single event of that day was happening right on schedule. God's sovereign decrees were being carried out down to the smallest detail.

Let me remind you of three texts that all teach this same truth. The first verse, Romans 8:28, presents the assurance and hope that comes when we understand and apply the other two verses.

> And we know that in **all things** God works for the good of those who love him, who have been called according to his purpose. (NIV, emphasis added)

You might be tempted to think that the words *all things* are not quite big enough to include the specific painful situation that you face right now. The second text expands that phrase *all things* in a way that makes it impossible not to include every event without exception.

Romans 11:36: *For from him and through him and to him are* ***all things***. *To him be the glory forever! Amen.* (NIV, emphasis added)

Previously, we noted that there are three different prepositions used in this verse.

1.   of him—*ek*—"out of"—God is the author and source of all things.

2.   through him—*dia*—"by means of"—God controls and brings to pass all things.

3.   to him—*eis*—"into"—God is the final and purposeful end of all things.

The third text adds the finishing touches. God really knows what he is doing. His plans and works are not purely arbitrary. God plans and brings to pass the particular things that he does simply because they are all, as Spurgeon said, "wise and good." God's plans are the best possible plans. Paul, in this text, is emphasizing that God's purposes grow out of the "counsel of His will."

Ephesians 1:11: *In Him also we have obtained an inheritance, being predestined according to the purpose of Him who works all things according to the counsel of His will....* (NKJV)

Someone has said, "If I were as sovereign as God, I would change a lot of things. If I were as wise as God, I would not change a single thing."

Outline of the Extent of God's Decrees

All Christians believe that God's plans have something to do with affecting the future. However, they disagree with what those plans are and whether God is going to be able to bring them to pass. The Pelagian, those who originally did battle with Augustine, denies that God has a plan, and the Arminian denies that the plan is specific and inclusive of all things. We believe that the Confession expresses accurately what the Bible teaches when it says, "God from all eternity did, by His most wise and holy counsel of His own will, freely and unchangeably ordain whatsoever comes to pass...." (Westminster & Philadelphia Confessions, Chapter 3, Section 1).

There are six specific areas clearly covered by the decrees of God. Let me list them and then cover them one at a time.

1. Every event of life—(including day of death) Job 7:1; 14:5. The answer to both questions in 7:1 is yes.

2. The smallest details of life—Matthew 10:29, 30.

3. The sinful acts of men—Genesis 50:20; Acts 2:23.

4. The plans of men, related to decrees—Proverbs 16:9; 19:21; 20:24.

5. "Accidents"—Deuteronomy 19:4-6; Exodus 21:12-14.

6. "Luck"—Proverbs 16:33; Acts 1:24-26.

First of all, God ordains every event in life, including the day of both our birth and death.

Does not man have hard service on earth? Are not his days like those of a hired man? Like a slave longing for the evening shadows, or a hired man waiting eagerly for his wages, so I have been allotted months of futility, and nights of misery have been assigned to me. (Job 7:1-3 NIV)

Does a hired man decide when his employment starts and when it ends, or is that totally determined by the one doing the hiring? The writer acknowledges that his time on earth, whatever time God ordains, has been "allotted" to him.

Man's days are determined; you have decreed the number of his months and have set limits he cannot exceed. (Job 14:5 NIV)

Death is an appointment set by God that no man can change in any way. See also Ecclesiastes 8:5-9.

Secondly, God's decrees extend even to the smallest detail.

Are not two sparrows sold for a penny? Yet not one of them will fall to the ground apart from the will of your Father. And even the very hairs of your head are all numbered. So don't be afraid; you are worth more than many sparrows. (Matt. 10:29-31 NIV)

Is Jesus being facetious, or is he being dead serious? Does God really know how many hairs are on your head? Does he know how many come out each morning when you brush your hair? Most people do not even read verse 29 correctly, let alone understand it correctly. They somehow think the text is saying that not a single sparrow falls to the ground without God taking notice that it happened. That is not what the text says. Jesus is saying that even an insignificant sparrow cannot fall if God has not decreed it to happen at that time. Jesus is not joking or stretching a point for effect. He is stating a fact and then making an application. If God is concerned whether a sparrow lives or dies, will he take care of you? Can you not trust him in all things and at all times?

Thirdly, the decrees of God include the sinful acts of men. We will look at one very familiar Old Testament text and one well-known New Testament text.

> You intended to harm me, but God intended it for good to accomplish what is now being done, the saving of many lives. (Gen. 50:20 NIV)

There is no question that Joseph's brothers had an evil motive. They hated Joseph and fully intended to do him harm. God purposed to use this very event to ultimately catapult Joseph into such a position of power that he would be able to save his whole family from famine. It is thrilling to read the whole sequence of events right down to the time when Joseph finally reveals himself to his brothers. They were afraid Joseph would "get even," but instead they heard the words of grace recorded above. Joseph is saying that a sovereign God purposed to use their sin to accomplish his purpose. God's sovereignty in no way excuses them for their sin.

> Men of Israel, listen to this: Jesus of Nazareth was a man accredited by God to you by miracles, wonders and signs, which God did among you through him, as you yourselves know. This man was handed over to you by God's set purpose and foreknowledge; and you, with the help of wicked men, put him to death by nailing him to the cross. (Acts 2:22-23 NIV)

The death of our Lord was neither an accident that could not be stopped, nor was it a victory of the Devil over God. Peter tells us that Christ had all of the credentials to prove he was the promised Messiah. God himself "handed Jesus over" to wicked men knowing full well those men would crucify him. The cross only happened because of God's "set purpose and foreknowledge." Men argue about who was responsible for the death of Christ. The men who engineered Christ's death and the people who knew he was innocent will be held accountable on the day of judgment, but at the same time it was God who was in total charge that day.

I can imagine the Jews who helped crucify Christ responding to Peter's words this way: "Are we ever glad to hear you say it was all God's fault. That means we are not accountable for what we did." But Peter does not stop with acknowledging God's sovereign purpose; he immediately says, "…you, with the help of wicked men."

No one can deny that the death of Christ was the event that brought this world the greatest blessing it has ever known, namely, the forgiveness of sins. That death was planned in eternity. Jesus was born in order that he might die on the cross. His death was his highest act of obedience to his Father. Everything that had to happen in order to bring the cross to pass was done willingly by wicked men out a hateful motive, but at the same time it all perfectly fulfilled exactly what God had sovereignly ordained. If you struggle with understanding the sovereign providence of God as it is related to the free-agency and responsibility of man, I refer you back to chapter one, "The Sovereignty of God in Providence."

Fourthly, God's decrees relate to our plans. Does the fact that God decrees all things mean or imply that I am not to plan for the future as wisely as I can? Not at all! Consider these texts that speak to this issue.

> *In his heart a man plans his course, but the LORD determines his steps.* (Prov. 16:9 NIV)

> *Many are the plans in a man's heart, but it is the LORD's purpose that prevails.* (Prov. 19:21 NIV)

> *A man's steps are directed by the LORD. How then can anyone understand his own way?* (Prov. 20:24 NIV)

The point in all three of these texts is that man plans as best he can, but he should do so knowing full well that he must always add, "If the Lord wills." A Christian man knows it is his duty to make decisions which are good, holy, and wise. He also knows that he cannot outwit God or beat his decrees. We pray for guidance, at the same time we use all available information in making choices for the future. If, in spite of all our best efforts, the roof falls in, we say, "Bless the Lord." There is a belief among many Christians that if trouble and difficulty follow a decision, then that proves you are out of God's will and made a wrong choice. What bad choices did Paul make that caused him to get beat up and left for dead? What bad choices caused Jesus to wind up on a cross? What did the early Christians do wrong that caused them to be fed to the lions?

Fifthly, are there such things as accidents? This can be a most difficult point to get into your mind and heart. I beg of you to "gird up the loins of your mind" and follow the texts carefully. The first text, Deuteronomy 19:4-6, instructs the Israelites to establish three cities of refuge. The idea behind these cites is spelled out in verses 4-6.

> *This is the rule concerning the man who kills another and flees there to save his life—one who kills his neighbor unintentionally, without malice aforethought. For instance, a man may go into the forest with his neighbor to cut wood, and as he swings his ax to fell a tree, the head may fly off and hit his neighbor and kill him. That man may flee to one of these cities and save his life. Otherwise, the avenger of blood might pursue him in a rage, overtake him if the distance is too great, and kill him even though he is not deserving of death, since he did it to his neighbor without malice aforethought.* (NIV)

The purpose of the cities of refuge was to protect a man who had "accidentally" killed someone from being killed in anger by that person's relatives. Moses gives the illustration of an ax head slipping off the handle and killing a neighbor or friend. A modern illustration would be this: a man and his 14 year-old son go deer hunting. The son sees a deer in a bush and shoots it. He rushes over and discovers he has shot and killed his father. We would say, "That was a horrible accident," and we would be correct from one point of view.

Let's look at another verse that is speaking about the identical kind of occurrence, but from a different perspective. Again, the same city of refuge is the subject.

> *"Anyone who strikes a man and kills him shall surely be put to death. However, if he does not do it intentionally, but **God lets it happen,** he is to flee to a place I will designate. But if a man schemes and kills another man deliberately, take him away from my altar and put him to death."* (Ex.21:12-14 NIV, emphasis added)

This is the same type of event as that depicted in Exodus 19:4-6, except this time it is explained from God's point of view. To view things only as accidents is to have the same mindset as pagan fatalism. A Christian must see the hand of God in all things. The NIV says "God lets it happen," and the KJV says, "If God deliver him into his hand." I admit that is a tough verse, but it is consistent with the rest of Scripture on the subject of decrees. You can say that the death of that father was a tragic accident, or you can say that God delivered that father into the hand of his son. Both of these things are true. We must acknowledge them both.

The sixth example, luck and the decrees of God, could be a subset of the fifth, but we will treat it separately. The first chapter of the book of Acts records the apostles choosing someone to take the place of Judas. The context and the method of choice are interesting.

> *Then they prayed, "Lord, you know everyone's heart. Show us which of these two you have chosen to take over this apostolic ministry, which Judas left to go where he belongs." Then they cast lots, and the lot fell to Matthias; so he was added to the eleven apostles.* (Acts 1:24-26 NIV)

First of all, we must see that casting lots was not "trusting luck" but was a method ordained by God to assure that God's will was accomplished. They prayed and acknowledged the sovereignty of God. They wanted to be sure the will of God was accomplished. That is why they used the method of casting lots. They knew God controlled the lot. It is sometimes argued that the apostles rushed ahead of God, since he had already chosen Paul as the twelfth apostle. I do not think we can prove that either way. I am not sure if they were right or wrong in choosing a replacement, but the method of casting lots was surely a biblical method.

Proverbs 16:33 is very specific: "The lot is cast into the lap, but its every decision is from the LORD." Casting lots was ordained by God as a means for Israel to know the Lord's will is some situation. On the Day of Atonement, they cast lots to choose which goat died and which one was taken into the woods and lost. When it came time to divide up the land, God insisted they do it by casting lots. The reason for this was that he controlled the lot, and this method would assure that his will was done. Casting the lot had nothing to do with luck, but everything to do with God's control.

By the way, our congregation does not have "pot-luck" suppers. We have "pot-providence" suppers. I am sure you see the difference. You come to a pot-luck supper and see what you are lucky enough to get. You come to a pot-providence supper and see what your heavenly Father has provided for you.

Texts that Teach God's Sovereign Decrees

1. God does all things deliberately—Psalm 115:3: *Our God is in heaven; he does whatever pleases him.* (NIV)

2. God does as he pleases—Psalm 135:6: *The LORD does whatever pleases him, in the heavens and on the earth, in the seas and all their depths.* (NIV)

3. God does all things according to his own eternal knowledge, power, and desire—Compare Isaiah 46:10 and Acts 15:18.

> Isaiah 46:10-11: *I make known the end from the beginning, from ancient times, what is still to come. I say: My purpose will stand, and I will do all that I please. From the east I summon a bird of prey; from a far-off land, a man to fulfill my purpose. What I have said, that will I bring about; what I have planned, that will I do.* (NIV)

> Acts 15:17-18: *that the remnant of men may seek the Lord, and all the Gentiles who bear my name, says the Lord, who does these things that have been known for ages.* (NIV)

4. Texts like Deuteronomy 2:30 give us a consistent picture of God's decrees and purpose: "But Sihon king of Heshbon refused to let us pass through. For the LORD your God had made his spirit stubborn and his heart obstinate in order to give him into your hands, as he has now done." (NIV)

A classic illustration of the above truth is found in 2 Samuel 17:1-14. In verses 1-3, Ahithophel gives Absalom good and wise (from a worldly point of view) counsel. In verse 4, the king is ready to act. If he had followed that advice, it would have been the end of David. In verses 5-13,

Absalom is deliberately given bad counsel, and verse 14 tells us that it was God who was behind the bad advice. God had purposed that Absalom would believe a lie. God used this method to preserve David's life. God "used" Absalom's vanity and pride to overcome his good judgment.

1 Kings 22:19–23 provides another example of the extent and involvement of God's decrees in the affairs of men:

> *Micaiah continued, "Therefore hear the word of the LORD: I saw the LORD sitting on his throne with all the host of heaven standing around him on his right and on his left. And the LORD said, 'Who will lure Ahab into attacking Ramoth Gilead and going to his death there?'*
>
> *"One suggested this, and another that. Finally, a spirit came forward, stood before the LORD and said, 'I will lure him.'*
>
> *"'By what means?' the LORD asked.*
>
> *"'I will go out and be a lying spirit in the mouths of all his prophets,' he said.*
>
> *"'You will succeed in enticing him,' said the LORD. 'Go and do it.'*
>
> *"So now the LORD has put a lying spirit in the mouths of all these prophets of yours. The LORD has decreed disaster for you."* (NIV)

Verse 23 could be written into the minutes of many church business meetings! How many times have manipulators and pressure groups received exactly what they wanted, only to suffer the consequences of God's judgment! The old saying is true, "Be careful what you pray for; you might get it."

Let me give one more example of how the decrees of God are carried out by God using ordinary means. This sordid story begins in 1 Kings 21:1:

> Some time later there was an incident involving a vineyard belonging to Naboth the Jezreelite. The vineyard was in Jezreel, close to the palace of Ahab king of Samaria. Ahab said to Naboth, "Let me have your vineyard to use for a vegetable garden, since it is close to my palace. In exchange I will give you a better vineyard or, if you prefer, I will pay you whatever it is worth."
>
> But Naboth replied, "The LORD forbid that I should give you the inheritance of my fathers." (1 Kings 21:1–3 NIV)

Ahab's wickedness lies in the fact that he is asking Naboth to sin against God's commandment. An Israelite was not allowed to sell the ground allotted to his family by God. He could mortgage it, but every fifty years all the land returned to the original owners.

> So Ahab went home, sullen and angry because Naboth the Jezreelite had said, "I will not give you the inheritance of my fathers." He lay on his bed sulking and refused to eat.
>
> His wife Jezebel came in and asked him, "Why are you so sullen? Why won't you eat?"
>
> He answered her, "Because I said to Naboth the Jezreelite, 'Sell me your vineyard; or if you prefer, I will give you another vineyard in its place.' But he said, 'I will not give you my vineyard.'"
>
> Jezebel his wife said, "Is this how you act as king over Israel? Get up and eat! Cheer up. I'll get you the vineyard of Naboth the Jezreelite."
>
> So she wrote letters in Ahab's name, placed his seal on them, and sent them to the elders and nobles who lived in Naboth's city with him. In those letters she wrote: "Proclaim a day of fasting and seat

Naboth in a prominent place among the people. But seat two scoundrels opposite him and have them testify that he has cursed both God and the king. Then take him out and stone him to death."

So the elders and nobles who lived in Naboth's city did as Jezebel directed in the letters she had written to them.

They proclaimed a fast and seated Naboth in a prominent place among the people.

Then two scoundrels came and sat opposite him and brought charges against Naboth before the people, saying, "Naboth has cursed both God and the king." So they took him outside the city and stoned him to death. (1 Kings 21:4–13 NIV)

If ever there was a pathetic couple that deserved each other, it was the spineless King Ahab and his treacherous wife Jezebel. What a pair of reprobates!

Then they sent word to Jezebel: "Naboth has been stoned and is dead."

As soon as Jezebel heard that Naboth had been stoned to death, she said to Ahab, "Get up and take possession of the vineyard of Naboth the Jezreelite that he refused to sell you. He is no longer alive, but dead." When Ahab heard that Naboth was dead, he got up and went down to take possession of Naboth's vineyard. (1 Kings 21:14–16 NIV)

It looked as though the wicked plan had succeeded. However, Ahab's joy did not last long. God sent the prophet Elijah with a message of judgment.

Then the word of the LORD came to Elijah the Tishbite: "Go down to meet Ahab king of Israel, who rules in Samaria. He is now in Naboth's vineyard, where he has gone to take possession of it. Say to him, 'This is what the LORD says: Have you not murdered a man and seized his property?' Then say to him, 'This is what the

LORD says: In the place where dogs licked up Naboth's blood, dogs will lick up your blood—yes, yours!'"

Ahab said to Elijah, "So you have found me, my enemy!"

"I have found you," he answered, "because you have sold yourself to do evil in the eyes of the LORD. 'I am going to bring disaster on you. I will consume your descendants and cut off from Ahab every last male in Israel—slave or free. I will make your house like that of Jeroboam son of Nebat and that of Baasha son of Ahijah, because you have provoked me to anger and have caused Israel to sin.'

And also concerning Jezebel the LORD says: 'Dogs will devour Jezebel by the wall of Jezreel.'

Dogs will eat those belonging to Ahab who die in the city, and the birds of the air will feed on those who die in the country."
(1 Kings 21:17–24 NIV)

Notice exactly what is decreed by God against Ahab and his family. First, Ahab is not only going to die, but dogs are going to lick up his blood on the very spot that Naboth's blood was shed (verse 19). Can you imagine how many things God would have to control in order for such a decree to be fulfilled in every detail? Secondly, Ahab and the males of his family will be completely destroyed (verse 21). Thirdly, dogs will devour Jezebel at Jezreel's wall and those of Ahab's family who live in the city, and birds will feed on the carcasses of those who live in the country (verses 22-24).

Three years pass and nothing happens to either Ahab or Jezebel. 1 Kings 22 records the episode of Ahab, king of Israel, and Jehoshaphat, king of Judah, going together to war against the king of Aram, who held Ramoth Gilead.

Read the dialogue between the prophet Micaiah and Ahab, especially the final word (verses 8-28). Ahab says, "Put this man in prison with only bread and water until I return." Micaiah responds, "If you come back alive, then I am not a prophet."

Ahab disguises himself before he goes into battle, and it appears to work.

The king of Israel said to Jehoshaphat, "I will enter the battle in disguise, but you wear your royal robes." So the king of Israel disguised himself and went into battle.

> *Now the king of Aram had ordered his thirty-two chariot commanders, "Do not fight with anyone, small or great, except the king of Israel." When the chariot commanders saw Jehoshaphat, they thought, "Surely this is the king of Israel." So they turned to attack him, but when Jehoshaphat cried out, the chariot commanders saw that he was not the king of Israel and stopped pursuing him.* (1 Kings 22:30–33 NIV)

It would appear that Ahab has outwitted God and frustrated his decree. The next verse is one those amazing statements that cause us to stand in awe of the greatness of God's power:

> *But someone drew his bow at random and hit the king of Israel between the sections of his armor. The king told his chariot driver, "Wheel around and get me out of the fighting. I've been wounded."* (1 Kings 22:34 NIV)

"But someone drew his bow at random," and the arrow went through the "sections of Ahab's armor." Perhaps the man had broken his bowstring and put a new one in place. He wanted to check it out so he shot an arrow over the hill "at random." The king had apparently loosened his armor a bit and that arrow went right into that small space where the two pieces were tied together, and Ahab was mortally wounded. The story is not yet over, though:

> All day long the battle raged, and the king was propped up in his chariot facing the Arameans. The blood from his wound ran onto the floor of the chariot, and that evening he died. As the sun was setting, a cry spread through the army: "Every man to his town; everyone to his land!"
>
> So the king died and was brought to Samaria, and they buried him there. They washed the chariot at a pool in Samaria (where the prostitutes bathed), and the dogs licked up his blood, as the word of the LORD had declared. (1 Kings 22:35–38 NIV)

Still the story is not over. What about the prophecy concerning that wicked Jezebel? Sometime later Jehu is anointed king of Israel. He is told to wipe out Ahab's whole family just as Elijah had said. He is also going to fulfill the prophecy uttered by Elijah years before concerning Jezebel. The story continues in 2 Kings 9:30-37:

> Then Jehu went to Jezreel. When Jezebel heard about it, she painted her eyes, arranged her hair and looked out of a window. As Jehu entered the gate, she asked, "Have you come in peace, Zimri, you murderer of your master?"
>
> He looked up at the window and called out, "Who is on my side? Who?" Two or three eunuchs looked down at him. "Throw her down!" Jehu said. So they threw her down, and some of her blood spattered the wall and the horses as they trampled her underfoot.
>
> Jehu went in and ate and drank. "Take care of that cursed woman," he said, "and bury her, for she was a king's daughter."

But when they went out to bury her, they found nothing except her skull, her feet and her hands. They went back and told Jehu, who said, "This is the word of the LORD that he spoke through his servant Elijah the Tishbite: On the plot of ground at Jezreel dogs will devour Jezebel's flesh. Jezebel's body will be like refuse on the ground in the plot at Jezreel, so that no one will be able to say, 'This is Jezebel.'" (NIV)

Every jot and tittle of God's Word will be fulfilled down to the smallest detail. Isn't it amazing how God accomplishes his sovereign decrees by ordinary means? He does this because he sovereignly controls each and every "ordinary" event, including an arrow "shot at random" and dogs licking up blood.

Relating God's Decrees to His Revealed Will

This is an important aspect of our subject. Deuteronomy 29:29 teaches us that God has a both a secret and a revealed will. The secret will consists of his decrees, and it belongs to God alone. We have no way of unlocking secrets that God has not revealed. It is a great comfort to know that God has decreed all things, but we do not try to understand God's decrees as a means of discerning God's will for us today. For instance, we are sure that God has decreed when the world will end and when Jesus will return. However, we have no way knowing when that is going to happen; therefore, we live each day as if it were going to happen today. God's revealed will is a different situation. The text says that it belongs to "us and our children," and it is given to us so that we might obey what God has revealed. We are responsible to understand what

God has revealed and order our lives in accordance with the principles he has laid down.

Revealed Will		Secret Will
Revealed Will		**Secret Will**
Found in the Bible	Source	Hidden from human view
For us today	Time	Deals with the future
Shows us our duty	Purpose	Teaches God is sovereign
Man CAN reject— disobey	Power	Man CANNOT resist or thwart

Our HOPE is in God's sovereign but secret decrees. Our rule of faith and duty is recorded in his revealed will. His revealed will includes both the law and the gospel.

Someone has well said, "Providence is a good DIARY but a very poor BIBLE."

The hyper-Calvinist, through pride of intellect, tries to use God's decrees for his rule of faith and practice, and the Arminian, through confidence in man's "free will," denies the reality of God's decrees. We dare not do either of these two things.

Difficulties in this Subject

When we discuss the decrees of God, we realize that there is an inscrutable relationship of the eternal to the temporal. We, as temporal beings, cannot see for certain anything beyond the immediate moment. God, who is eternal, does not operate in the sphere of yesterday, today, and tomorrow. With God there is nothing but "is." There is no "was" or "will be" with the everlasting God.

We also cannot totally see the relationship of the infinite to the finite. God's thoughts are not our thoughts. His ways and purposes are beyond our comprehension.

Even with all of our understanding, God's absolute sovereignty in relationship to man's true and total free agency is still beyond our grasp. We do not question any of these things, but we confess we do not understand them very clearly.

One of the most vexing of all questions is the origin of evil as it relates to the holiness, goodness, and power of God. How could a holy God deliberately choose to use evil as a means of revealing and magnifying his grace?

> These [the above problems] are peculiar to no system that acknowledges the existence and moral government of God, and the moral agency of man. They have perplexed heathen philosophers of old, Deists in modern times, and Socinians, Pelagians, and Arminians just as sorely as Calvinists. (A.H. Hodge, *Outlines of Theology*, p. 201)

Means Fulfill Ordained Ends

God sometimes uses miracles to accomplish his decree, but his usual method is to use ordinary means. A careful reading of Acts 27:9–44 will show this fact. Paul warns against sailing, but the captain rejects his advice, misinterprets providence, and proceeds to sail. A storm arises and makes control of the ship to be impossible. After many days, they begin to run out of food and water. Paul proceeds to give them assurance:

After the men had gone a long time without food, Paul stood up before them and said: "Men, you should have taken my advice not to sail from Crete; then you would have spared yourselves this damage and loss. But now I urge you to keep up your courage, because not one of you will be lost; only the ship will be destroyed. Last night an angel of the God whose I am and whom I serve stood beside me and said, 'Do not be afraid, Paul. You must stand trial before Caesar; and God has graciously given you the lives of all who sail with you.' So keep up your courage, men, for I have faith in God that it will happen just as he told me. Nevertheless, we must run aground on some island." (Acts 27:21-26 NIV)

The decree of God, according to Paul, was that no one would be lost even though the ship would be destroyed. Paul believed it would be just as God said. The ship started to come into more shallow water. Some of the sailors tried to flee the ship.

In an attempt to escape from the ship, the sailors let the lifeboat down into the sea, pretending they were going to lower some anchors from the bow. Then Paul said to the centurion and the soldiers, "Unless these men stay with the ship, you cannot be saved." So the soldiers cut the ropes that held the lifeboat and let it fall away. (Acts 27:30-32 NIV)

I am sure some of the sailors said, "Look, Paul, you are contradicting yourself. You told us for certain that no one would perish, and now you tell us that if we flee the ship, we will die." I do not know if Paul gave them a lesson on human responsibility and divine sovereignty or not. I do know they had to stay on the ship to be saved, and I also know they did stay on the ship. Staying on the ship was the means God had ordained to save them. Someone may ask, "What would have happened if some of the sailors had gotten off the ship?" I would reply, "That is a nonsense question. It is a question contrary to fact because nobody got off the ship. Don't ever get into a discussion about what would happen if something God decreed did not happen; because that is simply impossible. I am sometimes asked, "What would have happened the night you got saved if you had not believed the gospel?" I smile and say, "But I did believe. You are talking nonsense."

There were two-hundred and seventy-six people on board that ship. Paul assured them not a single person would "lose a hair from his head." The boat finally hit a sandbar, and all those who could swim jumped into the water and swam to shore. The last verse is both interesting and amusing.

> *The rest were to get there on planks or on pieces of the ship. In this way everyone reached land in safety.* (Acts 27:44 NIV)

I have no idea how many of those on board could not swim. But if the decree is to be fulfilled, they too must reach land safely. God very conveniently arranged to not just stick the ship on a sandbar, but also break it up so there were enough wooden life preservers to go around. God really does take care of all the details.

Conclusion

The concept of the decrees of God answers the age-old question of why events happen as they do. The Bible teaches that all things that come to pass are ordained by

God, and this includes even the smallest details of life. Joy and tragedy, obedience and sin, and "luck and accidents" all alike fall under the sovereign control of God. He is both transcendent over his creation and immanent in it. Man is still a responsible moral agent, required to obey what God has revealed, and held accountable when he does not; but God is ultimately the governing agent in the entire universe. Our good and wise God makes his plans, his power assures that they will be carried out, and his activity in his creation brings them to pass in the manner and time he has ordained. With the apostle Paul, we say, "To him be the glory forever! Amen."

CHAPTER THREE
THE SOVEREIGNTY OF GOD AND PRAYER

Introduction

In chapter one, "The Sovereignty of God in Providence," we showed that God not only sovereignly plans and purposes everything that happens; he also controls all events and uses every individual, including the Devil, in working out his sovereign plan. We showed how this truth is a "soft pillow for a weary head and a sorry heart." To be able to believe that "my times are in thy hands" is the beginning of hope even when we cannot understand.

This chapter begins by asking, and then seeking to answer, the logical question raised by the truth of the earlier chapter. "If God has ordained all things that come to pass, then why should I bother to pray?"

This is invariably the first response from someone who either rejects outright the truth of God's sovereignty or honestly sees it in Scripture but is having difficulty relating sovereignty to prayer. I suspect that every sincere Christian has, at one time or another, struggled with the relationship between the sovereignty of God and prayer. I am also quite positive that every person who has been confronted with the biblical fact of God's absolute sovereignty has wrestled with this question.

We have not attempted to write for the theologian even though we do deal with difficult problems. Our goal has been to bring biblical hope to God's sheep who are going through deep water. Another goal has been to show that the current doctrine of prayer taught by the "health and wealth" televangelists is very destructive to true faith. Some may feel we are a bit too strong, but we have seen much misery and unbelief created by preaching a false hope.

God's Sovereignty and Prayer Defined

Let's answer the question, "If God has ordained all things that come to pass, then why should we bother to pray?"

First, we must see that the apparent contradiction usually arises from one of the following sources:

(1) The questioner has an incorrect theology of either sovereignty or prayer. It is impossible to reconcile a biblical view of sovereignty with an unbiblical view of prayer, or vice versa. The doctrines of the Bible will dovetail together in harmony only when they are all truly biblical. Sadly, our generation has a very bad understanding of the theology of both sovereignty and prayer. This means that we are often trying to reconcile the biblical doctrine of God's sovereignty to a man-centered doctrine of prayer. In reality, we are attempting to reconcile truth and error, which is impossible. No one will ever grasp the true relationship between God's sovereign decrees and the absolute necessity of prayer until he sees that the popular view of prayer taught today is unscriptural.

Actually, the problem here is the same one faced when trying to reconcile the sovereignty of God and the responsibility of man. No one will ever see the truth of God's absolute sovereignty until he sees that the mighty "free will of man" is a myth. It is easy to see why Christians in this generation have such a problem with reconciling sovereignty to prayer. They do not really understand either truth when they are stated in biblical terms. Many contemporary evangelicals approach their doctrines with the presupposition of an unquestioning confidence in the free will of man. The Bible begins doctrinal teaching with God and his sovereign purposes.

(2) The second problem is often that the person who rejects God's sovereignty on the grounds that it contradicts the need to pray has never heard "the whole counsel of God." He invariably has a theology built on stock clichés like "prayer changes things" or "it is no longer the sin question but the Son question." Trying to discuss the Word of God with people like that can be an exercise in futility. In a former pastorate, one of the most "spiritual" men in the church was also one of the most dogmatic. He believed and proclaimed that his only authority was the Word of God, even though he would not sit down and discuss the Scriptures themselves. No matter what the Holy Spirit wrote in the book, this man would respond with a cliché. He knew a lot about the Bible but very little of the true message of the Bible. Although he asserted that he had no "system of theology," he was unbelievably consistent, predictable, and inflexible in his beliefs. His clichés dictated his response to every question and subject. The man's

clichés and system were more authoritative than verses of Scripture.

The fundamental question that we must answer is this: "Is prayer a necessary means of reaching a God-ordained end; or is man, by using believing prayer, the shaper and planner of our world and its events?" At first sight that may sound like an oversimplification, but it is not. That is really the bottom line.

First, let us be certain that we know what we are saying, and what we are not saying, when we talk about the sovereignty of God and prayer. Are we suggesting that the wall plaque saying "prayer changes things" is very wrong? Not at all. We are saying that the plaque does not tell the whole story. The plaque is a cliché that contains a half-truth. However, we must remember that a half-truth that stands for a whole truth is a no-truth that soon becomes anti-truth. That little plaque sets forth one-half of a very precious truth; but when it is allowed to stand for the whole truth, it creates some very bad theology, and bad theology will always be followed by bad experience.

Does the tenet expressed on that plaque mean that a six-foot-tall girl can change her height to five feet, four inches by sincere prayer? Does the word *things* in "prayer changes things" include my height or the color of my eyes? Does the theology of "prayer changes things," when combined with the power of my "free will," enable me to prove that Jesus was wrong in Matthew 6:27 about "adding an inch" to our height? Can a black man change his skin color to yellow or a white man change his pigmentation to red by fervent, believing prayer? Such a view of prayer is nonsense and contrary to the Word of God, and yet thousands of sincere Christians not only believe it, but they also send millions of dollars to the money mongers who build their whole ministry (dare we use the word?) on that very doctrine of prayer.

We must also emphasize that "prayer changes things" does not mean that prayer changes either God or his plans and purposes! Regrettably, that is what many people unconsciously (and some very consciously) think the plaque is saying. Any concept of prayer that allows me to persuade God to change his mind is a most unbiblical and extremely dangerous doctrine of prayer. Who in his right mind would even want God Almighty to change his mind, let alone actually try to get him to do so by means of a "believing prayer"?

If God changes his mind in any sense whatsoever, it must be either a change for the better or a change for the worse. If he could change for the better, then he was not perfect before he changed. If he could change for the worse, then he would be less than perfect after he changed. God alone can say, "I, the Lord, change not." The hymn writers have said it well:

> There is no shadow of turning with thee;
> Thou changest not, Thy compassions they fail not:
> As Thou hast been, Thou forever will be.
> Before the hills in order stood, Or earth received her frame,
> From everlasting Thou art God, To endless years the same.

We could make another plaque that says "prayer changes people" that would be just as half-correct as the first plaque. Sometimes prayer changes us and makes us willing to accept the very things that we have been asking God to change! Isn't that exactly what happened to Paul on one occasion (2 Cor. 12:7-10)? However, that again is only half of the story.

We will consider this aspect of prayer more fully a little later. John Calvin said that prayer is digging up the treasures that God has already prepared for us. Prayer, as we shall see, really does not originate in us or in our so-called free will. Effectual prayer is the ordained means that God uses to accomplish his ordained purposes. The true motivation for prayer comes from the Holy Spirit of God.

Let me establish several clear biblical truths that we dare not question or violate in any discussion about prayer and the sovereignty of God. First: we are positive that God has commanded us to pray; and, second: he has promised to hear and answer our prayers.

If we do not pray, then we are in deliberate disobedience to God. We are told that "men ought always to pray" (Luke 18:1), and that we are to "pray without ceasing" (1 Thess. 5:17). Paul's epistles are filled with his fervent petitions to God on behalf of the people to whom he is writing. If we have a doctrine of sovereignty that allows us to either deny or neglect the duty of consistent prayer, then our doctrine of sovereignty is wrong. If our prayer life does not see specific answers, then we ought to seriously question our relationship with God. James says, "The prayer of a righteous man availeth much," and no doctrine of prayer is biblical that contradicts that truth either theologically or experimentally. The truth that God commands, hears, and answers prayer is stamped on nearly every page of the Bible, and any doctrine of sovereignty that denies this truth is denying the clear teaching of Scripture.

However, many of the texts of Scripture used by modern-day teachers of prayer are taken far out of context. Let me mention two such texts:

> This is the confidence we have in approaching God: that if we ask anything according to his will, he hears us. And if we know that he hears us—whatever we ask—we know that we have what we have asked of him. (1 John 5:14, 15 NIV)

Is that promise for us today? Absolutely! Does it mean exactly what it says? Absolutely! Does that mean that I can get anything I want from God if I ask in faith? Is John saying that I can "name it and claim it"? If you believe that, I am sure that you will soon either deny your faith or refuse to face the real world in which you live. If you wholeheartedly believe that doctrine and sincerely and consistently put it into practice, you could easily wind up in a mental institution.

This text does not teach that I can ask anything that I want and believe it is covered in the blanket promise of verse 15. True, the verse says, "whatever we ask," but the previous verse qualifies it with "anything according to his will." I must see that the promise concerns everything, without a single exception, that is asked "according to HIS will." The promise does not begin with my wants or my will, but with God's sovereign purpose and glory. It presupposes that my mind and heart are so filled with God's thoughts and a desire to obey his will that my first concern in praying is to ask for grace to do his will. It means I am studying God's Word and praying for him to show me his will, instead of trying to impose my will on him regardless of whether it fits into his plans or not. The text is clear when examined in its context.

Compare this text in 1 John with another text in the book of James and the truth becomes even more pronounced. How do the following verses from James fit into your theology of prayer?

> *What causes fights and quarrels among you? Don't they come from your desires that battle within you? You want something but don't get it. You kill and covet, but you cannot have what you want. You quarrel and fight. You do not have, because you do not ask God.* (James 4:1, 2 NIV)

These verses state two things that concern our subject. First, the source of most of the frustration and many of the broken relationships in our lives is the desire of our flesh to use other people to get what we want. Secondly, such trouble is a direct result of our NOT praying — "ye have not BECAUSE ye ask not." We will push, pull, connive, cajole, threaten, pout, shout, and do a hundred other things to get our own way for the simple reason that we will not trust God in believing prayer for what he sees we need. We will kill relationships, betray confidences, and destroy anything or anybody that hinders us from getting our own way. Wrong desires and expectations that war inside of us are the exact opposite of confident prayer that seeks to know and to do God's will. "Ye have not because ye ask not" can be written across every futile day of frustration or depression that we experience in life. "You are frustrated and immersed in wars because you do not pray" should be put on a plaque and hung on the wall of our minds. It would remind us that we are trying to put ourselves in the place of God. Such an attitude is at the bottom of many of our problems.

The next verse in James 4 contains a devastating truth. When all of the efforts of our flesh fail to get us what we want, then we turn to God in what we wrongly call "prayer" and try to use him to get what we could not get with our pushing, pulling, pouting, etc. Notice how clearly James sets this forth:

> When you do ask, you do not receive, because you ask with
> wrong motives, that you may spend what you get on your pleasures.
> (James 4:3 NIV)

What a contrast that is to the current doctrine of prayer! Do you realize what James is saying? He is saying that we often hide a selfish, greedy motive under the pretense of prayer. He is accusing us of trying to use God for our own ends, and then daring to call it prayer. I have seen church leaders destroy entire congregations just to hold onto their position of authority, all the while claiming that they were "led by the Holy Spirit after much earnest prayer." Pure rubbish! Isn't it amazing that the Holy Spirit of truth and peace is blamed for so much of the bitterness and division that was done in the name of love "after much prayer"?

It is obvious that God does not view prayer the same way that many people do today. I wonder if the religious hucksters who are getting rich by peddling a doctrine of prayer that tries to use God to make us healthy and wealthy realize how neatly they fit into a warning given by the prophet Hosea:

> *And they have not cried unto me with their heart, when they howled upon their beds....* (Hosea 7:14)

The prophet is mocking Israel's supposed prayer. What they called prayer, God called "howling upon your beds." They were pretending to be crying out to God, but in reality they were whimpering like whipped puppies. How often are our prayers nothing but whimpering against God's sovereign providence? We so often demand from God what we want, instead of submitting to him and earnestly seeking the grace to trust him even when we do not understand.

My whole point is this: it is impossible to reconcile the truth of God's absolute sovereignty with a doctrine of prayer that is in reality nothing but "howling upon your beds." The false doctrine of prayer so prevalent today is nothing less than an attempt to dethrone God and his decrees. This makes him to be man's servant, thereby allowing man's own fleshly desires to use the mechanics of prayer to shape and control all of his own destiny. With such a view so widespread, it is little wonder there is such confusion in both theology and personal experience in twentieth-century Christendom. The worst part of this tragic situation is that the Bible is blamed for the problem because of the gross misinterpretation of texts like 1 John 5: 14, 15.

We must ask three questions of our hearts before we use this text as a "blanket promise."

1. Is it my earnest desire to do the will of God (John 7:17)? To pray for anything without this desire in our hearts is a waste of time.

2. Am I seeking God's wisdom in his Word in order to discover his will for me in all of my life? Again, prayer for "what I want" with willful ignorance of what God wants cannot be called prayer.

3. Can I honestly pray in the same attitude as my blessed Lord when he said; "Nevertheless, not my will, but thy will be done"? Am I greater than my Master when I pray?

If we are either unwilling or unable to answer these questions correctly, then we may well be trying to use God just to help us get our own way. We can be so determined to force our will upon other people that we will even try to employ God's power to do it. Our selfish nature wants our personal needs satisfied at any cost, whether it fits into God's purposes and plans or not. When our goal is our personal happiness, sought outside of God's nature and character, then our concept of both God and prayer becomes terribly distorted. We simply must understand that "whatsoever we ask" must be circumscribed with "according to his will" in our doctrine of prayer. 1 John 5:14, 15 and James 4:3 are two sides of the same coin, and neither of them can be ignored or denied. I am sure I need not remind you that our prayer life is one of the clearest barometers of our present spiritual state. It is much easier to preach and write books about prayer than it is to actually pray. There is no discipline in the Christian life over which I have lamented in tears of repentance as much as a cold heart in prayer. Sam Storms, in the introduction to his excellent book on prayer, describes my own "raincoat" experience. I cannot recommend this book too highly:

> My reason for writing this differs considerably from what one might expect. I was motivated largely by guilt. My prayer life simply is not what it should have been. I knew that as far as Scripture is concerned, prayer is a non-negotiable. Yet, I had come to treat prayer like a raincoat, hanging in the closet ready for use if the weather demanded, but hardly something to wear every day. Like my raincoat, prayer seemed unnecessary as long as the sun was shining. I had fallen into the snare of complacency, thinking that since my life was relatively free from discomfort and tragedy, prayer could take a back seat. (*Reaching God's Ear*, Dr. Samuel Storms, Tyndale House Publishers, page 7)

The second text we want to look at is probably the most misused of all texts. Every book or sermon about prayer will use—or misuse—this text. Notice carefully exactly what it says:

> ...*Whatsoever ye shall ask the Father in my name, he will give it you.* (John 16:23)

This text is sometimes used to teach that Christ has given us a book of blank checks that are already signed by him. We need only fill in the blank check with whatever we want. We are guaranteed anything we want if we only have enough faith. We immediately see that the emphasis is not on God's will but on our wants. All that is necessary for us to get whatever we desire is to believe that we have it, and it is ours. All we need to do is pray in the "name of Jesus." In such a view, the name of Jesus becomes a magic word that opens heaven in the same way as the famous words, "Open, sesame!" opened the mountain in Arabian Nights.

I assure you that praying in Jesus' name involves a lot more than just tacking his name onto the end of our prayers. Why do we not pray in our own name or in the name of the church where we have our membership? We pray in Jesus' name alone to acknowledge that we have no claim or merit before God, but we still dare to ask because we trust the merits and promises of Christ.

I remember attending the funeral of a member of the Masonic Lodge. The Masons had a part in the service. It was very serious and solemn and, at least to me, a bit amusing at times. A friend of mine who had some understanding of the gospel was standing in front of me at the grave. He and I had discussed the fact that many, but not all, Masons believe that they are going to heaven because of their Lodge membership. When the Masonic official commended "our dear brother into Thy hands in the name of the Masonic Lodge," I whispered to my friend, "But they do not have an account in heaven."

The only name that can be used on a check is the name authorized by the person that makes the deposits and owns the account. Our blessed Lord alone has earned the merits and grace upon which we can draw. It is true that he has given us permission to use his name, but not for the purpose of satisfying our own pleasure, irrespective of his glory and purpose.

Let me illustrate what I think it means to pray "in Jesus' name" and meet the conditions of John 16:23. Suppose I went down to a local bar in your town and asked for a bottle of whiskey. I then said, "I have no money to pay for this, but a friend of mine said I could charge it in his name, and he would pay the tab the next time he comes in." When the bartender asked for my friend's name, I would give him your name. Assuming the bartender knew you and knew that you were a Christian, he would say, "Mister, you are a liar. That person would not be caught dead in this place. He never sent you in here, and he surely never told you to use his name."

I wonder how many times God could say exactly the same thing to us. How often have we grossly misused the name of Christ and dared to ask for something we wanted without any thought of Christ and his glory? You cannot pray "in Jesus' name" unless you earnestly believe that Christ himself would ask for that very same thing. John 16:23 is not a blank check that enables me to get anything my selfish heart desires, irrespective of how it affects the cause of Christ and God's purposes for me, just because I add the words "in Jesus' name" to the end of my prayer.

Let me review a few things that we have learned so far about the biblical doctrine of prayer.

1. Prayer never makes God my servant to give me everything I think I must have in order to make me happy. God is not a "heavenly bellhop" who carries my suitcase of selfish desires any place I command.

2. Prayer never allows me to either dictate my will to God nor to make God in any way change his mind.

3. God has a fixed plan, and his plan is the best plan. God is determined to carry out his plan, and neither our sin nor our "believing" prayers are going to derail or in any way change God's ultimate decrees (cf. Job 23:13).

Spurgeon said it very well:

> It is, when properly understood, a matter of unspeakable consolation that God has a plan—for who could honor a God Who had no plan, but Who did everything by haphazard? It is a matter of rejoicing that He has one great purpose that extends through all ages and embraces all things; for then everything falls into its proper place, and has its appropriate bearing on other events. It is a matter of rejoicing that God does execute all His purposes; for as they are all good and wise, is it not desirable that they should be executed? It would be a calamity if a good plan were not executed. Why, then, should men murmur at the purposes or decrees of God? (From a sermon on Job 23:13)

A wrong view of prayer will quickly lead to despair and unbelief. This is one of the primary reasons for much of the depression and disappointment in the lives of many sincere believers today. This is especially true among those who listen to the so-called divine healers on radio and television. A woman who attended a weekly Bible class

that I taught was always in a state of depression when she
came, but she usually left rejoicing in God's grace. She
finally confessed to me that she listened to one healer after
another every Sunday. She even admitted that her
depression got worse by listening to the television
preachers. She would always wind up doubting her faith in
Christ because she was not healed. She sincerely believed
that God wanted her healed and that Christ had provided
for her healing. All that was lacking was her faith. I kept
urging her to stop listening to the lies that the healers were
telling her, but she would not. Both her physical condition
and her spiritual condition continued to get worse.

The doctrine of prayer and healing that is preached by
the healers sounds so loving. The healer seems to be a
sympathetic person genuinely interested in our well-being.
His God appears to be a most kind and generous God; but,
in reality, the healer, his doctrine, and his God are all very
cruel. Healers are not interested in us; they are interested
only in our pocketbooks. Many of them are religious
hucksters getting rich off the pain and misery of other
people's sicknesses. I am aware that these are strong
statements, but there is no language strong enough to
condemn those who knowingly peddle a false hope in the
name of Christ as a means of getting rich!

"But John, doesn't the Bible clearly teach that 'the prayer
of faith shall heal the sick'?" Let us examine the exact
words in James used by these healers, and see how closely
these "great men with the gift of healing" follow the truth
in the text:

Is anyone of you sick? He should call the elders of the church to pray over him and anoint him with oil in the name of the Lord. And the prayer offered in faith will make the sick person well.... (James 5:14, 15 NIV)

Exactly what is a sick person to do according to these verses? First, he is to "call the elders of the church." "Elders" is plural, and the sick person calls them. The elders (plural) are to come to the sick person and "pray over him." This is a bit different from a man setting up a tent and calling the sick person to come to him. Suppose a sick person was unable to come to the meeting. Suppose he was unconscious, and friends appealed on his behalf? Have you ever seen an unconscious man brought into a healing service? Have you ever heard of a healer answering an appeal for help and going to the hospital to heal the sick?

Secondly, the elders are "to pray over him" and anoint him with oil. Now, it is imperative that we notice who is doing the praying. The text says that it is the elders. There is not a word in this text about the sick person praying and turning his faith loose.

Thirdly, the "prayer of faith" offered by the elders "will make the sick person well." Now, it is clear that the necessary faith to see the healing take place has to be the faith of the people doing the praying, and the text says very explicitly that it is the elders alone who are doing the praying. The self-styled faith-healers totally distort this passage and put the entire responsibility for healing on the sick person! According to James, if the sick person is not healed, it is because the people praying the "prayer of faith" did not have enough faith. Why do television healers put all of the blame on the poor sick person? Just watch at the close of any of these media productions, and you will always see and hear the following "heads I win, tails you lose" routine.

First, the miracle worker declares how God has called him and given him the gift of healing. He then explains how the power of this gift flows through him. You must either touch his hand or lay your hand on the television for a "point of contact." After assuring the audience of his gift and power from God, the man will pray up an emotional storm and, with great gusto, demand and command that the "Devil set this person free from sickness." The following is commanded in a loud voice, "In the mighty name of Jesus, I rebuke you, Satan." As hands are waved and shouts are uttered, the man with the great gift of healing who has just "busted Satan on the snout" with the mighty "prayer of faith" turns to the sick person and says, "Now YOU turn YOUR faith loose and claim your healing."

Now that is really neat. The miracle worker has been boasting about his gift of healing, and he has just prayed his mighty prayer of faith, but nothing can happen until the sick man furnishes the faith to make it all work. If everything totally depends on the sick person's faith, why does he need the healer in the first place? The healer has rigged the situation so that it is impossible for him to lose. If a healing takes place, then praise the healer (and the Lord a little bit, too). If the sick person is not healed, then who is to blame? Not the healer, but the poor ailing individual who was unwilling to believe. What has really happened in this charade? The healer probably has a generous amount of the sick person's money given during the offering, and the sick person still has his illness. The healer is off the hook because the sick person would not do his part and believe hard enough. The poor sick person has now added a load of guilt to his physical infirmity. He not only still has his sickness, but he now doubts his faith in God. Under such a teaching, the victim cannot help being one-hundred-percent convinced that it is entirely his fault that he is not healed. The man responsible for loading that guilt on the conscience of the afflicted one is the charlatan who twisted the Word of God concerning the "prayer of faith."

I am sorry if someone feels that I am being unkind or unloving, but the cruelest and most hateful thing you can do to people in pain is to offer them something that God does not offer, and then blame them for not having enough faith to receive it! It is even worse when you are claiming that the power comes through you, and then you dump all of the responsibility of experiencing that power onto the sick person. That is both deceitful and cruel.

If you want to see how cruel the faith-healing hucksters are, just visit an institution on Monday morning that cares for people with cerebral palsy or a similar disease. Try to talk to a person who has spent the entire night searching back through his life to find "that one sin that has not been confessed" which is "blocking his healing." Feel some of the pain as a helpless victim of an incurable infirmity asks,

"How can I get the faith I need to be healed?" or "I don't believe God loves me because he will not heal me." All of a sudden, you will have a desire to see the "loving" money mongers on television and radio horsewhipped and put in prison for inhumane cruelty.

I remember reading a booklet by a noted healer in which he describes praying for a lady in a wheelchair. She heard him on television and traveled many miles to attend his meeting. She had been "given hope in God's power and willingness to heal" through his many messages. Here is the man's account of what happened:

> I put my hand on the lady's head and prayed the prayer of faith. I could feel the power of God flowing through me and fully expected another genuine miracle to take place. When I opened my eyes, I could see the hope written across this dear lady's face and in her eyes. I took her by the hand and ever so gently began to pull her to her feet. She started to move forward and then suddenly stopped. A look of fear came into her eyes and she sank back in her chair in despair and unbelief.

I trust that you who are reading this feel as angry as I did when I first read those words. The worst is yet to come. As I read the next few sentences, I was angry at that man's cruelty:

> I slowly let go of her hand. I had done all for her that I possibly could do. I had delivered God's message of healing, I had earnestly prayed the prayer of faith, and I had pleaded with her to only believe, but she would not exercise the necessary faith to be healed. I left very sad even though I knew I had done my best to help.

Can you imagine anyone being as callous and cruel as that? That man pumped up a false hope in the woman, put on his theatrical display of "shackling the power of Satan," dramatically pretended to be "praying in faith," took the woman by the hand, and then totally blamed her for not standing up! He then had the gall to say, "I did all that I could to help her." You and I both know exactly what he did for her. I believe that he also knows down in his heart, but unfortunately, he does not care, as long as the money keeps coming in. I could not call that "loving and kind" unless I had a heart of stone.

Sadly, many Christians are not interested in theology and therefore rarely see the root causes of many problems. Few people understand the basic theology of the healers. It is the "Oh, but he is sincere" attitude that makes it almost impossible to criticize false preachers of any kind. When you expose the healing racket, you will see that it has a bad theological foundation. The healers have a wrong view of the atonement of Christ. They believe that Christ suffered the penal consequences for our bodily sicknesses in the same sense that he suffered the penalty for our sins. We may claim physical healing by faith in the same way we claim forgiveness of sins by faith.

Of course, if this theology of the atonement is true, then it would also mean that it is a sin to be sick. Just as it is a heinous sin to reject forgiveness of sins, so it would be a heinous sin to reject healing for sicknesses. If the awful sin of unbelief is the only thing that keeps lost people from being saved, then the same awful sin of unbelief is the only reason sick people are not healed. The sick are just as guilty for being sick and remaining sick, as the unrepentant are for being sinners and remaining in sin. One is doubly guilty for remaining in either state after he has heard the message that there has been a "full payment made by Christ" for his deliverance. If the basic doctrine of the healer is correct, then his conclusions are also correct. However, if his theology is wrong, his conclusions can wreak havoc in the lives of many suffering saints. Who can believe that doctrine, especially the doctrine of the true nature and purpose of the atonement, is not important?

Before we finish with the book of James, we should also look at what he said about Elijah shutting up heaven and causing a drought. The following verses are most instructive:

> *Elijah was a man just like us. He prayed earnestly that it would not rain, and it did not rain on the land for three and a half years. Again he prayed, and the heavens gave rain, and the earth produced crops.* (James 5:17, 18 NIV)

Are we to understand that God abdicated all control of the weather and turned it over to Elijah to decide when it should or should not rain? Is God telling you and me that since Elijah was a man like us, we too can control the weather by fervent prayer? What if a Christian farmer is pleading with God for rain to help his crops and, at the same time, a godly evangelist is praying for good weather for a two-week tent meeting? Whose prayers would determine God's action?

How would you like to be an Elijah? Imagine that you have shut up heaven and it has not rained for nearly three years. All the cattle are nearly dead for lack of pasture. The chickens are dead because there is no corn. Children are bloated and dying because of malnutrition. And it is all your fault. People would curse you and plead with you to pray for rain. You would be looked upon as a cruel monster with no feelings. Why would you not pray for rain? Why did Elijah not pray? Did he have a "mean streak" that enjoyed seeing people suffer? The answer is simple. God was the one who instructed Elijah not only what to pray but also when to pray. Read again the story in 1 Kings 17-18, and you will see that Elijah does indeed command the rain to both stop and start, but he does so only when God specifically instructs him to do it. We must understand that God was teaching a nation a much-needed lesson in repentance; and nobody, including Elijah, was going to make it rain before God had finished giving the lesson.

Imagine a group of sincere sentimentalists during this time, calling an all-night prayer meeting to pray for rain. (Maybe a guy from Oklahoma told them that a nine-hundred foot Jesus had told him to organize this "army of faith to batter the walls of heaven for rain.") They could get as many people to pray as they wanted, and they could plead as long and as hard as was possible, but they would be wasting their breath. Nothing could make it rain until God's purpose in sending the drought in the first place was realized. Elijah is indeed the ordained means that God used, but God was the Master of Ceremonies. The cruelest man in the country would be the tear-jerking, faith-peddling huckster crying, "God is a good God! He wants to send us rain, but we must have the faith to let him do it." That man would be fighting the very purposes of a sovereign God and actually be hindering the rain from coming.

I had better take time to clearly state that I firmly believe in divine healing. In fact, I believe that all healing is divine. Unless God blesses the medicine or the hands of the surgeon, even an unbelieving surgeon, there is no benefit. I also believe in miraculous healing, which is God directly intervening and healing without the use of any physical means at all. What I do not believe is that I can claim by faith a miraculous healing because Christ has supposedly already purchased and paid for the healing of every disease.

If you ask me, "What must I do to be saved?" I will point you to Acts 16:31 where Paul said, "Believe on the Lord Jesus Christ, and you will be saved." If you say, "What must I do to be healed?" I must respond, "Ask God for his perfect will to be done, and to give you courage and unwavering faith to trust him regardless of what he does." I cannot find a text in the Bible that guarantees that you can be healed in the same manner you can be saved from sin.

I repeat, I do indeed believe in divine healing, but I do not believe in divine healers. God performing a miracle by his grace and power, and God giving a man the ability to bestow grace and power on others, are two entirely different things. I deplore the total abuse of Scripture that is necessary for the self-appointed healer to practice his deceit. I also lament the misery and despair that he leaves behind.

Ask a healer if it is right to add "Nevertheless, not my will, but thy will be done" to the end of a prayer for healing. He believes that is a sinful cop-out simply because he believes it is always God's will for you to be healed of every sickness. All you need is the necessary faith. The healer's entire money-making scheme is based on this bad theology. I have buried at least five people who had been "gloriously healed" by big-name healers. These people "lost their healing because they did not hold onto it by faith." Show me where that happened to anybody whom Jesus healed!

The health and wealth gospel of the healers is an insult to every hungry or sick believer in Asia, Africa, and the rest of the world. It forces us to believe that people like Fanny Crosby and Joni Erickson were, in some sense, wicked unbelievers who did not have enough faith to receive the healing that Christ had purchased for them. This would mean that these Christians spent their entire lives in unbelief. What nonsense!

If someone reading this is saying, "This guy is really worked up about this," you are right. However, I think every person who loves people and believes the Bible's message of sovereign grace should be just as worked up. The sexual sins of prominent faith-healers will not hurt the true gospel nearly as much as the false doctrine that they preach. Sins of the flesh can hurt incomes and ultimately lead to imprisonments, but a distorted false gospel will destroy the souls of those who believe it. It is time somebody started to emphasize that the immorality of some of the televangelist superstars is not nearly as dangerous as the unscriptural message that they declare.

Before we continue, let us briefly review the major points we have covered. (1) It is impossible to reconcile two doctrines if one of them is not truly biblical. Many Christians today have a wrong view of both the sovereignty of God and prayer. It would be most foolish to try to relate the truth of God's sovereignty to the man-centered view of prayer so widely accepted today. (2) Christians are commanded to pray, and God has promised to hear and answer our prayers. Any view of the sovereignty of God that does away with the need of prayer or the joy of experiencing real answers to prayer must be biblically wrong (James 4:1-3). (3) John 16:23 is not a "blank check" that enables us to fill in whatever we want. The promise is governed by the phrase, "in my name." Likewise, the "whatsoever we ask" in 1 John 5:14, 15 is controlled by "according to his will." (4) The divine healers of our day twist James 5:14, 15 and blame the sick person if he is not healed.

We will now demonstrate from Scripture some basic principles about prayer as it relates to the sovereignty of God.

Six Basic Facts about Prayer and God's Sovereignty

BASIC FACT NUMBER ONE: Believers in both the Old Testament Scriptures and the New Testament Scriptures had no problem believing in both the absolute sovereignty of God and the necessity of prayer.

In Daniel, chapter 9, the prophet fervently prays for the very thing that he is positive the Sovereign God is going to accomplish. Daniel is told the exact time that God is going to fulfill a prior prophecy made through Jeremiah. Notice that Daniel's knowledge of exactly what God was going to do and the precise time that he was going to do it, in no way kept him from pleading with God to actually accomplish what had been promised. In fact, the exact opposite is true! The more certain we are about God's sovereign promises and providence, the more we will plead for the very things that we know belong to us through the provision of his covenant.

The first recorded prayer meeting in the early church after the day of Pentecost is a classic illustration of the biblical relationship of the sovereignty of God and prayer. Let us read the text in Acts 4:

> And being let go, they went to their own company, and reported all that the chief priests and elders had said unto them. And when they heard that, they lifted up their voice to God with one accord, and said, Lord, thou art God, which hast made heaven, and earth, and the sea, and all that in them is; Who by the mouth of thy servant David hast said, Why did the heathen rage, and the peoples imagine vain things? The kings of the earth stood up, and the rulers were gathered together against the Lord; and against his Christ. For

of a truth against thy holy child Jesus, whom thou hast anointed, both Herod, and Pontius Pilate, with the Gentiles, and the people of Israel, were gathered together, TO DO WHATSOEVER THY HAND AND THY COUNSEL DETERMINED BEFORE TO BE DONE. And now, Lord, behold their threatenings; and grant unto thy servants, that with all boldness they may speak thy word, by stretching forth thine hand to heal; and that signs and wonders may be done by the name of thy holy child, Jesus. And when they had prayed, the place was shaken where they were assembled together; and they were all filled with the Holy Ghost, and they spake the word of God with boldness. (Acts 4:23-31, emphasis added)

This special prayer meeting was in response to the first great persecution of the church. The apostles were beaten and told to never again preach in the name of Christ. Verse 23 tells us "they went to their own company" and reported all that had happened. They did not set up a committee, nor did they gather the clergy together. The whole church discussed the matter, and the whole church acted together.

Verse 24 gives us the response of the church to the horrible situation they were facing. Is it not amazing that they did not begin their prayers the way we would probably have done? They started by worshipping God and ascribing to him greatness and sovereignty. When our personal world is about to collapse, we do not usually begin our prayers by calmly saying, "Lord, you alone are God. You created all things, and right now you are in perfect control of all things and every person." No, we rush into God's presence, blurt out our problem, and tell God to do something quick or the whole cause will be lost. Why is it so important that we begin our prayers with true worship and praise?

First, God is worthy of our worship regardless of what our problems are. Secondly, it is only fitting that we always remember that entering God's presence is an amazing privilege. Remembering these truths will put both God and our problems into the right perspective; forgetting them will make us so self-centered that we may insult God with our prayers.

Suppose you had received a bad deal from the local authorities in your community, and you kept appealing for redress to higher authorities, all the way up to the President of the United States. Suppose the President himself agreed to see you. When the door to his office opened, would you rush in and say, "Do you know what those crooks in my town did to me? You are the President. What are you going to do about it?" No one would dare act like that. We would, first, sincerely thank him for taking the time to see us because we realize who he is. We would say, "Mr. President, I am amazed that you, the President of the United States, would condescend to hear my personal complaint. I sincerely and deeply appreciate this honor and privilege." When we started to think about the problems that he must deal with daily, we might even begin to feel ashamed that we were so distressed about such a minor problem. Actually, we might be so filled with awe that we would forget what our problem was! My point is that we often treat God with far less respect than we would a human authority. The early church knew better.

The third reason that it is good to begin our prayers with worship of God and praise to him for his greatness and sovereignty is that it will bring us an appropriate sense of calm and assurance. If all we see is the problem, we are sure to lose sight of God's power and control. The early church could wholeheartedly recognize the insignificance of those human authorities in comparison to the God who made heaven and earth. I am sure you can begin to see that the early Christians consciously prayed from a carefully laid foundation of faith in God's absolute sovereignty! They first reminded themselves and God that they were confident of his power and decrees. Dr. Lloyd-Jones suggests that this is why God shook the building (v. 31). It was as if God said, "I like the way you pray. I like your confidence in my power, and I will give you a little sample of it to reaffirm your faith," so he shook the building, literally! Yes, he can shake anything and anybody; he can shake a whole empire and cause it to crumble.

Verses 25 through 27 are very instructive. Why did the church remind God that David's prophecy concerning the world's hatred of Christ was so clearly fulfilled in the crucifixion? Everybody was against Christ. Every source of human authority purposed to destroy him forever. The Christians were reminding themselves and God that they were at that moment in the very same situation that their elder brother had been in before them. He was hated and in trouble; they were hated and in trouble. However, just as Christ was safe in the hands of his Father, so they were safe there as well. The cause was God's, not their own. They realized that they were only pawns, and God himself was the master of the game.

Acts 4:28 is one of those verses that makes me want to shout. Exactly what did all the enemies of Christ do to him? Why were they all brought together into one solid power block? Those early, persecuted believers reminded themselves and their God that those wicked enemies did only "whatsoever thy hand and thy counsel determined before to be done." The NIV says, "They did what your power and will had decided before should happen." That, my friend, is confidence in the absolute sovereignty of God. We may talk about the "free will of man" or blame all the bad things on the Devil, but in times of real trial, we will lose our confidence without a grip on a sovereign God. Those besieged Christians saw no conflict between fervent prayer and God's sovereign decrees. They knew that nothing could have happened to them that had not been decreed by God any more than it could have happened to Christ.

I just recently went through the worst experience of my Christian life. I was lied to and lied about. I watched people that I loved and trusted stick a knife in my back. I saw wrong prevail, and the truth dragged through the mud. The philosophy of "the end justifies the means" was used by professing Christians to lie and distort facts in order to get what they wanted regardless of the cost. Where was God while all of this injustice was taking place? He was the Master of Ceremonies and in control of the whole thing, just as he was at Calvary and just as he was in Acts 4, when the disciples were beaten. Nothing happened to me that my heavenly Father had not ordained. If I did not believe that, I could not help but be bitter and desire revenge. If I said I was not deeply hurt, I would be lying. However, I can honestly pity some of the people who were the most dishonest and malicious. I can face both God and those who tried to do me in and know that I did the right thing and acted in the right way. The results always belong to God. His will shall be accomplished regardless of who appears to win today. My only responsibility is a conscience void of offense before God and men.

Do you think the believers described in Acts chapter 4 believed they had done something wrong and felt guilty because of the bad results, or were they sure that they were in the will of God despite the attitude and persecution by the leaders? Can you imagine one of those nice, sweet, "peace at any price" people standing up and saying, "Well, you know, we really asked for a lot of this trouble by the way we went about our preaching. We should not preach those offensive doctrines that the Jews hate, and we surely should not have been so dogmatic." That may pass as "Christian love and godly wisdom" in this wishy-washy generation, but we all know it is an insult to the zeal and courage of those early believers who established truth on the earth with their very blood.

No, my friend, there is no contradiction between the sovereign decrees of God and fervent, believing prayer. Read the words in Acts 4 again and see that it was their confidence in the fact that God decrees all things that come to pass which gave those Christians the courage and faith to pray in time of affliction. It is in the text. Only a deliberate twisting of the words necessitated by a man-centered theology can get anything else out of this passage.

In verse 29, the people finally get around to asking for something. Isn't it amazing that they have been worshipping and praising God without asking him to stop the persecution or kill the persecutors? It is even more amazing that when they do finally ask for specific help from God, they ask for grace to boldly keep on preaching the very same message that got them into trouble in the first place. They leave the persecution with God and pray for boldness to declare what they know is the truth of God, regardless of the results. That, my friend, is real prayer. As you can see, real prayer is a joyful submission to a sovereign God in order to be used for his purposes. Little wonder that we are all half-scared to really cry to God to be used by him, in his way, and for his glory. It is much easier to listen to a health and wealth promoter, and pray for a new camper to use at the lake.

We could outline Acts 4:23-31 as follows:

I. Vv. 23-28: Confidence in God's sovereignty—the true foundation for prayer.

II. Vv. 29-30: Asking for the right things—the true test of prayer.

III. V. 31: The felt realization of God's presence and power—the true answer to prayer.

BASIC FACT NUMBER TWO: Prayer can be used as a means of refusing to submit to what we know is the will of God!

Brethren, I suspect we have come to one of the real problems in true prayer. We often try to use prayer to get around God's providence. We are unwilling to bow to God's sovereignty and dare to use prayer as a means of trying to get God to change his mind. As we have already stated, true prayer is nothing less than a joyful submission to the will of our Sovereign God! Have we not all been guilty of trying to get God to change his mind in a situation that goes against our flesh? What is even worse, we dare to call our whimpering to God to get him to do what we want "prayer"! We actually try to use prayer as a means of refusing to submit to the clear, revealed will of God. Even the best of God's children are guilty of this awful sin. Let us look at a classic case in the life of Abraham:

> *And the LORD said, Shall I hide from Abraham that thing which I do....* (Gen. 18:17)

In this verse and the context, we see that God informs Abraham that he is going to destroy Sodom. Abraham is told exactly what God is about to do. However, Abraham is not in agreement with God's purposes and decides to "pray" to God in the hopes of changing his mind. The dialogue is a beautiful illustration of the point I am trying to establish. Notice the exchange between Abraham and God:

> *And Abraham drew near, and said, Wilt thou also destroy the righteous with the wicked? Peradventure there be fifty righteous*

within the city: wilt thou also destroy and not spare the place for the
fifty righteous that are therein? That be far from thee to do after this
manner, to slay the righteous with the wicked: and that the
righteous should be as the wicked; that be far from thee: Shall not
the Judge of all the earth do right? And the LORD said, If I find in
Sodom fifty righteous within the city, then I will spare all the place
for their sakes. And Abraham answered and said, Behold now, I
have taken upon me to speak unto the Lord, who am but dust and
ashes: Peradventure there shall lack five of the fifty righteous: wilt
thou destroy all the city for lack of five? And he said, If I find there
forty and five, I will not destroy it. And he spake unto him yet
again, and said, Peradventure there shall be forty found there. And
he said, I will not do it for forty's sake. And he said unto him, Oh let
not the Lord be angry, and I will speak: Peradventure there shall
thirty be found there. And he said, I will not do it, if I find thirty
there. And he said, Behold now, I have taken upon me to speak unto
the Lord: Peradventure there shall be twenty found there. And he
said, I will not destroy it for twenty's sake. And he said, Oh let not
the Lord be angry, and I will speak yet but this once: Peradventure
ten shall be found there. And he said, I will not destroy it for ten's
sake. And the LORD went his way, as soon as he had left
communing with Abraham: and Abraham returned unto his place.
(Gen 18:23-31)

Now remember that this dialogue took place as a direct
result of God revealing to Abraham his purpose to destroy
Sodom and Gomorrah. Abraham is not in agreement with
what God is about to do. Verses 23 and 24 make it appear
that Abraham's only concern is for the reputation of God.
Did Abraham have the faintest notion that there were fifty
righteous people in Sodom, or do you think that his only
concern was his nephew Lot? It is interesting to note that
neither God nor Abraham ever mention Lot by name, even

though both knew that he was the real concern in Abraham's heart. Notice that God revealed that he was going to destroy both Sodom and Gomorrah, but he only mentions Sodom in his response to Abraham. Why mention Gomorrah when Abraham's only interest is in Sodom?

God graciously condescends to Abraham's terms and agrees to spare the city if there are fifty righteous people found. That should end the matter, but Abraham decides to "pray" some more. He first acknowledges how humble he is and then proceeds to show how deceitful he is. Verse 28 is a classic example of twisting the facts and loading the dice. The first request is to spare the whole city for the sake of fifty righteous people. If Abraham wants to drop off five, then he should have said, "Will you destroy the city if forty-five are found?" However, he frames the statement in such a way that the question is not forty-five but only a matter of five. It is like saying, "Lord, would you quibble over a mere five people?" Abraham sets up the equation backwards. At the end of verse 28, God corrects Abraham's math and promises not to destroy the city if "forty-five" righteous can be found.

We would surely expect Abraham to be satisfied and ready to be quiet. Not so! Abraham is determined to impose his will on God and correct God's purposes. As you read verses 29 through 32 while Abraham goes from forty-five to forty, to thirty, to twenty, and finally down to ten, you wait for the hammer of Almighty God to fall on this insignificant gnat for his impudence! However, that never happens, not even when Abraham piously says, "I will speak yet but this once." He has already done that five times. Why doesn't the hammer fall? Simply because God is Abraham's friend, and God dearly loves him. God is long-suffering with his children. He knows that Abraham's nose is out of joint, and he surely sees through the whole facade of Abraham's prayers. However, God is concerned with changing Abraham's heart and attitude. Notice that in the KJV, verse 33, God calls this exchange "communing." I would call it "badgering," but then I am not as powerful or as gracious as God.

This illustration teaches us that one (but not the only) function of prayer is to change us. God did not change his purpose, but he did use Abraham's prayer to change Abraham's attitude. Prayer changed Abraham. We all sometimes try to use prayer to get God to change his mind instead of gladly submitting to his sovereign purposes. On the other hand, God often, instead of clobbering us with his absolute sovereignty—which he has every right to do—will allow us to vent our fears and disagreements to show us how unreasonable we are acting. Did you ever blow something out of proportion that had been done to you? You kept nursing it inside of you, and it kept getting bigger and bigger in your mind. You had, in your mind, an ironclad case against the person for what he had done. Finally you told someone how terribly you had been treated, but the more you tried to explain why it was so bad, the more your ironclad case fell apart. You began to realize it was really a small thing that should have been dropped. You knew that you were making a fool of yourself by trying to justify your feelings, and you wished you could shut up because of how ridiculous you appeared for feeling as you did. It took the "verbalizing" of the event to make you objective.

God often does the same thing with us. He patiently listens to us until we begin to see how ridiculous we are in trying to get him to change his mind. As a result, our whole attitude and the content of our prayers are changed. We are humbled and brought to bow in worship to whatever his providence brings. We also praise him anew and afresh for his sovereign patience with us.

This brings us to the next point in our discussion of prayer.

BASIC FACT NUMBER THREE: It is not wrong for us to pray what has been termed "selfish prayer."

Is it wrong to ask God to keep my children safe as they travel, or that he enable them to find good employment? If my wife goes to the hospital for surgery, is it wrong to ask God to make the operation a success? In all of these cases, I have no knowledge of what God has decreed. Abraham may have been less than honest in the way he prayed, but was it right for him to be concerned for Lot and entreat God for his safety? Is it right for us to be concerned for the safety of loved ones and pray for their well-being? Perhaps another biblical illustration will help us. Let us look at David and one of his prayers:

> *And David said unto Nathan, I have sinned against the LORD. And Nathan said unto David, The LORD also hath put away thy*

sin; thou shalt not die. Howbeit, because by this deed thou hast given great occasion to the enemies of the LORD to blaspheme, the child also that is born unto thee shall surely die. And Nathan departed unto his house. And the LORD struck the child that Uriah's wife bare unto David, and it was very sick. (2 Sam. 12:13-15)

You will remember that David had committed both adultery and murder. God sent Nathan the prophet to David, and through his message, God convicted David of his awful sin. In the above verses, God clearly reveals what is going to happen. The child is going to die. As in Abraham's case, David has a clear revelation of God's will or decree. David still feels constrained to plead with God to spare the sick child:

David therefore besought God for the child; and David fasted; and went in, and lay all night upon the earth. And the elders of his house arose, and went to him, to raise him up from the earth: but he would not, neither did he eat bread with them. (2 Sam. 12:16, 17)

Was David wrong in praying as he did? Had not God said that the child would die and therefore it was a waste of time to pray, or does that conclusion not necessarily follow? We learn a great lesson about prayer from this incident in David's life. The child died in spite of David's plea. You will remember that the servants were afraid to inform David of the child's death. They thought his state of mind might make him do something foolish. When David perceived the truth, he asked, "Is the child dead?" When the servants said, "Yes," the Scripture tells us what David did:

Then David arose from the earth, and washed, and anointed
himself, and changed his apparel, and came into the house of the
LORD, and worshiped. Then he came to his own house; and when
he required, they set bread before him, and he did eat. (2 Sam.
12:20)

The moment David realized that the child was dead, he
totally accepted God's providence. He first worshipped
God and then proceeded to get on with his life. David's
servants were amazed. They expected David to weep and
wail and carry on in an uncontrolled manner. They
questioned David, and we see in David's answer the heart
of this lesson in prayer that we are studying:

Then said his servants unto him, What thing is this that thou
hast done? Thou didst fast and weep for the child, while it was alive;
but when the child was dead, thou didst rise and eat bread. And he
said, While the child was yet alive, I fasted and wept; for I said, Who
can tell whether GOD will be gracious to me, that the child may
live? But now he is dead, wherefore should I fast? Can I bring him
back again? I shall go to him, but he shall not return to me. (2 Sam.
12:21-23)

What is David saying? What is the attitude of his heart
as he pleads with God to spare his child? David is saying
this: "As long as that child had breath, I prayed to God
alone as the only one who could keep him alive. God was
pleased to answer my prayers with a 'No.' I said, 'Blessed
be the name of the Lord' and got on with my life. I will
bow in humble faith to God's sovereign providence."
David may not have said aloud, "Nevertheless, not my
will, but thy will be done," but that attitude was certainly
in his heart as he prayed. You and I may pray for whatever

our heart desires, as long as we can sincerely leave it up to God to decide if the answer should be "yes" or "no." I am aware that this is contrary to the basic premise of the current, typical teaching on prayer, but it is biblical. Even our blessed Lord had to pray, "Nevertheless, not my will, but thine be done." Are we greater than our Master?

Perhaps it would be well to give one more illustration of this clear, biblical principle. In chapter one, "The Sovereignty of God in Providence," I spent a good deal of time looking at the book of Habakkuk. That whole book is a classic example of the principle of prayer that we are discussing. In the first few verses, Habakkuk challenges God's apparent inactivity. When God informs the prophet that he is about to send the Chaldeans to invade and mop up the nation of Israel, Habakkuk does exactly what Abraham did. He tries to convince God that this would be inconsistent with his character of holiness. Of course, we realize that Habakkuk also does not want to see Israel nearly destroyed. After God reminds Habakkuk that "the Lord is in His holy temple," the prophet's whole attitude changes. Listen to a real prayer from a confident heart:

> *A prayer of Habakkuk the prophet. On shigionoth. LORD, I have heard of your fame; I stand in awe of your deeds, O LORD. Renew them in our day, in our time make them known; in wrath remember mercy....You came out to deliver your people, to save your anointed one. You crushed the leader of the land of wickedness, you stripped him from head to foot. Selah...I heard and my heart pounded, my lips quivered at the sound; decay crept into my bones, and my legs trembled. Yet I will wait patiently for the day of calamity to come on the nation invading us. Though the fig tree does not bud and there*

are no grapes on the vines, though the olive crop fails and the fields produce no food, though there are no sheep in the pen and no cattle in the stalls, yet I will rejoice in the LORD, I will be joyful in God my Savior. The Sovereign LORD is my strength; he makes my feet like the feet of a deer, he enables me to go on the heights. (Hab. 3:1, 2, 13, 16-19)

It is obvious that Habakkuk's confrontation with God in prayer radically changed the prophet's whole perspective and attitude. He learned that God was always in control and always working out his own purposes; in doing so, he uses everybody, including the wicked Chaldeans, to accomplish his purposes. Verse 2 is real prayer. Verse 13 shows a true understanding and application of God's purposes in history. Ultimately, everything that happens involves the people of God. Verses 16-19 describe a man worshipping in wonder and awe. Habakkuk knows his nation is about to be judged, but he has faith and hope that God will bring good out of it all, as well as glory to himself. That is the right way to pray, and such prayer is sometimes possible only after God has used our wrong prayers to change our attitude and us.

BASIC FACT NUMBER FOUR: Prayer is ASKING, not TELLING God what to do.

Real prayer must be seen as asking, but we cannot see it in this light until we realize that God has every right to say no. When prayer is understood biblically, it is seen to be an attitude as well as an act. It involves the response of the heart to revealed truth as well as words of petition. Let me mention two things that prayer is not:

1. Prayer is not giving God advice and telling him what to do, when to do it, and who to use to accomplish it. All of this is to treat God as if he had no plan of his own to resolve the problem.

2. Prayer is not giving God information that he did not have before we prayed and gave it to him. Have you ever "prayed" and carefully explained to God exactly what was happening, and when you were finished you felt, "Now God really understands what is going on and will be in a position to see the wisdom of my advice!" How conceited can we be?

You may have heard of the man who felt led to pray for the families of the people killed in a plane crash. He stood up in a prayer meeting and said, "Lord, I ask you to bless the families of the people who died in that plane crash over in...(and the man forgot where the crash had occurred)...in, ah, ah...Lord, I forget where it happened, but I'm sure you know. It was in all the papers this morning." I wonder if anyone felt like saying, "I hope God got the right edition of the paper." We may smile at that story, but do we not betray the same attitude when we feel "now God has the real story" after we have prayed?

By the way, nothing proves our faith as much as how we feel and act after we have prayed. We say that we "give up" and cast our burden on God. We confess to him that the matter is in his hands. So we say! However, in reality that is often not the case. We "give up to God" and then proceed to manipulate every situation we can. We "let go" and then scheme for all we are worth. We "roll it on God" and then push and pull with every means that our flesh can conceive. We cannot pray in faith and scheme in the flesh at the same time.

Jay Adams has an excellent illustration showing this truth. A certain man was always depressed and complaining about everything. His friends learned never to ask him, "How are you?" unless they had a free hour to hear his many problems. One day a friend met the man, and he was smiling and rejoicing. When asked why he was so happy, the man replied, "I do not have a single worry in the world." "Well," said his friend, "that is something new for you. Whatever happened that enabled you to get rid of all your worry?" The man replied, "I found a fellow that could worry better than I could, and I pay him to do all my worrying." His friend said, "Well, it sure seems to work. How much do you pay for this service?" The former worrier said, "I pay the man $500 a week." His friend exclaimed, "How in the world can you ever raise that kind of money each week?" "Oh," said the man, "that is his worry, not mine." I am sure you see the point. If we give God the problem, we must give him the entire problem.

How often do we lay something before God and pick it up again when we leave his presence? How often do we give it to God and then worry about how he can possibly find a way to do anything about it? Our real problem is that we cannot see how God can possibly do what we want him to do in the situation.

Let me make three clear statements that define biblical prayer. They will show us why real prayer is so difficult for us. We often try to get God to agree with what we want instead of honestly seeking to know and bow to his sovereign will.

1. True prayer is a frank admission that God is sovereign. When we really pray, we admit that the circumstance is in God's hands alone. We are saying that tomorrow, and all it brings, is not under our control but under his control. It is in his hands and not ours.

2. Prayer is a joyful surrender to God's sovereign purposes. We are acknowledging that God has the right and power to do whatever seems good to him. We are saying that regardless of what God does tomorrow, we know it is part of the "all things" in Romans 8:28.

3. Prayer is earnestly pleading with God for grace to glorify him regardless of what he does. We are really saying, "Father, give me grace to trust you and act like your child whether you say yes or no."

I remember using the above definitions for a message in Montreal. One of the women in attendance became angry and did not come back to the meetings for three nights. When she came back, she said to me, "Mr. Reisinger, last night was the first time I have gotten a good night's sleep in over two years." She proceeded to tell me what had happened. Her son had gotten involved in drugs. She had covered and lied for him. She had wept over him and gotten angry with him. She had threatened, pleaded, and promised. She had come to her wits' end. She said, "Last night I got down beside my bed and put my son in God's hands. I told him that he had every right to destroy my son and use him as an example of the folly of drugs. I pleaded with God to save my son and felt assurance that regardless of what happens, I was going to trust God. I went to bed and slept for the first night in two years."

In this woman's case, God was pleased to save her son about three months later. It does not always happen that way. However, we must learn to put our lives, our jobs, and our children in God's hands. They are there, whether we like it or not. Our commitment of them to God in heartfelt prayer is merely learning to rest in faith in God's sovereign providence.

I repeat, isn't that one of the primary reasons that real prayer is so hard? Is it not a fact that we find it impossible to fervently pray about something that we are pretty sure is not going to come out the way that we want it to come out? Isn't that part of James' accusation to us concerning our attitude toward tomorrow? We know what we want to happen in our business and in our life—we already have it planned out. It is difficult to get into that "nevertheless, not my will, but your will" attitude of heart. It is far easier to just say, "Lord, bless the plans that I already have figured out." Real prayer is acknowledging that we realize our own insufficiency and need. We are confessing our total dependence upon God for each day and all it brings. We should always remember what James says, especially when we don't pray:

> Now listen, you who say, "Today or tomorrow we will go to this
> or that city, spend a year there, carry on business and make money."

Why, you do not even know what will happen tomorrow. What is your life? You are a mist that appears for a little while and then vanishes. Instead, you ought to say, "If it is the Lord's will, we will live and do this or that." As it is, you boast and brag. All such boasting is evil. (James 4:13-16 NIV)

James is saying, "You either do not pray about your plans, or else you plan without considering God's sovereignty." Earlier we saw that James accuses us of either not praying at all or praying amiss with a concern for only our own selfish desires. When all that we are concerned about is God blessing our plans and ideas, it is nigh unto impossible to really pray sincerely.

BASIC FACT NUMBER FIVE: A belief in the sovereignty of God will not hinder real prayer, but instead it will foster it.

It is a belief in free will that kills biblical prayer. Free-will preaching may produce what Hosea called "howling on our beds," but even that will not last very long. I venture to say that you have never been in a prayer meeting where anyone believed in free will or denied God's sovereignty and prayed accordingly. I remember one deacon in my first pastorate who constantly tried to pray from the perspective of his free-will theology, but could never do it consistently. Every week he would say, "Lord, I know you love everyone in the entire world exactly alike. You love every person in the USA. You are trying to save every soul in our state. I know you love everyone in the town of Lewisburg (by this time he was talking more slowly). Lord, I know you love everyone living on Third

Street. You love both of my neighbors." Now about this time, the man would begin to cry and say, "But Lord, they will not listen to the gospel. They will not come to church. Oh, Lord, send your Holy Spirit and convict them. Oh, God, begin to draw them to yourself." The next week it would be the same routine. That dear man never did see that he was constantly forced to acknowledge God's sovereignty before he could pray (the first part of his oration each week was really not prayer, but preaching to me).

Isn't it amazing that Christians forget all about man's so-called free will when they get on their knees? Don't we all love the absolute sovereignty of God when we are calling on his name in desperate need?

I will never forget a dear lady in a Bible class I taught in Rochester, NY. I believe she loved the Lord, but she had never been exposed to the truth of sovereign grace. She greatly enjoyed the class in Romans until we came to the doctrine of God's sovereignty. She said, "This class is ruining my prayer life, and I am not coming back." I said, "I do not blame you. However, I would like to know what I said that would have a bad effect on your prayer life." She replied, "This business about free will and the sovereignty of God. If what you say is true, then why should I pray?" I asked her what she had prayed for that morning (always good to check up!), and she opened her purse and got out a worn prayer list. That morning she had pleaded with God on behalf of two nurses in an African country experiencing a civil war. I said, "What did you ask God to do?" Without hesitation, the woman replied, "I asked God to keep my nurse friends safe. I prayed that neither army would hurt their ministry or the workers. I also prayed that none of the bombs or bullets would destroy any of the property." I looked at her in pretended amazement and said, "Did you really ask those things? How could you? All of those soldiers have free wills. Would it not be better to entreat an ambassador to try to intervene with the military in that country? Surely you do not expect God to control a whole war, every soldier, and every bomb and bullet, just to keep two people safe?" The lady was rather elderly, and I do not think she followed me, but many other people did. That dear saint of God had cried to a sovereign God that morning without questioning his power or thinking about the free will of sinful soldiers. She unconsciously knew God could control every soldier, from the general down to the private, and direct every bullet and piece of shrapnel in answering her prayer and keeping her nurse friends safe. In her heart, that dear lady was talking to the Sovereign God.

It is amazing to me that new converts, especially those converted under the preaching of sovereign grace, have no difficulty with the sovereignty of God and prayer. Shortly after my daughter-in-law was converted, she attended a different church one Sunday when I was away preaching. I phoned that evening and asked her how she had enjoyed the service. Her answer was amusing. She said, "It was strange, Dad. The preacher sounded like he did not agree with you while he was preaching, but when he started to pray, he sounded like he agreed with you one-hundred-percent." She was right. You may listen to many "free will" sermons (they come out of the preacher's mind), but you will never hear a "free-will" prayer (real prayer comes out of the heart).

BASIC FACT NUMBER SIX: Prayer is essential because God has ordained it as one of the means to accomplish his decrees.

The question is not "Can God do something without prayer?" but rather, "Has God himself sovereignly decreed that he will use prayer as a means of accomplishing what he has ordained?" A real burden to pray does not begin with us, but with God. If you doubt this, all you need to do is make a decision to have a burden and see if it works. Pick a missionary or any other person, and decide you will have a burden for him and his ministry. Your burden will last about as long as the dew lasts after the sun comes up. Has it not been your experience that real burdens are often those that you would not particularly choose? Sometimes God lays an individual on your heart with whom you have little relationship. You may not even like the person, or you may have just recently met them. However, the Holy Spirit keeps bringing that person to your mind, and you feel compelled to pray for them.

I remember a girl getting upset with me the first time she heard the truth of God's sovereign election. She said, "If I believed that, I would quit praying for my mother to get saved." Her statement gave me a hint that I decided to pursue. "Do you faithfully pray for your mother's conversion?" I asked. She had tears in her eyes, and answered, "I pray for her almost constantly. Sometimes at work I silently raise my heart to God, and I feel myself beginning to cry and I have go to the washroom. I have a real burden for my mother's soul." I said, "You did not mention your father. Is he a Christian?" "No," she replied. "How often do you pray for him? Have you ever shed tears pleading with God to save him?" She got a strange look on her face and said, "Now that you mention it, I rarely ever pray for my Dad, but I never fail to pray for my Mom." I smiled and said, "I think your Dad is the one you better worry about. I believe God is getting ready to save your mother. As long as you can plead to God with tears, you have every reason to believe that God's Spirit is moving you to pray. The Holy Spirit does not move us to pray in vain!"

I do not believe that girl could have worked up a real burden for her father, no matter how hard she tried. Likewise, she could not have been truly burdened to pray for her mother if God was not purposing to work in saving grace. God never burdens our hearts to plead for things that are not his will, and we can't arbitrarily choose what we want and then force God to include that particular thing in his purposes. This would mean that we control the world and run it with our prayers.

I am sure that some hyper-Calvinists will read this and say a loud "Amen." The only problem is that what I have said in no way justifies a cold heart that never prays! Let me make some very pointed remarks. I think they will help us to be sure that we have the theology of God's sovereignty straight.

One: prayer begins with God and grows out of his decrees or purposes. Two: the Holy Spirit burdens people to pray for those things that God has ordained and is about to do.

Now if these two facts are true, and they are, then you and I can tell whether we are in the will of God and under his blessing by whether we have a burdened heart. My friend, if you shed no tears at the throne of grace, it proves that God is not using you. You are on the shelf, or maybe you are not even converted! It is possible that God is not accomplishing any of his gracious purposes through you simply because your heart is cold as an iceberg. I did not say that God was not accomplishing his purposes, but I did say that he was not using you to do it.

Follow me carefully for a moment. If God is the one who burdens our hearts, and if he must either give us the desire of our heart or break our hearts by saying no, then where does that leave us if we have neither a burdened heart nor a broken heart? My friend, burdens begin as we seek God's throne and ask him to burden our hearts. We tell him that we want to be used by him. We plead with him to interrupt our complacency and revive our hearts. We seek him until we feel his Spirit moving in our hearts. We ought to pray the following chorus:

Lord, lay some soul upon my heart, and love that soul through me.
And may I humbly do my part, to win that soul to Thee.

That chorus is acknowledging that the very desire and burden to faithfully witness must begin with God. It pleads with God to burden our hearts so that we will want—and be able to—love and pray and witness. Can any true Christian desire less? No, my hyper-Calvinist friend, you cannot get off the hook that easily. We will not let your cold heart hide behind a pile of theology books, even if the theology in the books is correct. Jesus told us to ask, seek, and knock. He promised that we would receive, we would find, and it would be opened to us. Are you receiving, and finding, and are opportunities being opened up to you? The single most important question for us to ask in this matter is, "What are we asking for, what are we seeking, and what are we knocking for?" If we agree that God has sovereignly ordained prayer as a means to accomplish his decrees, then we should see that we are not being used by God if we are not earnestly asking, seeking, and knocking as part of that process. Let me summarize and repeat this last point with some personal questions:

1. Are we burdened to pray for anything specific? If not, then God is not using us to accomplish any of his gracious purposes.

2. Who are the specific people for whose salvation we feel burdened to pray? If there are none, then God is not using us to gather his elect to himself.

3. How many groanings for revival has God heard from our congregations? James says, "You have not because you ask not." I think I can say without fear of contradiction that we will cry to God for the things that we really want. That

being true, our prayer life is a good barometer of the spiritual condition of our Christian life. When we really want something and plead with God with a burdened heart, then, as I said before, God must either grant the request or break our hearts and say, "no." Again, how often have we neither a burdened nor a broken heart?

4. If God opened the windows of heaven this very moment and poured into our hearts every single spiritual blessing that we have been burdened to pray for in the last month, how many of us would be precisely as spiritually empty at this very moment as we were then? If such is our case, dare we blame that on God's sovereignty?

I hope I have convinced you that a firm belief in the sovereignty of God in no way conflicts with, or in any way hinders, true prayer. To the contrary, nothing is as contradictory as believing in the sovereignty of God and not praying. I wish I could write the following words in gold and put them over the pulpit of every Calvinistic or Reformed Church (and also tattoo them on my own brain):

> A day without prayer is a day that totally denies the sovereignty of God and glorifies the free will and self-sufficiency of man.

Let me summarize thus far. We saw that (1) the believers in both the Old and New Testament Scriptures never had any problem "reconciling" God's absolute sovereignty with the need to pray. They simply believed both truths. We noted that (2) prayer is often used as a means of trying to evade the clearly revealed will of God. We emphasized that (3) true prayer is asking God, not giving God information he did not have or instructions in how he should go about answering our prayers. We finished by stating that a day without prayer is a denial of our boast that we believe in the sovereignty of God. Let us continue with some positive statements about prayer and sovereignty.

Why is Prayer so Important?

Why is it so essential that we see the great importance of prayer? Prayer is commanded, and God has promised to answer prayer. The people who base everything on the myth of man's free will distort prayer in one direction, and hyper-Calvinists distort it in another direction. Let's look at some biblical facts that steer us clear of both these two errors.

ONE: Prayer is essential to the fulfillment of God's purposes. Some may wonder at the validity of such a statement, and standing alone with no reference to the rest of Scripture, the statement would be very wrong. However, when stated in conjunction with God's revealed purpose to use prayer as an ordained means to accomplish his purposes, the statement is very biblical, and only a hyper-Calvinist would object to it.

I trust that these truths on prayer and God's sovereignty are beginning to make the foregoing facts clear. I hope that we have started to grasp the reality of the absolute necessity of prayer. God is not helpless to accomplish his purposes without our prayers, but prayer is essential just because our Sovereign God has decreed that he will work through our prayers. The God that ordained to spare Israel when they made the golden calf also ordained that Moses would stand and intercede lest they be consumed (Exod. 32:1-11). True prayer always begins with "according to his will" simply because God is the first mover in prayer, and not us. Since true prayer is always "according to his will," then it follows that it is impossible for us to be consciously walking in God's will and at the same time to be prayerless. To be prayerless is to prove that God is not working in and through us.

We can safely draw two clear biblical facts: (1) Prayer is essential in accomplishing God's purposes because God himself has decreed to accomplish his will (or purposes) through the prayers of his people. In fact, prayer itself is one of the things decreed by God. (2) Because prayer is so tied in with God's will for us, one of the best barometers of our spiritual condition is our daily prayer life. I am aware that stating this truth so bluntly will send most people (including me) on a guilt trip—and it should! There is no one sin for which I must ask forgiveness as much as a failure to pray consistently with a warm heart.

What we are saying is this: prayer is one of the greatest means at our disposal to truly glorify God and prove our love and faith. For instance, even if you are a millionaire and own the largest bakery in town, you are still commanded in Scripture to "pray for your daily bread." God knows our needs before we ask, and it would seem we could surely supply our own bread under such circumstances, but we are still told to pray for our daily supply. Of course, we realize that "daily bread" means all of the things necessary to life, including life itself. Understood correctly, praying for our daily bread is just another way of acknowledging that every day, and everything in that day, is under the sovereign control of God. It is basically the same exhortation as James 4:13-15.

God desires that we commune daily with him as our heavenly Father. He delights to commune with us, as well as shower us with good things from his storehouse. Daily prayer demonstrates that we are conscious that every present blessing is from God, and our dependence is in him alone for any future blessing. You cannot be praying and be self-sufficient at the same time; likewise, it is simply impossible to neglect prayer without being self-reliant. I will repeat what I said earlier: the greatest denial of God's sovereignty is a day without prayer!

I can illustrate this principle with a parent who has a son in college. A parent can pay his son's expenses at college in one of two ways. He can give him one check for the entire semester, or you can give him enough for one week. Both ways will supply his need, with the only difference being how often you would like to have a letter or phone call from him. The "once a week" will get far more letters and phone calls. I heard of a boy who wrote home from college and said, "Dear Dad, no mon. No fun. Your Son." The father wrote back, "Dear Son, too bad. How sad. Your Dad." I am sure you see the point. God delights in hearing from his children, and one of the ways he assures this will happen is to put things on a daily basis.

We must learn to see that prayer is essential for the simple reason that a sovereign God has purposed to use prayer as the means to reach an end. At the same time, we must never think of prayer as "giving God a chance" to exercise his power. God's absolute sovereignty and the necessity of prayer may appear to be in direct opposition, but they are both true. The Bible teaches that prayer is a necessary means appointed by a sovereign God, but in no sense does the Scripture teach that God's desires or purposes are crippled and unable to succeed because of a lack of prayer. We may, as individuals, fail to experience the joy of being used by God in a given instance, but not a single thing that God has decreed will ever be hindered by our failure or our lack of prayer. God's decrees do not change moment by moment according to the various options opened up to him in a given situation by our prayers. God plans and carries out his purposes without any change. A. W. Pink said it well:

> Such thoughts of prayer as we have been citing are due to low and inadequate conceptions of God Himself. It ought to be apparent that there could be little or no comfort in praying to a God who was like the chameleon, which changes its color every day. What encouragement is there to lift up our hearts to One who was in one mind yesterday and in another today? What would be the use of petitioning an earthly king, if we knew he was so changeable as to grant a petition one day and deny it another? Is it not the very unchangeableness of God which is our greatest encouragement to pray? Because He is "without variableness and shadow of turning" we are assured that if we ask anything according to His will we are most certain of being heard. Well did Luther remark, "Prayer

is not overcoming God's reluctance, but laying hold of His willingness." (*The Sovereignty of God,* A. W. Pink, Banner of Truth, p. 113)

I recently read where a basketball coach in a Christian college told the team that if they had enough faith and prevailed in prayer, they could win every game and become the national champions. What horrible theology!

Imagine Team A praying for one hour and God saying, "Great, fellows, you are going to win." Team B, their opponents, pray for two hours, and God says, "Sorry, Team A, but Team B out-prayed you; they are going to win." Team A gathers the whole school together for an all-night prayer meeting, and God is again forced to change his mind and says, "Sorry, Team B, but Team A has overcome your volume of prayer, and they will win." Team B could then get the whole town involved in a prayer and fasting day, forcing God to again reverse his decree. I am sure we can see how wrong such a view of prayer is when we layout its implications. This view makes prayer, or the amount of prayer, like either the volume of noise at a pep rally or the pressure exerted by a political group on Congress. Whoever exerts the most pressure gets what he wants. According to such an idea, we could buy what we wanted from God by employing enough people to pray — meaning "pressure" — God for our wants (I deliberately did not use the word *needs*). This is a denial of God's sovereignty and an insult to both his wisdom and his purposes.

Perhaps someone is thinking about the lesson Jesus taught in Luke 11:5-10. This is known as "the parable of the importunate friend," and it certainly teaches us to persist in prayer. However, Jesus is encouraging us to pray by making a deliberate contrast. He is not telling us that God is like the man who was asleep and did not wish to be bothered. The God of Israel neither slumbers nor sleeps. Jesus is telling us that our heavenly Father is exactly the opposite of that man. The application is this: if a man that does not wish to be bothered can be forced into granting your request just to keep you from pestering him, how much more ready is your heavenly Father, who delights to have you come any time of the day or night, to hear and answer the prayers of his children. That passage does not contradict what I have been saying; it reinforces it.

As another illustration, suppose you were God and one of your earthly children was a farmer who desperately needed rain to save his crops. The farmer pleaded faithfully and fervently for rain and claimed the promise in James. At the very same time, the Bible conference on the adjoining property was pleading in prayer for sunny weather with no rain so that the "biggest mission conference in the history of the denomination" would be a success. How would you decide which one to answer? Do you see why it is essential that we understand that prayer does not begin with our wants but with God's purposes?

TWO: What about unanswered prayer? The above illustration brings us to our next point. How do we reconcile the fact of "unanswered prayer" with the "clear promises of Scripture"? Should the farmer believe that God did not answer his prayers if there was no rain? Would no rain prove that the Bible conference crowd was more spiritual or had more "prayer power" because of its size? To ask such questions is to demonstrate how terribly wrong we are in our concept of prayer. To even entertain such an idea of unanswered prayer is to be driven to believe that God is either less than sovereign or else our faith is not strong enough to force his hand to move.

Once we see the true nature of prayer, there is no problem. If we understand that prayer is asking God and not telling God, then "no" is just as much an answer as "yes." A child of God who understands the truths we have been stating will realize that there is no such thing as unanswered prayer. Actually, a heart of faith and confidence in God's wisdom and sovereignty will view an answer of "no" from God to be just as kind and gracious as a "yes." God's "no" answers are not based on either reluctance or a lack of power on his part; they are based just as much on his love and grace as when he says "yes." I am sure that all of us can look back and praise God for graciously saying "no" to some of the requests for which we desperately pleaded.

We must see that every prayer is answered with either a yes or no. Sometimes the "no" is a "wait, it is not yet the right time." I repeat, the believing heart is just as grateful for the answer "no, my child, that is not good for you" as he is for the positive answer. An indulgent parent may have difficulty saying "no" to a spoiled child, but God loves his children too much to allow them to become undisciplined brats. He is too kind and gracious to allow us to destroy ourselves with our own unbridled selfishness. We ought to gratefully acknowledge God's "no" answers just as enthusiastically as his "yes" answers.

If we keep reminding ourselves of what we have been saying, it will clear up a lot of confusion and apparent contradictions. Instead of thinking of prayer as the means of getting God to give us what we want, we will see that true prayer is first concerned with honoring God himself. When we pray correctly, we gladly acknowledge his universal rule over all things. We confess that our God controls even the sun and the rain. Biblical prayer makes us realize that only God himself can keep us from sin or deliver our loved ones out of ignorance and darkness. Proper prayer calls out and proves our faith and love. In showing God that we are truly dependent on him, we please him and glorify his very person. Prayer is an act of worship. We praise God for all that he is and has revealed himself to be, and this gives us the confidence to ask even greater things. Our Lord Jesus called the temple the "house of prayer" and not the "house of sacrifice." Every approach to God, including our singing and giving, is a form of prayer.

Prayer is one of the appointed means of obtaining spiritual blessings, and as such, it is one of the methods by which we grow in grace and the knowledge of God. Prayer humbles us and delivers us from self-sufficiency. It increases our faith and worship. It is one of the best barometers of our love and thankfulness to our God. If our prayers are correct, the following words of the Psalmist will aptly describe us:

> I love the LORD, for he heard my voice; he heard my cry for mercy. Because he turned his ear to me, I will call on him as long as I live. (Ps. 116:1, 2 NIV)

Concluding Thought

Billy Bray was a godly Christian known for saying; "I must speak to my Father about this." He felt he had to pray about everything. When I read about him, I was reminded of the following story.

An elderly believer felt that God wanted him to attend a two-day Bible conference in a city about ten miles away. He packed a lunch and decided that he would walk and save the bus fare. On the way, he met a young seminary student who was also going to the conference. At noon, they sat down to eat their lunch. The young man prayed and thanked the Lord for the food and asked his blessing on the conference.

The old man did likewise but added some "personal" requests. "Father," he prayed, "I really need a pair of shoes, and I am asking you to supply them for me. And, Father, I believe you really want me to hear the messages at the conference and you know I cannot hear too well, so I am trusting you to get me a good seat. And lastly, Father, I have enough money for a motel, but perhaps you might move one of your children to exercise Christian hospitality and open their home to me for the weekend."

The seminary student was obviously upset and chided the old man for the way he prayed. It was bad enough to ask for a pair of shoes, but to expect God to supply a home to stay in was just a little too much. When they arrived at the church, the place was packed. There was standing room only. The old man and the student were leaning on a railing that went across the back of the church. The old man had his hand cupped up to his ear trying to hear the preliminary announcements. The student was smirking from ear to ear and thinking, "So much for the good seat."

There was only one empty seat in the whole place, and it was in the front row. A young lady was sitting in the next seat and kept turning around and looking to the rear of the church. When the announcer said, "We will open the service with our first hymn," the girl called an usher over and, pointing to the rear of the church, whispered in his ear. The usher walked directly back to the old man and said, "Are you hard of hearing?" "Yes," the man replied. "Well, a young lady in the front row is saving a seat for her father who is a surgeon. He told her if he was not here when the service began, it meant he was still in surgery and she was to give the seat to someone else. The young lady would like you to come up and sit with her." The old man raised his eyes and said, "Thank you, Father," and the student stood with his mouth wide open.

In this particular church, it was the custom to kneel in front of your seat to pray. When the old man turned and kneeled in the front row, everyone on the platform could see both the seat of his pants and the bottom of his shoes.

After the service was over, the chairman of the meeting came up to the old man and said, "Brother, I don't know how to say this since I have never in my life done anything like this before. I do not in any way want to embarrass you, but I noticed when you prayed that your shoes are so worn that your socks are showing. I own a shoe store, and it seemed to me that God kept telling me to offer you a couple of pair of shoes. They are last year's style but brand-new. Would you accept them as a gift?" The old man smiled and said, "Yes, I will. I prayed about that need today, and my Father has answered." The shoe storeowner was overjoyed and said, "Praise God for the privilege of being the answer to your prayer."

The young lady was amazed. She asked the old man where he was staying during the conference, and he said, "I am not sure. I think my Father has a room reserved for me." She said, "Your father? Why, you look like you are over 70." Then she laughed and said, "Oh, you mean your heavenly Father. Please, wait right here until I get back." She went into the pastor's study, in a few moments came out, and said, "I phoned my Dad, and he is out of the operating room. I told him about you, and he said, 'I must meet that good brother. Ask him if he would please spend the weekend with us.'" The old man smiled, raised his eyes, and said, "Thank you, Father."

Do we believe things like that really happen? Do we ever see them happening to ourselves? I wonder if we have become so sophisticated and self-sufficient that we do not "bother God with small things." Maybe we ought to adopt

Billy Bray's theology. Maybe we ought to resolve to "talk to my Father about everything." After all, our Father sovereignly controls all things.

CHAPTER FOUR
TOTAL DEPRAVITY

Introduction

There are basically only two religions in the whole world. The one begins with the free will of man, and the other begins with the sovereignty of God. The first one keeps telling you what "you must do" for God, and the second declares what "God has done for you" that you could not do for yourself. The religion of "free will" pictures salvation as a possibility for all men if they are willing to cooperate with God by believing. The religion of free grace presents salvation as a certainty for all of the elect of God because God gives faith as a gift. Does your preacher keep emphasizing "do," or does he talk about "done"?

The many varieties of the religion based on man's free will differ only on what man must do in order to find acceptance with God. One says he must go to Mecca and kiss the sacred rock; another says he must bathe in the Ganges River; another says he must be baptized by immersion; and others say he must produce faith with his free will. The theological term for this view is *auto-soteriology*, which means "self-salvation," or salvation depending, in some sense, on man's cooperation with God. The religion of free grace is called *theo-soteriology*, which means "salvation depending wholly on God's grace and power." The biblical gospel is "God saves sinners"–period. That means God (all by himself with no help at all from the sinner) saves (actually and truly and not merely "tries to save") sinners (helpless, hopeless, guilty, hell-deserving people who can do absolutely nothing to earn or merit God's favor). The gospel is not "God gives every man a chance to be saved if the sinner will only cooperate by furnishing the necessary faith." In theo-soteriology, all of the glory belongs to God alone because his sovereign grace and power alone is what makes the difference. In auto-soteriology, the glory is shared by God and the sinner because it was "the sinner's willingness" that ultimately made the real difference between himself and other lost people that enabled God to effect salvation.

Genesis 11:1–9 shows these two basic ideas in the words *let us* as these words are uttered by man and the same words are uttered by God. "Let us [man] build us a city and a tower whose top may reach unto heaven..." (auto-soteriology) is the religion based on man's will. It begins with man and his effort. "Let us [Triune God] go down" (theo-soteriology) is the religion of sovereign grace that comes to a depraved sinner and enables the dead sinner to repent and believe.

When a knowledgeable believer says, "The Lord saved me," he does not mean the Lord Jesus Christ saved him. He means, "The Lord God the Father saved me in electing grace; the Lord God the Son saved me by his atoning death; and the Lord God the Holy Spirit saved me by opening my heart and giving me faith." Each member of the blessed

Trinity has a specific, and essential, part to play in every sinner's salvation.

One of the clear proofs of how man-centered our theology has become in the last one hundred years is the nearly total absence of either hymns or sermons depicting the sovereign electing grace of the Father or the regenerating work of the Holy Spirit. Remember that we have been saved by a triune God. Should we not gladly acknowledge and worship the Father for his electing grace even as we praise the Son for his vicarious death? Are we not duty bound to acknowledge and worship the Holy Spirit for raising us out of spiritual death and giving us the gift of faith and life? There is an absence of good hymns depicting the work of the Father and the work of the Holy Spirit because of the failure to grasp the biblical doctrine of *total depravity*. That is the subject of this chapter.

What Does the Phrase *Total Depravity* Mean?

I remember a college professor who constantly depicted the Puritans as kill-joys. He blamed their problem on their belief in total depravity. The professor's caricature was, "A puritan is a man who cannot sleep at night because he is afraid that somewhere in the world someone may be having fun." The Puritans really got bad press in that man's class.

The carnal mind hates the doctrine of total depravity. Nothing cuts across the grain of the modern religious, psychological, and philosophical view of man and his basic nature as much as the truth that man is a depraved sinner.

The unchallenged absolute in academic circles today is that "man is basically good." Biblical depravity says the exact opposite. The Bible clearly sees that environment plays a great part in shaping an individual. However, it traces the root cause of all man's problems to a wicked and selfish heart. The sun and rain cannot bring a single plant out the ground that is not already there in seed form, nor can a bad environment produce any fruit that is not potentially already in our hearts. Every one of us is capable, apart from grace, of being as wicked as any person who ever lived. If you balk at that statement, you have probably never become a Christian!

Once the fact of total depravity is accepted, then sovereign grace is man's only hope. As long as this fact is rejected and man's fictitious goodness is exalted, men will merely find more ways to justify their rebellion to God and his revealed truth.

Here is Webster's Dictionary definition: "depraved - characterized by corruption; perverted; evil…" The word *total* means what it says and needs no comment. The word *depraved* is not in your concordance, nor is the word *Trinity*. However, both of these truths are stamped on nearly every page of the Bible.

Here is the doctrine of total depravity in a nutshell. "Man is bad, but he is not that bad, but he really is bad." That means (1) man is a sinner, but (2) he is not nearly as sinful in actual practice as he could be. However, (3) he is really is a totally depraved sinner in the sight of God.

It takes both a negative and a positive wire to form a complete electrical circuit and thereby conduct electricity. Often times it is essential to clearly spell out what we do not believe before it is possible to understand what we actually do believe. We will begin our study with things that we do not believe, even though we are often very wrongly accused of believing these things.

First: Negative—let me show what we do not mean by total depravity.

1. Total depravity does not mean that man is without a conscience or any sense of right and wrong.

People often have a strong impulse to do "right," and they often feel remorse for doing "wrong." However, this only proves that man still has some remnants of his original creation. He still has a conscience and, depending on environment and training, it can be very strong. Conscience often drives people into a mental institution, and, in some cases, even to suicide. The following texts clearly show that man has a conscience.

> *And they which heard it, being convicted by their own conscience, went out one by one...." (John 8:9)*

> *For when the Gentiles, which have not the law, do by nature the things contained in the law, these, having not the law, are a law unto themselves: Which shew the work of the law written in their hearts, their conscience so bearing witness, and their thoughts the mean while accusing or else excusing one another; (Rom. 2:14, 15)*

C. S. Lewis spoke of the universal "ought" in every man. Every person will accuse others (and themselves in their conscience) of not doing what they ought to have done.

This universal admission by every creature of a "right and wrong" will be one of the righteous grounds upon which God will judge all men as guilty. Man's constant moral judgment of other people is absolute proof that man is a moral being created in the moral image of God. Man is not an animal without any consciousness of his creator. Man is a rational and moral creature who makes volitional choices based on both his rationality and moral consciousness.

Suppose the day that you were born God hung an invisible tape recorder around your neck. Every time you said either "you should have done such and such," or "you should not have done such and such," the invisible recorder went blip, blip, blip and recorded what you said. In the day of judgment, imagine God getting out the tape, with your own words of moral judgments on it, and saying, "I want to be fair in judging you. Therefore I will judge you on the exact standards that you boldly professed to believe. I will use your own words. I will not use either the Ten Commandments, or the words of Christ in the Sermon on the Mount; I will use what you yourself fervently acknowledged (by judging others) was right and wrong." Could anything be fairer? Would we not all be proven guilty before God? Do you realize that very thing is going to happen!

Man indeed has a consciousness of right and wrong. We need only read Ann Landers or visit a mental institution to see that people often have a very deep consciousness of morality that sometimes screams at them. However, this does not mean that these people are convicted of sin in

God's sight. A "guilty conscience" is not the same as "conviction of sin." People have great remorse for the results of sin who are not in the least concerned that they have offended God.

2. Total depravity does not mean that every sinner is devoid of all of the qualities that are both pleasing to men and useful to society when those qualities are judged only by a human standard.

Mother Teresa and Albert Schweitzer were great humanitarians. The world is a better place for many people because of them and their service. They rightly earned and deserve our praise for their humanitarian labors. However, they were still guilty sinners in the sight of a holy God. All the "good" they did will not earn them grace in God's sight. They too are included in the "you" who must be "born again." Were these two people "much better persons" than a Hitler or a Manson? Of course they were, if you judge only on the basis of a human standard. Is it possible that a Manson or a Hitler can be saved by grace and go to heaven, and a Mother Teresa and a Schweitzer be lost and go to hell because of self-righteousness? The answer is yes, both situations are possible, if you judge by God's revealed standards.

A parent's love and willingness to suffer even death for their child's well-being is certainly a "good" thing that deserves to be admired and applauded. However, such actions do not prove the parent has grace in his heart, nor does it prove he is not totally depraved in God's sight. All it proves is that man still has vestiges of the image of God from his original creation. A patriot's sacrifice for his country is another illustration of the same principle.

A bombed and ruined religious temple may have fragments of beautiful columns or parts of painted walls that are perfectly intact. However, it is not a fit place for worship. It is "totally" ruined for the purpose for which it was built even though a few isolated parts are not totally destroyed. Man has remnants of his creation in Eden, but he is totally ruined by sin as far as ability or desire to love and worship God.

Suppose a doctor in the Navy lead a crew into mutiny and took control of a Navy ship. He then uses the ship in piracy. The Navy finds him and demands that he either surrender, or they will destroy the ship. Upon his refusal, the Navy brings in the necessary firepower and begins to fight. During the battle, many men on the rebel ship are wounded. The doctor works without rest or food and risks his life over and over again in order to give his men the necessary medical treatment to keep them alive. When the Navy finally captures the ship, they will hang both the captain and his men because of their mutiny. The heroic "good" which the captain did in risking his life for his men will help neither him nor them at the trial. The judges who sentence the man to die may admire his courage, but he is still a traitor against the government and will therefore be put to death. None of his good will count for anything. The same principle applies to the all of the "good" that sinful men do.

It is this principle that is being taught in Proverbs 21:4: "A high look, and a proud heart, and the plowing of the wicked, is sin." It is not the actual plowing of the man that is sinful, but the sinful attitude of the man's heart.

a. His plowing is an exhibition of his faith in the seasons. If he did not believe that spring and summer were sure to follow, he would not plow and plant. His very act of plowing is an expression of faith in God's providence and will condemn the man's unbelieving heart for refusing to worship the very God he constantly acknowledges.

b. The man will curse God if there is too little or too much rain, but he will not praise God for a good harvest. His very cursing shows that he knows God is real and that he is in control of the weather. The man's pride and self-sufficiency will not allow him to give God the credit for the good weather. The whole situation shows that his very plowing will someday be the evidence that condemns him in his sin of unbelief.

3. We are not saying that every sinner is prone to every form of sin.

The Pharisees prove this point. Jesus acknowledges that some of the things the Pharisees did were right and "good." However, they also selectively omitted some other things. They will be condemned for the very good things they did because it proves they had an understanding of what God wanted. Their deliberate omissions prove the depravity of their hearts.

*Woe unto you, scribes and Pharisees, hypocrites! for ye pay tithe
of mint and anise and cummin, and have omitted the weightier
matters of the law, judgment, mercy, and faith: these ought ye to
have done, and not to leave the other undone.* (Matt. 23:23)

One form of sin will often exclude another form of sin.
(1) The miser will be delivered from the sin of
wastefulness. (2) The workaholic will be delivered from
sloth and laziness. (3) The pride of position will often
exclude immorality but only for fear of being caught.
Shakespeare said it well: "I see it has pleased Devil
drunkenness to give place to Devil wrath."

This truth explains the apparent change in some men
when elevated to a position of authority. Their nice
personality is replaced with a tyrannical attitude. Actually,
the man did not really change at all. His true self came to
the surface for the first time. The man was always like that
in his heart, but he never had the authority or opportunity
to demonstrate it.

4. We are not saying that every sinner is as intense as he
can be in his sin. Remember our original definition, "Man
is bad, but he is not that bad, but he really is bad."

No one person has ever expressed all of the sin of which
they were capable. The following texts demonstrate this
fact:

*In the fourth generation your descendants will come back here,
for the sin of the Amorites has not yet reached its full measure.*
(Gen. 15:16 NIV)

*But evil men and seducers shall wax worse and worse, deceiving,
and being deceived.* (2 Tim. 3:13)

Every year we are convinced that society and the world simply cannot possibly get any worse. However, it does get worse and will continue to do so until our Lord returns. The old saying is true: "You ain't seen anything yet!" I would not want to live in the same city, county, or state where God permitted one individual to express all of the rebellion of which he was capable. We ought to constantly thank God for his restraining grace.

We now put the positive wire into place and show what we actually do believe about total depravity.

Second: Positive—what we do mean by total depravity, or, what the Bible does teach on the subject.

Total depravity means that man is totally dead in sin and not just sick and dying. The sinner is not an emergency room case who desperately needs attention before it is too late—the sinner is a graveyard case. He is dead, not dying. He is not incurably sick and on the verge of death—he is already dead! Ephesians 2:1 is clear: "And you hath he quickened, who were dead in trespasses and sins."

1. Total depravity means that every sinner, including you and me, is destitute or without that love of towards God which constitutes the fundamental and all-inclusive demand of God's law. The one great thing that all men owe to God is the one thing that they adamantly refuse to give Him.

Then one of them, which was a lawyer, asked him a question, tempting him, and saying, Master, which is the great commandment in the law? Jesus said unto him, Thou shalt love the

Lord thy God with all thy heart, and with all thy soul, and with all thy mind. This is the first and great commandment. (Matt. 22:35-38)

All men, without a single exception, are guilty of this sin. They simply do not love God and put him first in any sense. They are commanded to do this twenty-four hours every day, but lost sinners have never consciously done one single thing in their whole life for the express purpose of glorifying God. They live to please themselves and have no thought of their indebtedness to God. I once pressed this fact on a high school teacher, and he claimed that his three children were produced out of obedience to God's command to "be fruitful and multiply." When I asked if that was the only motive involved, he grinned and said, "Well, maybe not entirely."

This is what Jesus meant in John 5:42: "But I know you, that ye have not the love of God in you." That is, we lack the one thing essential in order to please God. We are not at all motivated by either duty or love of God. We are motivated entirely by sin and self.

2. Total depravity means that every sinner is guilty of elevating some lower affection or desire above regard for God, his law, and the gospel. This is the opposite of #1. Sinners not only do not love the true God and put him first, but they do love some other god and put that false god first.

...lovers of pleasures more than lovers of God. (2 Tim. 3:4)

It is not that pleasures are wrong in themselves. It is when pleasure becomes the cause for living and is a higher goal than knowing God himself. God can justly charge that this attitude controls the hearts of all lost men.

A son honors his father, and a servant his master. If I am a father [in the sense of creation], *where is the honor due me?* (Mal. 1:6 NIV)

Sinners do not give God the love and worship that he deserves because they are filled with love for something else. They feel no obligation to God and therefore they cannot help but be unthankful. Chapter 1 of Romans is a perfect picture of sinful man's ungrateful and proud heart.

3. That "something else" that men love is an idol called *self* or *me*. Every sinner is determined, in his whole inward being and outward life, by a preference of self instead of God. The sinner treats himself as if he were the only true god.

People will be lovers of themselves.... (2 Tim. 3:2 NIV)

Light has come into the world, but men loved darkness instead of light because their deeds were evil. (John 3:19 NIV)

It is bad enough to dethrone God the Creator, but to enthrone the creature, to enthrone self as God, is the height of sin (see Romans 1:21-23).

Sin, in the garden of Eden, created a monster called happiness that literally consumes people. To be happy is to have everything and everyone act the way that I want them to act. To be unhappy is to wish that I could make everything that disagrees with me to unhappen, or cease to exist. It is to earnestly desire to have everything and everybody line up in the way that I want them to so I can get everything I desire.

4. Total depravity means that every sinner is possessed with a nature, inherited from Adam's fall, that is completely hostile toward God. We were all born with a "positive" aversion to God and his authority. By nature, every sinner wants his own way. Romans 8:7 makes this fact very clear. "…the sinful mind is hostile to God. It does not submit to God's law, nor can it do so."

The obvious question is, "Why does man not feel this awful hostility that, according to the Scripture, is in his heart?" The answer is simple.

> *But sin, taking occasion by the commandment, wrought in me all manner of concupiscence. For without the law sin was dead. For I was alive without the law once: but when the commandment came, sin revived, and I died. And the commandment, which was ordained to life, I found to be unto death. For sin, taking occasion by the commandment, deceived me, and by it slew me.* (Rom. 7:8–11)

This hostility, or enmity, is against God's authority, and as long as a man is not forced to think about God's authority, that man will not feel the hostility that is in his heart. However, when God's law, or authority, is pressed on the man's conscience, then the enmity that is buried in his nature will surface. As long as the sinner sincerely believes that he is free to do as he chooses, and as long as he has a false view of God, especially God's sovereignty and his duty to God, he will never feel either guilty or angry toward God. However, when God's true character as sovereign Lawgiver and Judge is pressed on the sinner, then the sparks begin to fly. This rarely happens today simply because our generation has been lulled to sleep by a totally false view of a "God of love."

Let me illustrate this fact. A truly virtuous woman may smile in mild amusement at a "wolf whistle" as she enters the grocery store. However, if the man would follow her into the store and literally force her into a corner, she would lash out in rage and indignation. Her true nature would manifest itself. You would see what she is really like. So it is with the lost man. It is not until his conscience is pressed with God's true claims that his true nature of hostility comes to the surface. That is when the "nice man" tells you, in anger, to "Leave me alone to do as I please."

Preaching the "love of God" makes no one angry. Preaching man's duty to God as his Creator and Judge will make the sinner gnash his teeth. We must remember that all men think they love God. However, the god they love is a god of their own imagination and not the God of the Bible.

Let me illustrate what I mean. The ancient Greeks "sincerely loved" and "fervently worshiped" God. On any given day, you could find several "worship services" in process. We know that these religious feasts were nothing less than drunken orgies, but they were done in the name of Bacchus, one of the Greek gods. If we would have rebuked the "worshipers" for their drunken immoral behavior because in their heart of hearts they knew better, they would not have thanked us. They would have been furious. They knew that the one true living God hated such behavior. However, they did not care and did everything they could to forget that fact. They would hate us for reminding them of what they knew in their conscience. They would have raised their wine goblets and shouted, "Away with your God, Bacchus is God! Bacchus is God!"

We come down a little farther in history and meet a pirate named Eric the Red as he is about to go on a "business" trip. Of course, his business was to capture ships, steal what was worth stealing, and kill every one of his helpless victims. If we said, "But Eric, have you fear or love for God?" the poor man would be horrified. He would say, "Why, of course, I love God. Look at his image on the front of my ship. I pray to him before I go to sea, and I sacrifice to him when I return." If we reminded this man that in his conscience he knew that the one true God who made the heavens and earth hated such behavior, Eric would be furious. He would put his sword under our chin and walk us off the gangplank backwards while he shouted, "Thor is God! Thor is God!"

Let us move down to the twentieth century liberal preacher who lives down the street from you. He is a hard working "do-gooder" sentimentalist. He "loves" God but when asked what God is like, the man admits he does not have a clue. When we begin to talk about the God who revealed himself at the cross in the atoning blood of Christ, we notice the man's neck is getting red. He finally grits his teeth and blurts out in anger, "I hate your religion of blood and the God who requires it." You see, he "sincerely loves God," but it is a god of his own imagination and not the

God of the Bible. He hates the true and living God revealed in the Scriptures.

The same reaction will come from the super-church leaders who insist on being "positive thinkers." When we mention Romans 9 and its awesome picture of God's sovereignty, we are hated and ridiculed. Put it into your memory system: men sincerely love a god of their own imagination, and he is always a god that they can control. Our duty is to confront men with the God of the Bible. He is the Creator, the Lawgiver, the Judge, and the only Redeemer. **We must begin with Genesis 1:1 and not John 3:16.** We are making a mistake when we begin with the God of John 3:16.

Let me illustrate this point. Suppose a man named Harry bitterly hated a next-door neighbor. The very sight of his neighbor made Harry furious. The neighbor finally moved to California. Several years later, someone visiting Harry said, "You really hated that guy who used to live next door." Harry would probably say, "Well, I did not like him too much, but I would not say I actually hated him. That is a strong word." No amount of arguing would convince Harry of how deeply he had hated that neighbor. You see, Harry has not seen the man for a long time. There was nothing confronting him that aroused his strong feelings.

Five years later, someone knocks on Harry's door and says, "I am collecting money to buy flowers for the widow of that man who used to live next door to you." It seems the former neighbor had died a tragic death. All of a sudden, the person at the door says, "Oh, I'm sorry; I forgot how deeply you hated the man. You would not be interested in helping. You are probably glad he is dead." Harry would protest that he was being misrepresented. "I admit we had our differences, but as I look back, I am sure part of it was my fault. He really was not all that bad. Here is five dollars for the flowers." It would be impossible to convince Harry that he had truly hated his former neighbor. The hatred had long settled in the bottom of his heart.

Five more years pass by and a moving van pulls up next door to Harry's house, and the man he hated starts to move back into the same house. There had been a mix-up, and the man had not died; it was his brother. How long would that man have to live there before all of Harry's buried hatred would once more be felt and expressed? The old saying, "out of sight, out of mind" is true. Man's hatred of God is like the dirty mud puddles on the road right after a heavy rain. Those same puddles become clear as crystal after several days. The mud is still there, but it has all settled to the bottom and is not visible. However, if you started stirring the puddle with a stick, the mud would soon come to the surface. Man's sinful heart is the same way. As long as Harry is not directly confronted with his enemy, he can never be convinced of the depth of his hatred. As long as men are not being directly confronted with a true picture of God, they do not feel the natural enmity towards God that is in their hearts. However, the moment we begin to tell them what God is really like, their rebellion against God's authority and their love of self will come to the surface. The God of the Bible is a forgotten God in our society. The weak and wishy-washy god that is preached in most churches, even evangelical churches, would never stir up any valid feelings of any kind. This is why men can hate God while being deeply religious. Because men today love a god of their own imagination, there is neither deep faith nor visible antagonism in the churches today.

Regardless of what we think or what any individual believes, we must accept what the Word of God says—all men by nature hate God! We need only preach God's revealed will to sinners, and press on them their absolute duty to do that will, and we see that Romans 8:7 is a fact. The one indelible mark of every lost man is Romans 8:7.

> *Because the carnal mind is enmity against God: for it is not subject to the law of God, neither indeed can be.*

Likewise, the one indelible mark of a true believer is the exact opposite:

> *For this is the love of God, that we keep his commandments: and his commandments are not grievous.* (1 John 5:3)

Before we were converted, we hated God's authority over us simply because we wanted to "do our own thing." We hated anyone who tried to tell us the awful consequences of our rebellion. We hated God's commandments because they condemned us, and we hated those who reminded us of those commandments. We felt God was unreasonable and too strict. When the Holy Spirit gave us a new nature, we then loved the very same law that we previously hated. Our problem then was not with the strictness of God's law but our total inability to keep it because we now wanted to keep it with all of our being.

5. By total depravity, we mean that every part of man's being and nature has been affected by sin. This is what the word *total* means. Total depravity means that sin has affected every part of man's being, and this includes his will. The primary difference between Calvinism (the religion of free grace) and Arminianism (the religion of free will) is whether man is totally depraved (meaning everything including his will) or whether he is partially depraved (meaning everything except his will).

Romans 6:17 is a key text.

> *But God be thanked, that ye were the servants of sin, but ye have [1] obeyed [the will] from [2] the heart [emotions] that [3] form of doctrine [mind] which was delivered you.*

This text shows the order of biblical conversion to be as follows: (1) the mind must be illuminated by the truth. God does not save us in a vacuum. We must hear, understand, and believe the gospel facts about our sin and Christ's death. (2) The heart must be penetrated by the truth. It is not enough to believe intellectually; we must literally feel the power of truth in our inward man (cf. 1 Thess. 1:4, 5). (3) The will must be liberated with the truth (cf. Acts 16:14). Lydia's heart must indeed be opened, and she must hear and believe the gospel in order to be saved. However, Lydia cannot understand or even desire the truth of God with her nature of sin. The Holy Spirit must "open her heart" (regeneration) before she is able to understand and believe. When the Holy Spirit gives Lydia a new heart, she will gladly be ready to believe. You will notice that all three of these things are mentioned in Romans 6:17.

The mind, or understanding, receives the form of doctrine, or facts of the gospel. Our natural minds are described as being totally incapable of understanding truth (cf. 1 Cor. 2:14; Eph. 4:18). Whenever a sinner understands and gladly receives the gospel, it is not because of their so-called free will; it is, as in Lydia's case, because God sovereignly opened that heart in regeneration.

The heart, or affections, by nature is not able to feel the power of truth (cf. Jer. 17:9). Whenever the gospel effects a real change in us, it is because the Holy Spirit has powerfully and savingly applied the truth to the core of our being. When a girl says, "He gets me," that can mean different things. If she sighs and almost faints when she says, "He gets me," that means one thing. If she grits her teeth and shakes her fist when she says, "He gets me," that means something entirely different. In both cases, the girl is saying, "Just seeing him or hearing his name evokes an uncontrollable feeling inside of me." In one case it is anger, and in the other it is love. In both cases, it is automatic because the girl's emotions are controlled by the attitude of her heart. It is the same with a child of God. He cannot hear the name of Christ without feeling deeply a heartfelt gratitude for such great salvation. The gospel really gets to a Christian and literally gets the Christian.

The will, or the power of choice, does not (indeed, it cannot) operate either independently of, or contrary to, man's sinful mind and wicked heart. Our will is not an independent faculty or "little man inside the man that is unaffected by sin." The will is chained to our sinful nature, and it is impossible for the will to operate independently of that sinful nature. The Scriptures are clear that man can no more change his sinful nature by an act of his will any more than an Ethiopian can "change the color of his skin" (cf. Jer. 13:23). To say, "A sinner can change if he sincerely wants to" is the same as saying, "An Ethiopian, who loves being black and hates any idea of being white, can change the color of his skin if he sincerely wants to." In both cases, the problem does not lie in the power of the will but in the "want to," or power that controls the will, and that power is the sinner's totally depraved nature. The sinner always wants to please himself. We will come back to this point later.

Let me repeat that the word _total_ in total depravity does not mean man is as wicked as he can be. It means sin has affected every part of our being in such a way that our autobiography reads, "I know that in me (that is, in my flesh) [that is, in no single part of me] dwelleth no good thing" (Rom. 7:18). It means that the sinner's heart, which is the seat of his thinking, feeling, and choosing, is "deceitful and desperately wicked" (Jer. 17:9). The word _total_ in total depravity means the same thing as putting a drop of deadly poison into a glass of water. The entire glass is totally (meaning every single particle of the water) poisoned and unfit to drink. If you pour that glass of water into a gallon jug, you will dilute the intensity of the poison, but you will still totally poison the entire gallon of water. Pour the gallon into a barrel of water, and you have totally poisoned the entire barrel of water. Remember our definition: "Man is bad, but he is not that bad, but he really is bad."

The primary objection to everything I have said goes like this: "If the sinner does not have the innate power or ability to repent and believe, then God cannot hold him responsible." In other words, man's ability is always the measure of his responsibility. If God holds the sinner responsible to repent and believe when He knows the sinner is unable to do so, then God becomes unjust and grossly unfair. This objection totally misunderstands both sin and responsibility. It also denies the reality and effects of the fall. It is beyond the scope of this chapter to fully develop this point, so for now let me show how absurd the argument is: is a sinner able to perfectly obey the Ten Commandments? All will answer, "Absolutely not!" Does God hold sinners responsible for perfectly obeying the Ten Commandments and punishing them for breaking those commandments? The answer will be, with a bit of hesitation and without the *absolutely*, the exact opposite, or "Yes!" So then God can, and does, hold men responsible for doing something they are totally unable to do! The objection is exploded.

What we will see is that the reason sinners can neither obey the commandments nor repent and believe the gospel is the power of their sinful nature to totally control the sinner's whole being. The only question is this: "Who is totally responsible for man's sinful nature?" Did man acquire his sinful nature by an act of his free will, or did

God force him to sin against his will? If man is totally responsible for his sin, then he is also totally responsible for the effects of that sin, and the awful affect is the sinner's total depravity and total inability to change that sinful nature.

I can say without hesitation that the sinner is "totally free to do exactly as he pleases." However, that kind of freedom is the sinner's greatest problem. An unregenerate sinner, because he is totally controlled by a sinful nature, will always, every single time, freely, or deliberately, choose to please himself. We always do, or choose to do, things which are consistent with what we are. If we are sinners by nature and choice, then every decision will be affected by our sinful nature. Adam is the only man that ever had a truly free will that was free from sin. Adam is also the only person who ever became a sinner by sinning, or by an act of the will. You and I sin because we were born sinners; we did not become sinners the first time we consciously disobeyed. Our first act of sin did not produce our sinful nature. The sinful nature inherited from Adam produced the sinful act.

6. Man has a nature that will not permit him to choose God or righteousness. Man's inability grows out of his depravity.

A lost man can choose between two evils according to which benefits him the most. He may choose a "good," as judged by the world's standard, instead of a "bad," but in every case he is motivated by his own interests. The sinner cannot choose between God's glory and his own selfish ends. Romans 8:7 stands as a biblical truth and a historical fact.

A Complete "Spiritual" Examination

We will now give man, the depraved sinner, a complete and thorough spiritual examination. We will use the Bible to test man spiritually the same as medicine and science test a man physically. We will look at all of man's faculties exactly as they are each described in the Bible. We are not concerned with how man looks at himself. We will not consult philosophy, psychology, medicine, sociology or popular sentiment. What does the Word of God say about the spiritual condition of man? We will use the following procedure:

1. The Physician's Report: After "Doctor" Bible carefully examines each faculty of man, the conclusion will be irrefutable. "The patient is totally unable to respond to any spiritual stimulus in any of his faculties. He is blind, deaf, dumb, has no pulse, can't breathe, mind totally gone, etc. Not one spiritual organ is functioning."

2. The Coroner's Report: The coroner administers every known test and cannot find any evidence of life. "There is absolutely no question, the man is spiritually dead."

3. The Autopsy Report: The dead sinner is opened up, and each part of his being is examined. The autopsy report establishes that the man died because of the cancer of sin. "Every part of his being was infected and ruined by sin. Not one part was left untouched and uncontaminated. He was totally depraved by sin."

I. The Physician's Report

"Doctor" Bible is going to examine seven individual faculties of the sinner. In each case, the result will show total inability. Here are seven things that God says a sinner cannot do. It is essential that we see that the Holy Spirit uses the word *cannot* in all seven instances. To say, "Well, the sinner really can do these things if he only wants to" is to not only misunderstand the Bible; it is to flat out contradict it! As we shall see later, man's "will not," or his refusal to repent and believe the gospel, is the direct effect of the "cannot" of total depravity. More about this in a moment.

First, the man is totally blind.

A lost man *cannot see*! "I tell you the truth, no one *can see* the kingdom of God unless he is born again" (John 3:3). The *see* means to realize, or to experience, or to appreciate. Christ is saying that man does not have the spiritual ability to even desire the kingdom of God until he is first "born again."

We must understand the relationship between *sight* and *seeing*. Once we grasp that, we will understand the relationship between the new birth and faith. Do you get sight by seeing, or do you see because you have sight? Which is the cause, and which is the effect? For instance, does it help a blind man to see if we shine a 1,000 watt bulb in his eyes instead of a 100 watt bulb. I am sure you will say that is a stupid question. We all know that the problem is not the amount of light; the problem is in the man's eyes.

He needs sight before he can see. Of course, we must have light to see, but people who are blind need more than light. They need the gift of sight.

The sinner's problem is the same. He needs far more than light simply because he is spiritually blind. He is not near-sighted. He does not have defective vision that can be corrected by an act of his will. He needs the gift of sight. Jesus said that a sinner cannot even see the kingdom of God unless he is first born again or regenerated. We agree that man needs the light of the gospel. It is true that no one can see spiritual reality without the light of the gospel. However, the sinner is blind until God gives him the spiritual ability to *see* in regeneration. The problem is with his spiritual eyes. Every regenerate believer can say a hearty "amen" to these words of Christ: "But blessed are your eyes because they see...." (Matt. 13:16).

Second, the man is mentally deranged.

He *cannot understand* a single thing that is spiritual. "But the natural man receiveth not the things of the Spirit of God: for they are foolishness unto him: neither *can* [emphasis mine] he know them, because they are spiritually discerned" (1 Cor. 2:14). Again we must notice the cause and effect. The word *because* in this text is very important. The natural, or unregenerate man, cannot understand spiritual things because those things are spiritually discerned, and the lost man does not have the Spirit until he is "born of the Spirit."

When we trusted Christ because we found Him to be most desirable, it was not our old blind mind that gave us that knowledge. That understanding came from the new nature given to us in regeneration. If we carefully compare 1 Corinthians 1:18–29 with 2 Corinthians 4:4–6, we will see that God's shining in the darkness at the first creation is the same as his shining into our dark and dead hearts to give us the knowledge of salvation. Can the old heart and depraved, incurable affections ever give us spiritual knowledge and desires? The will cannot choose something that the mind cannot truly understand and the affections truly desire.

Third, the man is stone deaf.

He *cannot hear* any spiritual truth. This is the verdict of Christ himself. "Why do ye not understand my speech? even because ye cannot hear my word" (John 8:43). Again we have the same cause and effect relationship. Jesus is more emphatic this time and adds the word *even*. Why did the Jews not understand our Lord's words? He said it was because ye *cannot*. Just as the ability to see is the gift of God, so is the ability to hear. All men are not given that ability (cf. Matt. 13:10–17).

I am sure we have all seen a dog responding to a special dog whistle. No human ear can hear the sound because our ears do not have the ability to hear that kind of pitch. A dog hears easily. So the sinner does not have ears to hear the gospel. He considers it nonsense (cf. 1 Cor. 1:18), but the Christian hears, understands and gladly believes by the grace and power of God.

I remember preaching at a picnic attended by deaf people. The interpreter and I were the only ones who could hear. The park was near the Toronto airport, and a large jet plane came in to land while I was preaching. The noise was so loud that the interpreter could not hear my voice so I stopped speaking and waited for the plane to land. I was facing the airport, and the congregation, because their backs were toward the airport, did not see the plane. Because they were stone deaf, they did not hear the roar. They kept watching the interpreter's hand and then looking at my lips. They began to look at each other with a look of bewilderment. I pointed up to the sky and as they turned around, they looked up and saw the plane. Having seen the plane, they smiled and nodded their heads in understanding.

My friend, that is the same way it is with an unregenerate sinner. The wrath of God against sin is clearly revealed from heaven and roars with its terrible threats. The gospel bells of promise and joy ring loudly and with clarity. Yet the sinner is totally deaf to both the law and the gospel until God, in regeneration, opens his ears.

Fourth, the man is completely powerless.

He *cannot* even want to receive spiritual help. A comparison of two verses of Scripture will establish this awful fact. The first verse shows us why a lost sinner cannot receive truth and grace.

> *Even the Spirit of truth; whom the world cannot receive because it seeth him not, neither knoweth him: but ye know him; for he dwelleth with you, and shall be in you.* (John 14:17)

Notice the following in this text:

1. The world cannot receive the Spirit because they cannot see him or know him. They are without spiritual sight and cannot perceive, or know, any spiritual reality.

2. Every Christian has seen (spiritually) and knows (experientially) the ministry of the blessed Holy Spirit. Remember that sight and knowledge were given in regeneration.

The second verse of Scripture is Jude 19. This is the best verse I know of that gives us the essence of man's total depravity and inability.

These be they who separate themselves, sensual, having not the Spirit. (Jude 19)

Notice the following in this verse:

1. The lost man is totally sensual. That does not mean in a sexual sense. It means the sum total of the man's knowledge and experience is that which comes to him through his physical senses.

2. He does not have the Spirit. The life of God, which is the Holy Spirit of God, left man when he sinned in the garden of Eden. Man's whole experience is now totally controlled by his fleshly nature and its senses. However, one does not know God through his eyes, ears, mouth, fingers, etc. God is a Spirit, and they that worship him must worship him in Spirit. Since the unsaved person is "sensual" and does not have either the Spirit or a spiritual nature, he cannot see or experience God until he is first

"born of the Spirit." He can only receive that which he is capable of *seeing* (John 14:17).

Let me illustrate this truth. Right this very moment, there is probably an airplane flying right through the room where you are sitting. There may also be a large ship, a herd of buffalo, and a line of pretty chorus girls dancing. If you look around, you will see none of those things. If you turn on a TV set and turn the channel changer, you will draw all of those things out of the air and "see" them. All of those TV waves are present even though unseen. God did not build a TV receiver into our heads. In the same way, there is a spiritual world and a real Savior that is just as real as the air we breathe. The unregenerate man does not see, hear, or feel a single evidence of that spiritual reality. The sum total of his potential experience is what he can taste, touch, feel, see, and smell, and God is not known or experienced through the physical senses.

Fifth, the man is a spiritual mute. He is unable to speak.

He *cannot* even "call on the Lord" until renewed by grace. See 1 Corinthians 12:3, Romans 10:9, 10, and Matthew 16:13–17.

Sixth, the man is unable to move a spiritual muscle.

He *cannot* even "come to Christ" until he is given spiritual life. The following two verses of Scripture should never be separated. The first one shows the total inability of the sinner apart from the regenerating work of the Holy Spirit. The second shows the certainty of repentance and faith in every single instance where the Holy Spirit does effectually call.

> *No man can come to me, except the Father which hath sent me draw him: and I will raise him up at the last day. It is written in the prophets, And they shall be all taught of God. Every man therefore that hath heard, and hath learned of the Father, cometh unto me.* (John 6:44, 45)

Verse 44 states what no man *can* do unless God does something first. No man *can* (has ability to) come to Christ unless the Father deliberately draws that individual by the power of the Spirit. That is human inability.

Verse 45 states what every man is certain to do when the Father does draw him. Everyone, without exception, who "hears" and is "taught by the Father" (the same thing as "draw" in verse 44) "comes (always) to me." Do you see the clear contrast? No man can—unless, but everyone will—when. Verse 44 is teaching inability, and verse 45 is teaching irresistible grace.

Seventh, the man is incapable of any kind of positive spiritual response.

He *can only* act out his nature of spiritual death. The indelible mark of the lost man is his hatred of God's authority, and the mark of a believer is a delight in God's truth. A lost man can no more give a spiritual response to spiritual truth than a physically dead man could respond to a ham sandwich.

We cannot leave this section until we at least mention another aspect of truth. Even though the above seven things are clear as crystal in Scripture, the following things are also true:

1. Every sinner is invited, commanded, and encouraged by God to do all of the above things which he cannot do.

2. Every sinner is held totally responsible for not doing all of the above things.

3. Every saved man has done all of these seven things and done them all most willingly! See John 15:5 and Philippians 4:13. The first verse shows inability, and the second verse shows the power of grace.

4. God has never commanded a sinner to do anything that the sinner is capable of doing! No, I did not say it wrong or backward. I said exactly what John 15:5 says, "Without me, you can do nothing." The *nothing* in that verse really means nothing.

The flesh can produce nothing that profits. Whenever a person does any of the above seven things, he does it only because he has been born of God and given spiritual life or ability.

II. The Coroner's Report

After the coroner has made every known test, he gives the following report. "The man is without a single evidence of spiritual life. He is dead" (Eph. 2:1-5).

There is an old saying, "Where there is life, there is hope." When it is discovered that someone is desperately sick, we rush them to the hospital in the hopes of keeping them alive. When they are dead, all hope is gone, and we take them to the graveyard. A lost sinner is not "sick nigh unto death"; he is really spiritually dead. He is not a hospital case who might respond to the right treatment. He is dead to righteousness and alive to sin. He loves his death in sin and hates both the doctor and the medicine. The sinner would rather perish than admit he is a sinner. He is a graveyard case that needs a life-giving miracle.

I sometimes try to picture the scene in John 11. I see the stone rolled away from the grave of Lazarus, and three men are there. The first one is looking into the dark tomb and passionately pleading with the dead Lazarus inside. "Lazarus, if you will only give God a chance, he will give you life. If you just take the first step, then the Holy Spirit will make you come alive. God honestly wants to make you live, but it's all up to you. Lazarus, this is a great deal that God is offering, but your 'free will' must decide to take advantage of it. You must get up and take that first step in faith." That may be just a bit of a caricature, but not much. That is exactly the way some free-will preachers talk.

I am reminded of a story told by C. H. Spurgeon about the Catholic saint whose head had been cut off. The man is supposed to have picked up his head, put it under his arm, and walked 10,000 miles back to Rome. Spurgeon said, "I would have no trouble believing that to be true, if the man could take that first step!" If man's will can enable him to get up out of the tomb of death, then he surely does not need any help to keep on going.

The second man I see at the tomb of Lazarus is what we call a hyper-Calvinist. He is sitting down and calmly writing a treatise on the futility of preaching to dead sinners. This pathetic creature never preaches or witnesses the gospel, and he discourages and condemns those who do. Since Lazarus is dead, this man concludes that it is a waste of time to address the dead sinner in any way.

The third man is a preacher of the biblical gospel. While the second man sneers and the first man gasps for breath, the third man cries out, "Sinner, believe! Lazarus, come out!" And Lazarus walks out of the tomb. If we interviewed the third man, the questions might go as follows:

"Were you fully aware that Lazarus was totally dead in that tomb?"

"Of course I was. Is not that what Scripture says?"

"Did you think that Lazarus had the ability to hear and respond to your message?"

"Not for a moment. How can a dead man respond to my voice?"

"Why did you command him to believe when you knew he was unable to comply because he was dead?"

The man would smile and say, "Friend, my confidence was neither in my ability to preach and invite, nor was it in the supposed (wrongly) power of Lazarus' "free will." My whole confidence was in the power of the words that I spoke. I spoke the words of Christ believing that Christ himself has the power to wake the dead and give them faith."

My friend, the gospel is the power of God that can "wake the dead" when it is attended by the power of the Holy Spirit. See John 5:21-25.

III. The Autopsy Report

The corpse is now sent to the morgue for an autopsy. After cutting open the sinner and examining every part, the report shows the cause of death. "The man was destroyed by sin. Sin penetrated every part of the sinner's being and left him in a state of total inability." The report listed the following:

(1) The Mind—"It was vain...dark...blind...deliberately ignorant." See 2 Corinthians 4:4-6 and Ephesians 2:3; 4:17-19 for a detailed description of the symptoms.

(2) The Heart—"It was saturated with a love of sin that could not be cut out. Sin had so entangled itself around the heart that it was incurable and inoperable." See John 3:19 and Jeremiah 17:9 for the symptoms.

(3) The Will—"The will was literally chained to sin and the love of sin in an indestructible union. The two had grown together so that they were not even distinguishable." See John 5:40 and 2 Timothy 2:24–26 for expert testimony and illustrations.

The autopsy report checklist shows that the words *totally destroyed by sin* appears after each of the items on the list.

Autopsy Report Checklist

Human faculty	Finding	Proof
Body	Totally destroyed by sin	Philippians 3:21
Head	Totally destroyed by sin	Isaiah 1:5
Throat	Totally destroyed by sin	Romans 3:13
Tongue	Totally destroyed by sin	James 3:6
Mouth	Totally destroyed by sin	Romans 3:14
Lips	Totally destroyed by sin	Romans 3:13
Feet	Totally destroyed by sin	Romans 3:15
Ears	Totally destroyed by sin	Mark 8:18
Eyes	Totally destroyed by sin	Isaiah 53:2
Hands	Totally destroyed by sin	James 4:8
Heart	Totally destroyed by sin	Jeremiah 17:9
Thoughts	Totally destroyed by sin	Psalm 56:5
Bones	Totally destroyed by sin	Job 20:11

IV. The Final Verdict: The sinner is totally depraved in sin and totally unable to do anything to help his recovery from sin and its effect.

We may think or reason in any manner we choose, but we dare not come up with conclusions that emphatically state that a sinner can, "if he only wants to," do things that the Bible specifically declares the sinner *cannot do!* The foregoing biblical facts are God's diagnosis of man's spiritual problem and man's true state. All the sentiment and sophistry in the world cannot change the Word of God and its final verdict.

V. The Big Problem: Moral responsibility versus moral ability, or free will versus free moral agency

Let us list several biblical facts that appear to be contradictory:

1. An unregenerate sinner *may* come to Christ for salvation, but an unregenerate sinner *cannot* come to Christ in true repentance and true faith until he is first born of the Spirit. See our tract, *God's Part and Man's Part in Salvation.* We are not fussing over words when we insist that "may not" and "cannot" are two entirely different things. One means permission, and the other means ability. A lawyer friend tried to teach his son correct grammar. When the boy asked, "Can I go out and play?" his father would reply, "You may go out and play if you are big and strong enough to be able to do so." That is more than proper grammar. That is solid theology.

2. Adam is the only man that ever had a truly free will in that he is the only man, apart from Christ, that ever had the spiritual ability, or power, to love and obey God. Adam used his free will to disobey God and forever lost the ability (free will) to love and obey God. See the chart on page 195 for a clear comparison of the difference in Adam's will at different periods.

If you can see three clear biblical facts, then you will clearly understand the doctrine of total depravity and man's responsibility.

1. Every sinner is free (is at liberty as a free moral agent) to obey God's commandments. Yea, he is commanded by God to do so and is condemned by God for not obeying them. He is both guilty and responsible even though unable to do his duty.

2. No sinner is free (has the moral ability) to obey God's commandments. The sinner can only live to please himself. He cannot choose God over sin and self.

3. The sinner, not God, is accountable for his spiritual inability to love and obey God's commandments. Adam was not created a sinner. He became a sinner by an act of pure free will. He cannot undo the effects of his sinful nature by an act of will. Adam did not fall and stub his toe; he jumped off a cliff and cannot "will" his way back up the cliff.

4. Man is only as free as his own sinful nature permits. Man cannot rise above his nature, or change his nature, by an act of will. See Matthew 12:33–35. A man may choose between the pieces of treasure in the chest (his heart), but he cannot by an act of will turn pieces of glass into diamonds, nor can he create a new treasure chest. The sinner can choose between sins, but he cannot choose between self and God.

VI. Man is Free to Do as He Pleases

In no sense whatever is man ever forced to do anything against his will, whether it is committing sin or believing in Christ. Every man is free to choose and act as he "pleases" within the limits of his ability and nature. See Proverbs 21:4; Matthew 27:14–28; and Acts 2:22–23.

What else can freedom or liberty be than to do as we please? However, we must carefully note that liberty is not identical with ability. Confusion of these two distinct things accounts for much false thinking on the subject of free will. Many people really mean _ability_ when they say _liberty_. They speak of man being free to do good or evil when they really mean to say that men are able to do good or evil. In this they seriously err. For the Bible clearly and consistently teaches that (1) man is free to do good or evil, that he is at liberty to do either, but it also clearly and consistently teaches that (2) man is able only to do evil because of his fallen condition (G.I. Williamson— _Westminster Confession for Study Classes_).

Man's freedom is like the freedom of water to run downhill. No one has to force it to run downhill. It does that naturally. However, it takes a power totally outside of the water itself to make it run uphill.

Man's freedom is like the bondage (freedom) of a mother's love. Give a mother a butcher knife and tell her to stab her child. She says, "I cannot." We say, "Of course you can. You have everything physically that is necessary. You do not mean _cannot_, but you mean you _will not_. You have the physical strength and ability. You just do not want to." She would reply, "In this case, *cannot* and *will not* mean exactly the same thing. I cannot want to kill my child because I love her." In other words, the woman is in bondage to her nature as a mother. Before she could ever kill her child, her nature would have to change. She would have to become totally insane and act in a manner contrary to her nature.

The sinner is in the same situation. He is controlled by his nature of sin. He cannot act contrary to that nature. The most revolting and impossible thing a sinner could imagine would be to renounce his self-righteousness and bow to the sovereign authority of Christ. His nature must be changed before he can even consider such a thing.

"FREE WILL" UNDER FOUR DIFFERENT CONDITIONS

Man perfect in Eden	Man fallen in sin	Man redeemed in grace	Man glorified in heaven
Man could sin but need not	Man can only sin	Man can sin but need not	Man cannot sin
Free to do as he pleases	Free to do as he pleases	Free to do as he pleases	Free to do as he pleases
Has freedom to do either good or evil	Has freedom to do evil only	Has freedom to do good but biased toward evil	Has freedom to do good only
Has no sinful nature	Has no spiritual nature	Has both sinful and spiritual nature	Has no sinful nature
Mutable	Immutable	Mutable/ immutable	Immutable

CHAPTER FIVE
UNCONDITIONAL ELECTION

Writers and speakers often use the words *predestination* and *election* interchangeably. However, this usage may create confusion. Predestination is the truth that God sovereignly purposes everything that will ever happen. He sovereignly brings to pass everything that he himself has planned (cf. Rom. 11:36, NIV). This includes every event of every person's life and everything about that person, down to the very hairs of their heads (cf. Matt. 10:30, NIV). The many verses that speak of "all things" being under God's sovereign control can only be true if predestination is true (cf. Rom. 8:28, NIV). Election is the truth of predestination applied to one specific area, or one category of the "all" things, namely, our personal salvation. The doctrine of election is the truth that God sovereignly chooses, or elects, certain individuals to be saved.

You have probably heard the following popular illustration about election. This is what I was taught in Bible School.

I believe in election because the Bible teaches election. However, it is a true *election* in that it involves voting. First, God votes for you. Then, the Devil votes against you. And lastly, you cast the deciding vote. Now that is a wonderful illustration, but it is the worst theology possible. Someone has noted that (1) this makes God and the Devil equal in power. The Devil has the power to deadlock God and frustrate his purposes; (2) man is mightier than both God and the Devil because he alone has the power to break the deadlock. Someone else has said, "In this election, the Devil was not a registered voter and since you were of non-age, you were not able to vote. That leaves only one vote—God's!"

I want to emphasize at the very beginning that not all sincere Christians agree with my understanding of the subject of election. If you have never heard this subject discussed or taught, it may "throw you for a loop" the first time you hear it. I urge you not to believe it just because someone else does; and likewise, do not reject it because your favorite preacher does not believe it. Prove that you have a Berean spirit and look at the texts of Scripture and see what they are actually saying. If you disagree with my understanding of election, that does not mean you do not love God. I have personal friends who love the Savior just as much as I do and disagree with me about election. John Calvin will not be at heaven's gate interviewing you about your view of election. You may be wrong about many subjects and still go to heaven, but you cannot be wrong about trusting the Lord Jesus Christ as your Lord and Savior. However, the Bible does say a lot about "God choosing some sinners," and we must understand in some way the many verses that use these words.

The Bible teaches something about both *predestination* **and** *election.*

The words *predestination, election, chosen, foreordained,* and *called* are used many times in the Bible. Whether we like it or not, we not only *must believe something* about this subject, but we must also realize that *everyone else believes* something about election. "I don't believe in predestination" does not mean, "I do not believe the words *predestination* or *election* are in the Bible," since everyone knows those words are in the Bible. No, "I do not believe in predestination" really means, "I do not believe the Bible means *what you are saying it does* when it talks about predestination." In other words, you must deny the very Word of God to reject predestination and election outright, but you are not necessarily denying the Bible just because you disagree with my interpretation. You cannot deny that Jesus said, "Ye have not chosen me, but I have chosen you" (John 15:16a), or you are denying the Word of God. You may, however, disagree with what I think those words mean without rejecting the Bible. You will, of course, be wrong in your understanding of election, but like me, you have been wrong before. Seriously, I repeat: sincere and godly Christians can, and do, disagree about what Jesus and the apostles meant when they talked about election.

Those familiar with the Doctrines of Grace will recognize that we are dealing with the second point of those five doctrines. We are discussing what is called "unconditional election."

Unconditional election, or grace *purposed,* deals with the work of God the Father in the scheme of redemption. All agree that God "chooses some people to be saved," but they differ greatly about *why* he chooses one and not another. The religion of free will says, "Yes, God chose some sinners to be saved just as he sovereignly chose Israel. However, he chose Christians purely on the basis of his foreknowledge." By foreknowledge, these people mean that before time began, God looked down through history and "foresaw" beforehand who would be "willing" to accept Christ, and on the basis of this "foreseen faith" in some people, God chose these particular people to be saved. It only takes a moment's reflection to realize that in such a scheme, God has not actually done any choosing at all. All God has done is ratify the sinner's pre-known choice. What else can that idea mean?

It is to counter this wrong idea that we add the word *unconditional* to the word *election*. We mean to emphasize that God's election of a sinner is totally unconditioned by anything known or foreseen in the sinner. Election is based solely on the unconditioned sovereign choice of God. If God *foresaw* what the sinner, with his free will, was going to do (namely, choose to be saved) and God then decided to "choose," based entirely on the foreknown information about that particular sinner, how can God be said to have chosen in any sense whatever? That sounds like double talk to me. The most that could be said was that God is merely agreeing with what he foresaw was going to happen and decided to ratify the sinner's choice. Thus, God looked into the future and foresaw I would be different from other people because I would be willing to believe the gospel. God's reaction to my foreknown decision was, "Great! I foresee your willingness, and that gives me a basis or foundation upon which I can choose you to be saved." If you believe that, please do not say that God, in any sense whatsoever, chooses in salvation. Be honest and say, "The one reason God was able to choose me to be saved was the fact that he foresaw that I would choose him first. He foresaw that I was not stupid like those who reject the gospel. God saw that I had a better heart, one that was willing to give him a chance to save me." I'm sure many will object and say, "But I never said that." Maybe you did not say that out loud, but that is exactly what your view of foreknowledge is saying.

On the other hand, the religion of free grace insists that apart from God first giving faith as a gift, no sinner would ever have any faith to be foreseen. God *sovereignly* chooses "whom he will" (cf. Rom. 9:10–13; 18–25), and his choice is totally "unconditioned" by anything foreseen in the creature. So the real question is not "Does God choose some sinners to be saved," but rather, is his choice "conditioned" by the foreseen willingness of the sinner or is God's choice totally "unconditional," or sovereign, based solely on his own good pleasure?

There are four basic questions that must be asked in any discussion of election. We will seek to answer these questions with specific texts of Scripture.

(1) Who does the electing—God or man? The biblical answer is "God." "Ye have not chosen me, but I have chosen you...." (John 15:16a)

(2) When did the electing, or choosing, take place—in eternity or in time? The biblical answer is "in eternity." "Who hath saved us, and called us with an holy calling, not according to our works, but according to his own purpose and grace, which was given us in Christ Jesus *before the world began....*" (2 Tim. 1:9)

(3) On what basis was the electing, or choosing, done: was it based on free grace (*i.e.,* unconditional), or was it based on man's choice (*i.e.,* conditioned by free will)? "Even so then at this present time also there is a remnant according to the election of grace. And if by grace, then is it no more of works: otherwise grace is no more grace. But if it be of works, then is it no more grace: otherwise work is no more work." (Rom. 11:5–6)

(4) Does this election involve personal salvation or only privileges and service? "But we are bound to give thanks alway to God for you, brethren beloved of the Lord, because God hath from the beginning *chosen you to salvation* through sanctification of the Spirit and belief of the truth...." (2 Thess. 2:13)

The Biblical meaning of *chose.*

Perhaps it would be well to fix in our minds how the Bible uses the word *chose.* Exactly what does God want us to understand when he says that he "chose us in Christ"? Look at the following text and ask yourself, "Exactly what did David do in this situation?"

And he [David] *took his staff in his hand, and chose him five smooth stones out of the brook, and put them in a shepherd's bag which he had, even in a scrip; and his sling was in his hand: and he drew near to the Philistine* (1 Sam. 17:40)

Whatever *chose* means in reference to those five stones, it means exactly the same thing that God did in reference to everyone whom he "chooses to be saved." Can anyone believe that those five stones somehow, possibly by wiggling a bit, indicated to David that they were *willing* to be chosen? No, everyone will see David sovereignly deciding which stones best suited his purpose. No one will dispute that the choice of the particular stones was totally in David's mind and purpose and not in the willingness of the stones. That is precisely what it means when the Scriptures say, "God *chose* us!" Just as David deliberately chose those five specific stones, and just as God chose one particular nation, Israel, out of all the other nations, so God deliberately chose specific individuals to be saved by his grace. Some may say, "Yes, but we are not lifeless stones." That may be true, but we were just as spiritually lifeless and dead as those stones were lifeless and dead. Our hearts were just as hard and cold as those stones, but the grace and power of God took out those stony hearts and gave us a heart of flesh (cf. Ezek. 36:26).

Election in the Old Testament Scriptures.

The nation of Israel is a classic proof of the doctrine of sovereign election. Deuteronomy 7:6–8 is a typical passage that describes Israel's unique relationship with God and how that relationship came about.

For thou art an holy people unto the LORD thy God: the LORD thy God hath chosen thee to be a special people unto himself, above all people that are upon the face of the earth. The LORD did not set his love upon you, nor choose you, because ye were more in number than any people; for ye were the fewest of all people: But because the LORD loved you, and because he would keep the oath which he had sworn unto your fathers, hath the LORD brought you out with a mighty hand, and redeemed you out of the house of bondmen, from the hand of Pharaoh king of Egypt. (Deut. 7:6–8)

Everyone agrees that Israel was "the *chosen* nation" of God. The question is *not*, "Did God sovereignly choose the nation of Israel out from among all of the other nations to be his special property?" You would have to literally deny the Bible before you could reject that clear truth. The only question is, "*Why* did he choose *that particular* nation as his special people?" And the only two answers you can give are either (1) because God foresaw they were "willing" to be chosen, or (2) because God sovereignly chose them simply because he wanted to choose them. What does the above Scripture say? Jacob's children were chosen because of the sovereign oath that God made to their father Abraham long before they were born. That choice had absolutely nothing to do with Israel's willingness. It is so with us who believe. We are saved by an oath the Father made to his Son long before we were born, and that oath has nothing to do with our so-called "free will."

Election is clearly taught in the New Testament Scriptures.

Our Lord Jesus taught the doctrine of election. We will confine our references to the gospel of John since that book is known as the *whosoever* gospel. Some verses from John are often used to refute election. Actually, no book in the whole Scripture is clearer on both absolute predestination and sovereign election.

> *I am the Good Shepherd, and know my sheep, and am known of mine. As the Father knoweth me, even so know I the Father: and I lay down my life for the sheep. And other sheep I have, which are not of this fold: them also I must bring, and they shall hear my voice; and there shall be one fold, and one shepherd.* (John 10:14–16)

These words cannot be understood without accepting the truth of unconditional election. Our Lord here speaks of certain people who belonged to him even though at that very moment they were lost—"other sheep I *have*." Notice the following things clearly taught in this text: (1) Christ calls some people "his sheep" long before he saves them. They belong to him at that very moment even though they are lost. (2) He declares that he "must, and surely will, find and bring them safely into the one true fold." Not a single sheep will be left not found. (3) Our Lord is positive that every one of those sheep "will hear his voice" and will come to him. That is sovereign grace choosing and bringing particular individuals to faith in Christ.

My dear friend, that is absolute sovereign election, pure and simple. Look at some other texts in our Lord's prayer in the 17th chapter of John. Notice the same expression is used time and again.

> John 17:2: *As thou hast given him power over all flesh, that he should give eternal life to as many as thou hast given him.*

John 17:6: *I have manifested thy name unto the men which thou gavest me out of the world: thine they were, and thou gavest them me; and they have kept thy word.*

John 17:9: *I pray for them: I pray not for the world, but for them which thou hast given me; for they are thine.*

John 17:11: *And now I am no more in the world, but these are in the world, and I come to thee. Holy Father, keep through thine own name those whom thou hast given me, that they may be one, as we are.*

John 17:12a: *While I was with them in the world, I kept them in thy name: those that thou gavest me I have kept…*

John 17:24: *Father, I will that they also, whom thou hast given me, be with me where I am; that they may behold my glory, which thou hast given me: for thou lovest me before the foundation of the world.*

Six times in our Lord's high priestly prayer, he refers to a group of people who have been "given to him" by the Father. Christ specifically says in verse nine that he does *not pray for the world* but for the elect who have been chosen out of the world and given to him as his sheep. Can anyone believe that Christ would die for an individual and then not pray for that individual?

Look at one more passage in the gospel of John. This is a key verse. It is probably the most misquoted, next to Romans 8:28, of any verse in the Bible. Many evangelists use this verse in every service when they give an altar call. The problem is that they only quote half of the verse. They begin in the middle and ignore the first part. Here is the entire verse:

All that the Father giveth me shall come to me; and him that cometh to me I will in no wise cast out. (John 6:37)

Notice that the verse contains one complete sentence with two distinct but vitally connected statements. Both statements contain a specific Bible truth. The statements are related to each other as cause and effect. As I mentioned, evangelists quote only the second half. They say, with arms outstretched while inviting people to come to the front of the church, "Jesus said, 'Him that cometh to me I will in no wise cast out.'" Unfortunately, they give the impression that "coming to Christ" and coming to the front are one and the same thing. It is true that Jesus said, "Him that cometh to me I will in no wise cast out," but he said those words as a conclusion to the first statement. Why can we be certain that everyone who comes to Christ will be accepted? Because those who come do so only because they already are one of his sheep. They come only because the Father is drawing them, and he is drawing them because he has given them to Christ in eternal covenant. The "coming ones" and the "given ones" are one and the same people. Those who believe in the free will of man (Arminians) will not freely preach the first part of John 6:37, which is unconditional election, and a hyper-Calvinist will not preach the second part of the verse, which is the free and universal proclamation of the gospel. We must preach both parts of this verse, and I might add, preach them both with equal enthusiasm and in the given order.

"All that the Father giveth me shall come to me..." is the truth of sovereign election. It is assuring us that there will be no empty houses in heaven catching cobwebs because someone was not willing to "claim by faith what Christ purchased for them." No, no, my friend, every chosen one will be there. The shepherd will seek, find, and save each one of his chosen sheep. After all, his reputation as the shepherd is at stake as well as the Father's purpose and glory.

The second part of the verse, "…and him that cometh to me I will in no wise cast out," is the message to a world of lost sinners. It matters not who you are, what you are, or what you have done; come to Christ, and you will be received. If you do not feel ready, come anyway, and you will be received. You say you have not felt your sin enough. Where, I ask, does the text say anything about feeling your sin enough? It says, "Come!" and assures all who come, regardless of their inadequacy, that they will be received.

People often ask, "Pastor, how can you reconcile election and the free proclamation of the gospel? How do you get those two things together?" I tell them that you never have to reconcile friends; you only reconcile enemies, and the free preaching of the gospel is not an enemy of sovereign election. The two doctrines are friends. As to getting them together, I insist that the Holy Spirit himself has put those two things together in John 6:37. The real question is, "How dare you try to separate them?" How dare anyone seek to put asunder what God has joined together!

The Apostle Paul taught sovereign election.

One entire chapter in Paul's letter to the Romans deals with the absolute sovereignty of God in election. We will look at that chapter in detail when we cover some objections to election. The following text cannot be understood except as teaching sovereign election unto salvation.

> *But we are bound to give thanks alway to God for you, brethren beloved of the Lord, because God hath from the beginning chosen you to salvation through sanctification of the Spirit and belief of the truth.* (2 Thess. 2:13)

Notice how the NIV translates the same verse.

> *But we ought always to thank God for you, brothers loved by the Lord, because from the beginning God chose you to be saved through the sanctifying work of the Spirit and through belief in the truth.* (2 Thess. 2:13)

You may have difficulty grasping this truth, but we dare not retreat and run away from God's Word. Read these words carefully, think about them, and ask the Lord to help you see and believe what they mean. *Don't ever be afraid of looking at the Word of God!* Don't ever take an attitude that refuses to look at passages that are "controversial." There are some who treat certain subjects in a manner that infers the Holy Spirit made a mistake by putting such "controversial issues" into the Scripture in the first place. *Don't run from any verse of Scripture even if you do not understand it!* Let's look carefully at this particular text.

First of all, *Paul specifically states that election is "unto salvation."* In Bible school, I was taught that election was true but had nothing to do with salvation. You choose to be saved with your free will, and then God sovereignly chooses where he wants you to serve. You could not force that idea into this text with a sledgehammer. The Holy Spirit says that election is unto personal *salvation*. God chose us "unto salvation," or as the NIV says, "to be *saved*." What can be clearer!

Secondly, *we are to give thanks to God for choosing us.* Election is always mentioned in the context of joy. *"Blessed be ...God...he hath chosen us..."* (Eph. 1:3, 4). "Blessed is the man whom thou *choosest,* and *causest* to approach unto thee..." (Ps. 65:4a). If the truth of sovereign election does not thrill your heart, then you either do not have a clue as to what it really means, or your heart is spiritually dead! Nowhere are we told to praise man for making a decision. No, no, we are to give thanks to God for every man's conversion, not praise to the man for his choice. Look at the text.

Thirdly, the text tells us *why it is necessary that we preach election.* People say to me, "Why do you preach about election when you know some people do not agree to it?" I always reply, "I do not have any choice. The Bible says I am "bound to." I have to preach election and give thanks to God for election, or I am deliberately disobeying this text."

Sometimes these people say, "But why do you have to preach about election so often?" Now, I really don't preach on the subject often, but preaching election one time is too much for the person who does not believe it. Again, I refer them to this same text. Notice Paul says, "We ought *always* to thank God" for choosing you. I remember a man in one congregation who really disliked me simply because I believed and preached election. His daughter got converted, but he still disliked me. The boy she was dating got converted, and the man still did not like me. I had the joy of marrying this young couple and during the ceremony I asked them both, "Do you believe that God in his sovereign purposes chose you for each other, and do you confess that his sovereign plan brought about this event this day?" After the service, the man was livid with anger. He said, "You can't even perform a wedding ceremony without talking about the sovereignty of God."

I believe we should preach sovereignty, pray and thank God for sovereignty, sing about sovereignty, and practice our belief in sovereignty in all we do. What else can James mean when he says:

> Go to now, ye that say, Today or tomorrow we will go into such a city, and continue there a year, and buy and sell, and get gain...For that ye ought to say, If the Lord will, we shall live, and do this, or that. But now ye rejoice in your boastings: all such rejoicing is evil. (James 4:13, 15–16)

Is not James accusing us of actual sin when we speak about our wills controlling things by failing to acknowledge the sovereign control of God over all things? "Rejoicing in our boastings" in this text is nothing less than thinking, speaking, and acting as if the events of tomorrow are in our hands and are our choices alone.

The fourth thing to note in the verse (2 Thess. 2:13) is the rest of the verse plus the following verses. Let me quote the whole section:

But we are bound to give thanks alway to God for you, brethren beloved of the Lord, because God hath from the beginning chosen you to salvation through sanctification of the Spirit and belief of the truth: Whereunto he called you by our gospel, to the obtaining of the glory of our Lord Jesus Christ. Therefore, brethren, stand fast, and hold the traditions which ye have been taught, whether by word, or our epistle. (2 Thess. 2:13–15)

Paul tells us that God not only chose us to salvation, but he also explains the means that God used to accomplish his goal. We were saved "through, first of all, the sanctifying work of the Holy Spirit." That is talking about regeneration giving us a new heart, enabling us to sincerely want to believe. This is more properly covered under the doctrine of regeneration. Secondly, we were also saved through "the belief of the truth" (verse 13b). We must be born of God in order to be able to believe, and we must believe in order to be saved. In other words, the God who chooses us to be saved guarantees salvation will happen by his sending the Holy Spirit to quicken us in regeneration. He also sends the gospel so we hear and believe it. God ordains the means to the end as well the end itself. 2 Thessalonians 2:13 is truly a powerful text of Scripture.

Probably no verse teaching election is as well-known as Ephesians 1:3, 4. Let us examine it.

Blessed be the God and Father of our Lord Jesus Christ, who hath blessed us with all spiritual blessings in heavenly places in Christ: According as he hath chosen us in him before the foundation of the world, that we should be holy and without blame before him in love: (Eph. 1:3, 4)

This text is clear and shows that in whatever sense the nation of Israel was "chosen" to be God's earthly nation, the church was "chosen" as the special spiritual people of God (cf. Ex. 19:5, 6 and 1 Pet. 2:9–10). Please note that God chose us in eternity, or before we were even born!

Peter taught the doctrine of election.

The following two verses both speak about the foreknowledge of God.

> *Peter, an apostle of Jesus Christ, to the strangers scattered throughout Pontus, Galatia, Cappadocia, Asia, and Bithynia, Elect according to the foreknowledge of God the Father, through sanctification of the Spirit, unto obedience and sprinkling of the blood of Jesus Christ… (1 Pet. 1:1–2a)*

> *Forasmuch as ye know that ye were not redeemed with corruptible things, as silver and gold, from your vain conversation received by tradition from your fathers; But with the precious blood of Christ, as of a lamb without blemish and without spot: Who verily was foreordained before the foundation of the world, but was manifest in these last times for you… (1 Pet. 1:18–20)*

One of the objections to our view of election is that "election is all based on foreknowledge," and then foreknowledge, as just mentioned, is defined as meaning "prior knowledge," or God's ability to "see into the future and make decisions based on that foreseen information." God is said to have purposed to choose us because he foresaw that we would choose him. If you will do a careful word study of "foreknowledge," you will see that the word really means "fore-loved" or "sovereignly chose." For now, look carefully at the above two verses from Peter.

The NIV translates 1 Pet. 1:1–2: "To God's elect...who have been chosen..." You can see that the NIV understands the word *foreknown* to mean *fore-loved* or *chosen*. We quoted both verses deliberately. We have a question for those who wish to argue that God's reason for choosing us was based on his looking forward into history to see what we would do and then basing his action of choosing us on that foreseen information. Would anyone dare say the same thing about "the foreordination of Christ" in verse 20? Can anyone seriously believe that God purposed, or chose, to give Christ up to the death of the cross only because he, the Father, looked into the future and "foresaw" that Christ would be willing to die, and, on the basis of that prior information, he decided to send Christ into the world to die? No! No! That is nonsense. Acts 2:22–24 is crystal clear that the Father consciously and deliberately foreordained the death of his Son. Well, the idea about God choosing us because he foresaw our faith is just as much nonsense. In whatever sense Christ was "foreordained to die," I was "foreordained to be saved!" It is just that simple.

God's foreknowledge of the church is like an architect's foreknowledge of a building. Would anyone say that a building is like it is because the architect had the ability to see into the future? He "foresaw" that Contractor A would get the brick contract. Since Contractor A liked white bricks instead of red ones, the architect put white bricks into the plan. He also "foresaw" that Contractor B would get the lighting contract and then used in the plans the kind of lights he "foresaw" that Contractor B would select. Because the architect had perfect foreknowledge of every contractor and exactly what specific thing each would use, he was able to design a building exactly like the one he knew all the contractors would build. You laugh at such an absurd idea, and so you should. You will say, "That architect knew exactly what that building was going to be like down to the last nail simply because he was the one who designed it." The contractors built the way they did only because the architect designed it that way. My dear friend, the church is exactly the same. God had perfect foreknowledge of the church for exactly the same reason. God did not need any foreknowledge to design and plan the church any more than an architect needs foreknowledge to design a building. God knew who would be saved because he sovereignly chose them to be saved.

How God taught me sovereign election.

God used a Mennonite farmer in a small country church near Lancaster, Pennsylvania, to open my eyes and heart to see and believe that sovereign election is a biblical truth. This man was in charge of the Wednesday evening Bible study and was going through the gospel of John. In the providence of God, he had started to study A.W. Pink's commentary on that book. The following verses were being discussed that particular evening:

> *Then came the Jews round about him, and said unto him, 'How long dost thou make us to doubt? If thou be the Christ, tell us plainly.' Jesus answered them, 'I told you, and ye believed not: the works that I do in my Father's name, they bear witness of me. But ye believe not! because ye are not of my sheep, as I said unto you.*

My sheep hear my voice, and I know them, and they follow me...' (John 10:24–27)

The teacher had two pieces of poster board which he set on separate chairs. On one poster board were written the words *heard and believed,* and on the other the words *heard and believed not.* The two chairs, thus labeled, represented the two groups of people spoken of in the verses being studied. Three questions were asked, and each one was answered by the words of Christ addressed to these Jews. The questions dealt with why some believed and why the others would not believe. The teacher's primary concern was to show the real reason that made the difference between the two groups. Why did some "hear and believe" and others "hear and believe not"? What made the vital difference between the two groups?

First question: "Why did the first group *refuse to* believe the gospel?" The teacher turned the first card over, and written on the back was the word *goat.* The Savior's words in verse 26 were unmistakably clear. "Ye believe not *because ye are not of my sheep."* It was impossible to argue about the meaning of such a concise statement. Why did they not believe? Christ gave the answer, "Because ye are not of my sheep." In other words, if they would have been his sheep instead of goats, they would have heard and believed. The fact that they would not believe proved they were goats and not sheep. Our Lord had earlier taught the same truth. In fact, his words in verse 25, "I told you, and ye believed not..." probably refers back to John 8 where Jesus said unto them, "...If ye were Abraham's children, ye would do the works of Abraham....Ye do the deeds of your father....If God were your Father, ye would love me: for I proceeded forth and came from God;...Why do ye not understand my speech? *even because ye cannot hear my words*....Ye are of your father the Devil...." (John 8:39–44). These people not only did not believe, but Christ said they *could not believe.* Why? They were not "of the Father." They were not "Abraham's seed." They were, in other words, not one of *God's elect.* They were not one of his sheep.

This does not mean that they wanted to believe but Christ would not allow them to do so. One of the wicked caricatures of our view states, "Many people want to be saved, but God refuses to save them because they are not elect." That is as big a lie as anyone ever told. We believe and preach that God has, does, and always will, save every sinner without a single exception that comes to him in the name of Christ! No, no, this verse means that they were totally unable to even *want* to believe because of their depravity, and God had sovereignly and justly chosen to leave them in that state. You can see in both John 10:26 and 8:39–44 the same "if" and "would have" relationship. Who and what these people *were* determined what they did or did not do. Our teacher reminded us that we all, without exception, were born with that same nature and into that same state of sin and unbelief.

Second question: "Why did the second group hear and believe?" The teacher turned over the second card, and it had the word *sheep* written on it. This question logically followed the first one, and again the Savior's word gave a clear answer. Verse 27 said, "My sheep hear my voice..." The teacher kept contrasting the two cards representing the two groups. "The gospel came to all of them, but one group believed and the other group would not. Why? What made the difference in the two groups? Why did the group called "my sheep" hear and believe? Did they have better hearts? Stronger wills? Keener minds? No, they believed because they were sheep.

I got the message! The "heard and believed" group did so only because they were "sheep," and the "heard and would not believe" group did not believe because they were not sheep; they were goats. Now I had always known the Bible divided men into two classes: sheep and goats. I also knew that the sheep were God's people and the goats were not. However, I never knew until that night why some people were sheep and others were not, and more specifically, that I had believed the gospel only because I had been chosen to be a sheep in eternity. It was always clear, as the poster cards showed, that "sheep" and "hear and believed" belonged together, and likewise, "goat" and "would not hear and believe" went together. However, no one had ever shown me which was the cause and which was the effect. I had thought, as my free-will teachers had carefully taught me, that I had decided to change my goat nature into a sheep nature by an act of my "free will." Oh, how those who love free will would like to make John 10:26 say, "You are not my sheep because you are unwilling to believe; if you would be willing to believe you would become one of my sheep." Ah, my friend, the text clearly says the opposite. Jesus said, "You believe not *because* you are not my sheep!"

The farmer's third question opened up the whole truth of God's sovereign election and forever silenced the nonsense of free will as the decisive factor in my "hearing and believing." The third question: "According to our Lord's words in verses 26 and 27, *does hearing and believing make you a sheep, or do you hear and believe because you have already been chosen to be a sheep?*" In an instant, God assured my heart of the answer. I knew which was the cause and which was the effect. The words of Christ were clear as crystal. The Spirit of God assured me that I had heard the shepherd's voice only because I had previously been chosen to be one of his sheep. I had willingly come to Christ only because I belonged to Christ by his sovereign election, and he was claiming, by his power, in time, what had been given to him in eternity. I was not a goat that had become a sheep by a decision of my so-called free will, but rather, I was a lost sheep that had been found! And I had been found only because I was a chosen to be sheep from eternity. A goat had not become a sheep; rather a lost sheep had become a found sheep.

Christ did not become my shepherd when he brought me to faith and repentance. He sought, found, and brought me to himself in salvation only because the Father, in eternity, had given me to him to be one of his sheep. That word "because" in verse 26 forever settled the reason of why some people reject the gospel. "My sheep hear" in verse 27 could only mean that I had heard and believed because I was a sheep from eternity. The texts can mean nothing else! Put down in your *Book of Indisputable Facts* these two things: (1) only those who have been eternally chosen to be sheep will ever come to Christ, and (2) every one of the sheep, without a single exception, will come when Christ draws them.

My mind was flooded with this amazing truth. *I was one of God's elect from eternity!* Why had I heard and believed the gospel? I knew the answer. Only because I had been chosen in Christ before the foundation of the world. I was not redeemed because I had believed, but rather the One who had redeemed me before I was born had now found me and revealed himself to me. Christ had sought me because I was his property. I did not become his sheep when he found me, but he had sought me and found me because I was one of his lost sheep.

As I left that little church in Lancaster County, I looked up into the heavens with tears in my eyes. I knew that before a single star had ever shown a beam of light, God had sovereignly chosen me as a sheep and purposed to draw me to himself and give me faith. With a heart filled with amazement and praise, I gladly acknowledged that I owed every part of my salvation to God's grace in sovereign election. I knew I was in possession of eternal life only because the Father had chosen me, the Savior had died for me, and the Holy Spirit had given me faith and a new heart.

Thus far we have covered the textual proof that the Bible clearly teaches the truth of God's sovereign unconditional election, the precise points of difference among sincere Christians on this subject, the basic meaning of the word *chose*, the doctrine of election in both the Old and New Testament Scriptures, our Lord's and the apostle's uniform teaching on election, and lastly, how God taught me the truth of his electing grace.

We now want to clear away some gross caricatures or misconceptions. Some of these arguments demonstrate that many sincere saints have never heard the truth of election clearly taught, and unfortunately, some of the caricatures are deliberate, wicked, and willful distortions of God's clear truth by people who really know better. The former group is often godly saints who need to be taught. The latter are wolves in sheep's clothing whose hearts have never been changed by sovereign grace. These people need to bow to God in true humility and repentance and be converted.

Election is not the Gospel.

The first misconception confuses the doctrine of election with the gospel message. There are some men who think that preaching election is preaching the gospel. It is true that no one would ever be saved if there were no sovereign election, but it is just as true that preaching election alone will not convert sinners. We believe election is what makes the gospel work, but we do not believe that election is the gospel. When the jailer asked Paul, "What must I do to be saved?" the apostle did not say, "Believe in the doctrine of election and you will be saved." When Paul, in 1 Corinthians 15:1–4, gave a summary of the gospel that he preached, he did not mention the word *election*. Many well-meaning preachers whose motives I do not question are actually doing more harm than good by trying to exalt God's sovereign electing grace as the gospel itself.

I know of no verse that teaches election any more clearly than Acts 13:48. However, that text does not set forth the gospel message. Look at what is said:

> *And when the Gentiles heard this, they were glad, and glorified the word of the Lord: and as many as were ordained to eternal life believed.* (Acts 13:48)

It is essential that we notice that Luke is not preaching a gospel sermon, but he is giving a *report* of what happened earlier that day when Paul had preached the gospel. The first part of the chapter is the evangelistic message referred to by the words "when the Gentiles heard *this.*" The heart of the gospel message, found in verses 37–40, is the apostolic gospel. It involves telling sinners about the death, burial, and resurrection of Christ and then assuring them that all who believe that message will be forgiven of every sin. Verse 48 is the report of the results, or effects, the Holy Spirit accomplished through the preached gospel earlier that day.

How different was the reporting done by the apostles than that which is done by the "evangelists" of our day. The apostles gave God all the credit for every conversion. The apostles "glorified the Word of the Lord" because they knew that the Word of the Lord alone had produced the amazing results. Today the report would read quite differently. An evangelist would boast, "I had ten first-time decisions today," or, "twenty people opened their hearts and gave God a chance to save them." The statistical boasting today is a result of men wrongly believing that conversion is effected by a combination of the power of a sinner's free will and the "soul-winning ability" of a preacher. The apostles knew nothing of such man-exalting and God-denying nonsense. They always credited God's sovereign electing grace with being the cause of every sinner's faith.

It amazes me to see the lengths that men will go in attempting to deny the truth of God's sovereign electing grace. Kenneth Taylor, in his *Living Bible*, which is marketed as a translation even though it is really a paraphrase, translates Acts 13:48b this way: "...as many as wanted eternal life, believed." In the margin he gives "disposed to" as an alternative meaning for "wanted." He then gives "ordained to" as a third option. It is not possible to make the verse say, "As many as *wanted*, believed." This is not paraphrasing in order to better understand the truth; this is radically and deliberately changing the meaning in order to hide the truth. If "were disposed to" is a legitimate translation, which it is not, it would still not settle the question as to why those particular individuals were disposed to believe, or who was responsible for disposing them. The word *ordained* as a third option shows that Taylor knows what the text means. It also shows his total bias against the truth of sovereign grace by passing off his interpretation as translation.

Spurgeon answered Taylor's distortion long before it was ever made. The great Baptist preacher explained Acts 13:48 well:

> Attempts have been made to prove that these words do not teach predestination, but these attempts so clearly do violence that I will not waste time in answering them... I read, "As many as were ordained to eternal life believed," and I shall not twist that text but shall glorify the grace of God by ascribing to it every man's faith....Is it not God Who gives the disposition to believe? If men are disposed to have eternal life, does not he in every case dispose them? Is it wrong for God to give grace? If it be right for him to give it, is it wrong for him to PURPOSE to give it? Would you have him give it by accident? If it is right for him to purpose to give grace today, it was right for him to purpose it before that date—and, since he changes not—from eternity.

A.W. Pink's comments are just as clear and concise:

> Every artifice of human ingenuity has been employed to blunt the sharp edge of this Scripture and to explain away the obvious meaning of these words, but it has been employed in vain, though nothing will ever be able to reconcile this and similar passages to the mind of natural man. "As many as were ordained to eternal life believed."

There are four things we can learn. First, that believing is the consequence and not the cause of God's decree. Second, we can see that a limited number only are "ordained to eternal life," for if all men without exception were thus ordained by God, then the words "as many as" would be a meaningless qualification. Third, this "ordination" of God is not to mere external privilege but to "eternal life," not to service but to salvation itself. Fourth, we understand that that all of the "as many as," not one less—who are thus ordained by God to eternal life, will most certainly believe."

Again, I remind you that election is not the gospel but is what makes the gospel work. If there were no sovereign election, we could preach the gospel until our tongues fell off, and not one single soul would be saved. Likewise, we could preach and teach election every Sunday for a lifetime, but unless we also preached the gospel facts, not one conversion would take place. We must understand that a man may preach a great sermon on election and never preach the gospel; and likewise, he may preach a clear gospel message without mentioning election. However, we must hasten to add that, first of all, no true biblical gospel sermon will ever say, or in any way infer, anything that denies or contradicts the truth of sovereign election, and secondly, no biblical sermon on election will ever deny or contradict either the gospel or its free and unfettered preaching to all sinners.

"But election isn't fair!"

Some years ago, I was at a weekend retreat with a group of university students. During a discussion period, someone raised the subject of predestination and election. One girl asked, "Where does the Bible clearly teach that God sovereignly chooses some people to be saved?" I asked her to read Romans 9 aloud. She paused a second with a surprised look on her face as she slowly read, "Before they were born or had done good or evil." When she got to 9:13b and read, "Jacob have I loved, but Esau have I hated," she stopped and said, "But that's not fair." I asked her to read the next verse. The King James Version says, "What shall we say then? Is there unrighteousness with God? God forbid." She had a modern speech translation and it said, "You will object and say, 'but that's not fair.'" The surprised girl blurted out, "That's what I just said!"

Now listen very carefully. If you object to election on the grounds that you think it is unfair, you are using an objection that has *already been used and answered* in the Scripture. The moment you say, "Election is unfair," you are admitting that you disagree with Paul's teaching in Romans 9:11–13 because that is the very objection he is presupposing his opponents will make. In his answer, Paul does not back up or soften his statement. He declares that God has every right to show mercy to whomever he chooses.

The young lady continued to read Romans 9. She read verse 18, "Therefore hath he mercy on whom he will have mercy, and whom he will he hardeneth." She literally gasped, "Then man cannot be held responsible. He is only a robot." Again I asked her to read the next verse. The King James says, "Thou wilt say then unto me, why doth he yet find fault? For who hath resisted his will?" The young lady's modern speech translation read, "You will say to me, 'Then man cannot be held responsible. He is only a robot.'" The poor girl said, "I did it again!" Let me repeat what I just said. If you object to election on the grounds that you think it makes man a robot, you are using an objection that has *already been used and answered* in the Scripture. The moment you say, "Election means man cannot be held responsible," you are admitting that you disagree with Paul's teaching in Romans 9:18. Again, we see that Paul did not soften his statement. He declares that the potter has the sovereign right to fashion, as he chooses, the lump of clay, which is sinful man.

Both of the above objections forget the fall of Adam and the doctrine of depravity. They treat sinners as if God created them sinful instead of remembering that we all chose, in Adam, to sin. Let me try to illustrate how ridiculous these objections are.

Suppose a very wealthy lady in your town chooses to adopt two or three orphans. She gives them her name, her love, and her fortune. Everybody in town would automatically accuse her of being mean and unfair because she only adopted three orphans instead of ten! You know that would not happen. Everyone would applaud her for adopting two or three simply because she did *not have to adopt any!* However, let God choose *some* sinners, when he could justly bypass all sinners since he owes no sinner anything but death, and God somehow becomes unfair or mean. In the case of the wealthy lady and the orphans, we magnify her gracious act. In the case of God and sinners, some will ignore his grace and vilify his character.

The writers of Scripture say very little about the dark side of election, called reprobation, simply because they are not at all surprised that God justly leaves some sinners to perish. The biblical authors are constantly amazed that God chose *anyone to be saved,* and even more amazed that he sovereignly *chose them.*

Since the objection of "unfairness" is so common and easily appeals to sentimentality, we need to say a bit more about it. A good friend of mine was covering the subject of election while teaching a high school and college class in Sunday School. There were seven kids in the class. My friend, Bob Dittmar, took an envelope out of his pocket and said, "There is a one-dollar bill in this envelope. I am going to choose one of you seven and give it to you as a gift. Do I have the right to choose anyone of the seven?" All seven vocally agreed that it was his money and he could do with it as he chose. Bob handed the envelope to a boy, and he opened it, took out the dollar and said, "Thank you." Bob asked the other six how they felt about not getting the dollar, and none of them were upset. They, of course, would have been happy if they had been chosen but were not upset since it was "his money to do with as he chose."

Bob then got two more envelopes out of his pocket and gave them to two girls. The girls opened the envelopes, took out a dollar and said, "Thank you." When asked how they felt, the other four said, "Something does not ring right about all this." The three with envelopes insisted that all was fair and right since it was Bob's money and he did not owe any of them anything. My friend then gave three more kids envelopes, and now six of the seven kids each had a dollar. He asked the one person out of the seven who had no envelope how she felt, and she immediately replied,

"I was cheated. It was not fair." The other six young people all reminded the girl how she had agreed that the teacher had a right to choose anyone since he owed none of them anything. It was a free gift, and she could not accuse Bob of being unfair. They really ganged up on her and put her down. They were all firm believers in Bob's right to "sovereignly choose" since it was his money and he owed none of them anything.

Bob then gave the last girl an envelope, and when she opened it, she discovered a *five-dollar* bill. Guess what the other six all cried. "It's not fair! I was cheated!" My friend said, "Aren't you the same people who were just arguing that I could not possibly cheat this girl since I owed her nothing? How can I all of the sudden cheat you when you just said I owed you nothing? Besides, you are holding a dollar as a gift you did not earn or deserve."

I am sure you can see that the "it is not fair" argument is utterly ridiculous. What makes the situation even worse is the fact that God freely offers to give sinners a full pardon for all sin if they would only be willing to receive it; but they all, without exception apart from his sovereign grace, say, "No."

Why does God predestinate some people to go to hell?

The answer to this misconception is simple. HE DOESN'T! God does not predestinate people to go to hell. This is a straw dummy that preachers who reject election often erect. Instead of dealing with the verses of Scripture that we show them, they make statements like the above.

All we need ask is this: "Did not anyone ever tell you about a man named Adam and how he used his free will to choose sin and plunge his whole posterity into depravity." How can God possibly predestinate someone to go to hell who is already on his *way to hell by the choice of his own "free will?"* The coming of Christ has absolutely nothing to do with people going to hell. It only affects people going to heaven. All men were lost long before Christ came. His death has nothing to do with any man's condemnation. If Christ had never come and died, all men would have justly perished in hell. How can his coming and dying have anything to do with the sons of Adam being lost sinners? Ask the question this way: "Why does God predestinate some SINNERS to go to hell?" and you have a whole new discussion.

Election sends no one to hell, but it does get some people into heaven. We could bring up from hell sinners who are now there, or who will ever be there, and not a single one of them would blame election for their being in hell. The so-called pagan who supposedly "never heard" will say, "My testimony is recorded in Romans 1. I did not follow the light God gave me, nor did I follow my conscience. I deliberately pushed away the truth. In my heart, I knew when I cut down a tree and used half of it to build a fire and the other half to carve an idol that it was the same wood."

The Jew will say, "I am in hell because I would not obey the light that God gave my nation. I trusted in the fact that I was a Jew and would not repent and believe the gospel promises of a Redeemer." We could go on and on and listen to one testimony after another, and every lost sinner would blame his or her own wicked heart for their lost estate. There will never be a single soul in hell who will say, "I wanted to be saved from sin but God would not save me because I was not one of the elect." The very throne of grace would collapse and be destroyed if that were true.

However, we must quickly add that the reverse is true for those in heaven. Bring any one of the saints who praise our God day and night from heaven, and not a single one will say, "I am here because of my free will. I am feasting on the riches and glories of grace because I decided to let Jesus save me." No, no, the uniform song from heaven will forever more be:

'Tis not that I did choose thee, for, Lord that could not be;
This heart would still refuse thee, hadst thou not chosen me.
Thou from the sin that stained me hast cleansed and set me free;
of old thou hast ordained me, that I should live to thee.

'Twas sov 'reign mercy called me and taught my op 'ning mind;
the world had else enthralled me, to heav 'nly glories blind.
My heart owns none before thee, for thy rich grace I thirst;
this knowing, if I love thee, thou must have loved me first.

But election is based on God's foreknowledge.

This is the favorite argument of the "Bible-believing fundamentalist" of our generation. "Oh, yes, God indeed chooses some sinners to be saved, but his choice is based on the fact that he foresees which sinner will be willing to accept the gospel. God, then, on the basis of this foreknown information, chooses those who are willing to choose him. Romans 8:29 makes this very clear." This is like a big rug that Arminians use to sweep the truth of election under. The problem is the big lump in the rug that cannot be hidden!

First of all, I agree that God indeed has the ability to look into the future. However, he has never yet found anyone with a willingness to believe. There is no "foreseen faith" to see. Romans 3:11, 12 tell us exactly what God foresaw:

> *There is none that understandeth, there is none that seeketh after God. They are all gone out of the way, they are together become unprofitable; there is none that doeth good, no, not one.* (Rom. 3:11–12)

It is impossible to find some way for God to foresee a willingness of someone to seek God in the crowd Paul describes in these verses. There is *none,* and that really means *no, not one,* who is willing to seek God until God first seeks him. The only faith that God foresees in any man is the faith that he himself purposes to give that man.

Foreknowledge is not an attribute of God that gives him the ability to see into the future. He, of course, can do that. When the Bible says that God foreknows, it means God purposes *to do something.* Foreknowledge is an *act of God,* not merely God having prior knowledge of something that will happen in the future. God only "foresees" what is absolutely certain to happen, and not one single thing can be absolutely certain to happen unless God has chosen to fix it so it does happen. Nothing happens that is not part of God's foreordained plan.

It is impossible for anyone, even God, to foreknow for certain that something is going to happen unless it is certain that it will actually happen. There can be absolutely no possible contingencies that will keep it from happening if it is truly foreknown. That is why you and I cannot foreknow one single thing in the future for certain. We cannot perfectly control any of the contingencies, and we have no control at all over many of them. Many unknowns may keep our plans and purposes from happening. God alone foreknows, simply because he alone can fix any given thing so it will positively happen. God does control every contingency. This is why Romans 8:28 is such a comfort. If man has a true "free will," then even God could not be absolutely certain of any event since the man might change his mind at the last second.

The word *know* basically means *to love*. Look at the following texts of Scripture.

> *You only have I known of all the families of the earth: therefore I will punish you for all your iniquities.* (Amos 3:2)

It is obvious that God "knew all things about every single nation," but he *knew,* or *loved,* Israel in a special way. This text means that God knew, loved, or chose Israel alone out of all the other nations.

> *But if any man love God, the same is known of him.* (1 Cor. 8:3)

In this text, *love* and *known* are used interchangeably.

And then will I profess unto them, I never knew you: depart from me, ye that work iniquity. (Matt. 7:23)

This verse cannot possibly mean that Jesus did not "know all about" the people to whom he was speaking. It was because he did know all about them that they were rejected. He knows everything about every nation and every person. Jesus is saying that he did not know them *in a way of love.* He did not love them redemptively. There is a sense in which it is not nearly as important that we know the Lord as it is that *he knows us!*

For the LORD knoweth the way of the righteous: but the way of the ungodly shall perish. (Ps. 1:6)

Again it is obvious that God sees and knows everything the ungodly do just as much as he sees and knows what the godly do. However, God *knows,* or watches over *in love,* the way of the righteous.

We could produce many other texts that clearly prove that the word *know* means *love.* When God knows someone, it means he loves that person. When he "fore" knows someone, he fore-loves them. The word *foreknow* really means the same thing as *choose* or *elect.* God's "fore" knowledge is his "fore" love, or his sovereign choice of a person. When God foreknows a person, he knows them in a way of special electing love. It means that he chooses them unto salvation.

In the next chapter, we want to show the effects the doctrine of election had on the life and ministry of the apostle Paul.

Shortly after I came to understand the truth of sovereign grace, I did a study of the effect of the doctrine of election on the life and ministry of Paul. I tried to look up and analyze every reference Paul made to election, predestination, calling, etc. I was amazed at how Paul's life and ministry not only clearly established the truth of sovereign grace; but it also totally refuted most of the objections that people offer to election and predestination. Here is what I discovered.

Paul attributed his own conversion, and the conversion of all of his converts, to God's sovereign election!

Paul never once mentioned the so-called free will of man when talking about anyone's conversion. He never considered the will of man the decisive factor in anyone's salvation. This is not to say that man does not have to be willing to believe, but it does mean that Paul viewed that willingness as a gift from God and not a product of man's so-called free will. Notice the great joy Paul expresses as he gives the right person the deserved credit for salvation. He always praises God's sovereign electing grace for every conversion.

First of all, he praised God for *his own conversion*. Paul's conversion experience is recorded several places in Acts and his epistles. In every case, God is credited from beginning to end as the reason Paul is saved. Notice one instance of his testimony:

> But **when it pleased God,** who separated me from my mother's womb, and **called me** by his grace, To **reveal his Son in me,** that I

might preach him among the heathen; immediately I conferred not
with flesh and blood. (Gal. 1:15–16, emphasis added)

Notice how strikingly different that statement is from
the "I decided to give Jesus a chance," or the "I'm glad I
was willing to let God save me" kind of testimonies we
hear today. Notice the following things: (1) Paul's
conversion did not take place "when I decided to accept,"
but *"when it pleased God."* (2) It was not when Paul decided
to "open my heart and let Jesus come in," but when (a) God
"called me [effectually, or regenerated me] *by his grace,"*
and (b) *"revealed his Son* in me." A new heart is not the
result of a dead sinner's willingness to be made alive but is
the direct result of a divine revelation of the Holy Spirit's
power to give a dead sinner a new heart. (3) Paul did not
need a personal worker or counselor to convince him that
he had been converted. He did not have to "confer with
flesh and blood" and be assured that "Jesus has indeed
come into your heart." When the Lord of glory takes up his
abode in a poor sinner's heart, that sinner knows
something amazing has happened. If a sinner has to be
badgered and argued into believing that Christ has indeed
"come into your heart," would we not be justified in asking
if it was worthwhile to have such an experience?

It is interesting how insistent Paul is that his readers
understand that it was not his will, but God's sovereign
will and purpose, which was totally responsible for his
conversion.

> *But now, after that ye have known God, or rather **are known of***
> ***God**…* (Gal. 4:9a, emphasis added)

Notice that the "or rather are known of God" is a very conscious and deliberate little insertion. It is almost as if Paul was saying, "I do not want you to misunderstand. I surely believe knowing God is vital, but I know [love] God only because he first knew [loved] me." Today we might paraphrase Paul's words this way: "Just in case a 'free will' enthusiast thinks I agree with him, let me set the record straight. I believe in sovereign electing grace. I was known by God long before I knew God."

Secondly, all of his converts were saved only because of election. Paul is not at all vague about why some people responded to the gospel under his preaching and others did not. He always made it clear that when anyone was converted, God alone was to have the praise. Since Paul believed that God's sovereign electing grace was responsible for every conversion, he consciously gave God the praise for every conversion. The following text is typical:

> But we are bound to give thanks alway to God for you, brethren beloved of the Lord, because God hath from the beginning chosen you to salvation.... (2 Thess. 2:13a)

The NIV translates this verse "chose you to be saved." We looked at this verse in the first chapter. I mention it again only to prove the point that Paul never congratulates the sinner on his "wise choice" or his good sense in "accepting Christ," nor did he praise himself or some other preacher for the "great message." He credited God with the whole of every man's salvation from beginning to end, including the gift of faith.

Further, Paul not only attributed his own conversion and the conversion of all of his converts to the electing grace of God, but he did the same *for all conversions.* Acts 13:48 is a statement concerning conversion in general. Again, we noted earlier how radically different this report is from the "I had ten first-time decisions last week" brag sheets published today. My purpose in quoting it again is to emphasize that this is a deliberate statement by Paul giving conscious praise to God's electing grace as the sole cause of all of the conversions that afternoon. Free will does not enter the picture.

> And when the Gentiles heard this, they were glad, and glorified the word of the Lord: and as **many as were ordained to eternal life believed.** (Acts 13:48, emphasis added)

Predestination was the foundation of Paul's life and call to the ministry!

How strange to read what Paul says about the effect that the truth of God's sovereign electing grace had upon him and his ministry and then hear sincere Christians say, "We should not preach about election and predestination since it is a dangerous doctrine." These people are especially afraid of hurting new believers with heavy doctrine, and they are even more concerned that lost people not be discouraged by hearing about the sovereignty of God. Let me answer these two objections with Paul's own testimony. Examine the following verses carefully, and you will see how unfounded these objections are.

> And I said, What shall I do, Lord? And the Lord said unto me, Arise, and go into Damascus; and there it shall be told thee of all

things which are appointed for thee to do. And when I could not see for the glory of that light, being led by the hand of them that were with me, I came into Damascus. And one Ananias, a devout man according to the law, having a good report of all the Jews which dwelt there, Came unto me, and stood, and said unto me, Brother Saul, receive thy sight. And the same hour I looked up upon him. And he said, The God of our fathers hath chosen thee, that thou shouldest know his will, and see that Just One, and shouldest hear the voice of his mouth. (Acts 22:10–14)

Let's make sure we get the message Paul was conveying. (1) Paul freely admits that he was not seeking after God. He was filled with blind rage against Christ and Christians and fighting them both as hard as he could. (2) He was testifying that he was blinded: spiritually by his religious ignorance, and physically by the miraculous intervention of God. (3) Jesus spoke to him from heaven. No man was ever more amazed than Paul when he learned that this "Lord" who had struck him down was none other than the very Jesus he was persecuting. (4) Ananias said, "Receive thy sight," and Paul was able to see. There is no hint of a suggestion that Paul had to be willing to comply before he would see. This incident is a manifestation of sovereign grace and power from beginning to end. Paul says, "And the *same hour* I looked…" The *looking* by Paul did *not give* his *sight*. The looking was the *result* of *God giving* him sight by the command of Ananias.

This passage clearly answers the two objections we are discussing. First of all, it proves that the first Christian doctrine that Paul learned as a brand-new convert was the doctrine of election. Notice again what Ananias said: "The

God of our fathers hath *chosen thee*...." The very first truth that Paul, a brand-new convert learned, was that he was saved because God had chosen him in electing grace. And, I might add, that was a truth that Paul never forgot nor did he ever cease to be amazed that it was true.

Notice the following in verse 14. (1) Paul states that he was chosen *in order to know* God's will. He did not first know that will and then decide to believe. (2) He was chosen so that he would be *able* to "see" that Just One. He did not first see, like what he saw, and then decide to believe. (3) He was chosen to "hear" and did not choose because he first heard and then decided to accept salvation. Isn't it amazing how carefully the Holy Spirit chooses his words?

I think the Holy Spirit is explaining that it is essential to start off one's Christian life with the clear realization that one is a child of sovereign grace. You are not your own but you have been bought with a price, and he who purchased you has every right to do with you as he pleases. We did not enter into a partnership with God at conversion; we were slaves and have been purchased out of slavery. We have neither the ability nor the right to boast about either the power of our wills or our rights to make our own choices. There can be only one boss, and the sooner we learn that God is that boss, the better off we will be. Paul's experience shows that God's purpose is that we learn that truth at conversion.

I believe that one of the primary reasons preachers and other church leaders are experiencing "burn-out" can be traced to the truth we are talking about. We cannot tell sinners that they did God a favor by *allowing* him to save them and then get them to live like they owe everything to God's grace. We cannot lead a sinner to believe that he alone, with his "free will," was the one decisive factor in his conversion and then urge that person to feel a deep and life-changing obligation to God's sovereign grace. In other words, if we want to get ulcers, we need only "fast-deal" sinners into making a decision that is totally designed to help them to "be happy" and then try to get those people to willingly make sacrifices that just might infringe on their happiness. We cannot get goats to act like sheep, but we can surely get burned out trying. If we teach the sinner he is "the master of his fate," don't be surprised if he lives as if that were true. Teach him he is a bondslave of sovereign electing grace, and it is a different matter altogether.

The second thing that Paul's conversion teaches us concerns election and gospel preaching. Not only was election the first Christian doctrine Paul learned, but when he was telling about his conversion in the Acts 22:10–14 passage, *he was giving his testimony to a group of lost people.* Now that ought to close the mouth of the objector who is frightened that a lost person should never be told about election. *Paul* was not afraid to talk about election in evangelism.

I am not at all suggesting that we must talk about election every time we preach or witness to the lost. We have already emphasized that election is not the gospel or part of the gospel. Election is what makes the gospel work.

However, there are times when election is the very truth that some sinners need. Nothing kills self-sufficiency like the truth of election. Nothing humbles a proud religionist like sovereign grace. How do you respond to a sinner who says, "Leave me alone; when I get ready to believe, I will believe"? I clobber them over the head with election. I tell them they cannot get ready. I press on them the truth that God does not have to send another witness to them but can leave them alone and let them go to hell for sure. Romans 9 is not a secret for only God's sheep. It is the message for every proud "Pharaoh" in this world. It is the hammer of God that destroys the damning myth of the power and rights of one's "free will." Sovereign election, rightly preached, will lead men to seek grace.

Predestination was the foundation of Paul's missionary zeal to preach the gospel.

How often have we heard the cry, "If I believed election, I would never witness"? Actually, if I did *not* believe election, I would not witness! If I believed that the sinner alone had the power to make God's plan of salvation work, I would realize that no one would ever be saved. "But," we are told, "preaching election will destroy all missionary effort." Again Paul's life proves this objection to be groundless. Notice first how election motivated Paul:

> *Then spake the Lord to Paul in the night by a vision, Be not afraid, but speak, and hold not thy peace: For I am with thee, and no man shall set on thee to hurt thee: for I have much people in this city.* (Acts 18:9, 10)

We don't usually think of Paul as a man who was afraid, but here is one instance where the Holy Spirit tells us that Paul was afraid. We can imagine that the Devil was whispering in Paul's ear about how hopeless the situation was as well as how useless were Paul's efforts. "You really don't believe you can persuade anyone in that wicked city to become a Christian. You may well lose your life." And how did God encourage Paul? He used the truth of election! God said, "Paul, you are safe wherever I call you to go. I have some elect in that city, and they are going to respond to the gospel when I open their hearts by my power." That is the thing that motivated our Lord in John 10:14–16. Some people, very particular people, simply *must* be saved because their salvation is the determined purpose of God. Paul was willing to suffer anything and everything for that purpose to be accomplished.

> *Therefore I endure all things for the elect's sakes, that they may also obtain the salvation which is in Christ Jesus with eternal glory.* (2 Tim. 2:10)

Why would Paul suffer for something that did not exist? Why would he endure all that he did unless he was sure of the outcome? John Patton was a missionary to the New Hebrides islands. He lost his wife and child to disease. He was nearly killed on many occasions. He labored for nearly twenty-five years with no "success." Do you think he ever felt discouraged? Do you think the Devil ever whispered in his ear as he did Paul's? What would keep someone preaching in such a situation? John Patton stood over the grave of his wife and child and prayed, "Father, you have chosen a people out of every tribe and tongue to be saved.

Some of those chosen ones are on this island, and I will not leave until they are safely in the fold." That is what biblical election will do for missions. In God's time, Patton saw the island swept into the kingdom of God. It was the doctrine of election that kept Patton on that island all that time.

I freely admit that the truth of God's electing grace, and the absolute necessity of the Holy Spirit to enable a person to be able to believe, will kill a lot of fleshly zeal that has hatched up some very "successful" carnal methods of "getting decisions" (and the sooner such practices are killed the better); but I assure you that both the Bible and history testify that election is the only thing that can produce and maintain true gospel mission work. Many sincere people have gone to the mission field with genuine pity and human love for those "poor people who are just waiting to hear the gospel" and after two break-ins of their homes, the loss of their possessions and constant threats to their lives, they have changed their minds and feelings about "those poor people."

Let me note one more passage that proves that believing in election did not adversely affect Paul's ministry.

> *Brethren, my heart's desire and prayer to God for Israel is, that they might be saved.* (Rom. 10:1)

Now remember, the above words immediately follow those awesome words in Romans 9. There is no chapter in all of the Word of God that exalts sovereign election like the ninth chapter of Romans. "Therefore hath he mercy on whom he will have mercy, and whom he will he hardeneth" (Romans 9:18) does not sound very "freewillish" to me. That is high, high Calvinism. And yet the man who wrote those awesome words immediately says that he longs to see those same people described in chapter nine converted. He sincerely prays for them and continues to witness to them. Human logic may say it is a waste of time, but that did not stop the great apostle from preaching the gospel to all men and pleading with God to open their hearts to believe.

Predestination was the ground upon which Paul appealed to believers when he urged them to worship and praise God.

We have already covered one of the most obvious texts that teaches this truth. You might want to look again at the first chapter and review the comments on 2 Thessalonians 2:13. Notice especially that election is the source of joy and thanksgiving. The next text is one my favorite verses in all of Scripture. I will never forget the way God taught me its meaning.

> *For who maketh thee to differ from another? and what hast thou that thou didst not receive? now if thou didst receive it, why dost thou glory, as if thou hadst not received it?* (1 Cor. 4:7)

In my first pastorate, I had to work part time. One morning before I went to work, I read the fourth chapter of 1 Corinthians. Verse 7 jumped out at me, and I could not quit thinking about it. On my way to work, I picked up an elderly African-American man. He told me some of the horrible things that had happened to him because of the wicked prejudice against the color of his skin. As he talked, I kept thinking, "Who maketh thee to differ from another?"

Why did that man suffer all those injustices of which I knew nothing in my life? Why was the color of his skin different from mine?

I have often asked the congregation to look at the color of their hands. Some may be black, others white or red or yellow. However, regardless of the color, the individual's "free will" had nothing to do with choosing that color. No person is either white or black by his or her own choice. It was God himself who made every Indian red, every Chinese person yellow, every African-American black, and every white man white. Our so-called free wills had nothing to do with our births. The very first sight that every person reading these words could have seen at birth was a mother in a loincloth carrying you off to the Ganges River to throw you in as a sacrifice. None of us said, "If I cannot be born in a middle-class home in America, I simply refuse to be born." No! No! "Who maketh thee to differ from another" in the color of your skin or the national and economic conditions of your birth? And, as Paul adds, since it was God alone who made the difference, how dare anyone boast or be prejudiced?

As I pulled into my boss's driveway, I saw his twenty-four-year-old son wearing only a large diaper. He was playing with a little rubber hammer. He had the mentality of a one-year-old. I kept thinking, "Who maketh thee to differ from another?" I had graduated from high school and seminary. I had two healthy children who were doing well in school. Did I, with my "free will," or my children, with their "free will," refuse to be born mentally retarded?

Did you decide with your "free will," if I cannot have at least a good enough IQ to graduate from high school, I simply refuse to have anything to do with this thing called life? No! No! Every person who reads these words could have been born a Down's syndrome child. "Who maketh thee to differ from another" includes not only the color of one's skin but also the capacity of his brain.

I pastored a church where there was a boy with Down's syndrome in the congregation. We would always hug each other, and I would say, "How is my friend David?" He would smile and say, "I am fine. How is my friend John?" One Sunday evening I preached on God's sovereign providence. After the customary hug and greeting, I said, "David, I do not know how much you understood of what I said tonight. However, someday all of the Christ rejecters, who were too "educated" to believe the gospel, will wish they had been like you. They will cry to the rocks to hide them from the face of God and wish they had been born with Down's syndrome. I do not understand mental illness but I know what I just said will surely happen."

The evening of the day of which I am speaking, I stopped at the post office on my way home from work to get my mail. As I put my key into box 221, I heard a guy use my name with a string of curse words. "John Reisinger, you blankety-blank so-and-so, how are you?" I turned around and saw a man I had not seen for years. We had been in the Navy together, and the last time I had seen him was on Guadalcanal, when we had been drunk all night. He said, "Let's go have a beer and talk over old times." I said, "Ah, well, ah, I don't do that anymore." I then told him the gospel and that I was a preacher. He was silent for several minutes and then burst out laughing and said, "That is the best one you ever told yet." He thought I was putting him on. I had to take him around the corner and show him my name on the bulletin board of the church before he would believe me.

As the man walked away shaking his head, the tears rolled down my cheeks as I thought, "Who maketh thee to differ from another." I think I would have gotten angry if someone would have said to me, "John, the difference between that man and you is this: you were willing to believe but he was not." I knew the difference between us was nothing at all in either him or myself. The difference was in the sovereign electing purposes of God.

My dear Christian brother or sister, I do not care if we are talking about your nationality, or the color of your skin, or your salvation. In every case, it was decided by God's sovereign predestination and had nothing to do with your so-called free will. The same thing is true of your physical health and mental ability. Whether you are a genius or a slow learner, you did not choose your IQ with your so-called free will. You must say, "It was God who made me to differ from another." Your personal salvation must be treated the same way. If you are one of Christ's sheep and rejoice in his free forgiveness, it is only because he chose you to be a sheep. Your free will did not enable a goat to change itself into a sheep. It was God's sovereign electing grace that "made you to differ from another."

I trust you can see the point that Paul is making. He is using election to destroy both our arrogant self-sufficiency and our constant tendency to stupid prejudice. No one who understands and feels the truth of 1 Corinthians 4:7 can ever again look down his or her nose at anybody. That person cannot boast, because, as Paul says, "Whatever you have you received is from God alone."

Paul based his appeals to believers to be holy on the fact of their election.

It is no accident that Paul's epistles always begin with doctrine. He does not appeal for a right response until he first gives a clear and convincing reason for demanding that response. In other words, doctrine precedes duty as the essential foundation for the duty. Duty is urged as the only logical response to the doctrine set forth. 1 Corinthians 6:19, 20 is the typical Pauline method of appealing to believers to be holy.

> *What? know ye not that…ye are not your own? For ye are bought with a price: therefore glorify God in your body, and in your spirit, which are God's.* (1 Cor. 6:19, 20)

Do you see the force of the argument? The appeal to glorify God in all things is based on a logical and doctrinal *therefore*. Why do I owe God perfect obedience in all that I do? Because I am not my own but belong entirely to him, and I belong to him simply because he bought me with the blood of his Son.

Does the object purchased choose its purchaser, or does the one who pays the price choose what he wants to buy?

The purchaser is the one acting, and the object being purchased is passive. Did you choose God and ask him to purchase you, or did God purchase you because he first chose you to be purchased? How can a believer not want to glorify God? It would be insane for a true child of God not to sincerely want to please the one who purchased him out of sin, shame, guilt, and death! And, I might add, God has given all of his sheep, without a single exception, a "sound mind" (cf. 2 Tim. 1:7).

A careful study of all of Paul's epistles will find this principle to be the norm: first doctrine and then appeal to personal behavior. To say, as many sincere sentimentalists today say, "Never mind doctrine; let's just have practical living," is to miss Paul's message. The message of Paul is this: "It is impossible to have godly practical living without first laying a foundation of sovereign grace where the only possible response can be holy living. Look at two examples.

I therefore, the prisoner of the Lord, beseech you that ye walk
worthy of the vocation wherewith ye are called. (Eph. 4:1)

This appeal for a worthy walk is the first such exhortation in the epistle. The first three chapters talk about doctrine. The truth of sovereign election is set forth in chapter one; the depths of depravity out of which we have been raised in regeneration is laid out in chapter two; and the amazing grace of God and its attendant blessings which have been freely given to every believer is explained in chapter three. All of this is through our union with Christ. Ephesians 4:1 is Paul's first use of the word *therefore* in the "doctrine/response" sense. Paul did use the word *therefore* previously in Ephesians 2:19, but that was not as the basis of an appeal but to establish a point of doctrine. Chapters one through three are pure theology. They show the great blessings a child of God has just because of being joined to Christ. The *therefore* in Ephesians 4:1 is the same as saying, "Now because everything I said in the three previous chapters is true, the only possible logical and sane response is for you to walk in your daily life in a way that brings glory to the one who lavished all these aforementioned blessings on you."

Paul does the same thing in Romans. Romans chapters 1 through 11 is doctrine, doctrine, and more doctrine. The first appeal of any kind whatever does not appear until 6:11. The exhortation in Romans 12:1 can only be understood by seeing that "the mercies of God" are referring back to the first eleven chapters.

> *I beseech you therefore, brethren, by the mercies of God, that ye present your bodies a living sacrifice, holy, acceptable unto God, which is your reasonable service.* (Rom. 12:1)

Notice Paul's appeal to reason. It is only reasonable that a child of God should present himself, and all that he is, to God because of God's sovereign electing grace (Rom. 1–11). Anything else is insane and irrational, and I repeat, God has given all of his true saints a "sane mind."

Is doctrine important? According to Paul, it is if you want to earnestly appeal to believers to live a holy life. Have you ever noticed that the hymns that glorify God's amazing grace are the ones that inspire you to be "lost in wonder and praise"? The more a hymn exalts God's amazing grace, the more it moves us to want to love and serve our great God and Savior. That is Paul's approach.

Let me quickly say a word about some of the specific effects the doctrine of election should have on us as individuals. It must make us humble and make us grateful for special grace. This was Paul's goal in writing to the Corinthians.

> *For ye see your calling, brethren, how that not many wise men after the flesh…But God hath chosen the foolish things of the world …God hath chosen the weak things of the world…That no flesh should glory in his presence….That, according as it is written, He that glorieth, let him glory in the Lord.* (1 Cor. 1:26, 27, 29, 31)

For just a moment, imagine that you are responsible — because of your free will — for your faith in Christ. You are saved only because you were willing to believe the gospel with your so-called free will. You could not in honesty utter the above words. You would have to say, as some Arminians are quite willing to do, "I, with my *own free will,* am the decisive factor that enabled God to save me. The only reason his eternal plan of salvation worked in my case, and not in another case, is the simple fact that I, with my free will, was willing to repent and believe the gospel." If that is the case, then what specific thing do you owe to God any more than any other person? Put another way, did God do everything for every lost man that he did for you? If not, then exactly what has God done for you that he did not also do for every lost person in this world?

You may be saying, God loved the whole world just as much as me, *"But I…I alone* made the difference between myself and other people. The difference has nothing at all to do with the electing love of God. It has to do with my free will."

You may be saying, Christ died for every person in this world in the same sense in which he died for me, *"But I...I* took advantage of what Christ equally provided for everyone. I accepted the redemption that was made for me and all other sinners. Christ redeemed all men in the identical same sense that he redeemed me, but I took advantage of it and believed. The only real difference between me and the man in hell is that *I, with my free will,* enabled the atonement of Christ to be effective and actually save me."

You may be saying, the Holy Spirit convicted others in the same sense and to the same degree that he convicted me, *"But I...I* allowed, with my free will, the Holy Spirit to give me a new heart. I was not, as others, unwilling to cooperate with Holy Spirit in regeneration. I wanted, with my free will, to be born again."

My sincere question is this: which approach leads to glory in self and the power of free will, and which approach leads to worship and praise of both the grace and the power of the triune God? Does the clear answer to that question possibly explain why there is so little genuine amazement and praise in the life and worship of believers today? How can we expect believers to fall flat on their faces in worship and praise to God for any kind of special grace when we constantly tell them, "God has done all he can do; it is now entirely up to you and your free will"?

The depth of your gratitude to God will be in direct proportion to the depth of your understanding of what you really owe to him in salvation. The *But I* theology of free will can only have a shallow gratitude because it has a shallow view of debtorship.

My dear reader, *you* may approach the throne of mercy and say, "Sovereign Lord, I am so happy that I decided to give you a chance to save me. I'm so delighted that my free will allowed you to do what you longed to do but could not do until I agreed to allow you to do it." I say, you may speak thus, but as for me and my house, we will sing the following hymn:

> Why was I made to hear thy voice,
> And enter while there's room,
> When thousands make a wretched choice,
> And rather starve than come?

> 'Twas the same love that spread the feast
> That sweetly drew us in;
> Else we had still refused to taste,
> And perished in our sin.

It is an undeniable fact that God chooses some sinners to be saved and leaves others to perish. However, we know that none are chosen because of either their own goodness or their willingness to be chosen. "But," says an objector, "the Bible specifically says that God is not a respecter of persons" (Rom. 2:11). If God, as an objector will assert, looked down through history and saw that some sinners would be willing to be chosen, then God could say, "I have found some sinners with a willing heart, and I now have a basis upon which to choose them to be saved." In such a scenario, God is a respecter of man's foreseen faith. Such a view truly makes God a respecter of persons.

Romans 2:11 does not mean that God cannot or does not show grace to only some men but not all men, since the Bible clearly teaches that he does that very thing. It means that there is nothing about any man's person or personage, especially foreseen faith, which makes him different in God's sight from any other sinner. There is nothing that any man has ever done or will do that God can respect and reward. Therefore when God chooses a particular sinner to be saved, it must be purely on the basis of sovereign grace and not foreseen faith.

I cannot emphasize strongly enough what we said in the first chapter. There is both a sovereign election of *some* unto salvation, and there is a sincere and universal proclamation of the gospel to *all* men without exception or distinction (cf. John 6:37 and Matt. 11:20–28).

Ah, my dear reader, may I say a pointed word to you? If you perish in hell, your lips will never accuse God of being unjust or unfair. You will never blame God's election for your eternal destruction. If you have read this far, or if you have been in meetings where I have preached, then you have heard the gospel. You have been urged to trust Christ. If you refuse to repent and believe the gospel, you will perish with that gospel in your ears. You will plead guilty and will never even think of accusing the most high God or his sovereign electing grace as the reason you are in hell.

However, just the opposite is true of the saint who makes it to heaven. In that land of glory, no one will even know how to spell the words *free will*. No saint will talk about "giving God a chance" or "allowing God to save him." All boasting in the free will of man will be left behind. Let the saints come down from heaven and testify, and their theme will be sovereign grace. They will, without exception, cry, "Salvation is of the Lord, from beginning to end."

Imagine you are a four-legged sheep caught in a thicket from which you cannot free yourself. You are cold, hungry, thirsty, and your throat is sore from bleating. The more you struggle to get free, the more the briars dig into your flesh and cause the blood to flow. Finally, in utter despair, you resign yourself to your pitiful situation, quit struggling, and prepare to die. If, in that most hopeless situation, you heard the familiar voice of a shepherd calling your name, what would you do? You would cry, "Baaaa! Baaaa!" as loudly as you could.

Well, let me tell you that if you are a two-legged sheep in the same condition, you will react exactly the same way. If you are caught in a thicket of sin and cannot get loose, and the harder you try to get free the more you fail because the bonds of sin get stronger, and you are hungry, tired, and thirsty, then I have *good news*. There is a gracious shepherd calling your name. Cry out to him. Cry, "Baaaa! Baaaa!" as loudly as you can. Tell him how sick you are of sin and its awful consequences. Tell him how totally helpless you are and how desperately you need his grace and power. He will be at your side in a moment. He will free you from the thicket of sin, bind up your wounds, give you bread and water, and put you on his shoulder and carry you safely back to the fold.

The only person who will not cry out, "Baaa! Baaa!" is the person who either does not believe he is caught in a thicket of sin but imagines he is totally free, or the person who loves the sin despite the misery it brings.

If you are a chosen sheep, you know what it is to be set free from the thicket. You have tasted the Bread of Heaven and have drunk the Water of Life. You will praise forever him who loved you with an everlasting love and washed you in his own precious blood.

CHAPTER SIX
LIMITED ATONEMENT

The central theme and message of both the Old Testament Scriptures and the New Testament Scriptures is the person and work of our Lord Jesus Christ. His atoning, or sacrificial, death on the cross is the watershed of all history (*cf.* Luke 24:25-27; Acts 8:32-35; 1 Cor. 2:2). It is no accident that even the secular world divides history as it relates to the birth of Christ. All men and events are recorded as being either BC or AD. Christ is not only the center of the Bible; he is also the center of history and all creation. The central concern and singular purpose of the mission of the Son of God was the work of atonement (*cf.* Matt. 1:21; 20:28; Luke 2:11; 19:10; 1 Tim. 1:15; 1 John 4:14). God's character of holiness and truthfulness demands that sin cannot be merely overlooked or ignored, but it must be punished by death. Either the sinner bears that punishment of death himself, or an acceptable substitute must be provided. It is safe to say that one will understand the Word of God to the same degree that one understands the person and work of Christ. To be ignorant about the atoning work of the Lord Jesus Christ is to be ignorant about salvation by grace.

The following principles should be carefully remembered and put into practice in all of our thinking and discussion of this vital subject. First of all, the doctrine of the atonement is a subject known only by *special revelation.* We do not learn about this truth in any place except the Bible. We are not looking to philosophy, psychology, science, sentiment, etc., to teach us the meaning of the death of Christ. We are looking to the Scriptures alone. No human mind could dream up the doctrine of atonement by the blood of Christ. This great truth is foolishness to the carnal mind.

Secondly, a right understanding and application by faith of the glorious truth of the atonement will cause us to see (1) the nature and depth of the sin out of which we have been redeemed, and (2) the amazing love and power of God that accomplished our salvation. As we look at the sufferings of Christ on the cross and understand what he really accomplished on that horrible instrument of shame, we will be led to adoring worship and praise.

Thirdly, I want it clearly understood that sincere Christians disagree about the biblical meaning of the nature and purpose of the atonement. Some godly believers think Christ died and "redeemed" all men without exception. In their view, Christ died for Judas in exactly the same way that he died for Peter. Judas perished, not because his sins were not paid for, but only because he was unwilling to claim by faith the redemption Christ had provided for him and all other men. We had a special speaker in my first pastorate who declared, "The worst drunk and immoral person in the gutter tonight is just as redeemed as you and I. He only need be willing to claim his redemption, and he will be saved. Whether he believes or does not, he is still redeemed by the atonement of

Christ." This view is called *universal* or *unlimited* atonement.

Other Christians, and I am in this second group, believe that Christ died for the sheep (*cf.* John 10:11), that is, those given to him by the Father (*cf.* John 17:2, 6, 9), in a way that he did not die for the goats. We believe that Christ died and paid Peter's debt in a way that he did not die and pay the debt of Judas. We believe that Judas, and every other lost sinner, will suffer in hell for their sins. If Christ died for Judas in the same sense that he died for Peter, then Judas would also have been saved.

We insist that the heart of the issue is this: did Christ on the cross actually redeem and make certain the salvation of some sinners, or did his death merely make it possible for all men without exception to be saved if they would contribute faith with their free wills as their essential part in salvation? Is the only real and vital difference between Peter and Judas the "willingness" of Peter and the "unwillingness" of Judas? Is Cowper's hymn correct, or incorrect, when it says:

Dear dying Lamb, Thy precious blood
Shall never lose its power,
Till all the ransomed Church of God
Be saved to sin no more.

The hymn writer clearly saw "being saved," or coming to faith in Christ, as a sure and certain result of "being redeemed," or having Christ die in one's place. He saw the power of the blood of Christ as truly a *redeeming* power. The blood did not make *all men* redeem*able*, but that precious blood actually made salvation sure, not for all men, but for "the ransomed Church of God." Cowper could not conceive that some of those who had been ransomed (redeemed) by the blood of Christ could ever perish because of their unwillingness to claim the redemption "provided" for them and all others. All of the ransomed people of God will be brought to believe and be saved.

Fourthly, let's be absolutely certain we understand what we are, and are not, saying. In no sense whatever are we even remotely implying that there are some poor sinners who sincerely want to be saved, but God refuses to save them because Christ did not die for them. Every sinner in the whole world who comes to Christ will be received and accepted. Revelation 22:17 means exactly what it says:

> *And the Spirit and the bride say, Come. And let him that heareth say, Come. And let him that is athirst come. And whosoever will, let him take the water of life freely.*

The problem is not with "whosoever will;" the problem is that all men, without exception, are "whosoever *will-nots.*" None are willing to come until God opens their hearts and brings them. We believe and fervently preach the words of our blessed Lord in John 6:37:

> *...him that cometh to me I will in no wise cast out.*

Can anything be more true and certain than these words that guarantee that every sinner without exception who comes to Christ will be saved? We preach that. We do not, however, do what some preachers do and begin in the middle of the verse. We also preach the first half of the verse. The first part tells precisely why the second part is true. All who come to Christ will be received because they, and they alone, are the elect for whom Christ died:

> *All that the Father giveth me shall come to me; and* [it is just as true] *him that cometh to me I will in no wise cast out.*

The "coming ones" and the "given ones" are one and the same people. All who come will be saved, and all who have been given by the Father and redeemed by the Son will come.

It is at best a caricature of our position to suggest that we believe that some sinners go into heaven kicking and screaming. They do not want to go, but since they are elect and Christ died for them, God throws them into heaven against their will. This was discussed when we covered the doctrine of election. We insist that the most willing thing any sinner ever did was to freely repent and believe the gospel. The question is never, "Must we repent and believe?" but rather, "Why do some sinners repent and believe and other sinners refuse to do so?" The biblical answer is not, "because of their free will," but rather, "because of the sovereign purpose of God in the death of Christ."

The essence of God's being is holiness. "Holy, holy, holy" is the theme of heaven's worship (cf. Isa. 6:3; Rev. 4:8). Those perfect beings in God's immediate presence do not say, "Love, love, love," but "Holy, holy, holy." A holy God, by his very nature, must not only hate sin, but he must also punish sin. All the love in the world, including all of the love in the heart of God, will not, because it cannot, forgive one single sin. Sin must be paid for by an atoning sacrifice. Grace and mercy are optional with God. He can, and does, show mercy to whomever he chooses (Romans 9:15), but righteousness and justice are not optional. God may choose to either act in mercy or choose to withhold mercy. Nonetheless, he must always act in righteousness. He may choose to love some sinners and not others, but in both cases he must act righteously. This is why the cross is so essential. The death of Christ does not make God love us, but Christ's atonement was essential so God could love us righteously and in true holiness.

I. The Necessity of the Atonement—Why Did Christ Have to Die?

Once God determined to save sinners, there was but one way of accomplishing this purpose that would be in harmony with God's own character and law, and consonant with the nature of sin and the needs of man. This one way was the *substitutionary blood atonement* of the incarnate Son of God. The unregenerate man cannot believe the gospel because he cannot see the real need of an atonement. He does not believe that he is a helpless depraved sinner who cannot save himself. One reason for this blindness and ignorance lies in the sinner's wrong view of the character of God and his holy and righteous demands as revealed in his law. As long as he views God as nothing but love, the sinner will miss seeing God's absolute holiness, perfect righteousness, and unflinching justice. The necessity of these attributes being satisfied by an atoning sacrifice will be ridiculed as pagan and inhumane.

II. The Nature of the Atonement—Exactly What Did Christ Accomplish by His Atoning Death on the Cross?

The *necessity* of the atonement addresses the question of "why?" The *nature* of the atonement speaks to the question of "what?" It is over the *what* that Christians disagree.

We have prepared a chart—*Two Views of the Atonement, Appendix One*—which contrasts the theological views of the two main groups and presents the Scripture verses that each uses. It is easy to see the differences in their views of the nature of the atonement. One group sees an atonement—a payment that forever removes sin—as merely a *possibility* until the sinner does his part with his free will to make the atonement effectual. In this view, the sinner's faith is "his contribution" in salvation. The other group sees the atonement of Christ as a real atonement that removes forever the sin of all those for whom it was made. This view presents the death of Christ not as merely making salvation possible for all men but actually guaranteeing that all those for whom Christ died will be saved. It is also clear that the two views are miles apart. It might be helpful to review the central differences between the two. Remember that *both groups* believe that the atonement was absolutely essential and that it is only through the atonement of Christ that any sinner can be saved.

Study the chart in *Appendix One* carefully and note the radical difference in the (1) intention of God in the atonement, (2) the actual success of the atonement, (3) the power of God alone to make the plan of salvation work, and (4) the real character, or nature of the atonement.

It is important that we recognize that salvation is the work of a triune God. When we say, "The Lord saved me," we do not mean that only the Lord Jesus Christ saved us. We mean that the Triune Lord saved us. The Lord God the Father saved us in electing grace; the Lord God the Son saved us by his atoning death; and the Lord God the Holy Spirit saved us by regenerating us and enabling us to savingly believe. We owe just as much to the Father and the Holy Spirit as we do to the blessed Lord Jesus, and our worship and praise should reflect our debt and gratitude to the Father and to the Holy Spirit for their work.

Not only is it true that each person in the Trinity has a distinct and necessary part to play in our salvation; it is just as true that the work of each will be *successful*. Success is guaranteed because all three persons in the Godhead work together toward the same goal. All those chosen by the Father were redeemed by the Son, and all those redeemed are brought by the Holy Spirit to believe the gospel. This is why the whole plan of salvation will succeed and accomplish everything God intended in its execution. Neither he who planned and brought about the death of Christ, nor those for whom that atoning death was intended, will ever be disappointed.

The core question: it is essential that we clearly understand the fundamental point of difference, as it concerns the atonement, between those who believe in free grace and those who believe in free will. The question is *not,* "For how many people did Christ die?" The essential question is, "Did the death of Christ, *in and of itself,* secure for certain the salvation of *some* people, or did his death merely make it possible for *all* men to be saved by an act of their 'free will'?" In other words, the discussion is not about *how many* people Christ died for, but rather *what Christ accomplished* by his death on the cross! What inevitably had to follow because of Christ's atoning sacrificial death? Put another way, the question is, "What is the one single ingredient that makes God's plan of salvation by grace through faith work in one person, who believes in Christ and is saved, but not in another, who rejects Christ and is lost?"

There is one sense in which it is impossible to *limit* the death of the Lord Jesus Christ. Our Lord suffered as the infinite Son of God. That is why he could suffer an eternal hell in a moment of time. It is also the reason that his death can avail for many poor sinners. Christ's death is not limited in its power in any way at all. If God had purposed to save all men without exception, Christ would not have suffered one more ounce of wrath. If only one person had been chosen to be saved, our Lord would not have suffered any less. The whole point involves the *purpose* of the Father in putting his Son on the cross. Exactly what did the Father plan to accomplish? Was it merely to give sinners a "second chance" to succeed where Adam failed, or was the atonement a carefully planned method of saving his elect? The answer of free-will religion to this vital question follows.

Answer of free-will theology: Christ died and paid the penalty for every man's sins, thereby providing, or making possible, salvation in the same way, and to the same degree, for *every man* without exception. Jesus died and paid for the sins of Judas in the identical sense that he paid for Peter's sins. All men are equally redeemed, but they must personally be willing to accept their redemption before it is effectual. An individual's redemption depends solely on his willingness to accept or reject the atonement. Either way, every man is redeemed (meaning *potentially* redeemed) because Christ died and paid for all the sins of all men. Peter was *actually* saved only because he was willing to accept the atonement that Christ had "provided" for all men. Judas was just as redeemed as Peter, and the only reason Judas was not saved was that he was not willing to accept the redemption that Christ would provide. The one and only difference between Peter and Judas was Peter's willingness to accept what Christ would do.

The gospel according to this view of free will is: Christ died for *you*. Your sins have already been paid for by the Son of God. It is no longer the "sin" question; that was settled at the cross. It is now the "Son" question. All your sins are paid for, and the only sin that will send you to hell is rejecting the redemption Christ provided for you.

In this view, all men are "redeemed" by the death of Christ. The individual need only "claim by faith" his redemption. You need only to be willing to "let Christ save you." It is Christ's intention and desire to save all men; nonetheless many will still perish. Christ can only save those who cooperate with their free will. The gospel of free will must always go back to man and his so-called free will as the ultimate *cause* of the success or failure of God's plan of salvation. It must make the affirmation that Christ died for "me personally" to be the foundation of assurance. This is radically different from the gospel message in the Scriptures.

It is obvious that the free-will view has no *real* redemption but merely a *potential*, or *hypothetical*, redemption. It is not the power of Christ's sufferings, but man, by his willingness, that is the one determining factor in every conversion.

Let us consider the answer that the religion of free grace gives to the question, "Did the death of Christ, *in and of itself,* secure for certain the salvation of *some* people, or did his death merely make it possible for *all* men to be saved by an act of their free will?" Did the atoning death of Christ actually redeem us, or did it merely make us redeem*able* if we would do our part and be willing to cooperate?

Answer of free-grace theology: although the death of Christ is of infinite value and could save ten thousand worlds of sinners, God's *intention,* or purpose, in putting his Son on the cross must be measured by its *accomplishments.* The redemptive work of Christ in and of itself *actually* redeems and assures the salvation of specific people, that is, all those given to Christ by the Father (*cf.* John 10:11, 14-16; 6:37). It does not make all men potentially redeemable *if* they will do their part by being willing to be saved. Christ's death is not just *provisional* in its nature; rather, it actually *secures* salvation for all of its objects.

The gospel, according to this view, is Christ died for *sinners.* He saves every sinner that comes to him; and every sinner that the Father has given to Christ will come to him. That promise of salvation includes sinners as bad as you and me.

In this view, Christ actually bought a people for himself out of every tribe and tongue. Christ's desire "to seek" and his success "to save" are fully realized because his intention and accomplishments involve the same people. He saves all without exception that he seeks. He does not *seek all* and save *some.*

III. The Problem with Terminology

Limited atonement sounds very narrow as compared to *unlimited* atonement. This comparison leads to misconception and meaningless controversy. We maintain that *all Christians believe in limited atonement.* The biblical doctrine of hell supports this statement. We all believe that the ultimate benefits of the atonement are limited to those who believe in Christ. The lost man does not share in the benefits of the death of Christ. Of course, the Arminian will insist that the only reason the lost man does not benefit from the atonement is that his free will chooses not to benefit. That is begging the question. The real question is *not*, "Is the atonement limited?"—as I just said, the fact that people are in hell and will be there for all eternity answers that question—but rather the question is, *"Who does the limiting, God or man?"* Does God's sovereign grace and purpose dictate the ultimate success or failure of the redemptive work of Christ, or does the "sovereign" and fickle will of man decide whether God's intentions and purposes will be realized?

To repeat, all Christians limit the death of Christ! The debate is over the *cause* of the limitation; is it God's grace or man's will? Those who teach free will believe that man's will limits the success of God's great plan of redemption. God then has an *unlimited* purpose—to redeem all men— but a *limited* power; he can only actually redeem those who make themselves willing and "allow" God to redeem them. We who believe free or sovereign grace hold to the exact opposite. We are convinced that God has a limited *purpose*—to redeem his people—and an unlimited *power*— to secure their consent and make them willing "in the day of his power" (Ps. 110:3).

It is not the *limited* aspect but the *particular* aspect of the atonement that the Bible emphasizes. Christ died for *specific people* and actually secured a complete salvation for each one of those for whom he died. He did not die for an undefined group, that is, for everyone in general but no one in particular, and then hope that some of that general group would be willing to give him a chance. Isaiah says,

"He shall see his seed." As our Lord died on the cross, he knew for whom he was dying and also knew they would be saved. The issue is not with *how many* but with the *nature* of his sufferings.

The terms *limited* and *unlimited* presented as opposites sound as if the *limited* view is narrow and the other, *un*limited, is magnanimous. We must remember that the "five points of Calvinism" have a negative slant precisely because they were negations (by the Synod of Dort) against the negations of the followers of James Arminius, who opposed the established truth of the Reformation.

We could, perhaps, more clearly present the issue by using the the terms *effectual* atonement versus *ineffectual* atonement, or *efficient* atonement versus *inefficient* atonement. These opposite terms are far closer to the crux of the matter than are *limited* and *unlimited*. Let the free-will universalist honestly admit that he preaches an *ineffectual* and *inefficient* atonement. Let him admit that he does not have a real atonement, but only a hypothetical one. The atonement of free-will religion can only be effective and actually atone for sin when man's free will allows it to do so. This makes salvation depend ultimately on man for its success. In reality, this view is teaching that man's free-will faith is the real redeeming factor in conversion. The mighty atonement of Christ is unable to accomplish God's earnest desire or purpose until the even mightier free will of man consents to allow it to happen.

The choice is *not* simply between *universal* and *particular* atonement. The choice is between an atonement that actually atones and an atonement that is purely *hypothetical* and does not really atone. If we are consistent and honest, the real difference is between particular *atonement* and universal *salvation*. Why are some men in hell paying the penalty for their sins if Christ has already paid the penalty for all of the sins of all men? What about those who *were already in hell when Christ died?* Surely the Father did not punish Christ for men like Ahab who were, at that very moment, in hell enduring the punishment for their sin.

We are not discussing the *extent* of the atonement in terms of *how many*. We are discussing the *nature* of the atonement, which does not pertain to the *number* of people for whom Christ died. The nature of the atonement deals with the question of the actual accomplishment of Christ in his death. If people insist on talking about the extent of the atonement, then we must ask, "The extent in relationship to *what?*" If we mean the extent of the atonement in relationship to God's sovereign purpose, then we will measure God's purpose in the atonement by what it actually accomplishes. The atoning work of Christ will secure every thing that God intended it to accomplish. If someone starts at the other end and asks, "For whom was the atonement made?" we will ask him, "Who will ultimately be saved?" In both cases the answer must be identical. If Christ died for all, then all will be saved; if only some sinners are saved, it is because it was for them alone that Christ died.

We must see that the disagreement is over salvation as merely a *possibility* (in which case the atonement is only hypothetical) and salvation as a *certainty* (because the atonement is a *real* atonement). That is the heart of the difference.

C.H. Spurgeon was often accused of preaching a very "narrow" atonement. His opponents said their atonement, or bridge to heaven, was as wide as the whole world, and his was not. Spurgeon responded by saying, "I grant that my atonement, or bridge to heaven, is more narrow than yours. However, your bridge only goes halfway across the chasm, and mine goes all the way. In your scheme, the sinner's will must furnish the other half."

IV. Particular Atonement is the Historic Doctrine of the Church

Augustine, Luther, Calvin, Knox, and the great Confessions of Faith neither deny the doctrine of limited atonement, nor do they confirm it. Until the actual question of the extent of the atonement was raised at the Synod of Dort, the church had not expressly declared the doctrine of limited atonement. Still, this does not deny that the church was in agreement with that which Dort confirmed. The church historically has been in essential agreement with the doctrine of limited atonement, but only implicitly. Universal atonement is the new and novel doctrine when one looks at all of church history. Neither creeds nor great leaders prove what the church *must* believe, but rather what she *has* believed. Being old or being found in a creed does not make a doctrine true. The historic creeds are like guardrails along the side of a highway. They must never be confused with the road itself. The Bible alone is the road, but the guardrails are a great asset in *keeping one on the road.* When anyone sees a doctrine that no one else in the history of the church has ever seen, he should have an abundance of very clear biblical proof to support his position. It is well to be concerned with any "new" truth that all of the great saints of God missed for nearly two thousand years.

V. What Does the Word of God Itself Say About the Death of Christ? Here are three preliminary biblical facts:

ONE: Christ's death was *voluntary,* therefore he has every right to totally control its results. In no sense whatever was God obligated to send Christ to die for sinners.

> *...I lay down my life....no man taketh it from me, but I lay it down of myself....* (John 10:17, 18)

> *For God so loved the world, that he gave his only begotten Son....* (John 3:16)

> *Him, being delivered by the determinate counsel and foreknowledge of God...* (Acts 2:23)

> *Yet it pleased the Lord to bruise him; he hath put him to grief: when thou shalt make his soul an offering for sin...* (Isa. 53:10)

God was in complete control at Calvary. This, as are all things done by God, was a most carefully planned and executed event. God was not compelled in any way to give his Son up to death, nor was Christ under any constraint to come and die. If it was completely a *voluntary* act on the part of God, should he not be permitted, and expected, to (1) dispense its benefits as he sovereignly chooses, and (2) assure the success of its planned results by the exercise of his power?

TWO: Christ's death was also *vicarious*. The word *vicarious* means "acting on behalf of or as representing another," or "something performed or suffered by one person with the results accruing to the benefit or advantage of another." The key idea is representation in such a way that one party literally stands in the place of another and is actually treated as if he were the other person. The classic text is 2 Corinthians 5:21:

> *For he* [the Father] *hath made* [treated him as if he were a sinner] *him* [the Son], *who knew no sin to be sin* [treated him as our substitute] *for us* [guilty sinners], *that we might be made the righteousness of God* [be treated as if we are as righteous as Christ] *in him.*

If Christ actually stood in my place and bore my sin, then I can never be punished for that sin. If Christ literally stands as a substitute in the place of any particular individual, then that individual must be brought to salvation and be eternally saved. Substitutionary, or vicarious, atonement must actually secure a real salvation for all for whom Christ died, or else it is not truly vicarious. If Christ acted as a real and true substitute for his people, then all of his people will be saved. If he actually collected the wages (death) which they earned by their sin, then all for whom he died will, yea *must*, collect the wages (righteousness) that he earned in his obedient life and death.

> For the wages of sin is death, but the gift of God is eternal life
> through Jesus Christ our Lord. (Rom. 6:23)

To say that Christ died a vicarious death in the place of all sinners but not all of those sinners will be saved is a contradiction in terms.

There are four Greek words used in the New Testament Scriptures that show the true vicarious nature of the sufferings of Christ. Each word contributes a distinct nuance of thought to the atoning work of Christ. When these four shades of meaning are put together, we see clearly that Christ's atonement was totally effectual in the salvation of all for whom that atonement was made. The biblical meaning of these four words, *ransom, substitute, reconciliation,* and *propitiation,* must be bled of their true meaning before it is possible to believe in universal atonement. Let us examine these four words.

The first word is λυτρόω *(lutroo)*, and it means "to release on receipt of ransom."[1] It is akin to the Greek word λύτρον *(lutron)* which, as *lutroo,* means "the ransom for a life...the redemption price of a slave...the price of a captive."[2] These words describe the process of releasing a person who is all tied up in debt and needs cash to get free. The cash is the ransom price that sets him free. It redeems him from the bondage of debt. Once the cash is paid, the debtor is set free. The same idea is set forth in our spiritual

---

[1] W.E. Vine, *Vine's Expository Dictionary of Old and New Testament Words* (Grand Rapids: Fleming H. Revell, 1981).

[2] Ibid.

redemption. We were in the marketplace of sin because we had "sold ourselves under sin." Christ shed his blood as the ransom price to "set us free." The key truth in the word *redeem* is that freedom *must* follow the price being paid, or there is no real ransom. When our Lord went into the marketplace of sin and paid the ransom price in his own blood to buy the freedom of sinners, he did not come out of the marketplace with his basket half empty. He did not leave behind any for whom he had paid the ransom price. Christ did not pay the price and purchase sinners, and then leave some of those sinners still in the marketplace of sin. "...the Son of man came...to give his life a ransom for many" (Matt. 20:28). The "many" for whom our Lord gave his life as a ransom are the elect. All that he redeemed will be saved. "...ye were not *redeemed* with corruptible things, like silver and gold...But with the precious *blood of Christ....* " (1 Pet. 1:18, 19). The blood of Christ did not make us merely redeemable, but it actually redeemed us.

One of the fundamental ideas in the word *redeem* is that of setting someone, or something, "free by buying it back with a redemption price." Think of a pawnshop where something is bought back that has been lost or pawned. In Scripture, sinners are bought out of the marketplace of sin by the redemption price of Christ's blood.

There are four different Greek words that are often translated *redeem* or *redemption* in our English Bibles. When put together, these words give us a good picture of redemption. However, they are also sometimes translated with other English words.

1. The first word is found in Romans 3:24, "Being justified freely by his grace through the redemption that is in Christ Jesus." It is απολυτρωσις *(apolutrosis)* and means "deliverance." The same Greek word, shown here in italics, is used in the following verses: "In whom we have *redemption* through his blood, the forgiveness of sins, according to the riches of his grace..." (Eph. 1:7). Hebrews 11:35 translates the same word differently: "Women received their dead raised to life again: and others were tortured, not accepting *deliverance*...." These women could have been "redeemed," or delivered, but they were not willing to pay the redemption price which was to deny their faith in Christ. They chose death over redemption.

The root from which this word comes is λυτρον *(lutron)* and is used as follows: "Even as the Son of man came not to be ministered unto, but to minister, and to give his life a *ransom* for many" (Matt. 20:28). "But we trusted that it had been he who should have *redeemed* Israel...." (Luke 24:21). "Forasmuch as ye know that ye were not *redeemed* with corruptible things, as silver and gold...But with the precious blood of Christ, as of a lamb without blemish and without spot" (1 Pet. 1:18, 19). The idea is that we are *delivered* from the wrath of God because we have been loosed from our sins and the punishment those sins deserve. The blood of Christ is always the ransom price that is paid to deliver or redeem us. This is why the child of God can never "come into judgment" (see John 5:24).

2. The second Greek word is αγοραζω *(agorazo)*, and it means to "go to market" or "buy." Here are some texts that

use this word. "Send them away, that they may go into the country round about, and into the villages, and *buy* themselves bread...." (Mark 6:36). "For ye are *bought* with a price; therefore, glorify God in your body...." (1 Cor. 6:20). "And they sang a new song, saying, Thou art worthy to take the book, and to open its seals; for thou wast slain, and hast *redeemed* us to God by thy blood out of every kindred, and tongue, and people, and nation" (Rev. 5:9).

The biblical writers deliberately placed particular emphasis on going to the market and buying something by applying a price. In reference to the gospel, it means that Christ went into the marketplace of sin, where we were slaves of sin, and he purchased our freedom with his own precious blood.

Slaves made up over fifty percent of the population of Rome in Paul's day. The largest markets by far were the slave markets. Men and women were stripped and examined the way horses and cows are examined at an auction and then sold and purchased by the highest bidder. Paul's readers would have clearly understood his meaning and use of this word. They would have realized that our Lord did not leave the market with his basket half full. He did not leave behind, still in their shackles, some for whom he had paid the ransom price.

The word *redemption* is one of the words sometimes changed in certain modern translations or paraphrases of the Scriptures. *Good News for Modern Man* totally eliminates the words *redeem* and *redemption* from the New Testament. They also eliminate, as much as is possible, the word *blood*.

They change *redeem* to "set free" and change *blood* to "his death." When Peter says we were "redeemed...by his blood," it comes out "set free...by his death" (*cf.* 1 Pet. 1:18, 19).

Now I'm sure some are thinking, "But John, isn't that exactly what you have been telling us that the word means?" It is true that redeem means to set free and to shed blood is to take life. However, there is one important ingredient missing in the meaning of each word when redemption becomes only "set free" and blood becomes only "his death." If I went down to the local jail and put sleeping powder into the jailer's coffee, I could, after he fell asleep, steal his keys and set every prisoner free, but I surely have not redeemed them. This word means more than merely to set free. It is setting free by paying a necessary ransom price. The ransom price is the blood offered to God as proof that a life had been sacrificed on the altar. It is not just his death that is vital; it is the *kind of death* that he died. Christ died under the just wrath of God in the place of guilty sinners. It was a vicarious death offered to God as a necessary price to appease his just wrath. This is Paul's argument in Galatians 3:13, 14. The atonement is first presented to God before it is presented to us.

Both liberals and proponents of free-will theology dislike this word because they misunderstand the essential character of God as being holy. The liberal actually changes the word, and the typical evangelical changes its meaning. The latter will speak of Christ redeeming sinners, when they really mean that Christ made it possible for sinners to redeem themselves by their faith. If their gospel offer is to be consistent with their doctrinal beliefs, they would say, "Christ has made your redemption a possibility but not a certainty. Only you can finish the job with your faith."

3. The third Greek word is a very interesting word. It is περιουσιος *(periousios)*, and it means "of one's own possession, one's own" and qualifies the noun λαος *(laos)*, "people," in Titus 2:14.[3] The idea of owning something that one dearly loves is bound up in the meaning of the word. It sets apart the people of God in this sense: "Christ's work of redemption has created for God a people that is a costly possession or special treasure."[4] The word is translated in our English Bibles by the word *peculiar*.

Words are losing their meaning in our society. I refuse to use the word *gay* to describe a homosexual. I have counseled many homosexuals in my ministry and have never yet met one that was *gay* or truly happy. There is no group of people who are more in need of love, affection, and attempts by Christians to give them the gospel than the homosexual community. They hate themselves, they hate God, and they hate everyone else. They desperately need the gospel of sovereign love and grace. They are anything but gay in the traditional sense of that word.

---

[3] Ibid.

[4] Gerhard Kittel and Gerhard Friedrich, eds., *The Theological Dictionary of the New Testament, Abridged in One Volume* (Grand Rapids: William B. Eerdmans Publishing Co., 1985).

Today the word *peculiar* is often used in the sense of *odd*, but originally it meant something entirely different. When I am teaching about this word, I will often say to a lady, "Suppose your husband publicly said, 'My wife is the most peculiar woman I have ever met.' How would you feel?" The lady usually says, "I would bop him on the head." I then add confusion by saying, "This word 'peculiar' originally meant *cows*." Now the lady is ready to bop *me* on the head!

The word *peculiar* comes from the word *pecus* and means cattle.[5] This word is found in deeds. A deed states that a house was bought for the "pecuniary value of $150,000.00." The word *pecuniary (pecus)* means the *real* value as measured in dollars. Originally the pecuniary value of things was measured in terms of cows. The more cows, the more pecus value. If the husband who said his wife was the most peculiar woman in the world was using the word in the biblical sense, then he was saying, "My wife is the most precious possession that I have."

Christians are indeed the most peculiar things in all of the universe. They have been purchased at the greatest price possible. God himself—in the person of his Son—is the purchase price with which he has bought Christians to be his own personal possession. With this definition in mind, we can better understand the meaning of Titus 2:14:

---

[5] *American Dictionary of the English Language,* 1828, s. v. "peculiar." PECULIAR, a. [L. *peculiaris,* from *peculium,* one's own property, from *pecus,* cattle.] Interestingly, none of the definitions given uses the word *odd.*

"Who gave himself for us that he might redeem us from all iniquity, and purify unto himself a *peculiar* people, zealous of good works."

4. The fourth word εξαγοραζω *(exagorazo)* is the same as the second word except it has an *ek* in front of it. This word "denotes 'to buy out' (ex for *ek*), especially of purchasing a slave with a view to his freedom."[6] The word *ek* means out of or exit. The word is used in the following passages: "Christ hath *redeemed* us from the curse of the law, being made a curse for us; for it is written, Cursed is every one that hangeth on a tree" (Gal. 3:13). "To *redeem* them that were under the law, that we might receive the adoption of sons" (Gal. 4:5).

This word does not just mean purchased *at* the market, but purchased *out of* the market. When a house is sold, it is placed on the market. If it does not sell in a given period, it is taken off the market for a while; it may be put back on the market later. The texts that use this word refer to God's effectual work of redemption in which sinners are purchased out of the market *forever*. The two texts in Galatians mentioned above means that believers are forever out from under the law and its just curse. The law cannot condemn them. They have been purchased and forever put out of its reach.

Once, a Van Gogh painting had been put up for auction, and the highest bid was nine million dollars. The owner

---

[6] W.E. Vine, *Vine's Expository Dictionary of Old and New Testament Words* (Grand Rapids: Fleming H. Revell, 1981).

refused to sell since he had paid over eleven million for the painting. He waited a year and then put it back on the market. Sometimes a painting is either purchased by, or given to, the National Museum of Art. When this is done, that particular painting can never again be put up for auction and sold. It is the "peculiar possession" of the museum to be enjoyed by the entire populace. Believers have been purchased by God and placed in his museum of grace. They can never again be put on the auction block in the market place of sin. The church will reveal the power and beauty of his grace throughout all eternity. Paul says that believers are "his workmanship." Just as an artist takes a piece of blank canvas and uses various colors of paint to produce a masterpiece or "work of art," so God has taken pieces of useless junk that were ruined by sin and created spiritual works of art that will shine throughout eternity. Redeemed sinners are living testimonies to the power of his love and grace.

Sometimes we read a verse and never stop to really discover its meaning. For many years, I read Romans 8:18 without recognizing its actual point. Paul is not talking about the amazing glory that shall be revealed *to* us in eternity. That, of course, is true, but it is not his point in this text. *Believers themselves are the glory of God!* The text says "the glory that shall be revealed *in* us" not "*to* us." Just as men and women walk through an art gallery and admire the amazing work of great artists, so the whole universe will admire the wisdom and power of God's grace as it is displayed in his people. What a tremendous thought! We should be living epistles now, even as we shall be revealers of his glory in eternity.

A classic illustration of the truth of redemption is found in Hosea 3:1-3.

> *Then said the LORD unto me, Go yet, love a woman beloved of her friend, yet an adulteress, according to the love of the LORD toward the children of Israel, who look to other gods, and love flagons of wine. So I bought her for myself for fifteen pieces of silver, and for an homer of barley, and an half homer of barley. And I said unto her, Thou shalt abide for me many days; thou shalt not play the harlot, and thou shalt not be for another man; so will I also be for thee.*

Hosea's wife, Gomer, was unfaithful to him. It is quite possible that his two sons were not really his own sons but had been fathered by a different man. Gomer left Hosea and openly practiced prostitution. She was finally reduced to slavery and was on the auction block to be sold to the highest bidder. God told Hosea to buy back his own former betrothed wife. Hosea was to love her "as I have loved Israel." She is a picture of Israel's (and our) nakedness, sin, and unfaithfulness.

Gomer did not come back to Hosea as a slave, as she actually deserved, but as a wife who was dearly beloved. She did not come back to be hated and punished, but to be "loved as I have loved Israel." That is grace.

There was once a preacher whose wife had become an alcoholic. She was a great embarrassment to him. One Sunday morning after his sermon, the preacher was shaking hands with the congregation at the door. A taxicab pulled up, and a drunken woman got out and lurched across the pavement. Just as she reached the place where the preacher was standing, she started to fall, and the preacher reached out and caught her in his arms. Everyone waited to see what he would do or say. While everyone was watching, he drew his wife to his chest and kissed her on her lips. She was his wife, and he loved her.

That is exactly what God has done many times with every one of us. We have played the harlot and given our affections to false gods. We have been drunk with the allurements of the world. How many times could God have justly divorced us and said, "I am sick of your sin and rebellion. I am tired of your halfhearted love. I am done with you forever!" Do not our hearts cry out, "Many times, many times"? But our God will never divorce his people that he choose in Christ and bought with the blood of his Son. He graciously brings us back to himself and opens the wellsprings of our heart; we weep in confession of our sin and with faith believe in the sure hope of his grace.

Bible translation is a very difficult job. This is especially so in a culture that has no written language and a very limited vocabulary. I once read about a missionary in Africa trying to translate the word *redemption* into a particular tribal language. No one could understand what he was trying to teach. He tried every way possible to explain the concept but got nowhere. Finally the oldest man in the tribe said, "You mean that Jesus died to take our necks out." The missionary asked what the man meant. The old man remembered the days of slave trading when men were caught and shackled with a steel ring around their necks and then tied with a chain to other men likewise shackled. As these helpless captives were being marched to the ship to be taken to England and America to be sold as slaves, a village chief might see one of his people in the line. If he chose to do so, he could trade with the slave trader and give him some ivory for the slave's release. The trader would then unlock the chain ring around the slave's neck and set him free. He would "take his neck out of the ring."

That is exactly what our Lord did for his people. He took their necks out of the chain of sin. The chains that held them were stronger than any steel and could not be broken by any human means. It took nothing less than the blood atonement of the Lamb of God to break those shackles. The Bible used by that particular tribe stills contains, "Jesus died to take our necks out," and everyone knows what it means. I am sure no one could imagine the village chief paying the price for a slave and watching that slave nonetheless go on in his chains into slavery.

Notice the contrast between the biblical use of the word *redeem* and that of those who hold to universal atonement. The latter teach that Christ's death merely made it *possible* for us to be redeemed, but *our faith* is the means whereby God is enabled to actually redeem us. In the final analysis, the implication is that we redeem ourselves by our faith.

The second of the four primary New Testament words used to show the vicarious nature of Christ's suffering is *substitute*. Often Christ's substitutionary death is mentioned as a deed on behalf of his people (cf. 1 Cor. 15:3; Rom. 5:8). The Greek word is υπερ (*huper*), which shows that Christ suffered on behalf of his people. He suffered in our place as our substitute. Something happened to him so that the same thing would not happen to us. That is the force of the statement *for us*. Christ died for his people. This is what is meant when we speak of Christ's substitutionary death.

There was an occasion when my daughter came home from high school all excited. She exclaimed, "We won! We won! We suffered a broken leg and got beaten up very badly, but we won." I looked at her and said, "I do not see a cast on your leg, and your skirt is not even wrinkled. What is this 'we got beat up' bit?" When she said, "*We* won!" she meant the high school football team had won the championship game. One player had indeed broken his leg, and most of the players were badly battered. However, my daughter said, "*We* won" instead of "*they* won." She meant that the football team represented her school, and therefore they represented her. When they won, she won, and when they lost, she lost. They did what they did as representatives of the school. This illustrates how Christ represented his people. When he conquered sin and death, his people did also, since he conquered those things in their place. Just as Adam, acting as the representative of his race, plunged all that he represented—the whole human race— into sin and death, so the Lord Jesus Christ, acting as the representative of a new race—the chosen of God—raised his people out of death and sin into life and righteousness.

A football player sitting on the bench does not feel the shoving and tackling taking place on the field. When the ball is snapped, two large guards from the other team may smash into a tackle on his team, but he feels nothing at all. If, however, the coach sends him into the game as a "substitute," he will feel something the next time the ball is snapped. This illustrates the meaning of Christ as a substitute. He took the place of his people as a substitute in a duel with sin, death, and the law. He endured, on the cross, the wrath of God in their place. When he defeated sin and death, they also defeated sin and death because he was doing that _for them_ as their substitute. When he fulfilled the law and died under its curse, they also met every claim of the law and endured its full wrath. Christ literally died _instead of them_. He alone did battle with sin, death, the grave, Satan himself, and the holy law of God. He defeated their full power _as his people's substitute_.

The third word is _reconciliation_. The Greek is χαταλλασσω _(katallasso)_, and it means "to change, exchange (especially of money); hence, of persons, to change from enmity to friendship, to reconcile."[7] Roman and Greek money was "profane" and could not be given as an offering in the temple. All secular money had to be "reconciled," or exchanged, into an acceptable form. It had to be exchanged into temple money. This is why the moneychangers were in the temple. Jesus was not angry with the moneychangers because they were in the temple, but because they were charging unfair exchange rates.

---

[7] Ibid.

The following text is important. It states exactly what it is that reconciles sinners to God. "...we were *reconciled* to God by the *death* of his Son...." (Rom. 5:10).

Question: what makes a child of God "different" (so as to be reconciled) in God's sight? Is it free grace and the blood of Christ, or is it the free will of man and the man's faith? What is the one essential difference between Judas and Peter? Were they both equally redeemed by the death of Christ, but Judas was not reconciled because he was not willing to claim, by faith, his redemption? Is Peter's faith the *essential* factor that reconciled him to God? It cannot be both ways. The answer is either reconciliation by free will or reconciliation by free grace. The biblical words which speak of the atonement must either be bled of their true meaning, or particular redemption must be accepted. There cannot be a true redemption and then a hypothetical reconciliation. Either both redemption and reconciliation are effective for all of those for whom the redemption was made, or else both are only hypothetical possibilities totally dependent on man's free will for success.

Those who are saved are indeed "justified by faith." Faith is absolutely essential in salvation. Faith as the *means* by which salvation comes to a sinner and faith as the *cause and foundation* of salvation are two different things. The Bible never teaches faith as the *ground* by which anyone is reconciled to God. *Faith* cannot be the ground of reconciliation. The atoning *death of Christ* alone is what makes the difference. Faith is the means, but even faith is a gift of God. Faith is not the sinner's contribution, actually the one essential component, by which he is redeemed and reconciled. No, faith is part of the salvation gift purchased by Christ and given to his elect through the preaching of the gospel and sanctification by the Holy Spirit. Believers were chosen to be given faith. "...God hath from the beginning chosen you to salvation through *sanctification* of the Spirit and *belief* of the truth" (2 Thess. 2:13). See also 1 Peter 1:2.

An examination of the places where the word *reconcile* is used will verify that the above fact is an essential aspect of the biblical doctrine of Christ's atonement (Rom. 5:10, 11; 2 Cor. 5:18, 19; Eph. 2:16; Col. 1:20-22).

The fourth word showing a specific aspect of the atonement is *propitiation*. The bitterest criticism I have ever seen against the biblical doctrine of the atonement has been that leveled by liberals against this word *propitiation*. Propitiation describes that priestly work of Christ by which he removed God's just anger and wrath against his people by satisfying the holy character of God through the substitutionary sacrifice of himself to God. Christ's propitiatory work secured, on righteous terms, his people's acceptance and reconciliation with God. This was accomplished by Christ enduring all of God's just wrath against his people's sin. See Rom. 3:25; Heb. 2:17; 1 John 2:2; 4:10 for the places this word is used in the New Testament Scriptures.

The reason why there is agreement between both the liberal and those of today's evangelicalism in opposition to the word *propitiation* is because the religion of free will does not fully take into account either the true nature of the sinner or the true character of God. Its adherents do not seem to believe that man is totally depraved and therefore justly under the wrath of God. Neither group can imagine that man is so desperately helpless that he is in reality "*dead* in trespasses and sin" (Eph. 2:1-3). Since both the liberal and the adherents of free-will theology teach that God is basically love instead of holy, they dismiss any idea of an offering of blood being necessary to turn away his just wrath. Love does not need to be appeased or placated. The very idea is an insult to God. Of course, they are right, *if God is nothing but love.* We agree that love does not need to be pacified since it cannot get angry. But God is more than love; he is also holy, just, and righteous. The psalmist says, "God is angry with the wicked every day" (cf. Ps. 7:11-13). The psalmist also tells us why God is angry with the wicked. "The LORD trieth the righteous: but the wicked and him that loveth violence his soul hateth. Upon the wicked he shall rain snares, fire and brimstone, and an horrible tempest: this shall be the portion of their cup. **For the righteous LORD loveth righteousness;** his countenance doth behold the upright" (Ps. 11:5-7). A true liberal cannot believe that man is totally depraved, and some evangelicals cannot see the awful, but very real, effects of total depravity.

Thus far it has been demonstrated from Scripture that the death of Christ is both *voluntary* and *vicarious.* We now look at the third and final aspect of the atonement and see that it was *victorious.*

THREE: The death of Christ was *victorious.* Every man for whom Christ died will be saved. His death will secure everything that God intended. It is at this point that the crucial theological difference between the religion of free will and free grace comes to the surface. There is nothing hypothetical about the following texts (emphasis mine).

> ...he **shall** save **his people** from their sins. (Matt. 1:21)

> ...the Good Shepherd giveth his life for the sheep. I am the Good Shepherd, and know my **sheep**.... other sheep I have... them also I **must bring**, and they **shall** hear my voice.... (John 10:11, 14–16)

These texts speak of Christ actually accomplishing something in his death. One cannot give the four words just covered (ransom, substitute, reconcile, and propitiate) their biblical meaning and still hold to universal *atonement* without also accepting universal *salvation.* One is forced to either give these words a hypothetical sense, and thus deny their biblical content, or else he must believe in universal salvation.

The universal atonement of free-will theology teaches the following:

(1) A *redemption* that leaves men still not free or actually redeemed. They are merely redeem*able* and will *actually be redeemed* only if they are willing to contribute faith as their part of the deal.

(2) A *reconciliation* that leaves men still estranged from God and lost. Reconciliation is potentially possible for *all* sinners, but it is not absolutely certain for *any specific* sinner unless the sinner does his part by being willing to believe.

(3) A *propitiation* that leaves men still under the wrath of God. The propitiatory sacrifice of Christ merely makes God willing to be propitiated but does not actually propitiate him until the sinner furnishes the necessary faith.

(4) A *substitutionary* death that still makes the sinner himself help pay the debt for sin. Christ did not actually bear the sins of his people on the cross as a substitute but he is willing to do so *if...*

In all four of these precepts, Christ's death is not victorious until the sinner makes his contribution. In each case, the universal atonement view is forced to have two different meanings for the same word. When the four words for atonement are applied to a believer, then the words are given their true biblical meaning. However, when the universalist, in his preaching, applies the identical words to the "world," then the words must be emptied of their biblical content. The same words now become only hypothetical possibilities. The nature of Christ's sufferings provide half of what is necessary to atone for sin, and the sinner's faith provides the other half.

I am glad that such a system is not the basis for my hope of heaven.

VI. Some Clear Implications

I was not always convinced that limited atonement was a biblical doctrine. I saw the other four points of Calvinism at least five years before God taught me the truth about the nature of the atonement. I remember tearing in half Arthur Pink's booklet, *Was the Sin Question Finally Settled at the*

Cross? and throwing it into the wastebasket saying, "I will never believe that!" I now not only believe the truth of limited atonement, but, along with J.I. Packer, affirm that this truth is the very heart of true evangelical faith.

Some have tried to convince me that I could not have been saved when I tore Pink's booklet in half. One man has vehemently urged me to repent of my false conversion and admit I did not become a true child of God until I became a five-point Calvinist. Many years ago, we published a booklet entitled *Decisional Regeneration*. We were trying to show that Arminianism really teaches that a sinner's decision has the power to regenerate his heart and make him a child of God. *"Doctrinal* Regeneration" would be a good label for the brand of Calvinism that insists that only five-point Calvinists are truly saved. In reality, these people give correct theology the same power that the Arminian gives to his decision. We insist that neither the sinner's will nor correct theology can give a dead sinner life.

Peter was a saved man when he said, "Not so, Lord." Our Lord rebuked him and said, "Get thee behind me Satan." J.C. Ryle correctly observes, "Just because God has sanctified your heart does not mean that he has totally sanctified your brains and taught you all the truth in one instant." A true child of God can be very mixed up, both theologically and emotionally, and still be in Christ. It is better to be a confused and emotionally upset saint on his way to heaven than to be a well-adjusted and theologically correct, but unregenerate, person on his way to hell.

Holding firmly to the truth of sovereign grace is not absolute proof that a person knows the sovereign Lord in a way of saving faith.

The importance of understanding the Doctrines of Grace is not to be minimized. One's theological understanding does not save his soul, but it does shape the way he understands and preaches the gospel. Sincere Christians, who in their hearts are right with God, can make injudicious statements which proceed from erroneous theology. That was my problem while struggling with limited atonement for over five years.

The following passage is part of a Christmas sermon preached and printed over forty years ago by a man named Noel Smith. He was a professor in a Bible Baptist seminary in the midwest, with a reputation of being a very godly man and a good instructor. Noel Smith rejected Calvinism and embraced universal atonement. This excerpt from his sermon is an example of a man's theology producing statements that are disturbing in their implications.

> Knowing God as I do through the revelation He has given me of Himself in His Word, when I am told that God is *not willing that any should perish but that all should come to repentance,* I know it means that the Triune God has done, is doing, always will do, all that the Triune God can do to save every man, woman, and child on this earth.
>
> If it does not mean that, then tell me I pray you, what does it mean?
>
> What is hell? It is infinite negation. It is infinite chaos. And it is more than that. I tell you, and I say it with profound

reverence, hell is a ghastly monument to the failure of God to save the multitudes that are there. I say it reverently, I say it with every nerve in my body tense; sinners go to hell because God Himself cannot save them. He did all He could. He failed.[8]

Noel Smith's candid statement is shocking. Few preachers, no matter how Arminian they are in their theology, will say publicly that they believe "hell is a ghastly monument to the failure of God." If, however, Noel Smith's understanding of 2 Peter 3:9 is correct, no other conclusion is feasible. Mr. Smith is both honest and totally consistent with his view of universal atonement.

If such a great effort on God's part does not accomplish his intention, then what other word can be used to describe the situation but failure? What is wrong with clearly and publicly stating that "God almighty failed" to accomplish the thing his heart desired the most? If, as Smith concludes, "sinners go to hell because God himself cannot save them," then God indeed failed! If God "did all he could" and still was not able to accomplish his heart's desire, then on what grounds is Noel Smith to be faulted for concluding, as he logically does, that "he (God) failed?" If the premise is correct, then the conclusion must also be true. The only real difference between Noel Smith and most evangelical preachers today is that Mr. Smith was honest and consistent with his theology. He rationally followed his position to its logical conclusion.

---

[8] Noel Smith, *Baptist Tribune,* 12, 13.

If universal atonement and Smith's interpretation of 2 Peter 3:9 are both accurate, adherents to the free will system should rejoice that Smith has stated their position clearly and logically. If (1) Christ endured the wrath of God for "every man, woman, and child on earth," and (2) if it was God's heartfelt purpose to save "every man, woman, and child on this earth," and (3) "God has done, is doing, always will do, all he can do to save every man, woman, and child on this earth," then Mr. Smith's conclusion is correct. God indeed failed in this system.

C.H. Spurgeon also clearly saw the same logical truth as Noel Smith. Spurgeon made almost the identical statement that Smith did, except he opposed Smith's position. Here is a classic statement from the prince of preachers:

> Once again, if it was Christ's intention to save all men, how deplorably has He been disappointed, for we have His own testimony that there is a lake which burneth with fire and brimstone, and into that pit of woe have been cast some of the very persons who, according to the theory of universal redemption [the view advocated by Noel Smith], were bought with His blood.[9]

The difference between Smith and Spurgeon is that they are on different sides of the "if." Spurgeon is decrying the very doctrine that Smith is holding up as a great gospel fact. Both men were Baptist preachers, proclaiming what they believed to be the gospel. The century that separates them has seen an astonishing change in that gospel. It is amazing that Spurgeon could openly denounce the exact

---

[9] C.H. Spurgeon, *Sermons on Sovereignty*, 11.

doctrine that men today preach as the foundation of their whole system of theology. Neither Spurgeon nor this author can be rightly accused of burning straw dummies. The zealous and honest Noel Smith took care of that with great clarity.

It may be embarrassing, and men may try to deny its implications, but the only alternatives to limited atonement are either (1) universal salvation, which is at least consistent with the belief that God is all powerful, or (2) the failure of God, as Mr. Smith's legitimate application shows. There really are only three choices. Either (1) everyone is going to be saved, (2) God miserably failed, or (3) particular redemption is true.

To those completely convinced of the validity of universal atonement and free will, the doctrine of particular atonement based on God's sovereign, electing love seems to be unfair and even cruel. The doctrine of universal atonement seems to magnify and broaden God's love. Actually, the exact opposite is the case, and Mr. Smith, by being consistent, honest, and courageous enough to set forth the ever present, but never spoken, legitimate conclusion and application of universal atonement, has proven the point better than any Calvinist ever could.

The result of the doctrine of universal atonement is manifested in the elevated position of man and his free will as the determining factor in God's plan of salvation. This exalting of free will and extolling of universal love may at first appear to honor God, but it will ultimately be seen as the first blow at dethroning God and corrupting the very spring of grace from which the gospel flows freely to sinful man. It is a hollow victory that proves that God is all love by reducing him to impotence before man's almighty will. There is no triumph in declaring that God's greatest act in history, the cross of Christ, was a colossal failure because man's "almighty" free will refused to give God a chance.

Bibically literate believers may wonder, "Whatever possessed Noel Smith to make such statements?"

The answer to that question is found in the statements themselves. Mr. Smith was possessed with a burning desire to exalt the love and grace of God. The title of his sermon was "The Middle Man," and he was extolling the incarnation of our Lord Jesus Christ. Mr. Smith was exalting the amazing love of God in giving his only begotten Son to die on the cross. It was Smith's purpose to so exalt this great display of God's love that his hearers might be gripped with the glory of the birth, death, burial, resurrection, and ascension of the Lord Jesus Christ. Noel Smith was setting forth Christ as the "Middle Man" who alone could stand between a holy God and sinful creatures and perform the ministry of reconciliation.

No preacher ever had a more glorious subject, nor could be possessed by a higher motive. I believe Noel Smith loved God and wanted to exalt his amazing grace. Unfortunately, Noel Smith also held the error of universal atonement. It is tragic but true that pure motives are not sufficient to correct either bad theology or its regrettable results. Mr. Smith sincerely *attempted* to exalt the love and grace of God. This he attempted to do in perfect harmony with his Arminian doctrine of universal atonement. Did this sincere attempt to glorify God's grace achieve its purpose, or did this consistent and conscientious man come close to blasphemy? I will leave it up to the reader to come to his own conclusion.

VII. The Atonement from Christ's Point of View

Isaiah 53 is the clearest and fullest description of the death of Christ in the Bible. It is amazing that this vivid portrayal of our Lord's sufferings on the cross is foretold in the Old Testament Scriptures. How did Christ feel as he experienced the things mentioned in this great chapter?

"Surely he hath borne our griefs, and carried our sorrows: yet we did esteem him stricken, smitten of God, and afflicted. But he was wounded for our transgressions, he was bruised for our iniquities: the chastisement of our peace was upon him; and with his stripes we are healed" (Isa. 53:4, 5). If Christ was truly "stricken, smitten, and afflicted" by God in our place, and if he was in reality "wounded, bruised and chastised" because our sins were actually laid on him, then does it not follow that we simply *must* ultimately "be healed"? Does not justice demand it?

Is it possible to have Christ actually experience, as a vicarious substitute, the things in Isaiah 53:4 and then make the things in verse 5 to be a mere *possibility?* This is exactly what a hypothetical atonement is proclaiming.

"All we like sheep have gone astray; we have turned every one to his own way, and the LORD hath laid on him the iniquity of us all" (Isa. 53:6). Are the two *alls* in verse 6 inclusive of every man without exception, or does it mean the Father has lain the iniquity of "every sheep that has gone astray" upon the shepherd? Who is the "we" and the "us" in this verse? If the first "all" includes you, then the second "all" also includes you. However, if you are not a poor lost sinner that has gone astray and needs to be saved, then you are not included in either "all." You are not the object of the death designed to save only poor sinners.

"...for the transgression of *my people* was he stricken" (Isa. 53:8). Who are "my people" in this verse if the atonement is for everyone without exception? Does the term *my people* include the Egyptians and Canaanites? This verse demands a particular application of the sufferings of Christ.

"Yet it pleased the LORD to bruise him; he hath put him to grief. *When* thou shalt make his soul an offering for sin, he *shall see his seed,* he shall prolong his days, and the pleasure of the LORD shall prosper in his hand" (Isa. 53:10). This verse contains one of the most amazing statements in all of the Word of God. It "pleased the Lord" to put his only begotten Son to death for sinners. It was the Father who made his Son "an offering for sin."

Our Savior was pleasing to his Father at the very moment that he cried out, "My God, my God, why hast thou forsaken me?" Paul writes in Philippians 2:5–9 that the height of the obedience of Christ to his Father's will was the moment when he *willingly* laid down his life in death under the sword of justice. "He became obedient unto death, even the death of the cross."

Our Lord knew the Father would turn his back the moment "he was made to be sin." God had to turn his back on Christ the instant Christ put on the sin and guilt of his people. The Father turned his back on Christ because holiness could not look on sin. God turned his back on his Son in order that he might turn his face towards us in *righteous* and *holy* love.

Our blessed substitute also knew that the Father would raise him from the dead! This was the height of his confidence in his Father's oath (*cf.* Acts 2:22-36). His obedience and faith were fully pleasing to his Father at that very moment when he fully trusted his soul into the hands of his Father's eternal purposes.

This same verse (Isa. 53:10) also contains one of the clearest proofs of particular atonement. At the very moment that Christ was made to be sin and treated as if he were guilty, he was conscious of what was sure to follow as a result of his sufferings. The verse states "when," or at the exact time his soul was being offered for sin, that he would, at that very moment, "see his seed." The church is his seed. When Christ was on the cross, he saw his sheep individually. He did not see an indefinable mass of humanity and hope that some of them would be willing to let him save them. *He saw his seed being brought to glory!* He saw the "many sons," the "sheep" given to him by the Father, being saved. He saw the elect receiving the benefits of his atoning work. Our Lord knew his work would not be in vain.

This is what Hebrews means when it says, "who for the *joy that was set before him* endured the cross, despising the shame..." (Heb. 12:2). That joy was nothing less than seeing his sheep safe and sound in the fold and forever delivered from sin and guilt. That ought to make us shout with joy!

What are the biblical answers to the following questions?

(1) Who are Christ's seed, and *when* does he *see* them? Dare one say, He saw the whole world as *potentially* saved if they could only somehow be persuaded to believe? No, the Bible does not allow this understanding. The text means that Christ saw the individual and specific people whom he was consciously representing and to whom he would give faith.

(2) Did Christ know for sure that *any one* person would be saved because he was at that moment purchasing that sinner by a real atonement? Did he see individual people and know he was actually redeeming them for certain, or did he see his death as a universal possibility for an indefinable mass? Was he positive that I would be with him in glory as a specific result of his propitiatory death, or did he see his death as only the down payment of my redemption, and hope that my "free-will" choice would provide the balance of payment that finalized the deal? Again, I leave the reader to answer the questions.

"He *shall* see of the travail of his soul, and shall be *satisfied*; by his knowledge shall my righteous servant justify *many*; for he shall bear *their* iniquities" (Isa. 53:11).

This raises the following two questions which must be answered from the words in this verse:

(1) Can Christ be satisfied if his travail ends in futility? I have visited hospital rooms where a mother's travail had ended in the birth of a dead child. I assure you that there were no expressions of great joy in those rooms. There was deep sorrow and a great sense of loss. If our Savior looks into hell and sees there those for whom he travailed unto death itself, how can he possibly be satisfied? No, no, everyone for whom he travailed will be saved. As the hymn writer put it:

> Till all the *ransomed* Church of God,
> Be *saved* to sin no more.

(2) Who are the "many" that are *certain* of being justified simply because Christ bears *their* iniquity? It is impossible to separate the certainty of the "many's" justification from the stated reason for that certainty. "The many," all of them and only them, will surely be justified because Christ bore *their* iniquities in his own body. That is *particular* atonement. It is a *real* atonement and not merely a hypothetical atonement! In no way do these verses say, "Christ bore the sins of all men but he is only able to justify those who are willing to let him."

Look at the logic of Romans 8:33. "Who shall lay anything to the charge of *God's elect?*" Not the Father, for "It is God [the Father] that justifieth." Not the Son, for he will not condemn those for whom he died, and because he died for them, he also makes intercession for them (*cf.* John 17:9). Isn't that clear?

"Therefore will I divide him a portion with the great, and he shall divide the spoil with the strong, because he hath poured out his soul unto death; and he was numbered with the transgressors; and he bore the sin of many, and made intercession for the transgressors" (Isa. 53:12). Carefully follow the logic and truth of this text, and it is impossible to get universal atonement into either this verse or any other verse in the fifty-third chapter of Isaiah. Christ receives a specific reward for his work, and that reward does not depend on the fickle, capricious will of sinful man. Our Lord was identified with specific people in his death (they are "many"). He makes intercession for all those given to him by the Father (*cf.* John 17:9). It is for these that he "poured out his soul unto death." All for whom he prays will be saved, and all who are saved are those for whom he died.

There are those who complain that election and particular atonement are narrow and unfair. We ask, "Unfair to whom?" To whom does God *owe* anything other than condemnation? How can he possibly be unfair to sinners who deserve nothing but wrath? Granted, he gives grace to some who do not deserve it, but the Holy Spirit has already stopped the mouths of all who would say that was unfair as the following passages clearly demonstrate.

> But when the first came, they supposed that they should have received more; and they likewise received every man a penny. And when they had received it, they murmured against the goodman of the house, Saying, These last have wrought but one hour, and thou hast made them equal unto us, which have borne the burden and heat of the day. But he answered one of them, and said, Friend, I do

thee no wrong: didst not thou agree with me for a penny? Take that thine is, and go thy way: I will give unto this last, even as unto thee. Is it not lawful for me to do what I will with mine own? Is thine eye evil, because I am good? So the last shall be first, and the first last: for many be called, but few chosen. (Matthew 20:10-16)

As it is written, Jacob have I loved, but Esau have I hated. What shall we say then? Is there unrighteousness with God? God forbid. For he saith to Moses, I will have mercy on whom I will have mercy, and I will have compassion on whom I will have compassion. So then it is not of him that willeth, nor of him that runneth, but of God that sheweth mercy. For the scripture saith unto Pharaoh, Even for this same purpose have I raised thee up, that I might shew my power in thee, and that my name might be declared throughout all the earth. Therefore hath he mercy on whom he will have mercy, and whom he will he hardeneth. Thou wilt say then unto me, Why doth he yet find fault? For who hath resisted his will? Nay but, O man, who art thou that repliest against God? Shall the thing formed say to him that formed it, Why hast thou made me thus? Hath not the potter power over the clay, of the same lump to make one vessel unto honour, and another unto dishonour? (Romans 9:13-21)

My questions to the objectors of sovereign grace and particular atonement are these: is God just and fair toward *his only begotten Son?* Will the Father fulfill every word and expectation of Isaiah 53 to the one who bore those pangs of death, or are those things promised to Christ only hypothetical possibilities, dependent upon the fickle free will of sinners? Will God condemn the sinner after having punished Christ in the sinner's place? How would you feel if you were the Savior on the cross and you knew that you were being punished (1) for many sinners who were already in hell at that very moment, and (2) for many more who were certain to go there? Is God only just and fair to sinners and not to his Son?

Some may object that these verses are in the Old Testament Scriptures and ask where the New Testament Scriptures teach that Christ died specifically for some men thus making certain their salvation. A few such references are John 10:11, Ephesians 5:25, and Hebrews 9:28.

The study of Romans 5:12–19—see *Appendix Two*—covers this objection. If you do not have Haldane's commentary on *Romans*, buy it at once. His unfolding of these verses is worth ten times the price of the book. Romans 5:12–19 teaches that all men represented by Adam *must* have imputed to them the consequence of Adam's *disobedience*, and likewise all the men represented by Christ *must* have imputed to them the consequence of his *obedience*. As "all" represented by Adam are made *sinners*, so "all" represented by Christ are made *righteous*.

VIII. Challenges

The main objection to the clear scriptural teaching of particular redemption comes from those who put logic in the place of the Scriptures. They reason like this: premise A—Christ died for sinners (Rom. 5:8); premise B—all men are sinners (Rom. 3:23); logical conclusion—therefore Christ died for all men. Both premises A and B, *by themselves,* are true, but the conclusion is false because (1) it contradicts the clear teaching of other Scriptures concerning Christ dying for the elect only, and (2) the premises, although true in themselves when standing alone, are not true in the format as set forth above. That Christ died for sinners as opposed to dying for good people, and all men are sinners because there are no good people, has nothing to do with how many sinners Christ did or did not die for. The formula mixes apples and oranges. That is like saying, all men have two legs; that bird has two legs; therefore, that bird is a man.

Luke 19:10, "For the Son of Man is come to *seek and to save* that which was lost," contradicts this conclusion. This shows that Christ *must save* all, without exception, that he *seeks*. Christ does not effectually seek *all* and only manage to save *some*. No, no, he saves all that he seeks.

Matthew 9:10-13 shows that (1) Christ did not come to save all men; (2) he does not call all men; and (3) not all men acknowledge themselves "sinners," but some are (in their own minds) righteous and therefore need no one to atone for them. Look at what the text says:

> *And it came to pass, as Jesus sat at meat in the house, behold, many publicans and sinners came and sat down with him and his disciples. And when the Pharisees saw it, they said unto his disciples, Why eateth your Master with publicans and sinners? But when Jesus heard that, he said unto them, They that are whole need not a physician, but they that are sick. But go and learn what that meaneth, I will have mercy, and not sacrifice; for I am not come to call the righteous, but sinners to repentance.*

John 17:9 certainly contradicts the logic that attempts to establish universal atonement. "I pray for them; I pray not for the world, but for them whom thou hast given me; for they are thine." Why would Jesus die for men and then not pray for them? His work of intercession must be co-extensive with his atoning work on the cross. When Aaron went into the holy place on the Day of Atonement, he carried the names of the twelve tribes of Israel on his breastplate. The Philistines, Caananites, and Jebusites were not included among those for whom the blood was shed or among those for whom Aaron interceded in the most holy place. He, like our Lord (John 17:9), prayed only for those for whom he offered the sacrifice.

IX. Some Problems for Universal Redemption to Solve

Here are some clear texts of Scripture that can only be understood in "particular" terms. I have yet to see a satisfactory Arminian universalist explanation of these texts.

(1) John 10:11, 15. Christ died for his sheep, not for his sheep and the goats. Compare John 17:9.

(2) Ephesians 5:25. Christ gave himself for the church, not the church and those who perish.

(3) Romans 5:12-21. See *Appendix Two*.

(4) Hebrews 2:10-17. Many "sons" cannot mean all men without exception. "Abraham's seed" is a particular people.

A second problem for the universalists is the *successful travail* of Christ. It "pleased the Lord to bruise him" — "he [the Father] put him to grief" (Isa. 53:10). Is God just as loving, kind, and just to his only begotten Son as he is to sinners? Is God honest and fair with sinners, but not with his Son? Will the Father give his Son *all* that he *earned* by his death?

A third difficulty is that Christ's office of shepherd becomes a failure. Free-will Arminianism would have us believe that some of those for whom Christ suffered and died will nonetheless perish. If he loses some of the sheep for whom he was made responsible, then he fails in his job as the shepherd. The following verses, as they respect Christ's work as the shepherd of the sheep, would have to be rewritten if universal atonement were true.

> *I am the Good Shepherd; the Good Shepherd **giveth his life for the sheep**.* (John 10:11)

> *I am the Good Shepherd, and **know my sheep**, and am known of mine.* (John 10:14)

> *That the saying might be fulfilled, which he spoke, Of them whom **thou gavest me** have I **lost none**.* (John 18:9)

> *Now the God of peace, that brought again from the dead our Lord Jesus, that **great shepherd of the sheep**, through the blood of the everlasting covenant.* (Heb. 13:20)

> *Who his own self bore our sins in his own body on the tree, that we, being dead to sins, should live unto righteousness; by whose stripes ye were healed. **For ye were as sheep** going astray, but are now returned unto the shepherd and bishop of your souls.* (1 Pet. 2:24, 25)

Yet another dilemma is that Christ's priestly work becomes a proposition that contradicts itself. He refuses to pray for the very people for whom he supposedly died. "I pray for them, *I pray not for the world,* but for them whom thou hast given me; for they are thine" (John 17:9). "For there is one God, and one mediator between God and men, the man, Christ Jesus" (1 Tim. 2:5). Notice that this last text says *men* (specific men) and not *man* (mankind indiscriminately). The world has no mediator, but the sheep have one whose mediatorial work never fails. Would Christ die for men and then not intercede for them?

The argument that convinced me that Christ could not have died for all men was Spurgeon's argument that there *were already sinners in hell when Christ died*. Can anyone honestly believe that the Father would punish Christ on the cross for men who were at that moment lost in hell? Who can believe that at the very moment Christ was suffering on the cross,s he could look into hell and see men there for whom he was being punished? Did the Father punish Christ for Ahab when Ahab was already in hell?

The very foundation of God's righteousness is destroyed by the doctrine of universal atonement. The ground of a believer's assurance is that God will not, yea, cannot, punish sin twice. Free-will universalism must hold that God punishes sin in Christ and then punishes the sinner in hell. The false idea that all sin is paid for except the sin of unbelief has been more than adequately answered by A.W. Pink and J.I. Packer.[10]

It does not seem to occur to the proponents of a universal atonement that the whole biblical plan of salvation is distorted by their system. In the Scriptures, the Trinity works in total unison in the purposes of salvation.

---

[10] See Vol. 4, No. 8 and Vol. 4, No. 9 of *Sound of Grace*.

The Son redeems all of those chosen by the Father, and the Holy Spirit regenerates all of the chosen and redeemed ones. In universal atonement, the persons of the Trinity work in different directions with varying degrees of success. At every turn the Holy Spirit cannot effect the gracious desires of the Father and the Son until the mighty free will of the sinner is willing to give God a chance.

Finally, the foundation of assurance of salvation must either collapse or be placed squarely on man's faith alone. If God did the same thing for Judas, and every other Christ-rejecter, that he did for Peter and the rest of the elect, how can we be sure that we will not eventually perish as Judas did? The religion of free will answers: because I am willing. I have faith! I used my free will to accept God's offer of grace. Such a system makes *faith,* not Christ's death, to be the grounds of assurance and the only vital difference between a lost man and a saved man. This teaches that all men are truly redeemed by Christ's blood, but it is the sinner's faith that makes the sole difference between him and those who perish. What happens when we doubt? Are we lost?

Conclusion: Read Exodus 28:6–12; 21–29

Consider the Old Testament Day of Atonement. Aaron wore only the names of the twelve tribes of Israel on his shoulders and breast as he stood before God. The blood shed on the altar and then sprinkled on the mercy seat was not for the heathen nations, but only for the nation of Israel. Just as the high priest carried the names of the tribes on his shoulder and heart as he stood before God on the Day of

Atonement, so our High Priest had our names on his shoulders and heart as he endured God's wrath, went into the tomb, and ascended into heaven. He breathes our individual names to the Father and pleads his merits on our behalf. He does this for every sinner that comes to him! He turns no one away that comes! If I am such a sinner, in need of such a Redeemer, I dare believe he died for even me!

CHAPTER SEVEN
IRRESISTIBLE GRACE

We want to begin our study of the new birth by looking at three texts of Scripture that speak to this vital subject. The first passage shows not only the absolute necessity of being born again, but also states that being born again is essential before one is able to even "see" the kingdom of God. In other words, we must have sight, the ability to see, before we can actually see. It is important to remember that seeing does not give us sight, but we see only because we have sight. The gift of spiritual sight is given to us in regeneration, and we see, or believe, because we have been given spiritual sight.

> In reply Jesus declared, "I tell you the truth, no one can see the kingdom of God unless he is born again." (John 3:3 NIV)

The second text also shows that the new birth must first take place before faith in Christ is possible; we will work this out in detail later.

> He was in the world, and though the world was made through him, the world did not recognize him. He came to that which was his own, but his own did not receive him. Yet to all who received him, to those who believed in his name, he gave the right to become children of God—children born not of natural descent, nor of human decision or a husband's will, but born of God. (John 1:10-13 NIV)

The third text shows that man has no more power over the new birth than he has over the wind. Both the wind and the Holy Spirit "blow" as they please. Everyone knows that man does not have the power to either make the wind blow or force it to stop blowing. However, many sincere Christians do not realize that the same thing is true of the Holy Spirit's work in regeneration. A sinner cannot cause the Holy Spirit to regenerate his dead heart, nor can he stop that work when the Holy Spirit purposes to do it! That is exactly what Jesus meant in this verse.

> *The wind blows wherever it pleases. You hear its sound, but you cannot tell where it comes from or where it is going. So it is with everyone born of the Spirit.* (John 3:8 NIV)

When studying the Scriptures, it is often necessary to isolate different aspects of truth. However, we must never try to isolate them in personal experience. Justification and sanctification are two entirely different things, yet it is impossible to experience one without the other. Both are an integral part of becoming and being a Christian, but they must be isolated to be studied. This is also true of regeneration by the Holy Spirit and personal faith in Christ for forgiveness. Regeneration is an essential part of salvation, but it is not to be equated with being saved. It is a misuse of the word *salvation* to limit it to just one aspect of being saved. Salvation has at least three different aspects.

1. A Christian is truly saved right now (Eph. 2:8, 9 — "have been").

2. A Christian is in the process of being saved every day (I Cor. 1:18 "…us who are being saved…").

3. A Christian is waiting in hope to be fully saved in the future (Rom. 5:10 "...we were [past tense] reconciled to him...having been reconciled...shall be [future tense] saved..."). Notice there is a clear distinction between reconciled and saved even though both are essential parts of salvation.

Sadly, our generation has confused "being saved" with "being born again." One of these, being saved, has to do with benefits, and the other has to do with power or life. One is the work and act of the sinner; the other, the work and act of the Holy Spirit. Notice the following two texts that show this distinction.

> *And brought them out, and said, Sirs, what must I do to be saved? And they said, [You must] Believe on the Lord Jesus Christ, and thou shalt be saved, and thy house.* (Acts 16:30-31)

> *Marvel not that I said unto thee, Ye must be born again. The wind bloweth where it listeth [pleases], and thou hearest the sound thereof, but canst not tell whence it cometh, and whither it goeth: so is every one that is born of the Spirit.* (John 3:7-8)

Acts 16:31 is teaching the necessity of a sinner having faith in order to be saved. God does not repent for us. The sinner must repent and believe. These are the acts of men and not the acts of God. Faith and repentance are not vicarious. If you have a problem understanding the relationship of these two things, see our tract, "God's Part and Man's Part in Salvation."

On the other hand, John 3:8 is referring to power and ability. The work of the Holy Spirit in regeneration is likened to the blowing of the wind. A sinner can no more command or stop the regenerating work of the Holy Spirit than he can make the wind blow or stop a tornado. This is why regeneration is sometimes called "irresistible grace."

Being born again and being saved are both essential. It is impossible to experience one without experiencing the other. The question is not one of time and sequence, that is, which is first and which is second, but rather one of cause and effect. Does our faith cause the new birth, or does the new birth cause faith? The question, "Why does one person believe and become saved, while another rejects Christ and is lost?" will be answered differently according to our understanding of the nature of regeneration. In one case, we will attribute the cause of man's faith to his free will, and in the other case we will give the Holy Spirit the glory for enabling us, by regenerating us, to believe and be saved. Perhaps the following will help.

Being saved— Acts 16:31	Being born again— John 3:3, 8
Benefits	Life and power
Our work—our faith essential	God's work—our faith not involved
Acts 16:30—"What must I do?"	John 3:7, 8—"What must I do?"
Answer—"you must believe"	*No answer! God must do something!*
Faith—an act of man	Regeneration—a sovereign act of God

God does not believe for us	God gives new heart—we believe
Receive benefits of salvation	Receive spiritual life and power
Acts 18:27	1 Peter: 1:2–3; James 1:18

I. Everyone agrees that man needs to be radically changed.

The Bible is quite clear as to the necessity of the new birth. My friend, Doctor Berry, frequently asked, "Do you know why Jesus said, 'you must be born again'?" And of course, his answer was, "Because you must be born again." George Whitefield preached over two thousand times on John 3:3. When asked why he preached so often on being born again, he replied, "Because you must be born again."

All churches believe you must be born again, but they radically disagree on what it means and how it happens. The Roman Catholic, Lutheran, Episcopalian, and Church of Christ all believe this happens through baptism. This is why they believe baptism is essential to salvation. Even Sigmund Freud had a doctrine of the new birth. He called it "an abrupt change in the continuity of the growth of the personality." Boy meets girl – boy falls in love – boy radically changes life style – boy is born again. In America today, we are told that over forty percent of our citizens have had a "born again experience." If this is true, it must be the kind that Freud talked about. Most of the misunderstanding of the true nature of regeneration grows out of a failure to see why the new birth is absolutely essential. One will never understand the *what* and the *how* until one clearly sees the *why*.

II. Why is regeneration, or the new birth, so essential?

The nature of God demands it. God cannot fellowship or approve of anything that is not perfect. No one can stand in his presence without a total absence of sin and a positive robe of righteousness. We are sinners by nature and practice, and a holy God has no choice but to reject us. We need a spiritual birth that changes us and makes us acceptable to God.

The nature of the sinner necessitates a new birth. To be happy in heaven, a sinner needs a new nature. Heaven would be a hell to a sinner without a new nature. Even if all his guilt was pardoned and a righteous standing imputed to him, until he is given a new nature, he would hate heaven. A friend has two sons that were constantly trying to impress their father that they loved Jesus and wanted to go to heaven. One day, on the way home from church, he asked them if they knew what heaven was like. When they had no answer, he explained that in heaven they sing a lot, they pray a lot, and they worship a lot. One of the boys said, "It sounds a lot like a church service." The father said, "Yes, that is a good description." The other son said, "You mean it's even longer than our church service?" About that time, I suspect that someone had changed his mind about going to heaven.

Actually, the sinner cannot even want to believe the gospel until he is first born from above. Some of the verses that speak of man's *cannots* were covered in the study of depravity. Only one of them will be reviewed here. A comparison of three texts will reveal why a man needs to be born spiritually before he can believe.

But the natural man receiveth not the things of the Spirit of God: for they are foolishness unto him: neither can he know them, because they are spiritually discerned. (1 Cor. 2:14)

Even the Spirit of truth; whom the world cannot receive, because it seeth him not, neither knoweth him: but ye know him; for he dwelleth with you, and shall be in you. (John 14:17)

These be they who separate themselves, sensual, having not the Spirit. (Jude 19)

One cannot receive and believe something about which he knows nothing, and one cannot know something that is totally beyond his ability to apprehend. 1 Corinthians 2:14 specifically states that a lost man cannot (that is, he does not have the ability to) understand spiritual truth, and therefore it is impossible for him to believe that truth. John 14:17 shows why this terrible reality is true. The lost man can only experience what he can touch, taste, feel, smell, etc., and God is not known by physical senses, but through the Spirit. Jude 19 is one of the best descriptions of a lost man that you will find in all of the Word of God. A lost man is merely a natural man who is totally limited in experiences to what his natural instincts can teach him. The sum total of his knowledge and experience is that which he can learn through his physical senses. This is what "sensual" means. They who worship God must do so in "spirit" as well as truth, and the lost man does not have ability to receive spiritual truth. He has all of the attributes of physical life but does not have the Spirit and can know nothing of spiritual life. He needs to be born of the Spirit before he can see, hear, feel, or experience spiritual things.

Man "died" spiritually in the garden when he sinned. The Holy Spirit, the spiritual life of God in man, left Adam, and he died spiritually. Now man is merely a "natural" man without the capacity to experience spiritual things. Regeneration is the Holy Spirit, or the life of God, coming back into the sinner and empowering him with spiritual life and ability.

As we mentioned, every church agrees on the necessity of the new birth, but they differ greatly on why it is essential and how it takes place. It is impossible to understand the *why* without grasping the truth of total depravity and its effect of total spiritual inability.

III. Exactly what is the new birth?

First of all, it is a literal implanting of life, as in conception, that gives real life. It is the cause of life and is evidenced later in a birth taking place. We are using "birth" to include conception and actual birth. The point is that we are talking about spiritual implanting by the Holy Spirit that gives spiritual life. Just as there is physical birth that gives physical life, so spiritual birth gives spiritual life.

Secondly, this birth is "from above." God is the sole author of this birth. The same Greek word translated *again* in John 3:3 is translated *from above* in John 3:31. Now it is true that the new birth is "second" in that it is after the first birth—first physical, then spiritual. However, the emphasis in the Scripture is not on the order or sequence of the birth but rather its source. It is from above. It is not from within us; it is not from around us; it is from above. It is a life-giving birth from God that comes down to us by his power. This new birth has nothing to do with heredity, education, environment, culture, or church ceremonies; it comes directly from God alone.

Thirdly, it is "new" in the sense of REgeneration. It is the sovereign implanting of life in the place of death. Two of the words which are used in the New Testament to describe the new birth or regeneration are *born* and *begotten*. They convey the fact of giving life through birth. Other words used are *regeneration* and *renewing*. These words show that life is put back into a place where it once was but where there is now only death. The Holy Spirit regenerates our hearts in the same sense that we regenerate a dead battery. Another phrase is *quickening* or *making alive*; "you hath he quickened who were dead in trespasses and sin" (Eph. 2:1). Regeneration is a "raising up" and bringing into being a "new creation." We could say, "The Holy Spirit brings dead sinners out of the grave of death, and resurrects the dead to life." Again, it is the idea of giving life to replace death. The new birth is literally a spiritual resurrection out of the spiritual death of sin. What Genesis 1:26, 27 was to physical creation, the new birth is to spiritual creation.

Comparing Genesis 5:1–3 with James 1:18 will help us to understand this by providing a picture of the nature and effect of regeneration.

(1) *This is the book of the generations of Adam. In the day that God created man, in the likeness of God* [that likeness was not physical but a moral, rational, volitional likeness] *made he him;* (2) *Male and female created he them; and blessed them, and called their name Adam, in the day when they were created.* (3) *And Adam lived an hundred and thirty years, and begat a son in his own likeness, after his image; and called his name Seth.* (Gen. 5:1–3)

Of his own will begat he us with the word of truth, that we should be a kind of firstfruits of his creatures. (James 1:18)

God created a son in "his own likeness," and Adam begat a son in "his own likeness." What does that mean? In both cases, it means there is a definite likeness between the father and the child. Adam's son looked like him, talked like him, walked like him because that son was Adam's true offspring. That son bore the physical image of his father. God created a child who had God's nature and bore God's spiritual image. That child was a physical creation, but he was also a spiritual being with a nature that saw and appreciated God in all of his works. Just as Adam's child was his true offspring and bore the physical image of his father, so Adam, at his creation, bore the spiritual image God. However, that original likeness to God was forever lost when Adam sinned. Regeneration is God "begetting" one anew in his image and making him his eternal spiritual child.

The first man, Adam, was created in the likeness and image of God. After Adam sinned, he begat a son in his own likeness, after his image. James tells us that Christians have been begotten by God. Ever since Adam fell, both God and men have been begetting true children in their own respective likeness and image. The children begotten, in both cases, share their father's life: bear his image, looks, nature, appetites, etc. In other words, through physical conception, one acquires physical life and bears the nature and likeness of his human father; and through spiritual conception, one acquires spiritual life and bears the nature and likeness of his spiritual Father, even God himself. In both cases there is true life, true birth, and in both cases, the child born is the true offspring of its parent. The Christian is God's child (John 1:12). We are God's seed (Isa. 53:10; 1 John 3:8). Just as Adam communicated to his posterity, in physical birth and life, his looks, appetites, habits, motivation, and image in physical conception, just so God implants spiritual life and communicates his nature, likeness, motivation, and desires in his seed, and they become a "new creation" by spiritual birth.

In James 1:18 we read, "Of his [God's] own will begat he us with the word of truth...." Christians are called sons of God. Just as Adam begat a son in his own likeness by procreation, so in regeneration God begets children in his own image from among sinners. He communicates to the "begotten ones" his likeness, his spiritual looks, and his desires. His children bear his image. They are truly God's offspring and bear God's likeness.

Now obviously the first question that one ought to face and seriously consider is this: have I been born of God? One may use a physical birth certificate as proof of birth, but one cannot use either a birth or baptismal certificate to prove any divine pedigree! We should ask ourselves: Do I bear the image of God? Am I a true Christian? Have I been born again? Do I have spiritual life?

When we are truly born of God, we bear God's spiritual image just as surely as we bear the physical image of our natural parents. We are "like God" simply because we are his true children. This should be evident in the way we think and live. Christians disagree about many ideas; nonetheless, there are some things that are true of every Christian who ever lived or will live. Let me explain. Some churches do not believe in mixed bathing. Many Christians do not believe that you can smoke and go to heaven. Other Christians believe that women ought not to wear makeup or cut their hair. (Why do preachers always pick on the women?) There are Christians who believe, and do not believe, all kinds of tenets. There was a man on the radio preaching against "loving the world." He was not doing half bad until he decided to clearly explain what God meant by "worldly." He said, "Now any fool who is honest with the Bible knows that God is talking about playing baseball." He then went into a tirade against baseball. One may smile, but I would suspect that any given church may have some ideas that are just as strange.

To repeat, I know that Christians disagree on many things, but I still insist that there are some things that are true of every Christian who ever lived. It does not matter if he is ten years old or one hundred years old; whether his face is yellow, red, black, or white; whether he lived in the fifth century or the twentieth century; or what his cultural or denominational background is or was. When a person is born of God, there are some things that simply must accompany his conversion.

Let me illustrate. I had the unforgettable privilege of visiting the mission fields in Africa. Once I was preaching in a place where four different tribes with different dialects were in attendance. There were four different translators. It took an hour to preach a fifteen-minute sermon. Several times I became so engrossed in observing the different faces as the different translators spoke that I forgot what had been said. I had never seen any of those people before that day, but I could have gone through the entire congregation of about two-hundred and fifty people and without a single mistake, pointed to any person and identified the tribe to which that particular person belonged. How? Each person had a tribal mark cut into his face. When they were seven years old, slashes were cut into their faces which left welts or scars. The number and direction or slant of the slashes was different in each case. You may have seen pictures of this in missionary meetings. Each tribe had its own mark. When a child is born into that tribe, he is marked so that no matter where he goes, he bears the tribal marks of his birth.

My friend, I assure you that the same thing is true of "God's tribe." Every Christian carries the tribal marks written in him by the Holy Spirit in regeneration. There are some distinguishing tribal marks on the people of God. When the Spirit of God brings the new birth, he always writes the proof of his work in the heart and experience of every "begotten one." 1 John sets forth nine tribal marks;

we have only listed four of them, which are true of every child of God. We may disagree about many facets of doctrine and practice, but every Christian wants to please God. He loves the revealed law of God and is committed to keeping it with all of his heart because it is the law of his heavenly Father and his Savior (1 John 2:3, 4). If a person does not love the brethren, he ought to doubt his salvation (1 John 3:13–16). Why is John so emphatic? Because the new birth communicates the nature of God to his offspring. This is one of the ways to test one's conversion.

A friend of mine from years past was a fine lawyer who worked as a district attorney for some time. A young lady came to him and accused a certain man of being the father of her baby. The man denied it and refused to marry her or do anything to help financially. At that time, it was difficult to prove in court who the father was if the mother had slept with more than one man. Five men testified that they had slept with this girl within the time frame of when the girl had become pregnant. It seemed impossible to prove that the accused man was really the father. When the baby was born, it had a very strange looking forehead. Instead of going straight up, the baby's forehead went back at about a forty-five degree angle. My lawyer friend had the mother sit where the jury could clearly see the baby's strange forehead. The accused man also had a strange forehead. In fact, his forehead was identical to the baby's. It also went back at a forty-five degree angle. The jury listened to all five men testify that they had slept with the girl. They listened to all of the technical, legal, and medical arguments. They looked at the baby, and they looked at the man, and said, "You are guilty." They knew that man was that child's father because the father's physical image was stamped in the child. My friend, the same is true in the spiritual realm. The Father's image is stamped in every one of his children. Do you and I bear the marks of the image of God in our hearts and lives? Do we exhibit the proof of the work of the Holy Spirit in the way we think and act? Can you and I prove our divine pedigree? Can we prove that we have been regenerated? Have we been born of God? Someone has said, "If there was a law that forbid being and acting like a Christian, would your life furnish enough evidence for you to be convicted?"

I must digress for just a moment and insist that regeneration is not merely a theological doctrine about which to argue. It is a spiritual experience that is essential to true conversion! God, by his power, works and writes his very nature in our hearts and lives, and he always leaves "living proof." I fear some reformed people preach their own election. They think that understanding and talking about sovereign grace is the same thing as experiencing it. Being born again is not something you believe; it is something that you personally experience. You do not look at either your birth or baptismal certificate to see if you are part of the elect of God. Do not examine your denominational creed or your knowledge of the doctrines of grace to discover your election. Honestly examine your heart and life to see whether the Holy Spirit of God has given you spiritual life. Have you been spiritually and powerfully drawn to know, love and worship God himself? That is the vital question.

This is what Jesus meant in John 6:44, 45. Too often verse 44 is used to prove "total inability" [and it clearly does so] and verse 45 is ignored. John 6:44 and 6:45 must never be separated, either in our theology or our experience. Look carefully at the verses beginning with verse 44:

"No man can come to me, except the Father which hath sent me draw him...." In John 6:37, Jesus has just taught the doctrine of election. The Jews started to murmur at him. In essence, he responded, "You want to murmur at what I said. I'll really give you something to chew on." He then hit them with the doctrine of total depravity. "No man can come to me, except the Father...draw him...." (verse 44). Jesus does not stop there. He goes on to declare the truth of irresistible grace in verse 45. "It is written in the prophets. And they shall be all taught of God. Every man therefore that hath heard, and hath learned of the Father, cometh unto me." Notice the comparison in these two verses. John 6:44 says, "No man can come," and John 6:45 says, "Every man who learns of the Father...comes to me." Drawing, hearing, and learning in these verses all refer to the same thing. Whatever "drawing by the Father" means in verse 44, the same thing is meant by "learned of the Father" in verse 45. Verse 44 is teaching inability. "No man can ...unless..." Verse 45 is teaching effectual calling. "Every man does...when ..." Verse 44 is affirming total inability, and verse 45 is showing that regeneration brings men to Christ in spite of that depravity.

Every man who "hears" or "learns of the Father" will always, without exception, come to Christ in faith, and no sinner ever will come, apart from the special regenerating work of the Holy Spirit. The new birth from God is a work that always produces saving faith and salvation. However, I repeat, we are talking about an experience and not just an abstract doctrine over which we argue. I ask you once more: Are you a Christian? Have you been born again? Or I could ask: Do you bear the marks, the pedigree, the tribal marks of the work of the Holy Spirit in your life? Regeneration is nothing less than the giving of spiritual life to a dead sinner. It is literally "being born of God."

IV. How does the new birth take place?

How is a man born of God? First of all, it is not produced by baptism. Neither the sprinkling of a child nor the immersion of an adult can regenerate a dead heart. Even if immersed by the apostle Paul or sprinkled as a child by John Calvin (or both), one still must be "born again." Baptism, in any form, can neither wash away sin nor create a new heart.

There are two texts of Scripture which I think should settle the question of baptismal regeneration forever. "For though ye have ten thousand instructors in Christ, yet have ye not many fathers: for in Christ Jesus I have begotten you through the gospel" (I Cor. 4:15). Paul is here addressing people who have been begotten by the gospel through his ministry. He was their spiritual father. He was the only person who could say, "You are, under God's blessing, one of my converts." However, the apostle also says the following to the very same individuals: "I thank God that I baptized none of you...." (I Cor. 1:14). Do you see the logic of the two statements? If a man is regenerated or begotten by baptism, it would be impossible for Paul to say, "I did not baptize any of you even though I have begotten you." If you put these two verses together, they prove beyond any doubt that baptism can have nothing at all to do with regeneration. If baptism is essential, or in any way contributes, to the new birth, then Paul could not have begotten converts without baptizing them. His argument and statements would be self-contradictory. The hymn writer was correct: "What can wash away my sin? Nothing but the blood of Jesus." Water, whether it is a few drops on our head as a child or a full tank into which we are immersed as an adult, cannot get into our heart where the change has to take place.

A missionary told of witnessing for many years to a Moslem friend. She was soon to go home and would not be returning because of ill health. She earnestly pleaded with God for one more opportunity to witness the gospel to her friend. One day she saw the Moslem woman start down the path to the sacred river to bathe. The missionary quickly put some clothes in a box, tied the box tight shut, and went down to the river and began dipping the box in the river. Her Moslem friend asked her what she was doing, and she replied that she was washing her clothes. Her friend smiled and said, "They will never get clean because the water cannot get inside to where the dirt is." The missionary asked, "Do you believe that water in which you are bathing can get into your heart where the sin is and wash it clean?"

Secondly, the new birth is not dependent upon church sacraments. Partaking of the Lord's table, no matter how regularly, cannot give one a new heart. Paul forever put the death knell to the foolish notion that church sacraments can give spiritual life.

> But God forbid that I should glory, save in the cross of our Lord Jesus Christ, by whom the world is crucified unto me, and I unto the world. For in Christ Jesus neither circumcision availeth any thing, nor uncircumcision, but a new creature. (Gal. 6:14-15)

We may substitute baptism, or anything else, for circumcision in these verses and not change the teaching of these verses. The new creation is regeneration by the Holy Spirit. That is all a poor sinner needs, but he vitally needs that great work.

Thirdly, being born again has nothing whatsoever to do with human authority. Dr. Billy Graham may have personally put his hand on your head and told you that you are a Christian. That does not make you a child of God. That does not prove that you are born of God.

Fourthly, the new birth is not merely a correct knowledge of theology. Some current Calvinists are reviving an old heresy. It is called "doctrinal regeneration." They associate true salvation with a clear knowledge of Calvinistic theology. Some of these people imply that John Calvin is going to stand at heaven's door and examine you on your knowledge of the "five points" (they call this the gospel) to see whether you get in or not. Not so, beloved! The five points are not the gospel. The gospel is, "Believe on the Lord Jesus Christ and thou shalt be saved." The five points are what makes the gospel work. Election never saved a single soul, but it does make certain that some will be saved.

Lastly, being born again has nothing to do with a man's so-called free will. Many people balk at this point. Look again at John 1:12, 13 and carefully examine the relationship of the two verses.

> *But as many as received him, to them gave he power* [or authority] *to become the children of God, even to them that believe on his name:* [notice the sentence does not end here] *Which were born, not of blood, nor of the will of the flesh, nor of the will of man, but of God.*

These Scriptures emphatically, categorically, and specifically state that we are "not born of the will of man." We are "born of God." Verse 12 tells what one must do to be saved. He must willingly receive Christ. The promise is that one will become a child of God when he receives Christ. The verse is clear. The tense of the verbs in these two verses is of utmost importance. John did not say that all who receive him, will be, as a result of believing, born of God. This would make faith to be the cause of the new birth. No, John said just the opposite. The people who receive Christ do so only because they have been (past tense) born of God. Their spiritual birth, given sovereignly by God, caused their act of faith. Verse 13 is not giving the result of verse 12, but rather the cause. Verse 13 tells exactly who the people are in verse 12 that received Christ. The people in verse 12 willingly received Christ only because they were (past tense "had been") born of God. Do not mix up a "would be" consequence with a "had been" certainty. Every man who is born of God (v. 13) will always gladly receive Christ (v. 12). Receiving Christ (v. 12) is the certain result of being born of God (v. 13).

1 John 5:1 teaches the same. "Whosoever that believeth that Jesus is the Christ is (already) born of God." John does not say that one will be born of God if he believes, but rather, if one believes it proves that he has been born of God. Faith is the fruit of being born again and not the cause. Some may say that I am just quibbling over words and say, "You cannot prove that from this text of Scripture." I am sorry, but the text can mean nothing else. This point may be proven by comparing 1 John 5:1 with 1 John 2:29. The identical construction is used but the subject is "doing righteousness" instead of being born again. The text: "...everyone that doeth righteousness is born of him." Is it just quibbling over words to insist that no one is born of God because he does righteousness? Do you not agree that we do righteousness only after, and only because, we have been born of God? We clearly know which is the cause and which is the effect in this verse. No one believes that "doing righteousness" causes one to be born of God. That destroys the gospel. The same identical truth is set forth in 1 John 5:1. Our faith does not cause the new birth, but, like "doing righteousness," our faith is a living proof that we have been born of God. To deny this clear fact is to destroy the biblical doctrine of regeneration. A man cannot born (active voice) himself, but he must be born (passive voice) from above.

When an evangelist announces that he is going to preach on what you must do to be born again, proceed with caution. This man is not making the biblical distinction between being saved and being born again. He may preach biblically about how to be saved, but certainly not about how to be born again. He will probably say, "You had nothing to do with your first birth, but you have everything to do with your second birth." He is dead wrong! You had no more to do with your second (spiritual) birth than you did with your first (physical) birth. There is no denying that a sinner must willingly repent and believe the gospel in order to be saved; however, we are talking about being born again. We are insisting that only God can give the power, or the "want to," that enables one to repent and believe.

Sometimes I like to tease people in order to stimulate them to think. When people argue for the doctrine of man's free will, I often say to them, "I do not discuss the doctrine of free will with anybody who doesn't believe in eternal security." They usually say, "Who said anything about eternal security?" I look rather puzzled and ask, "You surely do not believe a sinner has a free will and also believe that a saint can never be lost?" They almost always reply emphatically, "Yes, I do." In pretended surprise, I ask, "Are you saying that a sinner has the will power to either accept or reject Christ?" When they affirm that they believe this, I ask, "Can a saint will, or choose, his way out of grace?" When they say "No," I reply, "Well, if the sinner has power to both accept and reject, but once he accepts, he can no longer choose to be lost, it sounds to me that you believe a sinner has twice as much will power as a saint. You are saying that we lose part of the freedom of will that we supposedly had before we were saved." The dialogue usually ends at this point. It is nonsense to hold to a doctrine that teaches that man loses half of his will power when he is converted. It is impossible to believe both free will and eternal security. They are self-contradictory.

The new birth is something that God does in us, without us. It is his sovereign work, but it always produces fruit in our lives. Let me try to illustrate this. Suppose that I was away from home for a speaking engagement, and after the service, my car would not start. When I turned the key in the ignition, there was not even a buzz. I flipped the light switch, and there was not even a flicker. I pressed the horn, and there was not even a peep. Someone would probably say that he thought that my battery was dead. Suppose they were correct, and the battery was indeed dead. I leave the car in the church parking lot and go off to bed. The next morning, I once more try to start the car, and the motor immediately turns over. There are three possible explanations of what happened: (1) The battery was not really dead; I just thought it was. (2) A miracle took place. (3) Somebody re-charged, or "regenerated," the battery.

Now just suppose the various parts of my car had the power of speech. Suppose the evening before, I had said, "Lights, if you will only shine, that will put life in the battery." Or, "Horn, if you will only blow, that will put life in the battery." If my car could speak, it would have replied, "If you put some life in the battery, I guarantee you the horn will blow, the lights will shine, and the motor will start." So it is with the man who is dead in sin. His spiritual battery is dead. None of his facilities will work until he is regenerated. When God gives a sinner life, he will repent, believe, pray, etc. Appealing to a lost man's will as the source of power to save him is like appealing to the lights and the horn. It is life that the lost man needs just as the car battery needs life. The most powerful spiritual feat possible is the exercise of faith. It can move mountains. Does a dead man produce the spiritual power to perform the powerful act of faith, or does he do this because of regeneration and the gift of a new nature?

When I come back and find the battery working, I would assume that somebody had been fooling around underneath the hood. Wouldn't you? Some years ago, my wife and I took our son and daughter-in-law to a Bible conference. My son was a good "all-American" boy, but we weren't really sure if he had been converted. He knew all of the right answers but did not seem to have a thirst after God. I preached four messages on the doctrine of total depravity. After the second message, my son came up to me and said, "Dad, that's the first sermon I ever heard you preach. Something happened to me tonight. I think I got converted." He has not been the same since that night. He now exhibits the fruits of true conversion. I believe that night somebody was fooling around under the hood. My son had heard me preach for twenty-two years, but that night he "heard the voice of Christ." That night he was regenerated and believed the gospel.

Have you ever witnessed to a person for years, but they paid no attention to you? Then one day you see them reading a Bible, and they show up at church. What had happened? Somebody was fooling around under the hood. You prayed for your children and instructed them in the Word of God, but it seemingly went in one ear and out the other. Then one day, like my son, they say to you, "Why didn't you tell me this before?" You smile and realize that someone was fooling around under the hood. The Holy Spirit has been charging a dead battery. This is what the Bible calls regeneration, and this is what we need to see today. We do not need better buildings, preachers, or music programs. We need someone with the power to do something under the hood.

IV. Being born again is a creative act of the Holy Spirit.

We must emphasize again that being born again has nothing to do with heredity. It has nothing to do with our parents or church sacraments, and it surely has nothing to with man's so-called free will. Free will is to spiritual life exactly what evolution is to physical life. It is a blatant denial of God's creative power. It amazes me that sincere Bible believers do not see this awful fact. It causes them to make injudicious statements. The following quotation from the Scofield Bible's footnote on John 3:3 is an illustration:

> Regeneration: (1) The necessity of the new birth grows out of the incapacity of the natural man to "see" or "enter into" the kingdom of God. However gifted, moral, or refined, the natural man is absolutely blind to spiritual truth and impotent to enter the kingdom; for he can neither obey,

understand, nor please God (John iii.3, 5, 6; Psa. li.5; Jer. xvii.9; Mk. vi.21-23; 1Cor. ii.14; Rom. viii.7, 8; Eph. ii.3. See Mt. vi.33, note). (2) The new birth is not a reformation of the old nature (Rom. vi.5, note), but a creative act of the Holy Spirit (John iii.5; i.12, 13; 2 Cor. v.17; Eph. ii.10; iv.24). (3) The condition of the new birth is faith in Christ crucified (John iii.14, 15; i.12, 13; Gal. iii.24). (4) Through the new birth the believer becomes a partaker of the divine nature and of the life of Christ Himself (Gal. ii.20; Eph. ii.10; iv.24; Col. i.27; 1 Pet. i.23–25; 2 Pet. i.4; 1 John v.10–12.

How can a "creative act of the Holy Spirit" be "conditioned" in any sense whatsoever, and especially on something a poor sinner must do? That is like God saying, "I will create the world if you will agree to allow me to do so." Scofield confuses being saved with being born again. See Volume 5, Issue 1 of *Sound of Grace* for a detailed study of the difference between these two.

VI. The sinner is passive in regeneration.

In all the references to the new birth in the New Testament Scriptures, regardless of which word is used, the voice of the verb is always passive. No one ever birthed himself or regenerated himself. The sinner is always passive and not active in regeneration. He does not do anything. Something is done to him, but nothing is done by him. As mentioned earlier, the sinner has no more to do with his second birth than he did with his first birth. You did not decide to be born spiritually any more than you decided to be born physically.

Again, we insist that we are not talking about time sequence, but cause/effect. The new birth and repentance/faith are simultaneous; however, regeneration makes faith possible and not vice versa. Lydia's conversion is a classic example.

> And a certain woman named Lydia, a seller of purple, of the city of Thyatira, which worshipped God, heard us: whose heart the Lord opened, that she attended unto the things which were spoken of Paul. (Acts 16:14)

Everyone agrees that Lydia must have heard, understood, and responded in personal faith to the gospel message of grace before she could be saved. The text clearly shows that all of these things happened. Lydia heard, understood, and responded—and that most willingly—to Paul's preaching. The question is this: what was it that enabled Lydia to respond in faith? Did she, with her own free will, open her own heart and invite Christ to save her? That is not what the text says. The text says, "The Lord opened [Lydia's heart so] that she attended unto the things which were spoken...." Lydia's response was made possible by God regenerating (opening) her heart. The sinner's heart must indeed be opened, but a spiritually dead sinner cannot open his own dead heart. He bolts it shut with ignorance and fear. Only God himself can open a dead sinner's heart, and this he does for all of his elect. This is being born again. This is being made alive, or quickened (Eph. 2:1).

I am sure that some of my readers are saying, "You are preaching irresistible grace, and I know the Bible clearly teaches that the sinner can resist the work of the Holy Spirit. What do you do with Acts 7:51, 52?"

> *Ye stiffnecked and uncircumcised in heart and ears,* ye do *always* resist the Holy Ghost: as your fathers did, so do ye. Which of the prophets have not your fathers persecuted? and they have slain them which shewed before of the coming of the Just One; of whom ye have been now the betrayers and murderers... (Acts 7:51, 52)

Pay particular attention to the words in bold type. There is no question that the text specifically declares that men can and do resist the Holy Spirit. In fact, the text says more than that; it uses the word *always*. I think every reader will agree that they have resisted the Holy Spirit in their past. Who among us did not laugh at the people who first witnessed to us the truth of the gospel? By nature, every sinner will not only resist the gospel, but he will keep on resisting it. The question is this: why did every saved person decide to quit resisting and instead decide to repent and believe? Why is that word *always* not true of most of those who read this book? Again the text is clear. The people Peter was addressing were stiff-necked and uncircumcised in heart and ears, and could do nothing but resist. Every sinner will always resist as long as his heart and ears have not been circumcised. Regeneration is the Holy Spirit taking the resistance out of us and circumcising our heart and ears so that we want to believe. The verse does not refute irresistible grace but shows how essential irresistible grace is in true conversion.

One more concept is important in this text. The resistance spoken of in these verses concerns the voice of the Holy Spirit speaking in the prophets. Sinners can and do resist all of men's preaching and exhortations. My son totally resisted all my entreaties with him for twenty-two years. You may turn a deaf ear to the message when preached by men, but when that message is applied to the conscience directly by the Holy Spirit, the resistance is removed. The internal work of the Holy Spirit in regeneration is quite different from the outward work of human agency. The former cannot be rejected, but the latter can and is rejected by many.

The phrase *irresistible grace* turns some people off because they think of a steamroller rolling over a tube of toothpaste. That is not the irresistible grace of the Bible. We are not tubes of toothpaste. We are creatures with minds, hearts, and wills. The same mind, heart, and will that fervently resists the gospel is made willing in regeneration to stop resisting and sincerely repent and believe. Let me illustrate biblical regeneration. Two mothers were having a cup of tea, and the one mother's son came downstairs neatly dressed, his hair neatly combed, and his shoes shined. As he went out the door whistling, his mother said, "That really bugs me." The other mother asked, "What do you mean? I wish my son looked like that. He dresses like a slob." The first mother replied, "Oh, that is not what I mean. What really bugs me is that a blond head and a pair of blue eyes did in ten minutes what I could not do in sixteen years."

That is the kind of irresistible work that we are talking about. That boy did not have to dress neatly if he did not want to. From his mother's remarks, we gather that she had tried, without success, to get him to change his appearance. Then one day, an irresistible attraction made him want to change, and he did so immediately and most willingly. You did not have to receive Christ unless you really wanted to, but when the Spirit of God showed you your heart and then revealed the beauty and glory of the Son of God, you wanted to receive him with all of your being. Irresistible grace is nothing less than God taking the resistance out of us and making us "willing in the day of his power" (Psalm 110:3).

Man indeed needs to hear the gospel preached, but he also needs something more. He needs a new heart. The boy's mother gave him many correct and heartfelt instructions, but nothing worked until an irresistible force came along.

VII. The means God uses—his Word and the Holy Spirit.

Perhaps we should have added the word *normal* to the above heading. The classic text to show what we mean in the above statement is I Thess. 1:4, 5.

> *Knowing, brethren beloved, your election of God. For our gospel came not unto you in word only, but also in power, and in the Holy Ghost, and in much assurance; as ye know what manner of men we were among you for your sake.*

It is obvious that Paul had assurance that the people to whom he was writing were part of God's elect. How did

Paul know this? It had nothing to do with their pedigrees or baptismal certificates. It was because of the effect the Word of God had upon them. It is important to note that the gospel always comes in words. It does not come in dreams and visions, nor in a baptistery or communion cup. The gospel comes in words. It comes in propositional form. It comes as written facts of history. The gospel tells us, in concrete words, exactly who Christ is and what he has done.

However, words by themselves are not enough—even the words of God. This is why Paul adds the word *also*. The gospel always comes in words, but unless those words are attended with the power of the Holy Spirit, they do not prevail in opening a sinner's heart. This is why we said the means that God [normally] uses are his Word and his Spirit.

Two things need to be said: (1) many Scripture texts connect the Word of God with regeneration. However, (2) it would seem that regeneration may take place without the Word of God being applied to the mind and heart. Infant salvation would not be possible if the Word of God had to be the instrumental cause of regeneration. Having said both of these things, we can say that in nearly every instance where regeneration is specifically mentioned, it is always in connection with the Holy Spirit using the Word of God. Note the following instances:

> *The entrance of thy words giveth light; it giveth understanding unto the simple.* (Ps. 119:130) [This verse needs to be compared with 2 Cor. 4:4–6, *"In whom the god of this world hath blinded the*

*minds of them which believe not, lest the light of the glorious gospel
of Christ, who is the image of God, should shine unto them. For we
preach not ourselves, but Christ Jesus the Lord; and ourselves your
servants for Jesus' sake. For God, who commanded the light to shine
out of darkness, hath shined in our hearts, to give the light of the
knowledge of the glory of God in the face of Jesus Christ."*]

*Of his own will begat he us with the word of truth, that we
should be a kind of firstfruits of his creatures.* (James 1:18)

*For though ye have ten thousand instructors in Christ, yet have
ye not many fathers: for in Christ Jesus I have begotten you through
the gospel.* (1 Cor. 4:15)

*Being born again, not of corruptible seed, but of incorruptible, by
the word of God, which liveth and abideth for ever.* (1 Pet. 1:23)

These verses do not prove that the Word must be the
instrumental cause of regeneration, but they do show that
it is the emphasis in all of these recorded instances of
regeneration.

VIII. The new birth is a great mystery—so is physical birth.

John 3:8 and 1 Peter 1:23–2:1 demonstrate the mystery of
our subject. John tells us that being born again is as
mysterious and sovereign as the blowing of the wind. Peter
tells that the union of a man and woman that produces a
new life is also a mystery. We need to look closely at
Peter's words:

*Being born again, not of corruptible seed, but of incorruptible, by
the word of God, which liveth and abideth for ever. For all flesh is as
grass, and all the glory of man as the flower of grass. The grass
withereth, and the flower thereof falleth away: But the word of the*

*Lord endureth for ever. And this is the word which by the gospel is
preached unto you.* (1 Pet. 1:23-25)

Jesus told us that we must be born again, and Peter here
tells us how that takes place. Verse 23 compares our
spiritual birth to our physical birth. We were begotten
when a seed from our father was planted in the ovum of
our mother. That seed had the power to beget life itself.
That seed produced a new creation. That which was not
(you) "became" in the womb of your mother. You were
begotten and then born of a seed, but unfortunately that
seed was a corruptible seed. All that seed could produce
was a child that must die. No human seed has ever
produced a child with everlasting life. When we were born
of God, we were begotten with the seed of God, and that
seed in incorruptible. It produces children that have
everlasting life. That seed is nothing less than the Word of
God. As that word is eternal, so is everything that word
begets.

Peter then compares our existence on this earth to that of
a flower. All flesh is like the grass and the flower. You
plant a seed, a few days later there is a stem and then a
flower. Several more days pass, and it dries up and blows
away. Man is the same. Yesterday I was a little boy, today I
am a grandfather, and tomorrow I will be gone, and no one
will know I was here. However, the seed of God produces
plants of grace that are a sweet-smelling savor to God for
all eternity because they will not wilt and die. When the
Holy Spirit plants the seed of God in the ovum of a sinner's
heart, there is a new creation. We are truly "begotten of

God" through his Word of truth and the power of the Holy Spirit.

IX. The certain evidences — John 3:8.

The passage we quoted in 1 Thess.1:4, 5 goes on to show the radical change in those to whom the Holy Spirit has applied the Word in power. Look at verses 6–10:

> *And ye became followers of us, and of the Lord, having received the word in much affliction, with joy of the Holy Ghost: So that ye were ensamples to all that believe in Macedonia and Achaia. For from you sounded out the word of the Lord not only in Macedonia and Achaia, but also in every place your faith to God-ward is spread abroad; so that we need not to speak any thing. For they themselves shew of us what manner of entering in we had unto you, and how ye turned to God from idols to serve the living and true God; And to wait for his Son from heaven, whom he raised from the dead, even Jesus, which delivered us from the wrath to come.*

They faithfully "followed the Lord" even through times of great affliction. They were living examples of sovereign grace and witnessed their faith far and wide. They forsook their idols and turned completely to the true God, and they were keenly looking for the second coming of Christ.

One of the Puritans said, "If you get soundly converted, even your dog will know something happened to you." John 3:8 is emphatic about the absolute sovereignty of the wind's actions; however, the wind cannot blow without giving clear evidence of its work. The tree leaves move, and the clothes on the line wave back and forth. Some of us have seen firsthand evidence of the awesome power of a hurricane or a tornado. All of us have seen pictures on TV newscasts of a hurricane destroying a coastal town. The same thing is true spiritually. The Holy Spirit always leaves the marks of his work in the life of a true believer. Some of these marks that "accompany salvation" (Hebrews 6:9) are listed in 1 John. Look up each time John uses the words *we know,* and you will have a partial list of proofs of the regenerating work of the Holy Spirit. Galatians 5:22–26 is another list of evidences that the Holy Spirit is "blowing" in a person's life.

X. Summary

The nature of God and of man requires that man must be radically changed in order to be acceptable to God. That radical change is described in Scripture as a new birth that God works in man, without the assistance of man. It is a creative act of the Holy Spirit. The evidences of this creative act are faith and repentance, which in turn produce other distinguishing marks. The new birth is God's work, wrought in man through the Holy Spirit, which results in true spiritual life that is evident by the manner of life of the converted sinner.

CHAPTER EIGHT
THE PERSEVERANCE OF THE SAINTS

In this chapter, we will consider the fifth and final point in the study of the Doctrines of Grace, grace **victorious**. This explains the nature of true saving faith, or the doctrine of the perseverance of the saints. Thus far we have covered the following:

(1) Grace **needed**, which explains the doctrine of total depravity;

(2) Grace **conceived**, or the work of God the Father in salvation, which examines the doctrine of unconditional election;

(3) Grace **secured**, or the work of God the Son in salvation, which looks at the doctrine of limited atonement;

(4) Grace **applied**, or the work of the Holy Spirit in regeneration, which surveys the doctrine of irresistible grace.

Historic and Contemporary Positions

The basic question we are discussing is this: "Can a true child of God lose his salvation and be eternally lost?" Historically, some Christians known as Arminians answered "yes," and another group of Christians called Calvinists answered "no." The Arminian reply was consistent with the basic premise of that theological system. It holds that the one decisive factor in any individual's conversion is the sinner's free-will choice to accept Christ. The Arminian correctly and logically reasoned that if a sinner's free will could begin salvation, then that same free will could choose to end salvation. If the system based on free will is correct, then it indeed logically follows that a Christian can choose to quit following Christ, just as he chose to follow him in the first place. If the one is true, the other is also true.

The Calvinist was just as consistent and logical as the Arminian, but since the basic presupposition of his system was different, he naturally came up with a different answer. The Calvinist held that what God's sovereign grace and power began, it will also finish. A true Christian will be kept by the power of God and be given grace to persevere to the end. It is essential to understand that, at that point in history, all Christians, both the Arminians and Calvinists, agreed that only those who persevered in faith would ultimately reach heaven. A true Calvinist today is far closer to a historic Arminian in his understanding of the nature of saving faith than he is to the "eternal security, anti-Lordship" position.

Both of these groups quoted texts of Scripture that appeared to prove their particular position. The Arminians quoted texts such as the following to prove that one can lose his salvation:

> *For it is impossible for those who were once enlightened, and have tasted the heavenly gift, and have become partakers of the Holy Spirit, and have tasted the good word of God and the powers of the age to come, if they fall away, to renew them again to repentance,*

since they crucify again for themselves the Son of God, and put Him to an open shame. (Heb. 6:4-6 NKJV)

And you will be hated by all for My name's sake. But he who endures to the end will be saved. (Matt. 10:22 NKJV)

The Calvinists countered with verses in accordance with the following to prove that a Christian cannot lose his salvation.

For I am persuaded that neither death nor life, nor angels nor principalities nor powers, nor things present nor things to come, nor height nor depth, nor any other created thing, shall be able to separate us from the love of God which is in Christ Jesus our Lord. (Rom. 8:38-39 NKJV)

My sheep hear My voice, and I know them, and they follow Me. And I give them eternal life, and they shall never perish; neither shall anyone snatch them out of My hand. My Father, who has given them to Me, is greater than all; and no one is able to snatch them out of My Father's hand. (John 10:27-29 NKJV)

Today, most discussions about this subject are of a totally different nature than they were historically. The current tendency is to start in the middle of the subject and then proceed to go round and round in useless arguments. The discussion of this subject has radically changed in the last one hundred years. As mentioned above, it must be emphasized that in the beginning of this dispute, both Calvinists and Arminians agreed that only those who persevered unto the end would be saved. Both sides accepted Matthew 10:22 at face value. The Calvinist insisted just as strongly as the Arminian that one had to endure to the end, or he would indeed be lost. The argument was not over the necessity of perseverance but over the certainty of it. The point of disagreement was whether all Christians would be able to persevere unto the end. The doctrine of free will forced the Arminian to believe that some Christians would not be able to hold out and could, with their free wills, turn back to unbelief and be lost. The doctrine of free and sovereign grace forced the Calvinist to say, "We agree that only those who persevere to the end will be saved, but we also insist that God's grace and power will enable all true believers to persevere."

I am sure the reader will notice that I use the phrase "the perseverance of the saints" and not "eternal security." I assure you that the choice of words is deliberate. If we understand three vital points, we will not only understand the biblical doctrine of perseverance; we will also see how radically different that doctrine is from the idea of eternal security as it is believed and taught by most evangelicals today. Here are the three key questions:

(1) Exactly what, or who, is a true Christian?

(2) How does a person become a true Christian?

(3) How does any individual know for sure that he is a true Christian?

We could ask these same questions another way:

(1) Are you truly converted?

(2) Who told you that you were converted?

(3) Will your salvation enable you to endure to the end?

As you can see from the questions, the doctrine of perseverance is tied very closely to both the nature of salvation and the assurance of salvation.

Let's start with the first question, and discuss what we mean by the word *Christian*. We should get the drowning man safely onto the beach before we start arguing about happens to him if he falls back into the water. Before we argue about whether a true Christian can be lost, let's be sure we all agree on what kind of person we are calling a true Christian.

We are now confronted with the major problem in trying to answer the basic question. Even if we prove that a true child of God can never lose his salvation, we have really not answered the question or solved the real problem. The issue now becomes, "Exactly who is a real child of God?" As already mentioned, in the days when Arminians and Calvinists were arguing about losing one's salvation, they never argued about the necessity of the perseverance of the saints. Both groups taught that perseverance was absolutely essential to salvation. Historically, all evangelicals held that there were only two spiritual classifications of people. There were saved people and lost people. There were Christians, and there were non-Christians. All of that changed a little over a hundred years ago, and we are now told that there are two radically different kinds of Christians. There are "carnal" Christians, and there are "spiritual" Christians. The basic difference between these two clearly defined groups is that one group acts as if they are Christians, and the other one acts exactly like lost, or natural, men. The carnal Christians are said to be just as saved and just as eternally secure as the spiritual Christians. A carnal Christian will make it to heaven "by the skin of his teeth," but lose all his rewards. (This gross error is based on a wrong interpretation of 1 Corinthians 3:11-15). We will examine this theological shift in more detail in *Appendix Four*. For now, we are going to reject this two-fold division of Christians, and say that (1) all Christians are carnal in that they are not sinlessly perfect, and (2) all Christians are spiritual in that they are born of the Spirit, live in the Spirit, and walk—with varying speeds—in the Spirit. Carnality and spirituality are both qualities of degree, and all Christians without exception have varying degrees of both carnality and spirituality.

Definition of Terms

Perhaps it would be wise to explain a few different terms that are used when discussing this subject. Some people have said, "I do not believe in the perseverance of the saints; I believe in the perseverance of the Savior." I also believe in the perseverance of the Savior. However, I believe his perseverance includes the fact that he prays that I will be given grace to keep persevering in faith. The proof of the Savior's perseverance in my behalf is that God does indeed give me the grace to persevere.

Other people say, "I do not believe in the perseverance of the saints; I believe in the preservation of the saints." This is merely another way to express that which was previously stated. Every time I hear this statement, I think of a pickle in jar. It is preserved. The people who talk about preservation versus perseverance are usually teaching that once a man "accepts Christ," he is put into a jar of grace, the lid is sealed, and no matter what he does, he can't get out of the jar. Sadly, I am not caricaturing. That is exactly what the eternal security position means by preservation.

Let's begin with some basic foundation blocks. Our first question then is this: "Exactly who is a true child of God?" It would be both interesting and profitable to look at the many verses of Scripture that describe true Christians. They are designated as saved ones, called ones, elect ones, sheep, disciples, believers, children of God, brothers of Christ, etc. However, we will only look at two texts of Scripture that I think best describe a true Christian. The first is 2 Corinthians 12:2. Notice the following descriptive phrase:

I know a man in Christ… (II Cor. 12:2 NKJV)

That is the best description of a true child of God that I know of in the entire Bible. We cannot describe a true Christian in terms of his theological understanding. A wicked man may declare the truth of sovereign grace, but his theological knowledge about sovereign grace will not put grace into his heart. A man may be a member of the best and most orthodox church and still be as lost as the Devil. A man may go forward in a revival meeting, memorize John 3:16, be baptized by immersion, and still be headed for hell. In other words, theology, church membership, outward life style, and a testimony of faith all put together do not make or keep anyone a child of God.

To be "in Christ" means that a man is joined to Christ in spiritual life and union through a spiritual birth. It means that Christ lives in him, and he lives in Christ. A man in Christ is a living part of a new spiritual creation. Something has happened to him that produces a genuine transformation and change from the old creation of Adam into the new creation of Christ (See 2 Corinthians 5:17).

There is no other literature in all of the world's history that uses this phrase to describe the relationship between two people. It does not matter if it is poetry, prose, or history, nor does it matter in what time period it was written or in what language it was written. Never was it recorded that one person was "in" another person. This can only be understood when we grasp what happens when a sinner is truly "born from above." A real and vital union occurs, and this union is described from two different perspectives. The sinner is said to be "in Christ" (Col. 1:2), and Christ himself is said to be "in the sinner" (Col. 1:27). Paul describes this reality as being part of a "new creation" (II Cor. 5:17) and a "new man" (Eph. 2:15). It should be evident that such a union does not take place because someone walks down the aisle to the front of the church and utters a prayer and memorizes a verse of Scripture. We are talking about the result of a spiritual encounter that produces a radical change in the relationship between two persons.

What we insist on is obvious: a person cannot get "out of Christ" if he was never "in Christ" in the first place. Everything is going to hinge on what it means to be in

Christ and what happens to a sinner when he is baptized into Christ by the Holy Spirit—and every Christian without exception has been baptized into Christ.

The second verse we want to look at explains what happens in every true conversion. The text shows how the gospel affects every part of man's being. Notice how the sinner's mind, will, and affections are all involved in conversion:

> But God be thanked that though you were slaves of sin, yet you obeyed [the will] from the heart [the affections] that form of doctrine [the mind] to which you were delivered. And having been set free from sin, you became slaves of righteousness. (Rom. 6:17, 18 NKJV)

Notice that conversion always begins with acknowledging that God is the sole author of this work. "God be thanked" must always precede every single blessing we receive. Paul does not start by saying, "You are to be congratulated for giving God a chance." Likewise, Paul emphasizes that we were "delivered to the truth." He does not speak in this text about the truth being delivered to us, which, of course, truly happened, but he speaks here of God's sovereign grace and power delivering us over to the power of truth. Paul never misses an opportunity to emphasize sovereign grace!

The next thing to note is the change of masters, the transfer from our slavery to sin to our slavery to righteousness. Any person who is a "slave to sin" has never obeyed the gospel. The purpose of God in electing grace and particular redemption is to deliver his people from their bondage to sin. To think of people being both saved and still slaves of sin is contradictory. Please note that slavery to sin does not mean that saints do not sin or that they may not have besetting sins. It means that sin is not their master in the sense that they are no longer the willing slaves of sin. Likewise, being a slave of righteousness does not mean sinless perfection, but it does mean a willing change of ownership from self to Christ.

Now notice exactly how this transforming work of conversion takes place:

(1) The mind is illuminated with the truth.

(2) The heart, or affections, is penetrated by the truth.

(3) The will is liberated by the truth.

All three of the above must be involved in true conversion. If only the emotions are stirred, and a decision of the will is made based only on the emotions, there will be no true conversion. The individual cannot possibly make a valid spiritual choice while he is ignorant of what is involved in the choice he is making. This is the great tragedy of many "converts" in mass evangelism meetings. Many people sincerely make a decision, but unhappily very soon thereafter they make another decision to deny the first decision. What the emotions and will can do in their own power, they can also undo. With such pseudo-conversions, generally the problem lies not with the sincerity of the individual but with the content of the message. More often than not, the true gospel was not being preached. The listener had no clear knowledge of what or for whom he had decided. In reality, he was emotionally manipulated.

Likewise, if a person is merely intellectually convinced (as were many of the Pharisees) of the historical truth of the claims of Christ, he may decide to believe in Christ in the same way as he decides to believe that Columbus discovered America in 1492. Such a person may sincerely "take up Christianity," but, as Martyn Lloyd-Jones said, "he was never taken by Christianity." There is a great difference between those two things. The Reformed faith appeals to the mind. When correctly understood, it can run any and every philosophy off the campus. The Reformed faith will stand on its own as a valid world and life view. However, it can be held and taught as merely the correct philosophy of life. If the gospel of sovereign grace has not penetrated the very heart of a person, his decision to "accept the Reformed faith" is merely mental assent to the truth, and that is not the same as saving faith.

What are the specific truths that must illuminate the sinner's mind and penetrate his affections? There has to be recognition of God as holy and sovereign. This will produce a realization of actual sin and of being lost. There must then be an understanding of the gospel of God's amazing grace in Jesus Christ. The birth of the Son of God for sinners, his death to pay for our sins, and his glorious resurrection and ascension to the Father's right hand must be understood. We must grasp the cradle, the cross, and the crown of Christ. God does not save men in a state of total ignorance about either himself or their own miserable estate. The gospel is good news and must be heard, understood, and believed with the mind and felt, in some degree, with the heart.

Review

Let us review what we have covered thus far. We stated that the doctrine of the perseverance of the saints as it was taught by our forefathers and the doctrine of eternal security as taught by most evangelicals today are two radically different things. We insisted that we must begin any discussion of perseverance by defining what it means to be a true child of God. It is impossible to discuss whether one can be saved and then lost if we are not agreed on what it means to be saved in the first place. One cannot lose something one never possessed in the first place.

Several things should be obvious by this time. When we ask a person if he is a Christian, we are not asking him if he is a Baptist, Presbyterian, Catholic, Methodist, etc. It is possible that a person can be any one of these and be a truly converted person, and likewise it is also possible to be any one of these and be lost. No one is a Christian because he is a Baptist or Catholic, nor is anyone excluded from heaven because he is a Presbyterian or a Methodist. The question, "Are you a Christian" is the same thing as asking, "Are you in Christ?" We know that not all Presbyterians are saved, nor are all Baptists. Not everyone who goes forward in an evangelistic meeting and prays "the sinner's prayer" truly receives Christ in saving faith. We insist that the three elements of Romans 6:17 (changes in the will, the mind, and the affections) must be present in some degree before there is true conversion.

We are not insisting on correct doctrine alone, as if mere mental belief of the true gospel brings a sinner into Christ. Paul's words in 1 Thessalonians 1:4, 5 should be written in golden letters across every pulpit.

> *Knowing, brethren beloved, your election of God. For our gospel came not unto you in word only, but also in power, and in the Holy Ghost, and in much assurance; as ye know what manner of men we were among you for your sake.* (1 Thess. 1:4, 5 KJV)

In verse 4, Paul expresses his assurance that these people are truly part of God's elect. What made him so sure? Some would think he had seen their baptismal certificate; others would suggest they saw these people walk down the aisle to the altar; and still others might say, "These people are all Calvinists who understand sovereign grace." Paul was sure these people were part of the elect because of the gracious and powerful effect that the gospel had on them. There are several truths in this passage that demand a clear understanding.

First of all, Paul said the "gospel came not in word only." It is vital that we realize that the gospel always comes in words. It does not come in dreams, dramas, visions, or through the waters of baptism or communion cups. The gospel always comes in words or clear facts of history. The gospel is a story and must come to us in words that teach us the true story. However, the intellect can sincerely receive the information in the words and never receive the person of Christ himself. That is why Paul adds to "not only in words" the truth that the gospel words declared were accompanied by the power of the Holy Spirit. Stated another way, not only was the mind illuminated by the truth; the Holy Spirit also applied that truth to the heart and affections. The result was assurance and a wholehearted desire to follow the disciple's teaching.

Key Texts

One of the key texts that teach perseverance of the saints is 1 Peter 1:5, "Who are kept by the power of God through faith unto salvation ready to be revealed in the last time." Notice the following:

1.   God's people are kept persevering in faith, and none of them will ever be lost.

2.   They are kept in this good work by God's power, not their own efforts.

3.   They are kept through faith, signifying the means used, not because of their faith.

4.   This is not inconsistent with the exhortations in verses 13–16.

5.   The whole process begins with sovereign election in verse 2.

I mentioned earlier that until recently there were only two views on the subject of perseverance, but now there is a third. Perhaps it would be good to spell out these views clearly. I remember preaching a sermon entitled, "You are saved as long as you believe." I was with a group of university students, and a young lady come up after the message and said, "Mr. Reisinger, you don't believe the Bible." I don't know why people say that. Just because you don't agree with my interpretation does not mean that I don't believe the Bible. Most of the time when people say, "You don't believe the Bible," what they really mean is, "You don't believe my interpretation of the Bible." There is a man in Tennessee who is convinced I am not saved because I speak of "our Arminian brethren." He writes long letters warning me of my lost estate. He cannot see that he has placed his particular understanding of truth on the same level as inspiration. The poor man's entire theology is, in his eyes, just as verbally inspired as the Bible itself.

The young lady mentioned above went on to say, "You don't believe in eternal security." I replied, "I do not know what that phrase means to you." I learned a long time ago that labels can mean ten different things to ten different people, so I'm not about to say yes or no to any label until someone tells me what that specific label means to them. I asked, "What do you mean by 'eternal security'?" She opened her Bible and ran her finger over John 10:27–28. When she reached the "eternal life/never perish" part, she thumped the Bible with her finger and asked, "Do you believe that?" In response I asked, "Are you telling me that this verse means that not one of Christ's sheep can ever perish because they are all guaranteed eternal life?" She replied quite emphatically, "That's exactly what the verse is saying!" I replied, "Do you mean God gives every one of his sheep, without a single exception, eternal life, and it is absolutely impossible for even one of them to perish?" The young lady said, "That's what the text says."

I looked at the text for a few moments in silence and then asked her, "Who are his sheep?" She said, "What do you mean?" I asked again, "Who are these sheep who can never perish? Is everybody who comes down the aisle and comes forward in a church meeting a sheep with eternal life? Is everybody that has been baptized a sheep? Is everybody who has ever been led to make a confession of faith certain of never perishing because they have everlasting life?" To each of these questions she slowly answered, "No." I repeated, "Alright then, exactly who are these sheep that have everlasting life and cannot possibly ever perish?" She was looking a bit confused, and I pressed her again with the same question and received no answer. I then took my finger and ran it over another part of John 10:27. I said, "Jesus said that these sheep who have everlasting life and can never perish have two distinct marks that identify them as sheep. They all have a mark on their ear—they keep on hearing, and they have a mark on their feet—they keep on following. The text says, "My sheep hear (literally, keep on hearing) my voice and I know them and they follow me." You cannot put that sheep label on every outward professor and then assure that professor that he is "eternally secure."

The young lady asked, "But what if they don't follow?" I said, "What if Christ doesn't give them eternal life?" You can't take the one part of the verse without the rest of it. If you are going to attach the label of "sheep" to every person that you run through your particular ritual or "soul-winning system," whatever it might be (and every church has its own ritual of manufacturing confessions of faith), you are really going to run into trouble. You will indeed need a "carnal Christian" doctrine to explain why your converts do not act differently than lost people. We must insist that we take all of John 10:27–28, and when we do that, we will be teaching the biblical doctrine of perseverance of the saints. We must never deny the eternal security of the saints, but that is totally different from the eternal security of every person who merely makes a profession of faith. We dare not preach the eternal security of wicked and openly profane sinners and imply that there is security even in sin.

The confused girl said, "But all true Christians will keep on believing." "I agree," I said. "That is exactly what I said. You are a Christian as long as you believe and, as you say, if you have truly believed, you will keep on believing. I just said it a little differently. Listening to you, I get the impression that you think you can quit believing and still have everlasting life."

I sometimes read John 10:27–28 three different ways in order to clearly illustrate the three views concerning perseverance. The first time I add the word *if* and read, "My sheep hear my voice and if they follow me I give…" That is the saved-and-lost position. It makes ultimate salvation to be the reward for my perseverance. That is salvation by works. The second time, I leave out the words *follow me* and greatly emphasize the rest of the verse. "My sheep hear my voice, and I know them and [skipping they follow me] I give them eternal life and they shall never perish" That is the eternal-security/carnal-Christian view. Lastly, I read the verse correctly and remind the audience that Jesus emphasized both the following and the never perishing. We must never separate the great blessings of eternal life and never perishing from the mark on the sheep's ear and the mark on his feet.

Truth has Two Sides

We must preach the necessity of a faith that produces effects, but again we must be careful that we do not get into a works-sanctification. I have some friends that have twisted the doctrine of perseverance to the place that they are purely legalistic. They have exalted the law to the place that they are bringing the Christian's conscience under the condemning power of the law. Under such preaching, even the best of saints lose the joy and the assurance of God's so great salvation. We must avoid both of these extremes, which is no easy task.

On the one hand, we dare not hold assurance of salvation hostage to the fruits of sanctification, or we will become legalists. On the other hand, we dare not isolate justification from sanctification in such a way that sanctification is not an essential part of biblical salvation, or we will become antinomians. How we preach these two concepts will quickly prove whether we are legalistic, antinomian, or believe in biblical grace.

I believe any honest person will admit there are texts of Scripture that may appear to teach that you can be saved and lost. The answer to this problem is not to drown out these texts by amassing more texts that teach one cannot be lost after having truly believed. Nor is the answer to evade either the texts or the important truth that they teach. We must recognize that truth has two sides, and we must believe and teach both sides, even when we cannot fully understand how they fit together. Perseverance is essential in biblical salvation, and perseverance is absolutely guaranteed by God to every true sheep.

Let me correct a great error that posits that the truth of God is found "in the middle." Almost always, the people who dislike clear doctrine use this argument to blunt the edge of clear texts of Scripture. They are ready to "tone down the extreme" and strive to be nonoffensive by being in the middle of the road. The truth of God is not found in the middle of the road. It lies in daring to assert both of the extremes. Let me illustrate this with the doctrine of the person of Christ. The gospel confronts us with a person born of a human mother. He gets hungry, goes to sleep, and weeps. Obviously he has all the attributes of humanity, and any reasonable person would agree that this person is a man. And, of course, that is correct. Jesus is a true man.

The gospel also reveals that this individual could raise the dead, control the weather, forgive sins, and call God his Father. He even claimed that he was God. There is much evidence to support his claim of being deity, even as there is much evidence to prove he is a man. What shall we do with this apparent contradiction? Is he man, or is he God? Many would insist that he cannot be both God and man. It must be an either/or situation, but which one? Those dear "middle of the road" people will solve the problem and "reconcile" the problem by toning down both of the extremes. They will say that Jesus is half God and half man and avoid both wild extremes and reach the middle of the road. The only problem is they have lost the biblical truth of the person of Christ. They have a person who is half God and half man that in essence is neither. We must take both of the extremes at the same time and say that Jesus is "God of God and man of man" united in one unique person. I make no attempt to explain how it can be possible. I merely state that is what the Bible clearly teaches.

The Bible is also crystal clear that only those who persevere to the end will reach heaven. The perseverance of the saints is an essential part of the gospel of sovereign grace. The Bible is equally clear that not everyone who merely professes to be going to heaven is really going there. And lastly, the Bible is clear that all who persevere in faith and ultimately make it to heaven do so only because the sovereign grace and power of God enabled them to do so. We must insist on two clear facts: one, perseverance is essential, and two, perseverance is absolutely certain for all of the elect.

Objections

It might be well to mention the major objections to the doctrine of perseverance. The first objection concerns freedom of the will. The argument goes something like this:

"If man's will is truly free, then he can choose to be lost after he is saved. If this is not true, then man loses half of his will power when he becomes a Christian. Before he was saved, he had the power to choose to reject or to believe, but after choosing to believe, he is then no longer able to choose to reject." If this is true, then the sinner indeed has twice as much will-power as the saint. I personally do not think there is a valid answer to this objection. If the premise that man has a free will—the unencumbered or unaided ability to either accept or reject the gospel—is true, then that same free will can choose to renounce the gospel after one is saved. It is logically impossible to believe in free will and also believe you cannot be saved and then lost. Most evangelicals do not see that their free-will religion is untenable.

We must add that even though we reject the doctrine of the free will of man, we do believe that every person who savingly believes does so because he wants to with all of his heart. No one, including God himself, makes a person do something they do not choose to do. Every act of man is an act of free choice. But God can, and indeed he does, make us willing to do what we are totally unwilling and unable to do by nature. We covered this in chapter seven. The question is not, "Does the sinner willingly believe?" but, "Is the willingness a product of his free will or the sovereign work of the Holy Spirit?" Likewise, the question is not, "Must every sheep, and does every sheep, persevere unto the end?" but rather, "Does he do so by the power of free will or free grace?" Paul said the individuals at Achaia had "believed through grace." They had willingly believed, but it was sovereign grace that made them want to believe.

The second argument states that the doctrine of the perseverance of the saints will lead to immoral behavior. At its root, this argument is a form of legalism that cannot trust the awesome power of grace to transform and teach a child of God. This view is usually accompanied by a very weak view of regeneration. We must admit that the doctrine of eternal security and its twin sister, the carnal Christian doctrine, can indeed lead to immoral living. It must be remembered that the idea of the Holy Spirit giving a new heart and writing the law on the heart in regeneration is not at all essential to the proponents of the doctrine of eternal security/carnal Christians. This second argument is a valid evaluation and condemnation of much of evangelicalism today.

The old Methodist mourner's bench was far closer to the truth than modern day mass evangelism and the altar call system. There are two reasons for this statement. First, the old Methodists made the sinner keep praying until he "got through." They did not give very good directions on how to get through to God, but they did insist that no one had a right to tell you that you were saved except God himself! They did not have personal workers trained in how to badger you into an assurance of salvation. They believed the Holy Spirit alone could validate his own work and give you assurance. They were right on that point.

The second thing they taught was that if "getting through" did not make you a radically changed person on

Monday, then you must not have really gotten through, and you better come back and get another dose. In other words, they insisted that salvation made people holy in their hearts. The carnal Christian doctrine would have been just as odious to them as it ought to be to thinking people today.

The third argument is a modified form of the previous one. This argument states that "if the doctrine of the perseverance of the saints does not lead to overt sin, it will surely lead to an indolent 'could-not-care-less' attitude. If I am eternally secure, then I need never fear or worry about my soul." Again we must admit that this charge is valid when made against the "eternal security/carnal Christian" position. However, this is only because that position presents salvation as "insurance" and not as "biblical assurance." It distorts the truth of perseverance. Following are a few differences between the two views:

1. Perseverance is not merely "rely and relax," but it is "trust and obey."

2. Perseverance is not merely "let go and let God," but it is "pick up your cross and follow."

3. Perseverance is not "salvation is certain if we have once believed," but it is "perseverance (keeping on) is certain if we have truly believed."

4. Perseverance is not "persistent effort (holding out to the end) on the sinner's part is necessary to stay saved," but it is "if you are truly saved, you are certain of succeeding in your perseverance."

5. Perseverance is not "salvation is certain regardless
    of what you do once you are saved," but it is
    "perseverance (following) is guaranteed if we have
    truly believed."

6. Perseverance is not "you must keep yourself saved
    by your efforts," but it is "he whom we trust has
    promised that he will not let our faith fail."

It is easy to see from these comparisons that there is a
great difference in how different theologies view the
security of a true child of God.

God's Purpose, Promise, and Power

One aspect that is often overlooked in any discussion of
perseverance is the tremendous stake that God himself has
in the security of his children. I am sure you remember
how Moses pleaded with God to spare Israel when he
announced that he was going to wipe the whole nation out
and start all over with Moses as the new Abraham. Hear
again the exchange between God and Moses:

*And the LORD said unto Moses, I have seen this people, and,
behold, it is a stiffnecked people: Now therefore let me alone, that my
wrath may wax hot against them, and that I may consume them:
and I will make of thee a great nation. And Moses besought the
LORD his God, and said, LORD, why doth thy wrath wax hot
against thy people, which thou hast brought forth out of the land of
Egypt with great power, and with a mighty hand? Wherefore should
the Egyptians speak, and say, For mischief did he bring them out, to
slay them in the mountains, and to consume them from the face of
the earth? Turn from thy fierce wrath, and repent of this evil against
thy people. Remember Abraham, Isaac, and Israel, thy servants, to*

whom thou swarest by thine own self, and saidst unto them, I will multiply your seed as the stars of heaven, and all this land that I have spoken of will I give unto your seed, and they shall inherit it for ever. (Exodus 32: 9–13 KJV)

Notice how Moses argues that the very glory and reputation of God is at stake. The heathen will say that God's grace and power are not sufficient to fulfill his purposes. His professed love for this people is not strong enough for him to forgive and keep them. Moses pleads God's covenant promise and God's power. God's oath, power, purpose, and reputation are tied with Israel, his chosen people.

Our Lord realized that he was responsible for the safety of every sheep the Father had given him. This is clear in the following verses:

While I was with them in the world, I kept them in thy name: those that thou gavest me I have kept, and none of them is lost.... (John 17:1 KJV)

That the saying might be fulfilled, which he spake, Of them which thou gavest me have I lost none. (John 18:9 KJV)

Again it is clear that the both the glory and reputation of our Lord and his Father are tied up with the perseverance of every one of the sheep. There are three things involved in this subject. There is the stated purpose of God, the specific promise of God, and the sovereign power of God.

The stated purpose of God is clearly set forth in the five golden links in the chain of grace described in Romans 8:28–32. Every person who has been chosen and predestined to be conformed to the image of Christ is going to be effectually called and perfectly justified. They are already — past tense — glorified in the mind and purpose of God. If one of the sheep in the chain of grace is lost, the whole chain is broken and God's purpose is unrealized.

The specific promise of God is set forth in, among many others, the following passage from 1 Corinthians:

> *I thank my God always on your behalf, for the grace of God which is given you by Jesus Christ; That in every thing ye are enriched by him, in all utterance, and in all knowledge; Even as the testimony of Christ was confirmed in you: So that ye come behind in no gift; waiting for the coming of our Lord Jesus Christ: Who shall also confirm you unto the end, that ye may be blameless in the day of our Lord Jesus Christ. God is faithful, by whom ye were called unto the fellowship of his Son Jesus Christ our Lord.* (1 Cor. 1:4–9 KJV)

Notice the clear promise in verse 8. God has pledged to confirm the elect "unto the end." Verse 9 assures us that God is faithful to perform the things that he promises. Just as he faithfully called those he had chosen, so he will be faithful in keeping them in grace. I will grant that this has two sides. 1 Peter 1:5 tells us that we are "kept by the power of God," and Jude 21 exhorts us to "keep ourselves in the love of God." These are the two sides of one coin and are not in contradiction. We keep ourselves in the love of God purely through the grace and power of God that is given to us. Notice how John states the matter. "We know that whosoever is born of God sinneth not; but he that is begotten of God keepeth himself, and that wicked one toucheth him not (1 John 5:18 KJV). The "keeping" of ourselves is possible because of the truth that regeneration gives us a new nature. "...greater is he that is in you, than he that is in the world" (1 John 4:4 KJV).

The sovereign power of God in keeping his people is set forth in 1 Peter:

> Blessed be the God and Father of our Lord Jesus Christ, which according to his abundant mercy hath begotten us again unto a lively hope by the resurrection of Jesus Christ from the dead, To an inheritance incorruptible, and undefiled, and that fadeth not away, reserved in heaven for you, Who are kept by the power of God through faith unto salvation ready to be revealed in the last time. Wherein ye greatly rejoice, though now for a season, if need be, ye are in heaviness through manifold temptations: That the trial of your faith, being much more precious than of gold that perisheth, though it be tried with fire, might be found unto praise and honour and glory at the appearing of Jesus Christ: Whom having not seen, ye love; in whom, though now ye see him not, yet believing, ye rejoice with joy unspeakable and full of glory: Receiving the end of your faith, even the salvation of your souls. (1 Peter 1:3–9 KJV)

The salvation of God begins with God's abundant mercy in choosing us. We are then begotten by God's power unto a living hope. That same grace enables us to keep on believing in spite of many hindrances and temptations. We are enabled to rejoice even in tribulation because we are positively certain of reaching the final and full salvation of our souls.

Observations

The eternal-security position does not consider the biblical exhortations to perseverance, and the saved-lost view incorrectly proposes that such exhortations would never have been given if it were not possible to fall away. It has not occurred to adherents of these positions that the very means that God uses to assure our efforts to persevere are the warnings against apostasy. Someone has said, "To warn a traveler to keep to a certain path, and by the warning keeping him to the path, is no evidence that he will ever fall into a pit by the wayside just because you warned him about it. The very warning was necessary to keep him in the path." John Bunyan said, "There are two deep ditches on either side of the road to heaven. The one is the ditch of despair, and the other is the ditch of presumption. In front of the ditch of despair, God has placed a row of hedges made of promises to keep the poor pilgrim from despair in times of defeat. In front of the ditch of presumption, he has placed another row of hedges made of up of fearful warning to keep the poor pilgrim from presuming on the grace of God." J.C. Ryle said there were two thieves on either side of Christ. The one was saved in order to show there are death-bed conversions, and the other was lost to show that no one should wait and presume.

I must add one last observation. Whenever you say that a man was saved and is now lost, you make two possible grievous mistakes. You judge the man's heart in saying he was saved, and then you judge a second time when you say he is lost. We would all have pronounced Judas as saved for nearly three whole years, and we would have been wrong. We would also have labeled Peter a lying hypocrite when he cursed and swore, and again we would have been wrong. Judas was lost even when everyone would have put him on the saved list, and Peter, though backslidden, was a true believer, even though all of us would have put him on the lost list.

The nature of true salvation is covered in *Appendix Three*, which consists of those portions of The London Baptist Confession of Faith that deal with this subject, and in *Appendix Four*, which examines the carnal Christian doctrine.

CHAPTER NINE
THE SOVEREIGNTY OF GOD IN PERSONAL LIFE

And we know that all things work together for good to them that love God, to them who are the called according to His purpose. (Rom 8:28, KJV)

We could title this chapter, "A Soft Pillow for a Weary Head and a Sorry Heart." The truth and power of this text rests on what we have already established about the sovereignty of God. If God does not control all things, without exception, this verse cannot be true. The text reads better in the NIV, "And we know that in all things God works for the good of those who love him, who have been called according to his purpose." The key idea is not that all things turn out for the best, although that is true, but that God controls all things for the purpose of his children's good. We reject a mechanistic view of the world. The world does not run on its own, controlled only by natural law. God makes the sun to shine, and God makes the rain to fall. Rainfall and sunshine do not just happen; God makes them happen as he pleases. Things do not just work by themselves; God works, or controls, everything for the benefit of his people.

In the light of a promise as great as Romans 8:28, we wonder how Christians can ever be anxious or become depressed. It is, unfortunately, a fact that Christians sometimes are anxious and depressed—some more so than others. In this chapter, I want to offer eight reasons why

Christians do not receive the comfort that they should from this text and others like it.

One, we fail to grasp that *all things* really means ALL things.

The word *all*, in this passage, denotes all without distinction and without exception. The broader context (vv. 18-38) includes present suffering and subjection to decay, present frustration, possible future suffering and subjection, and future glory. The word *all* embraces things seen and unseen—everything in all creation. Thus, the text does not teach that God will work some things (all things of a certain kind, but not other things of a different kind) for our good, but that he will work all things for our good. It would indeed be a wonderful blessing if God made most things ultimately work for our good. We think it would be amazing if God worked many things together for the believer's good. Romans 8:28, however, goes beyond these possibilities and states that God works all things, without distinction or exception, for the good of his people.

We can better grasp the scope of the word *all* when we categorize what it encompasses: home, work, health, finances, church, and many other areas. The definition of *all* extends to time, as well: when I am young, when I am middle-aged, and "even down to old age."

To benefit, both intellectually and emotionally, from God's promise in Romans 8:28, we must believe, both intellectually and emotionally, that God really means all things, without a single exception. In this life, we may never understand or see how a specific event will serve God's purpose of good for us. We can be sure, however, that no matter what happens, God has designed it to serve his sovereign purpose of conforming us into the image of Christ. Regardless of what comes our way, we can be sure it was essential to accomplish God's ordained work in us.

Two, we confuse God's using something for a good end with the thing itself having a nature that is good.

In Romans 8:28, Paul is not teaching that God promises a pain-free life; rather, he is assuring his readers that God promises to bring good out of all things, no matter how ugly or painful those things may be in themselves. Many evil and painful things happen to believers. Sickness and pain are never good in themselves. Hateful and untrue gossip about us is extremely painful. God cannot and does not take the pain out of hurtful things, but he can and does give hope and comfort in the worst of times. I have heard many people testify after a serious and painful operation, "I would not have missed all that God taught me through this, just to avoid the pain that came with it." In effect, they were saying, "Romans 8:28 is true." They were expressing the comfort that Romans 8:28 brought to their weary heads and sorrowing hearts. We must not confuse the means with the ends. Remember those great words of Joseph, "You meant it for evil, but God meant it for good" (Gen. 50:20).

Someone may ask the logical question whether all things includes even sin. The text just quoted from Genesis helps to answer that. What Joseph's brothers did to him was mean, wicked, and painful, but God used it for his own glory. This concept extends to original sin, to our personal sins (those we commit), and to the sins against us (those others commit that affect us). In reference to original sin, we can say that because of Adam's sin, God's mercy is manifested in a way it never could have been otherwise. Apart from sin, there is no mercy, simply because if there is no sin, there is no need of mercy. The redeemed know God in a greater way than they ever could have apart from sin, because we have gained more in Christ than we lost in Adam.

In reference to our personal sins, God sometimes allows us to fall and bloody our noses as a means of keeping us from breaking our necks in the future. How often has God allowed us to be overcome in a specific instance as the means of teaching us just how bad our hearts really are? It is one thing to believe the doctrine of total depravity as a theological statement; it is another to see and feel that depravity in our own hearts and lives. God is serious about our sanctification and is always at work, moving it along.

Three, we tend to isolate one particular thing and try to figure out how it can possibly be used for good.

The word *together* is vital in this verse. Nothing operates independently of other things. Imagine trying to swallow the individual ingredients of a cake, one ingredient at a time. Try a mouthful of flour, then a teaspoon of salt, then a mouthful of butter. All of those things taken individually would make you gag, and none by itself is appealing. If, however, you mix them all together in the right proportions and bake them for just the right amount of time in an oven at 350 degrees, you have a mouth-watering cake. The same is true with the circumstances that God is pleased to bring into our lives. Everything is intertwined, but you and I see only a very small part of the picture. We must not dwell on one thing and allow it to control our thinking and living.

God controls all the variables and ingredients in our lives. He also controls the temperature of the oven and the length of time we spend there. We, on the other hand, cannot control all of the variables in our lives, and as a result, we often fail in a project. We may control six of seven essential variables, but not the seventh, and thus the entire project fails. We want the best for our children, but we do not always know what is best for them. Sometimes we are too close to be objective (maybe they need a good spanking; maybe they need words of encouragement). Sometimes we know what would be good for them, but we cannot afford it. Things such as college expenses may be beyond our means. Sometimes we know what is good for them, we have the finances to procure it, but we cannot get them to see that it would be good for them. God is not limited as we are! He knows what is best for us; he can bring into our lives exactly what we need; he is never hindered by lack of resources; and, praise his name, he can even make us willing to cooperate in the day of his power.

I once preached a funeral sermon for a twelve-year-old boy. His parents had recently been converted under my ministry. They were active in politics, were well-known, and were well-loved by the community. All the town officials attended the funeral. I prayed for God to help me illustrate the truth of Romans 8:28 in the sermon. I told how I used to work jigsaw puzzles. Inevitably, one or two pieces seemed not to belong to the puzzle. I would pick them up and move them around, trying to make them fit. I sometimes thought, "This piece must have fallen on the floor at the manufacturers, and they put it in the wrong box." The piece did not seem to have the right thickness or the same color as any of the other pieces. I would be tempted to throw it away, because it obviously did not belong to this puzzle. I would keep working the pieces and usually would put the troublesome piece in place at the very end. When I finished, the puzzle in front of me looked exactly like the picture on the box. It did not take many puzzles before I learned how stupid it would be to throw that piece away.

If we try to understand how a specific painful event in our lives makes sense and somehow works for our good, we waste our time and lose all sense of hope. Just like the mystery piece of the jigsaw puzzle, a particular incident may temporarily defeat our attempts to make it fit. We must not take hold of one piece of our life and demand an explanation of how and where it fits in the bigger picture. If we do that, all we will accomplish is to add the ragged edges of painful unbelief to our present suffering. Instead, we must lay that piece down at the feet of a sovereign God and live by faith (keep working the puzzle). Lay it down before God, and keep seeking to please him by faith. In the end, the picture of our lives will match what God has ordained.

When we say, "by faith, lay it down before God," we are not talking about treating God as though he were an Ouija board—all-knowing, but impersonal and indifferent. We are talking about a holy heavenly Father who loves us so much that he gave his Son to die for us.

Four, we fail to distinguish clearly the objects of the promise.

Sometimes, Christians think to offer comfort by generalizing the promise, "Well, you know the Bible says that everything will work out all right." If they mean that the Bible promises this positive outcome to all people without exception, they have misrepresented the actual claim. Clearly, Romans 8:28 does not apply to everybody. It can hardly mean that everything works out for good for the person who goes to hell. If people are lost and continue to reject the gospel, things will not, in any way, work out all right for them. Actually, all things will ultimately be bad for Christ-rejecters.

The word *all* in this text is indeed a universal *all*—all without exception—but it refers to things that happen, and not to the recipients of the promise. "In all things, God works..." This great promise does not apply to everyone without exception. The text explicitly limits the promise two ways: first, the promise itself is qualified—it applies to only "those who love God," and second, it defines this group as "those who have been called according to his purpose." The recipients of the promise are a specific and limited group of people, namely those who (1) love God and (2) have been called according to his purpose. This group does not include those who hate God and have never been called by grace.

Many Christians do not quote the text correctly. Ask the next ten Christians you meet to quote Romans 8:28, and likely nine of the ten will quote it incorrectly. They will either leave off the first three words, "and we know," or they will leave off the last phrase, "to them who are the called according to his purpose."

The phrase, *who are the called according to his purpose,* describes those who love God. Romans 8:28 is a promise given only to the people of God for their comfort and hope in times of trouble. It is indeed a soft pillow for a weary head and sorrowing heart for those who love God because he first loved them. If we leave off the qualifying phrase (who are the called...), we destroy the promise. If we leave off the opening (and we know), we lose the personal power of the promise. The words *and we know* are, in one sense, the best part of the verse. They refer to the knowledge of experience. This knowledge is not merely intellectual (although it must include that) but encompasses the experience of personal faith. When we apply the promise to difficult situations in our lives, we glorify God by believing that what he has said is true.

When I was in university, I had a professor who tried to teach us how to think. He spent one entire class period explaining the virtue of eating rats. He explained that they were high in protein, they were both free and accessible, and that eating them would solve more than one problem. The professor's arguments convinced all of our minds, but none of our stomachs. To my knowledge, no one in the class ever ate any rats. You could have said the whole class knew it was a good idea to eat rats, but no one in the class really knew by experience that it was good. There are many believers who know, intellectually, that Romans 8:28 and other promises in God's word are true, but they never act upon that knowledge. They do not experience the truth of the text. They do not see current problems in their own lives as included in *all things,* nor do they see the promise as meant for them. Thus, they fail to roll their problems or griefs onto the God of this text.

Many lost people know, intellectually, the way of salvation just as well as I do. I suspect that some such people are reading this book right now. However, they know it only in their heads and not in their hearts. They know that salvation is found in Christ alone and that a person must go to him in repentance and faith, but they have never approached Christ in personal faith and been saved. They cannot say, "I know, by personal experience, that Jesus saves, because he has saved me."

Five, we fail to put the promise in its context.

We touched on this briefly in our first point, when we discussed our failure to grasp that *all things* really means ALL things. When we read a text such as Romans 8:28, we might well wonder how Paul could have made such a sweeping statement. How could he have made such a dogmatic declaration? We find the answer in the next verse, which begins with the word *for* or *because.* Here, Paul provides the theological foundation for his confidence.

Without this theological foundation, the text is only a platitude.

Let us look at the context of Romans 8:28 and follow Paul's argument. Here are the verses that state the promise and then give the theological foundation for the promise.

> 28 *And we know that in all things God works for the good of those who love him, who have been called according to his purpose. 29 For those God foreknew he also predestined to be conformed to the likeness of his Son, that he might be the firstborn among many brothers. 30 And those he predestined, he also called; those he called, he also justified; those he justified, he also glorified.*
>
> 31 *What, then, shall we say in response to this? If God is for us, who can be against us? 32 He who did not spare his own Son, but gave him up for us all—how will he not also, along with him, graciously give us all things? 33 Who will bring any charge against those whom God has chosen? It is God who justifies. 34 Who is he that condemns? Christ Jesus, who died—more than that, who was raised to life—is at the right hand of God and is also interceding for us. 35 Who shall separate us from the love of Christ? Shall trouble or hardship or persecution or famine or nakedness or danger or sword? 36 As it is written: "For your sake we face death all day long; we are considered as sheep to be slaughtered." 37 No, in all these things we are more than conquerors through him who loved us. 38 For I am convinced that neither death nor life, neither angels nor demons, neither the present nor the future, nor any powers, 39 neither height nor depth, nor anything else in all creation, will be able to separate us from the love of God that is in Christ Jesus our Lord.* (NIV)

Verse 28 sets forth the promise. Verse 29 begins with the conjunction *for*, showing the connection of the promise to what follows. In verses 29-39, Paul explains why we can be so certain that all things, without exception, will work together for good for God's people. Then, in verses 29-31, Paul lists five links in a golden chain of grace. I have bolded the links.

29 For (1) those God **foreknew** he also (2) **predestined** to be conformed to the likeness of his Son, that he might be the firstborn among many brothers. 30 And those he predestined, he also (3) **called**; those he called, he also (4) **justified**; those he justified, he also (5) **glorified**.

Notice that this chain of grace occurs in eternity — outside of time. It begins with God foreknowing us, which is tantamount to choosing us unto salvation, and ends with our complete glorification before the throne of God. Nothing can break this chain. Every person, without exception, upon whom Gods sets his electing love will be conformed to the image of Christ, will be called, will be justified, and will be glorified. We experience the reality of God's action in time, but he established the entire chain outside of time.

The word *foreknew* in verse 29 does not refer to God's ability to look into the future and know what will happen. If God were subject to time in the same way that we are, then perhaps we could meaningfully talk about his ability to look into the future. But if God is not limited by time, then surely we cannot think about him looking into the future. Even if we were to grant the possibility, that is not what is conveyed by the word *foreknow*. Often in Scripture, the word *know* means love. Granted, it also sometimes means information and facts, as in Genesis 8:11.

> *And the dove came to him in the evening; and, lo, in her mouth*
> *was an olive leaf plucked off; so Noah knew that the waters were*
> *abated from off the earth.*

In other texts, however, such as Genesis 4:1, the word *know* does not simply mean factual knowledge. In those contexts, it means to love in an intimate sense. Compare the KJV and the NIV.

> *And Adam knew his wife; and she conceived....* (Gen. 4:1 KJV)

> *Adam lay with his wife Eve, and she became pregnant....* (Gen. 4:1 NIV)

From comparing the KJV and the NIV, as well as from looking at the context, it is clear Adam knew his wife means the same thing as Adam lay with his wife. There is no way in these verses that *know* means knowledge in the same way it means knowledge in Genesis 8:11. The same is true with Amos 3:2.

> *You only have I known of all the families of the earth....* (Amos 3:2 KJV)

> *You only have I chosen of all the families of the earth....* (Amos 3:2 NIV)

To know in this text means to love. It means, as the NIV correctly translates it, as to choose. Look at one last text from the New Testament.

> *And then I will profess unto them, I never knew you: depart*
> *from me....* (Matt. 7:23 KJV)

Clearly, the word *knew* in this text cannot mean informational knowledge. It was because Jesus had informational knowledge of these people that he sent them away. In this text, to know must mean, "I did not know you in a way of love," or "I never chose you as one of my own."

When we understand this facet of the word *know* and add the prefix *fore* to it, as it occurs in Romans 8:28, we have the concept of God loving us before he predestined us. In this sense, God foreknowing us is really God's rationale in his choosing us. Foreknowledge here is the love that precedes and causes election.

In Romans 8:28, Paul's use of the verb *foreknew* does not mean that God looked into the future and saw who would believe and, on the basis of this foreknowledge, chose those people to be saved. In such a view, God does not actually choose anyone; he merely knows beforehand that I will believe and, on that basis, he ratifies my choice. He foresees that I will be willing to believe and says, "Fine, on the basis of your free-will choice of me, I choose you." We must also point out that Romans 8:29 does not say that God foreknew something, meaning he had prior information, but he foreknew somebody. It is not facts he foreknew; it is people that he foreknew, meaning fore-loved.

The concept of *before*, denoted by the prefix *fore*, has a logical rather than a temporal sense. Everything that follows in the text grows out of this first step—God's foreknowing us in a way of electing love. The next link in the chain is predestination, which is God's purposing to conform all whom he has foreknown into the image of Christ. Notice carefully the wording. All those (and only those) whom God (1) foreknew, or fore-loved and chose, he also (2) predestined to be conformed into the image of Christ. All those he predestinated (and only them), he, as the first step toward ultimate glorification (which is complete conformity to the image of Christ), also (3) called; those whom he called, all of them (but only them), he also (4) justified; those, all of them (but only them) he justified, he also (5) glorified.

Each of the five links is inextricably bound to what precedes and what follows. The person who experiences one blessing experiences all five, and all of God's people experience all five blessings. Note that this is the only place in Paul's writings that he jumps from justification to glorification without mentioning sanctification (those he justified, he also glorified). This is not because he forgot, but because of the context. Paul is dealing with eternal realities. The sinner whom God chose in sovereign grace is certain of being called and justified. God, in his mind and purpose, has already glorified that same sinner in Christ. Paul, therefore, does not need to mention sanctification in this context.

Note also that the order and certainty of calling and justification destroys the Arminian concept of free will. Look carefully at the texts.

> *And those he predestined, he also called; those he called, he also justified; those he justified...*

"Calling" in these verses has to mean effectual calling or regeneration. The only reason that anyone is effectually called by the gospel is because that person has been foreknown and predestinated. Notice that everyone who is predestined is sure of being called. The text says, "also called." Likewise, every sinner, without a single exception, who is called is certain of being justified. Again, notice the text. All who are called (all of them, but only them), are certain of being justified. No amount of interpretive skill can recast the text to mean, "God calls all people without exception, and all those who are willing to believe will be justified." In Romans 8:29, all without exception who are called, and only them, will be justified. We agree that there is a sense in which the gospel invites all sinners, but that is not the sense Paul uses here.

In verse 31, Paul asks a logical question. The answer to this question determines the degree of comfort reasonable to expect from the great promise in Romans 8:28.

31 *What, then, shall we say in response to this? If God is for us, who can be against us?*

The KJV translates thusly, "What shall we say to these things?" This, or these things, refers to the five links in the chain of grace that Paul has just set forth. How ought the reader to respond to the certainty of this chain of grace? If God be for us means that he is for us in a way of electing love, for us in a way of predestination, for us by calling us in grace and power, for us in a way of justification, and for us in a way of certain glorification. Who (or what) can effectively be against the person upon whom God sets his love and sovereignly purposes to conform to the image of Christ? Who can even challenge the person whom God calls out of death and justifies from all guilt and shame, and then promises that nothing or nobody can stop his or her ultimate glorification? Remember, Paul asks this question in the context of his explanation of the foundation upon which the great promise of Romans 8:28 rests. All the devils in hell may be arrayed against you, but if you are one of the elect of God, you will prevail and make it to glory.

In verse 32, Paul continues to unpack the implications of "If God is for us, who can be against us?"

> 32 *He who did not spare his own Son, but gave him up for us all—how will he not also, along with him, graciously give us all things?*

This verse needs little comment. The logic is simple. If God gave us the best possible gift—his own Son—why would he withhold lesser gifts from us? The answer is that he will not—he will give us all good things. Implicit also is the idea that if God paid such a high price for us, he will protect his investment. Will he allow anything to keep him from fulfilling his promise to conform us into the image of Christ? *All things* in this verse refers to *all things* in verse 28. God guarantees that everything that comes our way is an essential part of his ultimate purpose—to conform us to Christ. We must remember that God has much at stake in our ultimate glorification.

Paul continues to explain why no one can be against God's chosen people. Verse 33 is one of those verses that elicits a hallelujah from those who understand it.

> 33 *Who will bring any charge against those whom God has chosen? It is God who justifies.*

Here, Paul restates the truth he already expressed, but now he emphasizes a slightly different aspect. Previously, Paul has highlighted the aspect of certainty. He wants his readers to grasp the absolute certainty of the ultimate and complete salvation of the people of God (those whom he has called and justified). Now he explains the basis for that certainty. The highest judicial authority has ruled, and no one can overturn his decision. We can illustrate this concept by looking at the American judicial system.

Our judicial system allows for appeal after appeal, from lower to higher courts. Finally, however, the appeal reaches the Supreme Court, beyond which there is no higher court. The only authority that is greater than the Supreme Court is the president. When the president of the United States pardons a person, no court, including the Supreme Court, or law enforcement agency can touch that person. When the president pardons, no one can legally challenge that pardon. President Ford pardoned Richard Nixon, and no one could bring an accusation against Nixon. The highest authority in the land had spoken. In our case, the highest authority in the universe has declared us to be justified in his sight, and neither humans nor devils can challenge his decree.

We can find comfort in times of great distress when we understand and apply verse 34.

34 Who is he that condemns? Christ Jesus, who died—more than that, who was raised to life—is at the right hand of God and is also interceding for us.

Paul, in verse 34, unpacks verse 33 a bit more fully. Verse 33 assures me that God has justified me. Verse 34 reminds me that the God who justifies is the one who has died for me. Christ Jesus is the judge into whose hands the Father has committed all judgment. He is also the one who died for my sins. Those sins were on him when he died, and were buried with him. They were left behind when he rose from the dead. The one who died for me, bore my sins, and buried those sins, now sits at the right hand of God and has the authority to save and damn whom he will. He makes intercession to the Father—specifically praying for those for whom he died. Do you see what Paul implies? Is it possible that Christ would die for me, pray out of one side of his mouth for the Father to keep me (because he died for me), and then pray out of the other side of his mouth for me to be condemned? Such a scenario violates the notion of Christ as undivided.

This assurance is a glorious truth. In Romans 8:26, the Holy Spirit, the third person of the Trinity, is in me and prays for me. In Romans 8:34, the Son of God, the second person of the Trinity, is at the Father's right hand making intercession for me. I believe I am going to make it!

When we understand the context of Romans 8, we see that it functions as a glorious song of assurance of complete salvation. This chapter is like an opera that goes from one crescendo of glory to another. It opens with no condemnation in Christ and closes with no separation from Christ. God's people cannot be condemned as long as they are in Christ, and no one and no thing can get them out of

Christ. Verses 35 through 39 conclude Paul's argument and list some of what is included in the *all things* of verse 28.

> 35 *Who shall separate us from the love of Christ? Shall trouble or hardship or persecution or famine or nakedness or danger or sword? 36 As it is written: "For your sake we face death all day long; we are considered as sheep to be slaughtered." 37 No, in all these things we are more than conquerors through him who loved us. 38 For I am convinced that neither death nor life, neither angels nor demons, neither the present nor the future, nor any powers, 39 neither height nor depth, nor anything else in all creation, will be able to separate us from the love of God that is in Christ Jesus our Lord.* (NIV)

Every time I read these five verses, I remind myself that somewhere in the world today, I have brothers and sisters enduring every one of those things. They suffer, but not without hope in eternal life. I marvel that Christ calls his bride to endure such suffering for his name's sake, and that they do so most willingly.

Thus far, we have considered five of eight reasons why Christians fail to receive comfort from the promise of Romans 8:28:

1. We fail to grasp that *all things* really means ALL things.

2. We confuse God's using something for a good end with the thing itself having a nature that is good.

3. We tend to isolate one particular thing and try to figure out how it can possibly be used for good.

4. We fail to distinguish clearly the objects of the promise.

5. We fail to put the promise in its context.

Let us continue with the final three reasons.

Six, we fail to personalize the promise for a present need.

As children, we learned that it was right to think of others and to stop saying, "Me!" When it comes to the promises of God, however, we must learn to say, "That means me!" Some Christians can lay hold of God and plead on behalf of a missionary far better than they can trust God for their own needs. They have no trouble believing that God was great and mighty "back in Bible times" and in the days of Spurgeon. They believe that God will manifest his immediate presence and power once more in the future. He will be great and glorious at the "second coming." The problem is that we live today, and we need grace for our present problems.

Seven, we fail to see the greatness of God.

Our faith and hope will never exceed our view of God's power and promise. How does God give us faith and hope? Does he have a big spiritual barrel in heaven labeled Faith? If we pray for thirty minutes, will he give us a quart of faith? If we pray for an hour, will he dish out several quarts of faith? Is there another barrel labeled Hope? If we keep his commandments exceptionally well, will he give us a pound of hope? Or do we grow in faith and hope as we behold God's character and power and review his promises? We look at the promise and say, "My God is able to do that!" Growing in faith begins with growing in the knowledge of God's word.

When I was in my first pastorate, I went to the hospital to visit one of the church members. When I got to the room, I discovered that the individual had gone home. An elderly man, lying unconscious in the bed, and his wife, who sat beside the bed, occupied the room. I introduced myself and apologized for intruding. The woman, Mrs. Steffen, explained that her husband had been hit by a train and had not regained consciousness. She then said, "We are old-time Methodist. Would you please pray for my husband?" The Lord knit my heart to the Steffens, and I visited them on a regular basis despite the fact they were not members of my particular congregation.

The doctors told Mrs. Steffen that her husband would probably never awaken from his coma. She continued to plead with God, who answered her prayer. Mr. Steffen not only awoke, but also started to recover. He was unable, however, to walk. The Steffens' doctor persuaded a noted surgeon from a large hospital in another town to look at Mr. Steffen's x-rays. The surgeon accepted the case, believing that he could apply a new operating procedure that would correct the problem. He told the couple that he believed Mr. Steffen would walk again. This surgeon was confident and persuasive, but he only visited this hospital once a week. By the time he would arrive for his weekly visit, Mrs. Steffen would be depressed. He would smile, take her hand and gently rub it, and say, "Now Mrs.

Steffen, did I not tell you that your husband was going to walk again?" Slowly her tears would dry, and she would smile and start to shake her head in agreement. She believed he was able to do what he had promised.

After the specialist would leave, Mrs. Steffen would gradually become depressed again. Her local doctor, the nurses, and I all would try to assure her, but to no avail. We would say exactly the same thing the specialist said, but our words did not have the same effect as his did. She never said it aloud, but you could almost hear her thinking, "What do you know?" It never occurred to her to treat the words of the specialist the way she treated ours. She believed his promise because she trusted his reputation and his character.

We need to trust God for the same reasons Mrs. Steffen trusted the surgeon. The reputation and character of God lie behind every promise he makes. If we realized this, we would trust him to fulfill his promises.

I should add here that God has not promised that he will keep us from difficulties and problems. Scripture contains no promise that God will deliver us out of the furnace any more than it contains a similar promise to the three Hebrew men who faced Nebuchadnezzar's fiery furnace. God's usual way is to give grace to endure, just as a child of God should endure, and not necessarily to provide escape from the situation. There is always (1) the assurance that he can deliver, and (2) if he does not, he has something better. Remember again those three Hebrew men. They knew in whose hands their lives rested, regardless of whether they escaped the fire or not.

Eight, we fail to distinguish between hurt and harm.

I was sitting in the dentist's chair, and I must have looked scared. The dentist smiled and said, "John, don't worry. I am going to hurt you, but I am not going to harm you." There is a great difference between those two things. Some things are painful, but they are essential or God would never allow them. The worst of pain does not contradict the truth of Romans 8:28 any more than needles or bitter pills harm us when we are sick. Sometimes, the only healing comes via painful treatments.

Mr. Steffen experienced hurt, but not harm, as he regained use of his legs after his operation. I was present during one of the surgeon's post-op visits. I started to leave, but the doctor said it was all right if I stayed. After examining him, the doctor said, "Mr. Steffen, today we are going to start moving your legs." The doctor took one leg and pulled it while slightly twisting it at the same time. Mr. Steffen let out one of the most blood-curdling screams I have ever heard. I could hear bedpans dropping and saw people running toward the room from every direction. I am sure they thought someone was being murdered. After things settled down, the doctor calmly said, "Now, Mr. Steffen, we are going to move the other leg," and he proceed to reach for it. Mr. Steffen turned white and cried, "No, please! Please don't! Leave it alone. I would rather be a cripple! Please! Please!" The doctor ignored Mr. Steffen's pleading and proceeded to pull and twist his other leg.

From my vantage point at that time, it sure seemed as though the doctor was harming Mr. Steffen. But if I had concluded that the doctor was cruel and was harming his patient, I would have been wrong

I was present later when Mr. Steffen walked out of the hospital, with only a cane to help him. I watched him, with tears in his eyes, kiss those same hands that had made him scream earlier. My dear child of God, you will do the same thing one day. At the present moment, when God raises the temperature in the furnace of a particular affliction, you are ready to cry, "No! No! Please don't! I would rather be a carnal Christian." God loves you too much to let you be a spiritual cripple. He will pull and twist when it is necessary to enable you to walk straight. You will kiss the hands that brought the necessary affliction. As my dentist said, "Hurt, but not harm."

I read somewhere (I think it was in Spurgeon) of a grandpa who took his grandson to church. The preacher graphically depicted the awful things people did to Jesus at the cross. On the way home, the little boy started to cry, and his grandpa asked him why he was crying. The little boy said, "I was thinking about all the wicked things those men did to Jesus." He bit his lip and said defiantly, "I bet if God would have been there, they would never have done those things to our Savior." Then his grandpa started to cry, as he said, "God was there. He was the one who allowed all those things to happen!" My dear reader, God is always there. In your darkest hour and in your deepest need, he is there. He knows all about it and has it all under

control. He is at work in his potter's shop, and you can rest
assured that you will come forth as gold—tried and refined
by sovereign grace. God has provided Romans 8:28 to give
us the grace we need to kiss his hands now, while we are in
the fire. We do not have to wait to bless him until the day
of our full redemption. Texts such as Romans 8:28 enable
us to joyfully sing hymns such as the following; one of my
favorites.

> What-e'er my God ordains is right:
> Holy His will abideth;
> I will be still what-e'er He doth,
> And follow where He guideth:
> He is my God; though dark my road,
> He holds me that I shall not fall:
> Wherefore to Him I leave it all.

> What-e'er my God ordains is right:
> He never will deceive me;
> He leads me by the proper path;
> I know He will not leave me:
> I take, content, what He hath sent;
> His hand can turn my griefs away,
> And patiently I wait His day.

> What-e'er my God ordains is right:
> Though now this cup, in drinking,
> May bitter seem to my faint heart,
> I take it, all unshrinking:
> My God is true; each morn anew
> Sweet comfort yet shall fill my heart,
> And pain and sorrow shall depart.

What-e'er my God ordains is right:
Here shall my stand be taken;
Though sorrow, need, or death be mine,
Yet am I not forsaken;
My Father's care is round me there;
He holds me that I shall not fall:
And so to Him I leave it all.

Conclusion

Christians fail to appropriate the power of God's promises, set forth in texts such as Romans 8:28, when they fail to understand the nature of God as depicted in Scripture, the definition of the terms the biblical author used, the conditions and extent of the promise, and the context in which the biblical writer places the promise. God controls all things, without exception, and arranges them all for the benefit of his people. His people's greatest benefit is to be conformed to Christ. While the outworking of God's purpose may sometimes result in painful events, God never harms his children. The painful experiences that God brings into the lives of his children, when correctly understood, serve to weld them more tightly to Christ. True harm would be to be severed from Christ, which is not possible.

Chapter Ten
Our Sovereign God

Two portions of Scripture will serve as a background for this chapter. The first is Psalm 115:1-3.

> *Not unto us, O LORD, not unto us, But to Your name give glory, Because of Your mercy, Because of Your truth. Why should the Gentiles say, "So where is their God?" But our God is in heaven; He does whatever He pleases.*

As we look at the second passage—Daniel 4:30-37—I want to give you a sermon outline on these verses. I could easily use this section as the basis for this entire chapter, but I feel constrained to take another direction. However, we will get a clear view of "our Sovereign God" in these verses. I am indebted to Pastor John Weaver of Jessup, Georgia, for this outline. This could be entitled "The Testimony of a Pagan King to the Absolute Sovereignty of God."

Sermon outline of Daniel 4:30-37:

I. v. 30—God's Sovereignty Ignored and Rejected

> *The king spoke, saying, "Is not this great Babylon, that I have built for a royal dwelling by my mighty power and for the honor of my majesty?"* One can feel the pride and arrogance of this pagan king. He has no thought of God but only his own self-appointed importance.

II. vv. 31–33—God's Sovereignty Experienced

While the word was still in the king's mouth, a voice fell from heaven: "King Nebuchadnezzar, to you it is spoken: the kingdom has departed from you! And they shall drive you from men, and your dwelling shall be with the beasts of the field. They shall make you eat grass like oxen; and seven times shall pass over you, until you know that the Most High rules in the kingdom of men, and gives it to whomever He chooses." That very hour the word was fulfilled concerning Nebuchadnezzar; he was driven from men and ate grass like oxen; his body was wet with the dew of heaven till his hair had grown like eagles' feathers and his nails like birds' claws. Today people say, "Oh, God would never do anything so cruel as that." If such treatment was the essential means necessary to bring this proud king to knowledge of God, then it was a very gracious act.

III. v. 34a-God's Sovereignty Gladly Acknowledged

And at the end of the time I, Nebuchadnezzar, lifted my eyes to heaven, and my understanding returned to me; and I blessed the Most High and praised and honored Him who lives forever....

There are three things in this verse that always go together, and they always follow the same order:

1. *I...lifted up my eyes*—A right view of God.

2. *My understanding returned*—A right understanding of reality.

3. *I blessed...praised...honored*—A right attitude of worship.

One may immediately think of Romans chapter 1 as showing how the exact opposite is true.

1. Instead of looking up to God, Paul says that men have deliberately turned their eyes away from God and rejected his revelation (cf. Romans 1:18-20).

2. Their foolish hearts were darkened because their mind had become vain and, like Nebuchadnezzar, they were given over to senseless insanity in morality and life style (cf. Romans 1:21-32).

3. They refused to "glorify God" and "thank him," but instead they exalted the creature and boasted about themselves and their own power (cf. Romans 1:21, 22).

Either the three things in Nebuchadnezzar's experience or the three things in Romans will always occur. Every person fits one of these two descriptions. There is no neutrality.

IV. vv. 34b–37—God's Sovereignty Described

1. v. 34b—The Superiority of His Kingdom. *...for His dominion is an everlasting dominion, and His kingdom is from generation to generation.*

2. v. 35a—The Insignificance of His Creatures. *All the inhabitants of the earth are reputed as nothing.*

3. v. 35b—The Sovereignty of His Will. *He does according to His will in the army of heaven and among the inhabitants of the earth. No one can restrain His hand or say to Him, "What have You done?"*

4. v. 36—The Sureness of His Purposes. *At the same time my reason returned to me, and for the glory of my*

kingdom, my honor and splendor returned to me. My counselors and nobles resorted to me, I was restored to my kingdom, and excellent majesty was added to me.

5. v. 37a—The Supremacy of His Person. *Now I, Nebuchadnezzar, praise and extol and honor the King of heaven....*

6. v. 37b—The Singleness of His Character. *...all of whose works are truth, and His ways justice.*

7. v. 37c—The Strength of His Position. *And those who walk in pride He is able to put down.*

That, my dear friend, is the God of the Bible! That is the God that you and I must face in eternity! That is our Sovereign Holy God!

Several years ago, I spoke at a conference where the sermon titles given to the evening messages were stated in terms of God himself. My topic was "Our Sovereign God." We are on solid biblical ground when we talk about God himself instead of speaking only of doctrines about him. I agree with A.W. Pink when he said, "To speak about the 'sovereignty of God' is to be theological, but to speak of a 'God who is sovereign' is to be biblical." The goal of our study is not to know things about God; it is to know God himself.

We must not get "lopsided" and think of God in terms of only one attribute. Our Sovereign God is also a most gracious God. His grace sweetens his sovereignty, and his sovereignty makes certain that his grace will accomplish its intended purpose.

Our study is not going to cover the ground so familiar to those who glory in the truth known as Calvinism. I do not hesitate to call myself a Calvinist because I believe the great truths set forth under that name. However, I have often found that many men and women, who rejected the sovereignty of God when it was set forth in theological terms, would bow in worship and praise to a sovereign heavenly Father when they were undergoing affliction. I hate to admit it, but my pastoral experience has convinced me that godly Arminians often exhibit more practical submission to our Sovereign God than the Calvinist who can win all of the theological arguments about the sovereignty of God versus free will. Calvinists have a tendency to have a better grasp of the "logic" of theology than they have of the grace and love of God himself!

I assume that you have read Pink's book, *The Sovereignty of God*. If you have not, then I urge you to do so as soon as possible. I hope that you are familiar with the ninth chapter of Romans and that you know that it clearly teaches that our God is indeed a most sovereign God. I am assuming that you accept without question that God has "mercy upon whom he wants to have mercy, and he hardens whom he wants to harden" (Romans 9:18).

My goal is more pastoral and is aimed at encouraging the heart. I have a sermon on Romans 8:28 entitled "A Soft Pillow for a Weary Head and a Sorry Heart" (see chapter 9). God has used this particular message to bring help and hope to many suffering sheep. There is no sweeter balm in Gilead to a true sheep of Christ than the knowledge that his

God is the Sovereign God who controls the whole universe. This is especially true when God's providence turns our personal world upside down. It is then that we must be able to say with David, "My times are in thy hands" (Psalm 31:15). The hymn writer has caught the truth we long to experience:

> My times are in thy hand; my God, I wish them there;
> my life, my friends, my soul, I leave entirely to thy care.
> My times are in thy hand, whatever they may be;
> pleasing or painful, dark or bright, as best may seem to thee.
>
> My times are in thy hand; why should I doubt or fear?
> My Father's hand will never cause His child a needless tear.
> My times are in thy hand, Jesus the Crucified;
> those hands my cruel sins have pierced are now my guard
> and guide.

Daniel 4:34 expresses what I pray might happen to all of us. Notice again the three specific things that happened to Nebuchadnezzar, and be sure to notice the sequence in which they occur.

1. *I, Nebuchadnezzar, raised my eyes to heaven....* When he did that, he saw a sovereign God sitting on a throne. Nebuchadnezzar describes what happened in his heart at this sight.

2. *...and my sanity was restored.* The most insane thing a man can do is look toward himself instead of up to God. Just as Nebuchadnezzar's insanity was directly related to his pride and exalting himself, so the return of his sanity was related to his humility and repentance in "raising his eyes to heaven." What a

lesson for the egotistical "me first" society in which we live.

3.   *Then* (note well the connection) *I praised the Most High; I honored and glorified Him who lives forever.* You cannot see God as he is and not want to honor and praise Him, and you cannot turn away from him without seeking to honor and praise yourself. A right sight of God will always give you a right sight of yourself.

I trust we are beginning to see how firmly these three things are tied together and cannot be separated. You will notice, of course, the similarity of this passage with the words of Stephen, the first martyr:

> *Stephen...looked up to heaven and saw the glory of God....*
> *"Look," he said, "I see heaven open and the Son of Man standing at the right hand of God." (Acts 7:56)*

Whenever you see "heaven open," you will always see a sovereign Savior at the "right hand of God," and when you see the exalted Savior, you will always see the "glory of God." When we really get that into our heart with a living faith, then we will be enabled to fall on our knees and pray for the people throwing the stones. That is the kind of power we need to experience in our personal lives as we think about "our Sovereign God." We need to know experientially in daily life what we can argue so effectively in debate.

Several years ago, I preached in a large church in Detroit. After the service, a young couple came up to me and showed me a copy of an old _Sword and Trowel,_ the magazine which I edited for several years. The young lady, Peg Rankin, gave me an autographed copy of a book she had written. She said, "You will recognize some of your own material in this book." The title of the book was _Yet Will I Trust Him,_ and her purpose in writing the book is the same as mine in this chapter. The back cover says: "_Yet Will I Trust Him_ is a practical, provocative guide showing how to yield to God's control and experience his peace and victory, no matter what!"

That is the kind of attitude we need as we study together. We cannot afford to come together just to confirm our theological convictions. We do not want to "hold fast our theology"—we want our theology to hold us fast in real life. I fear that too often we pass the test in the classroom of theology and then flunk the test in the classroom of life. It is a hollow victory for us as Calvinists if we can write better books and preach better sermons than Arminians but cannot live more contented and joyful lives than they.

Peg Rankin had just been witnessing to a girlfriend involved in divorce proceedings. The girl was bitter, frustrated, and left in anger. _Yet Will I Trust Him_ was probably conceived in Peg's mind in the next few moments:

> As I walked back into the kitchen, I answered the jangling phone. It was a friend. "Did you hear about Bob?" she queried.

"No, what?" I asked. I had seen Bob in the hall at the church on Sunday. We had chatted awhile about a mutual friend who was giving up a lucrative job to become a missionary.

"That's what I'd like to do someday," Bob had said, "become a missionary. I guess one of these days I'll just have to take the bull by the horns and do it. I'm not getting any younger, you know. Just turned forty last week."

With the conversation only a couple of days old, I expected my friend to announce that Bob had come to a decision to give his life to Christ in a full-time missionary effort. But it was not to be. The voice on the phone shattered my thoughts.

"Bob was struck by a car and killed on his way to work this morning," it said, hesitating between the phrases. "His wife is stunned. And the kids—they're so young to be without a daddy. What will they do?"

"They will have to cope with the crisis," I philosophized, startling myself with the starkness of what I was saying, "and go on from there. What else is there to do?"

As I hung up the phone, I had the same helpless feeling that I had experienced when dealing with the family whose rebellious daughter had just run away from home. Then I thought of Shirley and her divorce. Problems seemed to be multiplying everywhere.

Someone has said, "When your world is badly shaken, start with what you know you believe and build upward from there." I decided to put the advice into practice.

I thought, "I know that God is in control of all things. I believe that his plan for our lives is perfect. At least that is what the Bible says. But how can I toss such a platitude to someone caught in the maelstrom of a crisis? Especially when I'm not even sure that I have hold of it myself?"

I was confronted with what I felt has to be accomplished in my own life and in the lives of many others. Somehow we Christians have to get the sovereignty of God out of the closet and into the mainstream of living. But how do we go about doing it? Victory on the mountain peaks is easy. It is a natural result of success. But if Christianity doesn't work in the valleys, it isn't worth having at all, is it?

(From: *Yet Will I Trust Him*, by Peg Rankin, Gospel Light, pages 12, 13)

Shortly after this, Mr. and Mrs. Rankin were asked to teach an adult class in Vacation Bible School on the subject "The Sovereignty of God in Family Crises." Their first preparation consisted in listing all of the crises that their family, and all the families they knew, had faced or were facing. Their first reaction was, "All of life seems to be a crisis." They began to study and prepare for the course with deadly earnestness:

With anticipation, we tossed out the questions that would be covered during the course of study:

1.   Who is this God I'm trying to serve?

2.   Where is he when I need him most?

3.   Why are there crises in my life?

4.   What do life's crises accomplish?

5.   How can I have victory in the midst of crises?

We know teachers cannot integrate truth without spending hours in disciplined study. So before we laid our heads on

our pillows that night, we pledged ourselves to God afresh to
be diligent in our searching of his Word. Then we reaffirmed
our faith in a God who controls all things, working them for
his glory and to his children's good. (Ibid., page 15)

One of the things I enjoyed most about *Yet Will I Trust
Him* was the author's definition of the sovereignty of God.
In fact, I quoted all of the preceding just to get to this
definition:

Several years ago, Lee and I taught a class of very sharp
young married couples. We imparted to them the same truth
that we impart to every class we teach: God is sovereign in
the lives of men. We examined his sovereignty in creation,
proceeded with his sovereignty in history, and looked with
detail at his sovereignty in salvation. The entire course took a
year to cover. We ended with a challenge to the students that
if they would surrender their lives daily to the will of the
King of Kings, no limit could be placed upon their spiritual
victory.

Then we said to them, "OK, you've sat for a year in a
course entitled 'The Sovereignty of God,' now you define
God's sovereignty." I will never forget the statement that
came from Tom, a doctoral candidate in the field of physics.
Although he had not anticipated the question, he was
thoroughly prepared for the answer. He said, "The
sovereignty of God means that God can do anything he wants
to do, any time he wants to do it, any way he wants to do it,
for any purpose he wants to accomplish." (Ibid., page 23)

Wow! What an answer!

Now you and I must realize that "anything, any time,
any way" includes any and every person as well as all

events. More specifically, it actually means you and me and all of my loved ones and everything that pertains to them. Normally, this truth would be learned at conversion. However, with the current distortion of the gospel of grace in modern evangelism, many sincere Christians are ignorant of this awesome fact.

The heart of a sinner's rebellion to God is the sinner's implacable hatred of God's sovereign authority, and the essence of true repentance and faith is confident submission to God himself as absolutely sovereign. The Psalmist put it beautifully when he said, "Be still, and know that I am God" (Psalm 46:46). Moffitt translated it, "Give up, and admit that I am God." The contest since the garden of Eden has been, "Who is really God?" Are we the master of our fate, our own god? Or is the God who "made heaven and earth and the sea, and all that is in them" (cf. Acts 4:2a) really the Sovereign Ruler of everything including you and me?

I remember buying a book of poems compiled by a famous preacher. The poems were supposed to be "great aids in getting decisions." One of the preacher's favorite poems that he urged his readers to use when the altar call was being given was entitled, "The Invictus." Because of his theology, this man used the poem as if it were solid truth. He saw it as embodying the "right way to appeal to the free will of man." Apparently the man never checked up on either the origin of the poem or the author's intention in writing it.

The author of "The Invictus," W.E. Henley, was a militant humanist who hated the Christian faith. The word *invictus* means unconquered in Latin, and the author's intention in the poem was to shake his fist in defiance at the very thought of a sovereign God ruling over him. We could well entitle the poem, "The Rebel Sinner's Banner." The use of this particular poem during an altar call was actually reinforcing in a sinner's mind the very thought that must be destroyed before he can ever truly be saved. Henley's poem is pure blasphemy. The evangelist who advocated using it in altar calls may be excused for not knowing who Mr. Henley was, but he cannot be excused for not recognizing blasphemy when he hears it stated so blatantly.

The Invictus, by W.E. Henley

Out of the night that covers me,
Black as the Pit from pole to pole,
I thank whatever gods may be
For my unconquerable soul.

In the fell clutch of circumstance
I have not winced nor cried aloud.
Under the bludgeonings of chance
My head is bloody, but unbowed.

Beyond this place of wrath and tears
Looms but the horror of the shade,
And yet the menace of the years
Finds, and shall find me, unafraid.

It matters not how strait the gate,
How charged with punishments the scroll,

I am the master of my fate;
I am the captain of my soul.

Around 1900, a young lady who had been greatly enamored with Henley and his humanism was graciously converted to Christ. She wrote a response to Henley's blasphemy and set forth the correct attitude of a child of God toward the sovereignty of God. This is her poem:

Conquered, by Dorothea Day

Out of the light that dazzles me,
Bright as the sun from pole to pole,
I thank the God I know to be,
For Christ—the Conqueror of my soul.

Since His the sway of circumstance,
I would not wince nor cry aloud.
Under the rule which men call chance,
My head, with joy, is humbly bowed.

Beyond this place of sin and tears,
That Life with Him and His the Aid,
That, spite the menace of the years,
Keeps, and will keep me unafraid.

I have no fear though straight the gate:
He cleared from punishment the scroll.
Christ is the Master of my fate!
Christ is the Captain of my soul!

I trust we are beginning to see that the essence of true Christian faith involves submission to God as sovereign, and the essence of unbelief is deliberate rebellion to God as sovereign. It is essential we learn at conversion that a life of faith is nothing less than joyfully "giving up, and admitting that God is God." The word *joyfully* is very important in that sentence. A believer does not grudgingly acknowledge that God is sovereign; he does so with joy and confidence. The two parts of Romans 11:36 show this fact:

> For from him and through him and to him are all things: to him be glory forever! Amen. (Rom. 11:36 NIV)

There are three different Greek prepositions in this verse. They show the truth of God's absolute and total sovereignty. The verse states that all things, without any exception, are:

1. from God (the Greek is *ek* and means "out of" or "out from");

2. through God (the Greek is *dia* and means "by means of" or "because of"); and

3. to God (the Greek is *eis* and means "into").

In other words, all things have their source in God's decrees or purposes; all things that happen do so only because God's power has brought them to pass; and finally, everything that God plans and then brings to pass will ultimately bring glory to him since they all move into him or unto him as their final end. Now that is the biblical truth about our Sovereign God. That is acknowledging that "God can do anything he wants to do, any time he wants to do it, any way he wants to do it, for any purpose he wants to accomplish." However, the response of faith is not to grit our teeth and submit to that truth because God is stronger than us and we can do nothing about it (implying that we would if we could). No, no, the child of God bows his head in worship and says, "To him be glory forever." We can do this because we know that Romans 8:28 is just as true as God himself is true.

The unbeliever gnashes his teeth and cries, "I am the master of my fate, and I am the captain of my soul." The cry of the rebels in Luke 19:14 is the real heart attitude of every lost person—"But his subjects hated him...(and said) 'We will not have this man to reign over us.'"

Brethren, it is the preaching of God as sovereign that brings man's hatred of God to the surface. C.H. Spurgeon was exactly right in stating the following:

> The householder says, "Is it not lawful for me to do what I will with mine own?" and even so does the God of Heaven and earth ask this question of you this morning, "Is it not lawful for me to do what I will with mine own?"

> There is no attribute of God more comforting to His children than the doctrine of Divine Sovereignty. Under the most adverse circumstances, in the most severe troubles, they believe that Sovereignty has ordained their afflictions, that Sovereignty overrules them, and that Sovereignty will sanctify them all. There is nothing for which the children of God ought more earnestly to contend than the dominion of their Master over all creation—the throne of God, and His right to sit upon that throne.

> On the other hand, there is no doctrine more hated by worldlings, no truth of which they have made such a football, as the great, stupendous, but yet most certain doctrine of the Sovereignty of the infinite Jehovah. Men will allow God to be everywhere except upon His throne. They will allow Him to be in His workshop to fashion worlds and to make stars. They

will allow Him to be in His almonry to dispense His alms and bestow His bounties. They will allow Him to sustain the earth and bear up the pillars thereof, or light the lamps of Heaven, or rule the waves of the ever-moving ocean; but when God ascends His throne, His creatures gnash their teeth; and when we proclaim an enthroned God, and His right to do as He wills with His own, to dispose of His creatures as He thinks well, without consulting them in the matter, then it is that we are hissed and reviled, and then it is that men turn a deaf ear to us, for God on His throne is not the God they love. They love Him anywhere better than they do when He sits with His scepter in His hand and His crown upon His head. But it is God upon the throne that we love to preach. It is God upon His throne whom we trust. It is God upon His throne of whom we have been singing this morning; and it is God upon His throne of whom we shall speak in this discourse.

(From: "Is It Not Lawful For Me To Do What I Will With Mine Own?" a sermon by Charles H. Spurgeon on Matthew 20:15)

The last vestige of old Adam that we are willing to give up is our fancied "free will." The last truth that we will submit to in heartfelt worship is God's absolute sovereignty over us. The greatest obstacle in man's conversion is his conviction that his free will alone is "master of his fate." Is it not tragic that so many sincere but misguided preachers confirm and harden that folly in the sinner's heart? To tell a lost man that "God has done all he can do, and it is now totally up to you" is to point the poor sinner to his own dead heart as the only ground of hope. It is telling the sinner that his power of will is stronger and more powerful than God.

There has probably never been a more classic illustration of the foregoing truth than the conviction and conversion of David Brainerd. The one exception could be the great apostle Paul; especially if we understand the words concerning "kicking against the goads" (cf. Acts 26:14) to mean that he really knew in his heart that Jesus was the true Messiah. David Brainerd's biography is one of those books that it would be good to read once a year. Here are his own words describing the rebellion that went on in his mind and heart when he was under real conviction of his lost estate:

> The many disappointments, great distress, and perplexity I met with, put me into a most horrible frame of contesting with the Almighty; with an inward vehemence and virulence finding fault with his ways of dealing with mankind. I found great fault with the imputation of Adam's sin to his posterity; and my wicked heart often wished for some other way of salvation, than by Jesus Christ. Being like the troubled sea, my thoughts confused, I used to contrive to escape the wrath of God by some other means. I had strange projects, full of atheism, contriving to disappoint God's designs and decrees concerning me, or to escape his notice, and hide myself from him. But when, upon reflection, I saw these projects were vain, and would not serve me, and that I could contrive nothing for my own relief; this would throw my mind into the most horrid frame, to wish there was no God, or to wish there were some other god that could control Him, etc. These thoughts and desires were the secret inclinations of my heart, frequently acting before I was aware; but, alas! they were mine, although I was affrighted when I came to reflect on them. When I considered, it distressed me to think, that my

heart was so full of enmity against God; and it made me tremble, lest his vengeance should suddenly fall upon me. I used before to imagine, that my heart was not so bad as the Scriptures and some other books represented it. Sometimes I used to take much pains to work it up into a good frame, an humble submissive disposition; and hoped there was then some goodness in me. But, on a sudden, the thoughts of the strictness of the law, or the sovereignty of God, would so irritate the corruption of my heart, that I had so watched over, and hoped I had brought to a good frame, that it would break over all bounds, and burst forth on all sides, like floods of water when they break down their dam. (*The Works of Jonathan Edwards,* Banner of Truth Trust, Vol. II, pp. 317–318)

Brainerd graphically describes four specific truths that made him exceedingly angry while he was under conviction of sin. Men today hate the same truths, but these very truths are the only hope that poor sinners have. This is why a necessity is laid on us to preach these specific truths. Unless we preach God on a throne of holiness and sovereignty, we will only be stirring up the dust and not really helping poor sinners at all. We will never see men on their knees seeking mercy until they see God on his throne of sovereignty and holiness.

And while I was in this distressed, bewildered, and tumultuous state of mind, the corruption of my heart was especially irritated with the following things.

1. The strictness of the divine law. For I found it impossible for me, after my utmost pains, to answer its demands. I often made new resolutions, and as often broke them... I was extremely loath to own my utter helplessness in this matter: but after repeated disappointments, thought that, rather than

perish, I could do a little more still; especially if such and such circumstances might but attend my endeavors and strivings... This hope of future more favorable circumstances, and of doing something great hereafter, kept me from utter despair in myself, and from seeing myself fallen into the hands of a sovereign God, and dependent on nothing but free and boundless grace.

As you can see, at the bottom of every objection and problem in Brainerd's mind, the sovereignty of God was always the center. He could not bear the thought of putting himself solely into the hands of a sovereign God and trusting in nothing but "free and boundless grace." Herein lies the heart of every sinner's problem, and most modern-day preachers compound that problem instead of helping it.

2. Another thing was, that faith alone was the condition of salvation; that God would not come down to lower terms, and that he would not promise life and salvation upon my sincere and hearty prayers and endeavors. That word, Mark 16:16, "He that believeth not, shall be damned," cut off all hope there: and I found, faith was the sovereign gift of God; that I could not get it as of myself, and could not oblige God to bestow it upon me, by any of my performances, (Eph. 2:1, 8.) This, I was ready to say, is a hard saying, who can bear it? I could not bear, that all I had done should stand for mere nothing, who had been very conscientious in duty, had been exceeding religious a great while, and had, as I thought, done much more than many others who had obtained mercy.

3. Another thing was, that I could not find out what faith was; or what it was to believe, and come to Christ...

4. Another thing to which I found a great inward opposition was the sovereignty of God. I could not bear that it should be wholly at God's pleasure to save or damn me, just as he would.

That passage, Romans 9:11-23, was a constant vexation to me, especially verse 21. Reading or meditating on this, always destroyed my seeming good frames: for when I thought I was almost humbled, and almost resigned, this passage would make my enmity against the sovereignty of God appear. When I came to reflect on my inward enmity and blasphemy, which arose on this occasion, I was the more afraid of God, and driven further from any hopes of reconciliation with Him. It gave me such a dreadful view of myself, that I dreaded more than ever to see myself in God's hands, at His sovereign disposal, and it made me more opposed than ever to submit to his sovereignty; for I thought God designed my damnation.

It was the sight of the truth concerning myself, truth respecting my state, as a creature fallen and alienated from God, and that consequently could make no demands on God for mercy, but must subscribe to the absolute sovereignty of the Divine Being; the sight of the truth, I say, my soul shrank away from, and trembled to think of beholding. (Ibid., p. 318)

How can sinners be humbled under the mighty hand of God when preachers are telling them that their "free will" is more powerful than God? Why should men bow and seek grace from a God who "has done all he can do" and whose "hands are tied" until sinful man decides to "give him a chance?" It is little wonder that we see so few believers today like David Brainerd. The God before whom Brainerd bowed in saving repentance and faith is almost unknown in our land. We must declare Romans 9 to proud, self-sufficient sinners, but we must be certain that we do it in the spirit of Romans 10:1, 2. The God who is sovereign is also most gracious. We must seek to drive men to despair in their own efforts only as a means of bringing them to hope in the gospel of God's sovereign mercy.

Strange as it may seem, some of the people that appear to be the most humble and earnest about their soul are really the most self-sufficient. David Brainerd is a classic example of this fact. He would have been looked upon as an "earnest and most sincere man seeking after God." However, his own testimony reveals his deep-seated hatred of God.

What should we say to the sinner who weeps and says, "I am too wicked to be saved"? We must tell them that they are deceived and are being deceitful! If they really believed they were helpless, they would fall at the feet of sovereign mercy. They are still trying to change and save themselves on their own terms. Their tears of "hopelessness" are really an expression of their unwillingness to put themselves entirely into God's hands. Their vaunted humility is like Brainerd's before he was ready to admit to the awful truth that he was both hopeless and helpless in himself and his own strength. False humility is backhanded self-righteousness.

If we really want to see sinners converted and saints edified, we must confront them with the truth of God's awesome sovereignty. We must tell them, as Rolfe Barnard did, "Son, all you need to do to be saved is bow to Jesus the

Lord." We must assure people that no sinner who ever bowed to Christ in repentance and faith was ever turned away. He was welcomed into the arms of grace. However, we must also tell them that the only way they can come to Christ is with a heart that is ready to submit to him as the only Lord. The sovereignty of God and the lordship of Christ is not only the one safe and sure place for a **saint** to rest; it is also the one and only safe and sure place for a poor lost **sinner** to rest.

Let me close with a quotation from a great preacher blessed by God in bringing many souls to a living faith in Christ:

> The fact, that conversion and salvation are all of God, is an humbling truth. It is because of its humbling character that men do not like it. To be told that God alone must save me if I am to be saved, and that I am in his hand, as clay is in the hands of the potter, "I do not like it," saith one. Well, I thought you would not; whoever dreamed you would? If you had liked it, perhaps it had not been true; your not liking it is an indirect evidence of its truthfulness. To be told that "he must work all my works in me," who can bring me so low as that? Where is boasting then? It is excluded. By what law? The law of works? No, but the law of grace. Grace puts its hand on their boasting mouth, and shuts it once and for all; and then it takes its hand off from the mouth, and that mouth now does not fear to speak to man, though it trembles at the very thought of taking any honour and glory from God. I must say—I am compelled to say—that the doctrine which leaves salvation to the creature, and tells him that it depends upon himself, is the exaltation of the flesh, and a dishonouring of God. But that which puts in God's hand

man, fallen man, and tells man that though he has destroyed himself, yet his salvation must be of God, that doctrine humbles man in the very dust, and then he is just in the right place to receive the grace and mercy of God. It is a humbling doctrine.

Again, this doctrine gives the death blow to all self-sufficiency. What the Arminian wants to do is to arouse man's activity; what we want to do is kill it once and for all, to show him that he is lost and ruined, and his activities are not now at all equal to the work of conversion; that he must look upward. They seek to make the man stand up; we seek to bring him down, and make him feel that there he lies in the hand of God, and that his business is to submit himself to God, and cry aloud, "Lord, save, or I perish." We hold that the man is never so near grace as when he begins to feel that he can do nothing at all. When he says, "I can pray, I can believe, I can do this, and I can do the other," marks of self-sufficiency and arrogance are on his brow. But when he comes to his knees and cries, "Oh, for this no strength I find, my strength is at thy feet to lie," then we think that God has blessed him, and that the work of grace is in his soul. O sinner! Think not that thy own unaided arm can get the victory. Cry unto God, and beg him to take your soul in hand, for you cannot be saved unless He doeth it for you. Bless Him for the promise that says, "Him that cometh unto me, I will not cast out." Oh! Cry to Him, "Lord, draw me by thy grace, that I may run after thee; work all my works in me, and bring me to thyself and save me!" Not to yourself do we bid thee look, nor to your prayers, nor to your faith, but to Christ and to his cross, and to that God who is "able to save to the uttermost them that come unto God by him." (C.H. Spurgeon, New Park Street Pulpit, Vol. 6, p. 257)

Maybe, just maybe, if we understood and preached the gospel as Spurgeon did, God would be blessed to convict and convert sinners under our ministry as he did under Spurgeon's ministry. Maybe, just maybe, if believers today really understood just how sovereign and gracious God is, the counseling couches would be empty, and the prayer and worship meetings would be full.

APPENDIX ONE
TWO VIEWS OF THE ATONEMENT

There are two views of the nature of the atoning work of Christ on the cross. One view is called "universal" atonement, and the other is called "particular" atonement. They are also called "unlimited" and "limited" atonement. One is based on the free will of man, and the other is based on the free and sovereign grace of God. The fundamental question is this: What did Christ accomplish in his death on the cross? Did his death make salvation possible for all men, or did his death make salvation certain for the elect of God? Here are the two answers. I have chosen every word with great care.

Answer of Free-Will Religion	Answer of Free-Grace Religion
Atonement is *universal* in *intention* and *provisional* in *character*. God has an *unlimited purpose* (to save all men), but his *power is limited* (by man's free will). The atonement of Christ, in and of itself, does not assure that	Atonement is *particular* in *intention* and *redemptive* in *character*. God has a *limited purpose* (to save his elect) and he is *unlimited in his power*. The atonement of Christ, in and of itself, guarantees that some men, all of the

anyone will be saved for sure but it does make it possible for all men to be saved by choosing to believe with their free will. 1 Tim. 4:10; 1 John 2:2; John 3:16.

elect, will be saved. Repentance and faith are part of the gifts purchased by Christ in his atoning death. Job 23:13; John 10:11; Eph. 5:25; Heb. 9:28.

Let me point out several clear facts from the above.

(1) The *intention* of God in giving his Son up to death is different in the two systems.

God's intention in giving his Son is universal in the sense that he sincerely desires and earnestly tries to save all men without exception.

God's intention is particular in the sense that he has purposed to make certain that some specific, or particular, individuals will be saved.

(2) The *success* or fulfillment of God's intention in giving Christ is different in the two cases.

God's intention to save all men without exception is thwarted and is impossible of attainment because of man's free will.

God's decreed intention to save his elect is fully realized because the atonement of Christ purchases the gifts of both repentance and faith.

(3) The *power* of God is different in both cases.

God's power is totally limited by man's free will. God has a limited power that cannot accomplish his unlimited purpose.

God has an unlimited power to accomplish everything his sovereign will desires. It is his purpose that is limited and not his power.

(4) The real issue is the *nature,* or character, of the atonement.

The sufferings of Christ are provisional in character. His death cannot really redeem anyone. The most that Christ's sacrifice accomplished was the opportunity for men to save themselves by *their* faith in Christ.

The sufferings of Christ were redemptive in nature. His death really and fully paid for sin in such a way that it guaranteed the redemption of those for whom it was made.

A careful comparison of these two views will show that one has an atonement that can only make redemption a possibility that is totally dependent on man's free will for its success while the other has an atonement that really redeems. We insist that the free-will view has only a hypothetical atonement that does not redeem. In reality, free-will religion has: (1) a *redemption* that does not redeem but still leaves many for whom it was made eternally in their bondage; (2) a *reconciliation* that still leaves many eternally unreconciled to God and in their sin; (3) a *substitutionary* death that still leaves the sinner eternally without forgiveness of sins and forever lost in hell; and (4) a *propitiation* that leaves some for whom it was made still under the wrath of God. One must change the biblical meaning of the above four words and empty them of their biblical content in order to believe in universal atonement.

Appendix Two
All *Equals* Many *but* Many *Does not Equal* All

Many commentaries on the book of Romans state that Romans 5:12–19 is the most difficult section in the whole book. Nevertheless, if the apostle's argument is followed closely, it is a very clear passage. A consistent exegesis of these verses will reveal the truth of particular atonement.

Let us read the verses carefully. As we do, we will immediately notice that Paul's use and interchange of the words *one, all,* and *many* does, at first reading, seem to be confusing. When we follow his argument carefully, we will not only understand exactly what Paul means by *one, all,* and *many,* but we will see how specific and selective Paul is with each use of the different words. I suggest you read the text carefully. All of the emphasis is mine:

*Wherefore, as by **one man** sin entered into the world, and death by sin, and so death passed upon **all men,** for **all have sinned.** (For until the law sin was in the world, but sin is not imputed when there is no law. Nevertheless, death reigned from Adam to Moses, even over them that had not sinned after the similitude of Adam's transgression, who is the figure of him that was to come. But not as the offense, so also is the free gift. For if through the offense of **one many** are dead, much more the grace of God, and the gift by grace, which is by **one man,** Jesus Christ, hath abounded unto **many.** And not as it was by **one** that sinned, so is the gift; for the judgment was by **one** to condemnation, but the free gift is of **many** offences unto justification. For if by **one man's** offense death reigned by **one,** much more they who receive abundance of grace and of the gift of*

*righteousness shall reign in life by **one**, Jesus Christ.) Therefore, as*
*by the offense of **one** judgment came upon **all men** to*
condemnation, even so by the righteousness of one the free gift came
*upon **all men** unto justification of life. For as by **one man's***
*disobedience **many** were made sinners, so by the obedience of **one***
*shall **many** be made righteous.* (Rom. 5:12–19)

I. The Overall Context

The argument in Romans 5:12–19 is an integral part of
the major argument in Romans. In Romans, chapters 1
through 3, Paul shows that all men without exception are
guilty sinners in the sight of God. Guilt means not only that
you are going to be punished, but also that you truly
deserve to be punished. This biblical perspective on guilt and
sin differs from that of a secular worldview. Modern
philosophy agrees that man does some very bad things, but
it is not the individual's fault. Man's wicked deeds are
blamed on bad parenting, poor social conditions, lack of
education and opportunity, plus many other excuses. The
actual wicked acts of man cannot be denied, but he is
always excused because "man is basically good and not
really depraved." The poor sinner was forced, by factors
outside of his control, to feel and act as he did. The sinner
may act wickedly, but he is not "guilty" in the sense that he
deserves to be punished. He needs unconditional love,
understanding, education, etc.

In Romans, chapter 4, Paul shows how ungodly sinners
are freely justified totally apart from works or their own
efforts. God justifies "the ungodly," not the "good." He
saves him who "works not" but instead "believes in Jesus

Christ." This method of justification by grace, through faith, has always been God's method of saving sinners.

Romans 5:1–11 lays out the results that follow justification. The justified sinner has "peace with God" and "access" into the presence of God. A justified believer is no longer God's enemy but has been totally reconciled. In Romans 5:9 and 10, Paul emphasizes the assurance of the future of all those who belong to Christ.

II. The Immediate Context

The word *wherefore* in verse 12 points back to verses 1–11. The sure blessings outlined in these verses flow from justification, and the guarantee of our full reconciliation and total redemption is now shown by Paul to rest on the fact of our *union with Christ as our representative.* This glorious principle of imputation is laid out in 5:12–19.

Verse 12 begins with the word *wherefore* and shows that this section is part of the argument being carried on in the preceding verses. Paul here introduces the conclusion of the truth just established in the preceding verses. He does not immediately spell out that conclusion, but (as he often does) goes into an explanatory parenthesis in verses 13–17. In verse 18, Paul will conclude the argument. The primary point summarized in verse 10 concerns our reconciliation to God. We were enemies, but we are now reconciled. Paul will now show just how God's wrath and its effects have been taken away.

III. The Exposition of Romans 5:12–19

Verse 12 gives us a historical explanation of sin. (1) *"Wherefore, as by one man sin entered into the world..."* Sin entered the world by one man's (Adam's) one act of sin. (2) *"...and death by sin"* Death, as the just and sure penalty of sin, followed Adam's sin. (3) *"...and so death passed upon all men, for all have sinned."* Death, because it is the just punishment of sin, proves guilt was present, or there would have been no death. In other words, wherever one finds death, one finds guilt being punished. God does not punish innocent people. If one soul ever dies who was not a guilty sinner, then God was unjust in inflicting death on that person. Only guilty sinners die; therefore, when we find death, we also find a guilty sinner being justly punished. Log this fact into your mind.

The point of Paul's argument is to prove that all men without exception, including infants, are guilty sinners because of their union with Adam. Let me repeat the argument. Paul states that death is the penalty for sin. If death only comes to guilty sinners, then all who die must indeed be guilty sinners who actually deserve to die. Only guilty sinners are punished. God does not punish "innocent" people. Paul is showing that wherever death is inflicted, guilt is being justly punished. Only guilty people are punished by God; therefore, finding death is finding guilt being punished.

We can stand at the grave of every child that died in infancy and say, "Consider now: Who, being innocent, has ever perished? Where were the upright ever cut off?" (Job

4:7 NIV). That child has just endured the penalty of sin—
death. In no sense is Paul saying the child is lost. Paul's
only point is to establish the guilt of every one of Adam's
children, including the newborn child. We must see in
verse 12 that Paul does *not* say, "All men die because *Adam*
sinned." He says that all men die only because all men
actually sinned in Adam. We do not die, nor does the
infant die, because Adam did something which was totally
unrelated to us. The entire human race was in the loins of
Adam when he acted as our representative in the garden.
We were part of him, and we all acted in him.

It is essential that we understand Paul's basic foundation
points. Paul does not say that all men die because *Adam*
sinned, but only because *all men* have sinned. When did *all
men* sin? The answer is, "They sinned in Eden in the person
of Adam, their representative." It is vital that we see this
fact if we are to understand the "guilt" aspect of Paul's
argument.

Verse 13 raises an obvious problem: *"...until the law sin
was in the world; but sin is not imputed when there is no law."*
Paul insists that "before the law" was given at Sinai, sin
was not only in the world; it was also punished with death.
All will agree that it is unfair to punish sin if there is no
guilt, and it would seem, at least on the surface, that since,
according to verses 12 and 14, there was no law to define
sin before Sinai, there could not have been true guilt.

Verse 14 shows that the answer to the problem is *the
truth of imputation.* Two things must be true: (1) Adam's sin

must have been unique, and (2) all humans (even babies) must have somehow participated in that one sin.

We know death reigned over all men without exception, including babies, prior to Sinai (or the time when the law was given). Death, the just penalty of sin, was experienced by those incapable of breaking a law, including babies, even if there had been a law. The guilt of Adam's sin is imputed to all of his posterity because they were all reckoned "in him" when he sinned. Adam was the representative of all men. When Adam sinned, all his posterity sinned in him.

Please observe: (1) Adam was the only person who could have brought sin into the world. Eve sinned first, but it was not until Adam sinned that "sin entered into the world" and the race fell. (2) There was only one single commandment that Adam could have broken in order to bring sin into the world: "Do not eat of the tree of the knowledge of good and evil." (3) Adam is the only person that ever became a sinner by sinning. You and I are born sinners, and sin because we are sinners.

Let's review and emphasize the points developed so far:

1. Sin entered this world through the one sin of one man, Adam.

2. Death followed that first sin as the just penalty for the guilt of sin.

3. Death was, and is, passed on through Adam to all of his posterity only because they are somehow held accountable for Adam's first sin.

IV. The *Many* and the *All*

We must distinguish between *the many* and *the all* in Paul's argument. This is the key to the passage. The *one* sin of the *one man* (Adam) brought sin, death, and condemnation to more people than just himself. The *many* who were affected by Adam's sin were really *all men without exception,* because the whole human race was represented by Adam. This *one* and *many* fact is set forth in verses 15–19. I have added some bolding and words for emphasis.

(15) *But the free gift is not like the offense. For if by the* **one man's** *offense* **many** *died, much more the grace of God and the gift by the grace of the* **one Man, Jesus Christ**, *abounded to* **many**. (16) *And the gift is not like that which came through the one who sinned. For the judgment which came from one offense resulted in condemnation, but the free gift which came in spite of many offenses and resulted in justification.* (17) *For if by the one man's offense death reigned through the one, much more those who receive abundance of grace and of the gift of righteousness will reign in life through the One, Jesus Christ.)* (18) *Therefore, as through one man's offense* **judgment came to all men** [represented by Adam], *resulting in condemnation, even so through one Man's righteous act the* **free gift came to all men** [*represented by Christ*] *resulting in justification of life.* (19) *For as by one man's disobedience many* [all Adam represented] **were made sinners,** *so also by one Man's obedience* **many** [all men Christ represented] **will be made righteous**. (Romans 5:15–19, NKJV)

Notice carefully the comparisons:

Verse 15:

1. By *one* man's [Adam's] offense *many* [the whole human race] died [because they were in some way represented by Adam and reckoned as guilty].

2. By one man [Christ] grace abounded to *many* [all of the new redeemed race, or the elect].

The *many's* in these two verses do not involve the same amount of people. The first *many* includes every person that was ever born. The *many* are all of Adam's posterity. The many—all of Adam's children—died because the guilt of Adam's one sin was imputed to them. This is the doctrine of *imputation*. It means that the guilt of Adam's sin was, by imputation, truly the guilt of each one of his posterity. It means that you and I are just as guilty as if our fingers took the fruit. It is only in this way that God could justly hold all men to be guilty of the consequences of Adam's sin. This same doctrine of imputation is likewise the only way we can understand and believe that Christ actually paid our sin debt before we were even born. If we reject the truth that Adam's guilt was imputed to us by representation, then we cannot accept the truth that Christ's righteousness was also imputed to us by representation. This is Paul's argument in this section of Scripture.

We can now see why Paul added verses 13 and 14 as a necessary explanation of verse 12.

For until the law sin was in the world, but sin is not imputed when there is no law. Nevertheless death reigned from Adam to Moses, even over those who had not sinned according to the likeness of the transgression of Adam, who is a type of Him who was to come. (NKJV)

These verses were added to prove Paul's assertion that "all (including infants) have sinned." Paul's argument in these verses can be understood several ways. He is definitely answering the objection that "sin cannot be imputed where there is no law." Paul's answer involves the guilt and death of infants, as well as the period of time from Adam until Moses when there was "no law." How can people be judged guilty when there is no law to break, and how can children break a law before they are even old enough to know right and wrong? It is obvious that people die who have not sinned "after the similitude of Adam's transgression." The NIV says, "by breaking a commandment as Adam did." Paul is proving that infants and others incapable of making a volitional choice to break a known commandment are nonetheless guilty sinners because they experience the penalty of sin which is death. If you establish that there was known law, then you must also prove the infant somehow broke that known law, and Paul's whole argument is destroyed.

One group of commentators has Paul agreeing with the objector concerning transgression and known law. Paul then would be saying that his opponent's argument proves too much. It proves there was law from Adam to Moses. There must have been law since men died under the curse of law. This law is the Ten Commandments that were given first to Adam and then later to Moses. True, this law was not written down prior to Moses but was written in the conscience. There is only one eternal moral law of God, and it has always been known since the dawn of creation. The death of men prior to Sinai proves there must have been known law in operation.

Other commentators have Paul saying: you are correct that guilt cannot be imputed without a deliberate transgression of a known law. You are also correct that there was no such codified law from Adam to Moses. However, you must still explain the fact that death, which is the penalty for sin and guilt, reigned over all men from Adam to Moses. Death even destroyed some infants and others who were not capable of breaking a commandment. Whether there was, or was not, a law in force, you must still explain the death of the infant. The baby cannot die if he is not guilty, and according to your argument, guilt can only come from deliberately breaking a law. The baby did not choose to break a known law. Why then did babies, and all others, die under the guilt of sin before Sinai?

It seems to me that the first interpretation, though textually legitimate, is more concerned with protecting a theological system than it is in exegeting Paul's words. Those who try to push the Ten Commandments back into the garden of Eden hold that view. Paul's concern at this point is not to prove whether there was, or was not, a law before Sinai. He is proving that all men sinned in Adam in the garden of Eden. Paul is saying that since death, as the penalty of sin, reigned during the period without law from Adam to Moses, it proves that the cause of that death in each case was the imputation of the guilt of Adam to each person, including the infant.

Paul is not arguing that the reign of death from Adam to Moses proves there was law in force. That would, in one sense, weaken his whole argument. He is showing that death comes to all men only because all that die somehow participated in that *one* sin of the *one* man, Adam. Paul is not concerned with the law/grace discussion concerning the "one eternal unchanging law." He is concerned with the doctrine of imputation.

The phrase "who is the figure of him that was to come" at the end of verse 14 is meant to introduce the contrast he is going to make. Just as some men were "made sinners" and treated as actually guilty because of what Adam did, so other men are "made righteous" and treated as actually justified because of what Christ did. Robert Haldane said, "Those who are saved fulfill the law just as others break the law, namely, in their great head or representative."[11]

Let's review and summarize Paul's argument in verses 12–14:

1. Death entered this world as a penalty for sin.

2. Where death is present, sin is being punished. There can be no death where there is no sin or guilt.

---

[11] Robert Haldane, *Exposition of the Epistle to the Romans* (The Banner of Truth Trust: Edinburgh, 1996), 211.

3. An innocent person will never be punished for any sin of which he is not personally guilty. God is neither unfair nor unjust. He only punishes those who deserve to be punished.

4. The only reason that any person is punished is because of their guilt, and since all men, including infants, die, it clearly proves that those who die are being punished because they truly are guilty sinners.

Problem: It is unjust to charge a man with the guilt of breaking a law of which he knew nothing. How could God declare men guilty before the law was given at Mt. Sinai? How could a day-old baby be declared guilty of breaking a law?

Answer: It is a clear fact that death was in the world before the Law of Sinai, and it is just as clear that death reigned over all men during the period of time from Adam until the Law was first written on the Tables of the Covenant at Sinai. Even infant children died during this period of time. Either they were truly guilty, or God was punishing the innocent. If they were not guilty of breaking a known commandment, then they must somehow be guilty because of their relationship to Adam. They must share in his guilt. They must have "sinned in Adam." That is the truth of imputation.

Let's move on to the argument of verses 15–19:

First: God has only ever dealt with two *public* or *representative* persons.

A. *The first representative person was Adam.* He was the head of the human race, and he acted in its behalf. What he did, the whole human race also did "in him," since all men were in his loins and were represented by him. What happened to him must also happen to each one that he represented. Since Adam represented all men without exception, it must follow that when *he* sinned, *all* sinned. When Adam was condemned, everyone that he represented—all persons without exception—was condemned as guilty. This includes infants as well as old men.

When God created man, he did not create him like a cornfield where each person was an independent stock. God created mankind like a tree where every limb, twig, piece of bark, and leaf came out of the one root.

B. *The second public person was Christ.* He also represented others and not just himself. All that Christ did and all that he suffered was for the benefit of others. He lived and died FOR others. The principle of representation that establishes the just condemnation of all those who were "in Adam" also establishes the sure justification of all those who are "in Christ." Just as everything that Adam did was, by imputation, also done by all those he represented, so everything that Christ did was, by imputation, also done by all those whom he represented. Just as each one of Adam's posterity must receive the rewards of Adam's sin, so each one of Christ's seed must receive the reward of Christ's work of redemption.

Second: There are some things which are exactly the same and other things which are exactly opposite when Adam and Christ are compared as representative persons.

The actions, and consequences of those actions, of both representative men are passed on to all those who are represented. In verse 15, the "offense" of Adam and the "gift" of Christ are passed on to others. Adam sinned, and *many* died. Christ earned grace and that grace is freely given to *many*. If the truth of this verse is missed, then the whole passage will be difficult. If Paul's clear meaning is grasped at this point, the rest falls neatly into place.

1. We must see the principle of representation. What happens to the head, or representative person, must of a certainty happen to all that are represented.

2. "*Many* are dead" because of one man's (Adam's) action. "*Many* receive grace" because of another man's (Christ's) action.

Question: Are the *many* the same in both cases? Do the exact same *many* that receive death for Adam's action also receive life because of Christ's action? The answer to that is the key to the whole passage.

Answer: Heed this very carefully. All whom Adam represented are not potentially or hypothetically guilty because he sinned. They are all actually treated as guilty sinners because of that one sin of Adam. All, without exception, who were in Adam, died in Adam. The identical principle holds true of Christ and his seed. All men, without exception, are not potentially or hypothetically righteous because of the work of Christ. All, without a single exception, whom he represented, will, of a certainty, be treated as righteous. If Christ, in his atoning death, represented all men, then all men will be declared righteous just as surely as all those whom Adam represented were declared guilty.

Question: But is not Christ the second Adam, or second head of the human race?

Answer: No! He is indeed the "second Adam," but he is the head of a *new race*. He is the "head of the *church*" (Eph. 1:22, 23; 5:23). He is the "shepherd of the *sheep*" and lays down his life for them.

Here is the root error of the universal view of the atonement of our Lord Jesus. It insists that the atonement only has a *potential* value to save men. It cannot and does not by itself guarantee that *any* sinners will be saved. The atonement, in such a view, merely makes it hypothetically possible for *all men* to be saved if they are willing to contribute faith as their part of the deal. It is impossible to read the idea of either a hypothetical *condemnation* (of Adam's race) or a hypothetical *justification* (of Christ's new race) into Romans 5:12–19. There is nothing hypothetical about either Adam's sin, or the guilt and death that was credited to all whom he represented. Likewise, there is nothing hypothetical about either the atoning work of Christ, or the crediting of righteousness and justification to all that he represented. If we try to make the work of Christ to be only hypothetically able to secure its designed benefits, we corrupt the meaning of Paul's words and totally destroy his argument in these verses.

The word *many* means exactly what it says. It means many more than just one. It means a *whole lot.* Only one man actually took the fruit, but many were affected by that one man and his one act of disobedience. The word *many* may mean all without exception. However, in the verses being discussed, it cannot mean every single person in the world without exception. It means every person without exception *who is represented!* The *many* represented by Adam are all of the human race without exception. The *many* represented by Christ are all of the new elect race, or the church.

Let me paraphrase these verses and insert in brackets what I have just stated. You will see why Paul goes back and forth with the words *many* and *all,* and why he sometimes says *"the* many." We will begin with verse 10:

For if when we were God's enemies, we were reconciled [not hypothetically but *actually*] to him through the death of his Son [and not on the ground of our faith]...through him we have now received [a real] reconciliation. Therefore [here is how that happened] death and righteousness both came into the world the same way. They both came from the actions of one individual. In one case, the person was Adam, and in the other case, the person was Christ. Both sin and righteousness were passed on as a certainty to every single person who was represented by either Adam or Christ.

You see, death came to all men only because all men have actually sinned. I realize that presents a problem. Since it is obvious that all men, especially infants, could not be guilty of breaking a known commandment [as Adam did], and since [as some objectors correctly state] there was no written law from Adam to Moses, then how do we explain the fact that death reigned over all men, without exception, including babies? If they could not themselves have broken a known commandment, they must have somehow been involved in Adam's sin, since it was at that time that death started its universal reign. That is the answer! All men sinned in Adam. He, like Christ, represented many others beside himself. Adam is a clear pattern of Christ.

As Adam plunged all whom he represented [and he represented all men without exception] into sin and death, so Christ will bring all those whom he represented [and he represented all those given to him by the Father] into righteousness and life. As everything Adam earned is imputed to his seed [the *many* whom he represented], so everything Christ earned is imputed to his seed [the *many* whom he represents]. However, the reward of Christ far outshines what Adam lost. Judgment followed one sin, but justification is from many sins. [End paraphrase]

Perhaps it would be good to look again at verse 15, the beginning of the point being argued, and verses 18 and 19 where the apostle concludes his point:

> ...*For if the many* [all whom Adam represented, or the whole human race] *died* [actually—not merely hypothetically]

by the trespass of the one man [simply because he represented them], *how much more did God's grace and the gift* [justification and life] *that came by the grace of the one man, Jesus Christ, overflow* [actually—not merely hypothetically] *to the many* [all whom Christ represented, or the church]!

Consequently [to summarize the whole matter], *just as the* [sure] *result of one trespass was condemnation of all men* [that Adam represented, or the whole human race], *so also the* [sure] *result of one act of righteousness was justification that brings* [actually—not merely hypothetically] *life for all men* [that Christ represented, or the new race]. *For just as through the disobedience of the one man the many* [all whom Adam represents, or the whole human race] *were made* [actually—not merely hypothetically] *sinners* [because they sinned in their "head"], *so also through the obedience* [unto the death of the cross] *of the one man* [Christ] *the many* [all whom Christ represents, or the church] *will be* **[must be actually—not merely hypothetically]** *made righteous.* (NIV)

The main thing that must be seen in the whole passage is the truth of imputation. What happens to the representative, must, of necessity, also happen to all those who are represented. That part is as clear as crystal. What is just as clear, but not as easily accepted by many people, is the fact that either particular atonement is true, or else all men are going to be justified. What happens to *the one* absolutely must happen to *the many*. If *the many* that Christ represents are exactly equal to *the many* that Adam represents, then all men without exception will be made righteous by the obedience of Christ, just as surely as all men without exception were made sinners by the disobedience of Adam. Either Christ died for his people alone, or else all men are going to be saved. Any fair interpretation of Paul's words can lead to no other conclusion.

Appendix Three
Perseverance and Our Baptist Forefathers

London Baptist Confession of 1644

Articles XXII through XXXII

XXII

That faith is the (1) gift of God wrought in the hearts of the elect by the Spirit of God, whereby they come to see, know, and believe the truth of the (2) Scriptures, and not only so, but the excellency of them above all other writing and things in the world, as they hold forth the glory of God in His attributes, the excellency of Christ in His nature and offices, and the power of the fullness of the Spirit in His workings and operations; and thereupon are enabled to cast the weight of their souls upon this truth thus believed.

1. Eph. 2:8; John 6:29; 4:10; Phil. 1:29; Gal. 5:22

2. John 17:17; Heb. 4:11-12; John 6:63

XXIII

Those that have this precious faith wrought in them by the Spirit, can never finally nor totally fall away; and though many storms and floods do arise and beat against them, yet they shall never be able to take them off that foundation and rock which by faith they are fastened upon, but shall be kept by the power of God to salvation, where they shall enjoy their purchased possession, they being formerly engraven upon the palms of God's hands.

Matt. 7:24, 25; John 13:1; 1 Peter 1:4-6; Isa. 49:13-16

XXIV

That faith is ordinarily (1) begot by the preaching of the Gospel, or word of Christ, without respect to (2) any power or capacity in the creature, but it is wholly (3) passive, being dead in sins and trespasses, does believe, and is converted by no less power, (4) then that which raised Christ from the dead.

1. Rom. 10:17; 1 Cor. 1:21

2. Rom. 9:16

3. Rom. 2:1, 2; Ezek. 16:6; Rom. 3:12

4. Rom. 1:16; Eph. 1:19; Col. 2:12

XXV

That the tenders of the Gospel to the conversion of sinners, (1) is absolutely free, no way requiring, as absolutely necessary, any qualifications, preparations, terrors of the Law, or preceding ministry of the Law, but only and alone the naked soul, as a (2) sinner and ungodly to receive Christ, as Christ, as crucified, dead, and buried, and risen again, being made (3) a Prince and a Savior for such sinners.

1. John 3:14, 15; 1:12; Isa. 55:1; John 7:37

2. 1 Tim. 1:15; Rom. 4:5; 5:8

3. Acts 5:30-31; 2:36; 1 Cor. 1:22-24

XXVI

That the same power that converts to faith in Christ, the same power carries on the (1) soul still through all duties, temptations, conflicts, sufferings, and continually whatever a Christian is, he is by (2) grace, and by a constant renewed (3) operation from God, without which he cannot perform any duty to God, or undergo any temptations from Satan, the world, or men.

1. 1 Peter 1:5; 2 Cor. 12:9

2. 1 Cor. 15:10

3. Phil. 2:12, 13; John 15:5; Gal. 2:19-20

XXVII

That God the Father, and Son, and Spirit, is one with (1) all believers, in their (2) fullness, in (3) relations, (4) as head and members, (5) as house and inhabitants, as (6) husband and wife, one with Him, as (7) light and love, and one with Him in His inheritance, and in all His (8) glory; and that all believers by virtue of this union and oneness with God, are the adopted sons of God, and heirs of Christ, co-heirs and joint heirs with Him of the inheritance of all the promises of this life, and that which is to come.

1. 1 Thess. 1:1; John 14:10, 20; 17:21

2. Col. 2:9, 10; 1:19; John 1:17

3. John 20:17; Heb. 2:11

4. Col. 1:18; Eph. 5:30

5. Eph. 2:22; 1Cor. 3:16-17

6. Isa. 16:5; 2 Cor. 11:3

7. Gal. 3:26

8. John 17:24

XXVIII

That those which have union with Christ, are justified from all their sins, past, (1) present, and to come, by the blood of Christ; which justification we conceive to be a gracious and free (2) acquittance of a guilty, sinful creature, from all sin by God, through the satisfaction that Christ has made by His death; and this applied in the manifestation of it through faith.

1. John 1:7; Heb. 10:14; 9:26; 2 Cor. 5:19; Rom. 3:23

2. Acts 13:38, 39; Rom. 5:1; 3:25, 30

XXIX

That all believers are a holy and (1) sanctified people, and that sanctification is a spiritual grace of the (2) New Covenant, and effect of the (3) love of God, manifested to the soul, whereby the believer is in (4) truth and reality separated, both in soul and body, from all sin and dead works, through the (5) blood of the everlasting Covenant, whereby he also presents after a heavenly and evangelical perfection, in obedience to all the commands, (6) which Christ as Head and King in this New Covenant has prescribed to him.

1. 1 Cor. 1:1; 1 Peter 2:9

2. Eph. 1:4

3. 1 John 4:16

4. Eph. 4:24

5. Phil. 3:15

6. Mat. 28:20

XXX

All believers through the knowledge of (1) that justification of life given by the Father, and brought forth by the blood of Christ, have this as their great privilege of that

(2) New Covenant, peace with God, and reconciliation, whereby they that were afar off, were brought nigh by (3) that blood, and have (as the Scripture speaks) peace (4) passing all understanding, yes, joy in God, through our Lord Jesus Christ, by (5) whom we have received the Atonement.

1. 2 Cor. 5:19

2. Isa. 54:10; 26:12

3. Eph. 2:13-14

4. Phil. 4:7

5. Rom. 5:10-11

XXXI

That all believers in the time of this life, are in a continual warfare, combat, and opposition against sin, self, the world, and the Devil, and liable to all manner of afflictions, tribulations, and persecutions, and so shall continue until Christ comes in His Kingdom, being predestined and appointed there unto; and whatsoever the saints, any of them do possess or enjoy of God in this life, is only by faith.

Eph. 6:10-13; 2 Cor. 10:3; Rev. 2:9, 10

XXXII

That the only strength by which the saints are enabled to encounter with all opposition, and to overcome all afflictions, temptations, persecutions, and trails, is only by Jesus Christ, who is the Captain of their salvation, being made perfect through sufferings, who has engaged His strength to assist them in all their afflictions, and to uphold them under all their temptations, and to preserve them by His power to His everlasting Kingdom.

John 16:33; Heb. 2:9, 10; John 15:5 ff.

APPENDIX FOUR
THE CARNAL CHRISTIAN DOCTRINE

The very term "carnal Christian" seems to be a contradiction in terms and as it is used by many today, it is indeed a contradiction in terms. Exactly what is meant by the "carnal Christian doctrine"? This appendix will try to answer that question and also show why we reject this doctrine. The arguments over the rightness or wrongness of this doctrine reach back all the way to the early church, and continue to appear throughout church history. The term "carnal Christian" as opposed to a "spiritual Christian" has not always been used, but the basic idea of the difference between the two has always existed. What is unique about the current carnal Christian doctrine are the extreme lengths to which its modern advocates have gone (consistently, I should add) in carrying out the logical implications of their erroneous theology.

One group of Christians insists that Christ must be both acknowledged and received as Lord as well as Savior before an individual can be saved. Another group of Christians vehemently opposes this position and insists that bowing to Christ in repentance and receiving him as Lord has nothing to do with salvation. When we insist that "Christ must be Lord of all, or he is not Lord at all," we are accused of denying the gospel of grace and preaching a false gospel of works. Two statements will demonstrate the two sides of the argument.

The thought of surrender is also implied in the exhortation to "believe on the Lord Jesus Christ" (Acts 16:31) and the declaration that we must confess "Jesus as Lord" (Romans 10:9) if we would be saved. To believe in him as Lord is to recognize him as Lord; and we cannot recognize him as Lord until we ourselves abdicate. This note in faith is today often overlooked or even referred to a later time of consecration; but the Scriptures connect it with the initial experience of salvation. (From: _Introductory Lectures in Systematic Theology_, by Henry Thiessen, page 359)

The second statement just as clearly sets forth the opposite view, namely that neither preaching nor receiving Christ as Lord is necessary in salvation.

The message of faith only and the message of faith plus commitment of life cannot both be the gospel; therefore, one of them is a false gospel and comes under the curse of perverting the gospel or preaching another gospel (Gal. 1:6-9). As far as sanctification is concerned, if only committed people are saved people, then where is there room for the Carnal Christians? (From: _Balancing the Christian Life_, by Charles Ryrie, Moody Press, page 170)

I think everyone will immediately see that Ryrie has radically changed the biblical meaning of "faith." He has reduced faith to mean nothing but an intellectual act of the mind. You can believe in Christ in exactly the same manner that you believe "Columbus crossed the ocean blue in 1492" and be a true Christian. The only thing in Dr. Ryrie's statement with which I agree is that Thiessen's position and Ryrie's position cannot both be the gospel of the Bible.

Ryrie is indeed correct when he states that one of the two is indeed "under the curse of God."

Let us first of all be sure we understand precisely what we are discussing. As Ryrie has correctly pointed out, the stakes are enormous! According to Ryrie, "heaven or hell" and "gospel truth or rank heresy" are the choices. The carnal Christian doctrine is the teaching that there are two distinctively different types or categories of Christians. The one is called a carnal Christian, and the other is called a spiritual Christian. Both types have distinct and radically different characteristics that are clearly discernible and easily categorized. Every Christian is in one of these two categories, and, according to the advocates of this doctrine, it is not difficult to know whether one is a spiritual or a carnal Christian. Several lists of traits are made available, and one only need pick the list that best represents his life. In a matter of seconds, he will know if he is to look upon himself as being in the "spiritual" category or the "carnal" category. One of the strange things about this teaching is that it is far easier to discern the difference between a carnal and spiritual Christian than it is to discern the difference between a carnal Christian and a lost person. This amazing fact alone ought to be enough to warn any thinking person that something is wrong.

There are several other things that are basic to, and an integral part of, the carnal Christian teaching. The very statements, when honestly faced, should force people to be skeptical.

One: Both carnal and spiritual Christians are genuine believers, even though the carnal Christian acts exactly like a non-Christian. The carnal Christian is just as "eternally secure" and sure of heaven as the spiritual Christian, despite the fact they are radically different in their respective life styles. This point ought to make anyone raise his eyebrows. It seems rather inconsistent to proclaim, as the advocates of this doctrine do, that the carnal Christian is headed for heaven even though he lives like the Devil.

Two: The carnal Christian's assurance and safety is in no way connected to, or to be examined by, the fruits of sanctification. One knows for sure that he is saved because he has "accepted Christ as his Savior," which actually means he has "professed to have accepted Christ." A profession of faith is never to be tested in any way by life and experience. Regardless of one's present state, he is to be assured he is "eternally secure" if he has "asked Jesus to come into his heart."

Three: A person may become, live, and die as a carnal Christian and still go to heaven—even if he has never bowed to Christ as his Lord. Such a person will suffer losses of rewards (either in heaven or the "millennium"), of a greater or lesser degree, but he need not fear for his soul's salvation. The absolute and unconditional security of every person, regardless of how they live, who has "made a decision of Christ" is to be protected at all cost.

Four: A wholehearted turning from all known sin is neither demanded nor considered to be an essential part of evangelism. The necessity of repentance is not to be preached to lost sinners since doing so would deny grace and bring in works and merit. The Saviorhood of Christ alone is the message to sinners and must not be confused with the Lordship of Christ, which is the message to believers in order that they might also become disciples. In the carnal Christian doctrine, being a Christian and being a disciple of Christ is not the same thing. Becoming a true Christian does not demand that a person bow to Christ as his Lord. When a Christian "accepts Christ as his Lord," which is usually at a later date, it is at that point that the Christian becomes a disciple of Christ. Not all true Christians are disciples. Discipleship is in no way related, or essential to, salvation, security, or assurance. "You accept Christ as your Savior, and you are ready for heaven regardless of how you live. You accept Christ as your Lord, and you are ready to live the Christian life. Carnal Christians are ready for heaven but not ready to live the Christian life." The three preceding sentences are the words of a professor of theology from Dallas Theological Seminary.

Five: The two classifications of Christians are clearly distinctive and opposite. It is a simple matter to know (1) whether you are in the spiritual category and, (2) if you are in the spiritual category, exactly when and how you got into this group. Incidentally, I have never met a person who was prepared to say they had ever crossed back over the line and become a carnal Christian again after having become a spiritual one. Listening to the testimonies of carnal Christians who became spiritual Christians is like hearing someone testify, "I used to be proud, and now I am humble." I fully expect any day to hear one of them add, "And I am quite proud of my spirituality" (humility).

Next, let us ask the question: "Where and when did the carnal Christian doctrine originate?" As mentioned above, the basic idea goes all the way through church history back to the New Testament. However, the carnal Christian doctrine is currently being defined in different terms and has taken on new strength in our generation.

The carnal Christian doctrine, as we are discussing it, was the immediate and logical consequence of the "new evangelism" of easy-believism that J. C. Ryle and others criticized. For a full discussion and proof of this, read B.B. Warfield's Christian Perfectionism and J. C. Ryle's Holiness. The _Scofield Reference Bible_ gave the teaching creditability and was probably the most significant factor in its spread. A single footnote in that Bible provides the supposed foundation of the whole carnal Christian concept. The footnote is found at 1 Corinthians 2:14 on page 1213 of the first edition of the _Scofield Reference Bible_.

> Paul divides men into three classes: psuchikos, "of the senses" (Jas. iii:15; Jude 19), or "natural," i.e. the Adamic man, unrenewed through the new birth (John iii:3, 5); pneumatikos, "spiritual," i.e., the renewed man as Spirit-filled and walking in the Spirit in full communion with God (Eph. v:18 20); and sarkikos, "carnal," "fleshly," i.e. the renewed man, who walking "after the flesh," remains a babe in Christ (I Cor. iii:1 4)..."

The phrase "after the flesh" used to describe a carnal Christian is obviously lifted from Romans 8:4, 5, and 13. However, Scofield's use of it makes it say the opposite of what Paul intended in Romans 8. Paul emphatically states in those verses that any man who "minds," "walks," or "lives" after the flesh will perish. It is impossible to impose the concept of a "...renewed man...walking after the flesh..." into "if ye live after the flesh ye shall die...." (Romans 8:13).

Lest anyone say we are reading more into Scofield's note than he intended, let me quote from his footnote on Romans 7:14:

> "Carnal" = "fleshly" is Paul's word for the Adamic nature and for the believer who "walks," i.e., lives, under the power of it."

What is a carnal Christian according to the *Scofield Reference Bible*? A carnal Christian is a renewed man who "walks after the flesh." What does *walks* mean? It means nothing less than "living under the power" of the Adamic nature. Stated another way, a carnal Christian is a Spirit-born, blood-washed, justified, adopted saint of the most high God who walks (that is, he lives) under the power and control of the Adamic nature. That is no caricature. That is precisely what the carnal Christian doctrine is saying. A man can be totally committed to obey the Adamic nature and still be a renewed man and secure in Christ. Seriously, what kind of salvation is that? Where is the freedom and liberty won by the Redeemer in his battle with sin and Satan (John 8:32, 36)? Where is the power and life infused by the Holy Spirit in his mighty work of regeneration? This is not a salvation from sin. It is a salvation in sin. The very essence of biblical salvation is expressed in the angel's announcement that Jesus would "save his people from their sins" (Matt. 1:21). Carnal Christian salvation is security and assurance in sin and makes Christ a minister of unrighteousness instead of righteousness.

It will do no good for the advocates of the carnal Christian doctrine to cry, "You grossly misrepresent us. We never teach that Christians should be carnal; in fact, the whole purpose of our preaching is to plead with them to accept Christ as Lord of their lives so that they will become spiritual. We advocate spirituality, not carnality." No, my friend, you don't! You may think you are advocating spirituality, and it may be your sincere desire to promote more holy living, but you are still apostles of carnality. Regardless of what the intention may be, the result of this most unbiblical doctrine has been disastrous. Rome may loudly proclaim that the confessional box and indulgences are an attempt to restrain sin, but history proves she has actually encouraged sin and hindered holiness by those awful practices. The modern doctrine of the carnal Christian is just as wicked as the doctrine that allowed Tetzel to sell indulgences for sins before they were even committed. The carnal Christian doctrine gives the same license to sin.

We admit that some souls may have been helped in a Roman confessional box by verbalizing their guilt and shame, but has this brought them closer to Christ and true forgiveness, or has it driven them farther away from both? Likewise, some true saints may have been raised to a new joy in Christ by elements of truth in the "higher life" teaching, but hundreds of others have been given carnal security to continue in sin. It is impossible to plead for a second type of Christian without dogmatically protecting the assurance and security of the first type. Practical sanctification and holy living cannot be considered optional without giving ironclad assurance that unholy living and true salvation are perfectly compatible as long as an individual has mentally "accepted Christ."

Listen carefully to a famous advocate of the carnal Christian doctrine:

> If you have received the Lord Jesus Christ as your Redeemer, then the Holy Spirit, as we have already seen, has come to take up residence within your human spirit, and you have been born again and God has set His seal upon you as His child. But if that old, Adamic nature, the flesh, still dominates your soul and monopolizes your personality by coloring your thinking, sparking your ambitions, capturing your affections and subtly persuading your will into submission to its claims upon you, then you are a Carnal Christian." (From: *If I Perish...I Perish,* by Major Ian Thomas, Zondervan Publishing House)

There are no *if*s or *but*s in this position, and certainly no possibility that the carnal Christian was never really saved. There is no suggestion that he should examine himself to see if his professed conversion was real. There is no warning or admonition that to continue in a carnal state may be disastrous. To do this is to be guilty of preaching salvation by works. On the contrary, Major Thomas emphatically assures that sin can "dominate your soul and monopolize your personality" but that in no way means one is to question his salvation. An advocate of this doctrine would emphatically deny that bondage to, and domination by, sin should cause you any alarm about your soul's security. You have "received the Lord Jesus Christ as your Redeemer" (true, he is a Redeemer that leaves you a victim and slave of sin). "The Holy Spirit has taken up residence in you" (true, he never made a particle of difference in your heart and life). "God has set his seal upon you as his child" (true, no one can see any evidence of that seal). How glorious! Redeemed by the Son of God, regenerated and indwelt by the Holy Spirit, justified and adopted by the Father; all of this and not one whit different than an "unsaved" sinner! A slave of sin, but nonetheless sure of God's stamp of acceptance—dominated and monopolized by the Adamic nature, but assured of being the temple of the Holy Spirit! Again, it may not be the deliberate intention of carnal Christian advocates to encourage the above, but that is what they are doing whether they realize it or not.

I want to emphasize that we are not implying that a true Christian may not act in a very carnal manner at certain times. We are not claiming that no Christian ever backslides, yea, very badly sometimes. We are just as opposed to the "spiritual" Christian concept as we are to the "carnal" Christian idea. Every Christian is both carnal and spiritual. It is a matter of degree. Some of the people who fight the carnal Christian doctrine are just as dangerous as those who uphold it. Unless you condemn the "spiritual" Christian concept, which in reality is a form of perfectionism, just as strongly as the carnal Christian idea, you are laying the foundation for the very atmosphere that made the carnal Christian doctrine possible in the first place. Most of the so-called Reformed responses to the carnal Christian doctrine have totally confused the issue of sanctification by grace. We will say more about this later.

Let no one who reads these lines think me unkind or unloving in writing this section. We "Lordship Preachers" whose concept of the gospel does not make "room for carnal Christians" have been accused of proclaiming a "false gospel" that "comes under the curse" of Galatians 1:6-9. If a "nobody" had made such bold and far-reaching statements, we could smile and go on our way. However, when the accusation carries the authority of the Systematic Theology Department of Dallas Theological Seminary as well as the endorsement of a publishing house of the stature of Moody Press, it is an entirely different matter. It is time for a church council to convene and determine who is adhering to God's Word and who is departing from it.

First Corinthians 2:14–3:3 is the basic "biblical proof" for the carnal Christian doctrine. This one portion of the Bible supposedly identifies three classes of people. Notice in the diagram on page 460 the two questions concerning how to identify which class you are in, and then how you can "right now" move from carnal to spiritual. I am sure you see how clearly they demonstrate most of the statements made at the beginning of this article. They fairly exude the notion that knowing for certain which of these three groups one is in is a matter that can be easily and quickly determined. Not only is it a simple matter to immediately classify oneself, but it is also just as simple to become a "spiritual man right now." In a matter of moments, one follows the steps and takes upon himself the title "spiritual Christian" with an unshakable assurance that such is really the case.

It is no accident or coincidence that Campus Crusade, the originators of the three circles, is such a strong advocate of the carnal Christian doctrine. They have a sure-fire evangelism approach that enables anyone with an effective salesman's personality to get "decisions" for Christ in a matter of moments. This approach grossly misrepresents and distorts some wonderful biblical truths into "Four Spiritual Laws." Sadly, their spiritual laws produce a host of carnal Christians who did not receive genuine spirituality from the so-called Spiritual Laws. Since they practice the easiest "easy-believism" in evangelism, it logically follows that Campus Crusade needs an "easy-believism" form of sanctification.

The Bible tells us that there are three kinds of people: *But the* **natural** *man receiveth not the things of the Spirit of God: for they are foolishness unto him: neither can he know them, because they are spiritually discerned. But he that is* **spiritual** *judgeth all things, yet he himself is judged of no man. For who hath known the mind of the Lord, that he may instruct him? But we have the mind of Christ. And I, brethren, could not speak unto you as unto spiritual, but as unto carnal, even as unto babes in Christ. I have fed you with milk, and not with meat: for hitherto ye were not able to bear it, neither yet now are ye able. For ye are yet carnal: for whereas there is among you envying, and strife, and divisions, are ye not* **carnal,** *and walk as men?* (1 Corinthians 2:14-3:3)

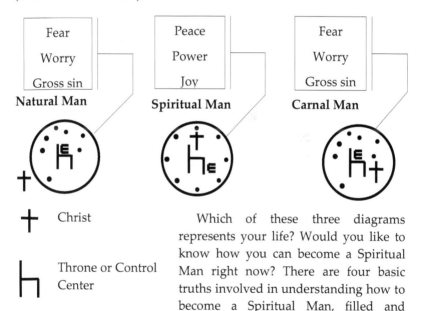

Natural Man

Fear
Worry
Gross sin

Spiritual Man

Peace
Power
Joy

Carnal Man

Fear
Worry
Gross sin

✝ Christ

⊓ Throne or Control Center

E Ego or finite self

● Various interests in life

Which of these three diagrams represents your life? Would you like to know how you can become a Spiritual Man right now? There are four basic truths involved in understanding how to become a Spiritual Man, filled and controlled by the Holy Spirit.

ILLUSTRATION

From: *Have You Made the Wonderful Discovery of the Spirit-filled Life?*

Campus Crusade

A careful examination of the three circles depicting the three classes of people demonstrates the basic error of the whole doctrine. The circle depicts one's life. The chair in the center of the circle represents the throne or control center of the individual's life. The "E" is the real person, i.e. the "ego or finite self." The cross is the symbol for the Lord Jesus Christ. The dots are the various interests, goals, and pursuits of life. The most important lesson being stressed is the fact that Christ bears three distinctly different relationships to the three kinds of people. This is the heart of the carnal Christian doctrine, and it is also the heart of the violent opposition to "Lordship preachers."

Carefully look at each of the three kinds of people and note especially the relationship that Christ bears to each one.

The Natural Man: Christ (represented by the cross) is outside of the life of the natural man. This man is unsaved. He is under the control of "E," or self. Scattered around the circle in a disorganized manner are dots of varying sizes. The picture is that of the meaningless, disorganized life of the man who has rejected Christ and has chosen to run his own life.

The Spiritual Christian: The second picture shows that all the dots have been changed to the same size and placed in perfect symmetry. Christ is on the throne. "E" is still part of the person (it is inside the circle), but it has been displaced as ruler.

The Carnal Christian: It is no accident that the third circle is identical to the first circle in every detail except one. One may be tempted to think the artist was lazy or the layout person wanted to skimp by using the same figure twice. Such is not the case. The dots are identical and in the same position in order to show that the life, habits, desires, etc., of the carnal Christian are exactly the same as the natural man! Further on in the booklet from which this diagram was taken, and in other material, the specific characteristics of both the natural man and the carnal man are listed, and the two lists are identical. In placing these two circles one on top of the other, the only difference will be revealed to be the position of the cross. In the first circle Christ is outside of life, and in the third circle Christ is just inside the circle but "E" is still on the throne. In other words, there need be no basic change in a person's mind, heart, will, or life as a result of regeneration. Both the natural man and the carnal Christian are controlled by the same sins. Here is Bill Bright's list of the attributes or characteristics of a carnal Christian:

> Fruitless witness for Christ, poor prayer life, no desire for Bible study, disobedient to God, legalistic life, impure thoughts, jealousy, worry, controlled by self, self-seeking, doubt, critical spirit, defeat, wrong doctrine, frustration, aimlessness and envy. (From: *Have You Made the Discovery of the Spirit-filled Life?* Campus Crusade, page 7)

The only difference between the person described in that quotation and a lost man is that the "carnal Christian" has made a mental decision to believe that Jesus is a real person who died on the cross. That is what it means to "accept Jesus as his Savior" and be "eternally secure in Christ."

It would be impossible to build a better bomb shelter for carnality or to give a greater sense of security to men in sin. A second or higher experience cannot be magnified without minimizing the first one. Carnal Christians who "live under the power of the Adamic nature" cannot be encouraged to become spiritual Christians without condoning carnality. Whether they admit it or not, the carnal Christian advocates are directly responsible for the arrogant assurance of many lawless professors who have no marks of grace. It is impossible to preach that carnality can rule in one's life as king and that Jesus can be denied as King in the same life, but in spite of those facts, that individual is still saved, secure, and certain of salvation. You cannot have two masters at the same time. You cannot preach that Jesus is willing to be the Savior from the penalty of sin and at the same time also to be rejected as King or Lord, without many people believing and living out in practice such a monstrous contradiction. God forbid that we should be accused of saying the carnal Christian advocates are deliberately aiming at producing a generation of people who sincerely believe they can serve sin in this life but still have glory and happiness in the next. Regrettably, their doctrine has produced just such a state of affairs, and it couldn't have been brought about much more quickly if they actually had intended to do so.

The very titles or headings in the above-mentioned booklet betray the fact that the whole carnal Christian system produces carnality because it is a system based on carnal human wisdom. I could hardly believe my eyes the first time that I read it. I thought I was back in a Wear-Ever (pots and pans) sales meeting. "How to Promote the Assurance of Christ's Presence in Life After One Commits His Life to Christ" is the main heading, and the first sub-heading is "How to Communicate Assurance." Of course, if we call attention to this obvious attempt to play Holy Spirit, we will be told, "Oh! We believe it is the work of the Holy Spirit to do this." Believe me; armed with the methodology of the Four Spiritual Laws to get decisions, and the "four basic truths involved in understanding how to become a spiritual man," the Holy Spirit is not at all necessary. If we have to "promote and communicate the assurance that Christ has come into a person's heart in cleansing power and saving grace" with psychology gimmicks and sales, then I humbly suggest that such a Christ is not worthy of being a guest in the first place. And while we are on the subject of "communicating assurance," I still have not found out how these people are able to look into other people's hearts and know for certain that said people really have genuine faith in Christ. Please don't respond, "But John, you must ask them if they were sincere when they prayed." If there is one thing I am sure about, it is the fact that a sinner is the very last person capable of being the judge of his own sincerity. The Word of God says that "the heart is deceitful above all things...and who can know it...." John Bunyan speaks well on this point of a man's heart being the judge of his own sincerity.

Christian: ...But why, or for what, art thou persuaded that thou hast left all for God and heaven?

Ignorance: My heart tells me so.

Christian: The wise man says, "He that trusteth in his own heart is a fool." (Prov. 28:26)

Ignorance: That is spoken of an evil heart, but mine is a good one.

Christian: But how dost thou prove that?

Ignorance: It comforts me in hopes of heaven.

Christian: That may be through its deceitfulness; for a man's heart may minister comfort to him, in the hopes of that thing for which he has yet no ground to hope.

Ignorance: But my heart and life agree together; and therefore my hope is well grounded.

Christian: Who told thee that thy heart and life agree together?

Ignorance: My heart tells me so.

Christian: Ask my fellow if I be a thief! Thy heart tells thee so! Except the Word of God beareth witness in this matter, other testimony is of no value....

(From: *The Pilgrim's Progress,* by John Bunyan)

Why do we reject the "carnal Christian" doctrine?

It hardly seems necessary to list specific reasons for rejecting such a non-biblical doctrine. Nonetheless, the following list contains some of the more obvious objections to this false doctrine.

1. It directly opposes the analogy of Scripture on the subject. Nowhere in the Bible is there a suggestion of three kinds of people (except 1 Peter 4:18, but there the sinners are divided into two classes). The Bible divides men as saved and lost, believer and unbeliever, sheep and goats, children of darkness and children of light, etc. Scripture knows nothing of a creature that looks and lives like those in one category but possesses the nature and benefits of those in the opposite group.

2. It breaks an important rule of biblical interpretation. A passage of Scripture must never be used as a foundation for a doctrine unless that passage is specifically dealing with that doctrine. Most certainly, a non-doctrinal passage cannot be used to contradict a passage where that specific doctrine is the subject of discussion. 1 Corinthians 3 is not a doctrinal passage and by no stretch of the imagination can it be thought of as providing the foundation of the doctrine of sanctification. Yet this is exactly what the carnal Christian advocates do with these verses. Examine Romans 8, where the subjects being dealt with are security and sanctification, and see what happens to every person who is dominated by carnality.

3. It leads to "security in sin" and spiritual pride. The moment a man is sure he is a spiritual Christian, one can be sure he is not. Where is the dividing line between the two classes? Is it a one-hundred-percent to zero situation? How does one test his heart in this classification? Can one be proud that he is no longer a carnal Christian and still be a spiritual Christian?

4. It denies what is (a) recorded of every Bible hero, (b) imprinted on the heart of every honest Christian, and (c) the uniform experience of the greatest saints in history; namely, that (1) every Christian is carnal and every Christian is spiritual, (2) that no Christian is dominated by carnality, and (3) no Christian is sinlessly perfect. It may well be that a believer is the most spiritual when he feels himself to be the most carnal, and vice versa.

5. It divorces what God has joined together. It separates justification from sanctification. These two are most certainly different. They may be isolated in order to be better studied and understood, but they cannot be separated in experience. He whose justification does not lead to practical sanctification has never been justified, and he who attempts to earn, or keep, his justification by means of sanctification knows nothing of the free and sovereign grace of God that "justifies the ungodly."

We call this "optional" sanctification and consider it to be the heart of this awful error. We believe a holy heart (not a sinless life) that wants to please God is wrought in every person born of God's Spirit. "Follow...holiness, without which no man shall see the Lord..." (Heb. 12:14) is not an option for carnal Christians; it is a command that is to be obeyed by every saved person. "Sin shall not have dominion over you..." (Rom. 6:14) is not a promise to be claimed by faith; it is the actual experience of every child of grace.

I remember reading an article where the author wrote, "No Christian would desire that type (i.e., carnal) of life"

Did the man mean by "would" that no Christian could desire that and be a genuine Christian? If such were the case, we would reply, "Amen, brother! That is exactly what we are contending for." However, such is not the case. Two paragraphs later, the same writer states, "The Lord desires a holy life of his people." What is he saying? God wants you to desire to please him, you will be far better off if you will desire to please him, and we earnestly urge you to desire to please him, but it is optional. It has nothing to do with your salvation or security. Desiring to live a holy life is like having a CD player or air conditioning in your car. It is an option. It plays no essential part in the car's ability to get you where you want to go. It merely makes the trip more enjoyable. God desires you to be a spiritual Christian because you will be happier now and also when your "works" are judged at the judgment seat of Christ, but it is optional and has nothing to do with whether you get to heaven or not.

Is that really what the Bible teaches? Listen to some clear words from Paul. "...to be carnally minded is death... if ye live after the flesh, ye shall die...." (Rom. 8:6, 13). That doesn't sound very optional to me, and it does not sound like something that God merely desires you not to do, but rather something that God demands. How dare anyone say that what Paul really means is, "to be carnally minded is to lose all your rewards and be saved yet so as by fire." I say for the third time, these dear sincere souls may be horrified at the suggestion, but they are apostles of carnality. You cannot continually put *should* where God says *must*, and add *ought* to where God says *has* without people being led to think and live as if holiness were merely an option in the Christian life. No matter how desirable you make such an option, you cannot help but say that it really is not an essential part of God's plan of salvation.

6. Carefully consider the following, and after searching the Scriptures, determine whether the carnal Christian doctrine is true.

A. The goal, or purpose, of God the Father in electing grace is denied and frustrated by the carnal Christian doctrine.

> *You did not choose Me, but I chose you and appointed you that you should go and bear fruit, and that your fruit should remain....* (John 15:16 NKJV)

> *But we are bound to give thanks to God always for you, brethren beloved by the Lord, because God from the beginning chose you for salvation through sanctification by the Spirit and belief in the truth....* (2 Thess. 2:13 NKJV)

> *Just as He chose us in Him before the foundation of the world, that we should be holy and without blame before Him in love...* (Eph. 1:4 NKJV)

> *Therefore, beloved...be diligent to be found by Him in peace, without spot and blameless....* (2 Pet. 3:14 NKJV)

B. The goal, or purpose, for which God the Son came into this world is denied and frustrated by the carnal Christian doctrine.

> *For whom He foreknew, He also predestined to be conformed to the image of His Son, that He might be the firstborn among many brethren.* (Rom. 8:29 NKJV)

I beseech you therefore, brethren, by the mercies of God, that you present your bodies a living sacrifice, holy, acceptable to God, which is your reasonable service. And do not be conformed to this world, but be transformed by the renewing of your mind, that you may prove what is that good and acceptable and perfect will of God. (Rom. 12:1-2 NKJ)

Now by this we know that we know Him, if we keep His commandments. He who says, "I know Him," and does not keep His commandments, is a liar, and the truth is not in him. But whoever keeps His word, truly the love of God is perfected in him. By this we know that we are in Him. He who says he abides in Him ought himself also to walk just as He walked. (1 John 2:3-6 NKJV)

C. The goal, or purpose, of God the Holy Spirit in his work of quickening and sealing is denied and frustrated by the carnal Christian doctrine.

There is therefore now no condemnation to them which are in Christ Jesus, who walk not after the flesh, but after the Spirit. (Rom. 8:1 KJV)

And you hath he quickened, who were dead in trespasses and sins; Wherein in time past ye walked according to the course of this world, according to the prince of the power of the air, the spirit that now worketh in the children of disobedience...For we are his workmanship, created in Christ Jesus unto good works, which God hath before ordained that we should walk in them. (Eph. 2:1-2, 10)

This I say then, Walk in the Spirit, and ye shall not fulfil the lust of the flesh....If we live in the Spirit, let us also walk in the Spirit. (Gal. 5:16, 25)

It is impossible to even remotely understand the implications of the above verses and still insist, "These are goals that God merely desires will come to pass, but whether they do or don't come to pass is of no eternal consequence."

Made in the USA
Las Vegas, NV
21 October 2023

79467846R00280